ISRAEL, THE ARABS
and
THE MIDDLE EAST

ISRAEL, THE ARABS
and
THE MIDDLE EAST

Edited by

Irving Howe and Carl Gershman

QUADRANGLE BOOKS

A NEW YORK TIMES COMPANY

Contents

Introduction   1

I   ISRAEL AS A SOCIAL EXPERIMENT

An Experiment That Did Not Fail/*Martin Buber*   5

Zionism, the Marxist Critique, and the Left/
   Walter Laqueur   16

The Problems of Israeli Socialism/*Ben Halpern*   45

The Kibbutz: An Experiment in Microsocialism/
   Chaim Barkai   69

Images of Israel: A Personal View/*Ronald Sanders*   100

Reflections of an Israeli Intellectual/*T. R. Fyvel*
   talks to Amos Oz   115

Israel: The Two Kinds of Jews/*Nissim Rejwan*   125

II   CONFLICT IN THE MIDDLE EAST

The Myth of Zionist "Original Sin":
   A Few Historical Notes/*Joseph Neyer*   135

The Palestinian Refugees: Resettlement,
   Repatriation, or Restoration?/*Marie Syrkin*   157

Nationalism, Internationalism, and the Jews:
   The Chimera of a Binational State/
   Michael Walzer   186

Self-Determination and the Palestinian Arabs/
   Julius Stone   200

The Failure of the Fedayeen/*Carl Gershman*   224

Israeli Policy in the "Administered Territories"/
   Michael Bruno   249

Civil Liberties in Israel: The Problem of
   Preventive Detention/*Alan Dershowitz*   266

Modernization and Arab Society: Some Reflections/
   Shlomo Avineri   300

Trapped in Vicious Circles/*Yehoshua Arieli*   312

III   INTERNATIONAL IMPLICATIONS

The Soviet Union and the Middle East/
   Walter Laqueur   323

Vietnam and Israel/*Irving Howe*   339

Imperialism in the Middle East/*Michael Harrington*   350

The Middle East Conflict and International Politics/
   Gil Carl AlRoy   366

The Return of Anti-Semitism as a Political Force/
   Seymour Martin Lipset   390

The Campus Left and Israel/*Irving Howe*   428

Index   431

Introduction

The survival of Israel is a major priority for everyone who cares about democracy; it should be a special obligation for people on the democratic left to speak out—passionately yet not uncritically—in behalf of the social innovations and achievements of Israeli society; such a view of the Middle East situation has nothing in common with any sort of chauvinism and in fact requires a commitment to policies leading toward Israeli-Arab amity—these are among the central premises of this book.

It is a book that represents a collective attempt by a group of writers to probe the underlying problems that have beset the Middle East in the last few decades. Our concern has not been primarily with the immediate negotiations of the competing states; that is best left to daily journalism. Our concern has been, rather, with the sources of the conflict, the entanglements of rival ideologies, the clashes between kinds of societies. Even if a peace treaty were to be signed tomorrow morning in the Middle East— and all of us devoutly wish that it would be—the problems discussed in these pages would persist.

We write as partisans, but not as propagandists. The essays that follow make, we believe, permanent contributions to the investigation of the Middle East conflict. Our contributors seek to probe, analyze, persuade. Yet we make no false claims to "objectivity." Who, in regard to so burning an issue, could?

For we believe that the survival of democratic Israel is an urgent moral-political necessity, even as we do not necessarily endorse one or another policy of the Israeli government. A few of our contributors have been associated with labor or socialist Zionism, but most of us do not identify with any branch of the Zionist movement. By

1

now, in any case, Zionist or anti-Zionist designations seem far less to the point than the fact that Israel itself exists as a vibrant human effort.

Hardly an article in this collection doesn't contain some criticism of Israeli policies. In this respect, our attitudes are very much like those of numerous Israelis themselves, who see in a vigorous but responsible criticism one token of their commitment to democratic Israel. During the several months before this book went to press there broke out within Israel—in part, because the lull of military hostilities allowed its citizens to turn their attention inward—extremely strong criticism of various social policies, especially in regard to the "oriental" Jews who suffer from poverty. We take such criticism to be a sign of the health of Israeli society, a vindication of its democratic and socialist commitments.

Most of us are people from the democratic left—that is, people who believe in the unity of democratic method and radical social change. It is this complex of values that enables us to regard the Arab peoples, if not most of their governments, with friendliness. We see them as fellow human beings with whom accommodations must be made; we write in the hope that peace and freedom, and thereby an improvement in the conditions of life, may yet come to the Middle East.

THE EDITORS

1

ISRAEL AS A SOCIAL EXPERIMENT

An Experiment That Did Not Fail

Martin Buber

MARTIN BUBER—one of the central figures of twentieth-century philosophy, student of Hasidism, author of *I and Thou, Paths in Utopia*.

The era of advanced capitalism has broken down the structure of society. The society which preceded it was composed of different societies; it was complex, and pluralistic in structure. This is what gave it its peculiar social vitality and enabled it to resist the totalitarian tendencies inherent in the prerevolutionary centralistic state, though many elements were very much weakened in their autonomous life. This resistance was broken by the policy of the French Revolution, which was directed against the special rights of all free associations. Thereafter centralism in its new, capitalistic form succeeded where the old had failed: in atomizing society. Exercising control over the machines and, with their help, over the whole society, capitalism wants to deal only with individuals; and the modern state aids and abets it by progressively dispossessing groups of their autonomy. The militant organizations which the proletariat erected against capitalism—trade unions in the economic sphere and the party in the political—are unable in the nature of things to counteract this process of dissolution, since they have no access to the life of society itself and its foundations: production and consumption. Even the transfer of capital to the state is powerless to modify the social structure, even when the state establishes a network of compulsory associations, which, having no autonomous life, are unfitted to become the cells of a new socialist society.

From this point of view the heart and soul of the cooperative movement is to be found in the trend of a society toward structural renewal, the reacquisition, in new tectonic forms, of the internal social relationships, the establishment of a new *consociatio consociationum*. It is (as I have shown) a fundamental error to view this trend as romantic or utopian merely because in its early stages it had romantic reminiscences and utopian fantasies. At bottom it is thoroughly topical and constructive; that is to say, it aims at changes which, in the given circumstances and with the means at its disposal, are feasible. And, psychologically speaking, it is based on one of the eternal human needs, even though this need has often been forcibly suppressed or rendered insensible: the need of man to feel his own house as a room in some greater all-embracing structure in which he is at home, to feel that the other inhabitants of it with whom he lives and works are all acknowledging and confirming his individual existence. An association based on community of views and aspirations alone cannot satisfy this need; the only thing that can do that is an association which makes for communal living. But here the cooperative organization of production or consumption proves, each in its own way, inadequate, because both touch the individual only at a certain point and do not mold his actual life. On account of their merely partial or functional character all such organizations are equally unfitted to act as cells of a new society. Both these partial forms have undergone vigorous development, but the consumer cooperatives only in highly bureaucratic forms and the producer cooperatives in highly specialized forms: they are less able to embrace the whole life of society today than ever. The consciousness of this fact is leading to the synthetic form: the full cooperative. By far the most powerful effort in this direction is the village commune, where communal living is based on the amalgamation of production and consumption, production being understood not exclusively as agriculture alone but as the organic union of agriculture with industry and with the handicrafts as well.

The repeated attempts that have been made during the last 150 years, both in Europe and America, to found village settlements of this kind, whether communistic or cooperative in the narrower sense, have mostly met with failure.[1] I would apply the word "failure" not merely to those settlements, or attempts at settlements, which after a more or less short-lived existence either disintegrated completely or took on a capitalist complexion, thus going over to the enemy camp; I would also apply it to those that maintained themselves in isolation. For the real, the truly structural task of the new village communes begins with their *federation*, that is, their union under the same principle that operates in their internal structure. Hardly anywhere has it come to this. Even where, as with the Doukhobors in Canada, a sort of federative union exists, the federation itself continues to be isolated and exerts no attractive and educative influence on society as a whole, with the result that the task never gets beyond its beginnings and, consequently, there can be no talk of success in the socialist sense. It is remarkable that Kropotkin saw in these two elements—isolation of the settlements from one another and isolation from the rest of society—the efficient causes of their failure even as ordinarily understood.

The socialistic task can only be accomplished to the degree that the new village commune, combining the various forms of production and uniting production and consumption, exerts a structural influence on the amorphous urban society. The influence will only make itself felt to the full if, and to the extent that, further technological developments facilitate and actually require the decentralization of industry; but even now a pervasive force is latent in the modern communal village, and it may spread to the towns. It must be emphasized again that the tendency we are dealing with is constructive and topical: it would be romantic and utopian to want to destroy the towns, as once it was romantic and utopian to want to destroy the machines, but it is constructive and topical to try to transform the town organically in the closest possible alliance with technological developments and to turn it into an aggregate composed of smaller units. Indeed, many countries today show significant beginnings in this respect.

---

[1] Of course, I am not dealing here with the otherwise successful "socio-economic organizations, used by governmental or semi-governmental agencies to improve rural conditions" (Infield, *Cooperative Communities at Work*, p. 63).

As I see history and the present, there is only one all-out effort to create a full cooperative which justifies our speaking of success in the socialistic sense, and that is the Jewish village commune in its various forms, as found in Palestine. No doubt it, too, is up against grave problems in the sphere of internal relationships, federation, and influence on society at large, but it alone has proved its vitality in all three spheres. Nowhere else in the history of communal settlements is there this tireless groping for the form of community life best suited to this particular human group, nowhere else this continual trying and trying again, this going to it and getting down to it, this critical awareness, this sprouting of new branches from the same stem and out of the same formative impulse. And nowhere else is there this alertness to one's own problems, this constant facing up to them, this tough will to come to terms with them, and this indefatigable struggle—albeit seldom expressed in words—to overcome them. Here, and here alone, do we find in the emergent community organs of self-knowledge whose very sensitiveness has constantly reduced its members to despair—but this is a despair that destroys wishful thinking only to raise up in its stead a greater hope which is no longer emotionalism but sheer work. Thus on the soberest survey and on the soberest reflection one can say that, in this one spot in a world of partial failures, we can recognize a nonfailure—and, such as it is, a signal nonfailure.

What are the reasons for this? We could not get to know the peculiar character of this cooperative colonization better than by following up these reasons.

One element in these reasons has been repeatedly pointed out: that the Jewish village commune in Palestine owes its existence not to a doctrine but to a situation, to the needs, the stress, the demands of the situation. In establishing the "kvutzah" or village commune the primary thing was not ideology but work. This is certainly correct, but with one limitation. True, the point was to solve certain problems of work and construction which the Palestinian reality forced on the settlers, by collaborating; what a loose conglomeration of individuals could not, in the nature of things, hope to overcome, or even try to overcome, things being what they were, the collective could try to do and actually succeeded in doing. But what is called the "ideology"—I personally prefer the old but un-tarnished word "ideal"—was not just something to be added afterward that would justify the accomplished facts. In the spirit of the members of the first Palestinian com-munes ideal motives joined hands with the dictates of the hour; and in the motives there was a curious mixture of memories of the Russian artel, impressions left over from reading the so-called "utopian" socialists, and the half-unconscious aftereffects of the Bible's teachings about so-cial justice. The important thing is that this ideal motive remained loose and pliable in almost every respect. There were various dreams about the future: people saw before them a new, more comprehensive form of the family, they saw themselves as the advance guard of the workers' move-ment, as the direct instrument for the realization of social-ism, as the prototype of the new society; they had as their goal the creation of a new man and a new world. But nothing of this ever hardened into a cut-and-dried pro-gram. These men did not, as everywhere else in the his-tory of cooperative settlements, bring a plan with them, a plan which the concrete situation could only fill out, not modify; the ideal gave an impetus but no dogma, it stimu-lated but did not dictate.

More important, however, is that, behind the Palestinian situation that set the tasks of work and reconstruction, there was the historical situation of a people visited by a great external crisis and responding to it with a great inner change. Further, this historical situation threw up an elite —the "halutzim" or pioneers—drawn from all classes of the people and thus beyond class. The form of life that befitted this elite was the village commune, by which I mean not a single note but the whole scale, ranging from the social structure of "mutual aid" to the commune itself. This form was the best fitted to fulfill the tasks of the cen-tral halutzim, and at the same time the one in which the social ideal could materially influence the national idea. As the historical conditions have shown, it was impossible for this elite and the form of life it favored to become static or isolated; all its tasks, everything it did, its whole pioneering spirit made it the center of attraction and a central influence. The pioneer spirit ("halutziut") is, in

every part of it, related to the growth of a new and transformed national community; the moment it grew self-suf-
ficient it would have lost its soul. The village commune,
as the nucleus of the evolving society, had to exert a
powerful pull on the people dedicated to this evolution,
and it had not merely to educate its friends and associates
for genuine communal living, but also to exercise a formative structural effect on the social periphery. The dynamics of history determined the dynamic character of the
relations between village commune and society.

This character suffered a considerable setback when the
tempo of the crisis in the outer world became so rapid,
and its symptoms so drastic, that the inner change could
not keep pace with them. To the extent that Palestine had
been turned from the one and only land of the "aliyah"—
ascent—into a country of immigrants, a quasi halutziut
came into being alongside the genuine halutziut. The pull
exerted by the commune did not abate, but its educative
powers were not adapted to the influx of very different
human material, and this material sometimes succeeded in
influencing the tone of the community. At the same time
the commune's relations with society at large underwent
a change. As the structure of the latter altered, it with-
drew more and more from the transforming influence of
the focal cells, indeed, it began in its turn to exert an influence on them—not always noticeable at first, but un-
mistakable today—by seizing on certain essential elements in them and assimilating them to itself.

In the life of peoples, and particularly peoples who find
themselves in the midst of some historical crisis, it is of
crucial importance whether genuine elites (which means
elites that do not usurp but are called to their central
function) arise, whether these elites remain loyal to their
duty to society, establishing a relationship to it rather
than to themselves, and finally, whether they have the
power to replenish and renew themselves in a manner
conformable with their task. The historical destiny of
the Jewish settlements in Palestine brought the elite of the
halutzim to birth, and it found its social nuclear form in
the village commune. Another wave of this same destiny
has washed up, together with the quasi halutzim, a problem for the real halutzim elite. It has caused a problem

that was always latent to come to the surface. They have not yet succeeded in mastering it and yet must master it before they can reach the next stage of their task. The inner tension between those who take the *whole* responsibility for the community on their shoulders and those who somehow evade it can be resolved only at a very deep level.

The point where the problem emerges is neither the individual's relationship to the idea nor his relationship to the community nor yet to work; on all these points even the quasi halutzim gird up their loins and do by and large what is expected of them. The point where the problem emerges, where people are apt to slip, is in their relationship to their fellows. By this I do not mean the question, much discussed in its day, of the intimacy that exists in the small and the loss of this intimacy in the big kvutzah; I mean something that has nothing whatever to do with the size of the commune. It is not a matter of intimacy at all; this appears when it must, and if it is lacking, that's all there is to it. The question is rather one of openness. A real community need not consist of people who are perpetually together; but it must consist of people who, precisely because they are comrades, have mutual access to one another and are ready for one another. A real community is one which in every point of its being possesses, potentially at least, the whole character of community. The internal questions of a community are thus in reality questions relating to its own genuineness, hence to its inner strength and stability. The men who created the Jewish communes in Palestine instinctively knew this; but the instinct no longer seems to be as common and alert as it was. Yet it is in this most important field that we find that remorselessly clear-sighted collective self-observation and self-criticism to which I have already drawn attention. But to understand and value it aright we must see it together with the amazingly positive relationship—amounting to a regular faith—which these men have to the inmost being of their commune. The two things are two sides of the same spiritual world and neither can be understood without the other.

In order to make the causes of the nonfailure of these Jewish communal settlements sufficiently vivid, in Palestine, I began with the nondoctrinaire character of their

origins. This character also determined their development
in all essentials. New forms and new intermediate forms
were constantly branching off—in complete freedom.
Each one grew out of the particular social and spiritual
needs as these came to light—in complete freedom, and
each one acquired, even in the initial stages, its own ideology—in complete freedom, each struggling to propagate
itself and spread and establish its proper sphere—all in
complete freedom. The champions of the various forms
each had his say, the pros and cons of each individual
form were frankly and fiercely debated—always, however,
on the plane which everybody accepted as obvious: the
common cause and common task, where each form recognized the relative justice of all the other forms in their
special functions. All this is unique in the history of cooperative settlements. What is more: nowhere, as far as
I see, in the history of the socialist movement were men
so deeply involved in the process of differentiation and
yet so intent on preserving the principle of integration.

The various forms and intermediate forms that arose in
this way at different times and in different situations represented different kinds of social structure. The people who
built them were generally aware of this as also of the particular social and spiritual needs that actuated them. They
were not aware to the same extent that the different forms
corresponded to different human types and that just as
new forms branched off from the orginal kvutzah, so new
types branched off from the original halutz type, each with
its special mode of being and each demanding its particular sort of realization. More often that not it was economic
and suchlike external factors that led certain people to
break away from one form and attach themselves to
another. But in the main it happened that each type looked
for the social realization of its peculiarities in this particular form and, on the whole, found it there. And not only
was each form based on a definite type, it molded and
keeps on molding this type. It was and is intent on developing it; the constitution, organization, and educational
system of each form are—no matter how consciously or
unconsciously—dedicated to this end. Thus something has
been produced which is essentially different from all the
social experiments that have ever been made: not a labora-

tory where everybody works for himself, alone with his
problems and plans, but an experimental station where, on
common soil, different colonies or "cultures" are tested
out according to different methods for a common purpose.

Yet here, too, a problem emerged, no longer within the
individual group but in the relation of the groups to one
another; nor did it come from without, it came from
within—in fact, from the very heart of the principle of
freedom.

Even in its first undifferentiated form a tendency toward federation was innate in the kvutzah, to merge the
kvutzoth in some higher social unit; and a very important
tendency it was, since it showed that the kvutzah implicitly
understood that it was the cell of a newly structured society. With the splitting off and proliferation of the various
forms, from the semi-individualistic form which jealously
guarded personal independence in its domestic economy,
way of life, children's education, etc., to the pure communistic form, the single unit was supplanted by a series
of units in each of which a definite form of colony and a
more or less definite human type constituted itself on a
federal basis. The fundamental assumption was that the
local groups would combine on the same principle of
solidarity and mutual help as reigned within the individual
group. But the trend toward a larger unit is far from having atrophied in the process. On the contrary, at least in
the kibbutz or collectivist movement, it asserts itself with
great force and clarity; it recognizes the federative kibbutzim—units where the local groups have pooled their
various aspirations—as a provisional structure; indeed, a
thoughtful leader of their movement calls them a substitute for a commune of communes. Apart from the fact,
however, that individual forms, especially, for instance,
the "moshavim" or semi-individualistic labor settlements
—though these do not fall short of any of the other forms
in the matter of communal economic control and mutual
help—are already too far removed from the basic form
to be included in a unitary plan, in the kibbutz movement
itself subsidiary organizations stand in the way of the trend
toward unification which wants to embrace and absorb
them. Each has developed its own special character and
consolidated it in the unit, and it is natural that each should

incline to view unification as an extension of its own influence. But something else has been added that has led
to an enormous intensification of this attitude on the part
of the single units: political development. Twenty years
ago a leader of one of the big units could say emphatically:
"We are a community and not a party." This has radically
changed in the meantime, and the conditions for unification have been aggravated accordingly. The lamentable
fact has emerged that the all-important attitude of
neighborly relationship has not been adequately developed,
although not a few cases are on record of a flourishing
and rich village giving generous help to a young and poor
neighbor which belonged to another unit. In these circumstances the great struggle that has broken out on the question of unification, particularly in the last decade, is the
more remarkable. Nobody who is a socialist at heart can
read the great document of this struggle, the Hebrew com-
pilation entitled *The Kibbutz and the Kvutzah*, edited by
the late labor leader Berl Kaznelson, without being lost
in admiration of the high-minded passion with which these
two camps battled with one another for genuine unity.
The union will probably not be attained save as the outcome of a situation that makes it absolutely necessary. But
that the men of the Jewish communes have labored so
strenuously with one another and against one another for
the emergence of a *communitas communitatum,* that is to
say, for a structurally new society—this will not be forgotten in the history of mankind's struggle for self-renewal.

I have said that I see in this bold Jewish undertaking a
"signal nonfailure." I cannot say: a signal success. To become that, much has still to be done. Yet it is in this way,
in this kind of tempo, with such setbacks, disappointments,
and new ventures, that the real changes are accomplished
in this our mortal world.

But can one speak of this nonfailure as "signal"? I have
pointed out the peculiar nature of the premises and conditions that led to it. And what one of its own representatives
has said of the Kvutzah that it is a typically Palestinian
product, is true of all these forms.

Still, if an experiment conducted under certain conditions has proved successful up to a point, we can set about
varying it under other, less favorable, conditions.

There can hardly be any doubt that we must regard the last war as the end of the prelude to a world crisis. This crisis will probably break out—after a somber "interlude" that cannot last very long—first among some of the nations of the West, who will be able to restore their shattered economy in appearance only. They will see themselves faced with the immediate need for radical socialization, above all the expropriation of the land. It will then be of absolutely decisive importance *who* is the real subject of an economy so transformed, and who is the owner of the social means of production. Is it to be the central authority in a highly centralized state, or the social units of urban and rural workers, living and producing on a communal basis, and their representative bodies? In the latter case the remodeled organs of the state will discharge the functions of adjustment and administration only. On these issues will largely depend the growth of a new society and a new civilization. The essential point is to decide on the fundamentals: a restructuring of society as a league of leagues, and a reduction of the state to its proper function, which is to maintain unity; or a devouring of an amorphous society by the omnipotent state; socialist pluralism or so-called socialist unitarianism. The right proportion, tested anew every day according to changing conditions, between group freedom and collective order; or absolute order imposed indefinitely for the sake of an era of freedom alleged to follow "of its own accord." So long as Russia has not undergone an essential inner change— and today we have no means of knowing when and how that will come to pass—we must designate one of the two poles of socialism between which our choice lies, by the formidable name of "Moscow." The other, I would make bold to call "Jerusalem."

Zionism, the Marxist Critique, and the Left

Walter Laqueur

WALTER LAQUEUR—a distinguished European historian, director of the Institute of Contemporary
History in London, professor of History at the
University of Tel Aviv, author of many books, including *Young Germany, The Fate of a Revolution, Europe Since Hitler,* and *The Struggle for
the Middle East.*

The opposition to Zionism is as old as Zionism itself; it
has come from many directions, Jewish and non-Jewish,
left and right, religious and atheist. It has been asserted
on the one hand that the Zionist goal was impossible to
achieve, on the other hand that it was undesirable, and
by some that it was both illusory and undesirable. Arab
opposition is not surprising, but attacks came from other
quarters too, including the Catholic Church, Asian nationalists suspicious of European intruders, Arabophile
European politicians and orientalists, and the Communists.
Pacifists condemned it as a violent movement; Gandhi
wrote that as a spiritual ideal Zionism had his sympathy,
but by the use of force the Jews had vulgarized and de-
based their ideal. Tolstoy said that Zionism was not a
progressive but basically a militarist movement; the Jewish idea would not find its fulfillment in a territorially
limited fatherland; did the Jews really want a state on the
pattern of Serbia, Romania, or Montenegro?[1]

Some anti-Semites welcomed Zionism, others denounced
it in the sharpest terms; for to them Jews and Judaism
represented a destructive element and their policy was

---

[1] *Graf Leo Tolstoi über die Juden*, ed. O. Pergament (Berlin,
n.d.), pp. 18, 23.

16

therefore aimed at reducing Jewish influence and getting rid of as many Jews as possible. It might seem that they should have welcomed a movement which intended to reduce the number of Jews in the various European countries, but in fact they frequently turned against it; Palestine was too good or too important to be given to the Jews, who in any case had lost the capacity to build a state of their own. They were bound to remain parasites and Zionism was therefore a sham; it was not a constructive effort, but on the contrary a mere ruse, part of the conspiracy to establish Jewish world rule. Confusing his metaphors, Alfred Rosenberg, the Nazi ideologist, wrote in 1922:

> Some of the locusts which have been sucking the marrow of Europe are returning to the promised land and are already looking for greener pastures. At its best Zionism is the impotent effort of an unfit people to achieve something constructive, but in the main it helps ambitious speculators as a new field in which to practise usury on a world-wide scale.[2]

Rosenberg demanded the outlawing of Zionism as an enemy of the German state, and the indictment of Zionists on the charge of high treason.

The present essay, part of a larger study, deals with the Marxist and neo-Marxist critique of Zionism. The topic is fascinating but now at least partly of historical interest. For with the emergence of a Jewish nation and the state of Israel the question whether Zionism was a good or a bad idea is no longer one of immediate political relevance. The nation and the state have become a reality, to the joy of some and the distress of others.

While socialism had many followers among the Zionists, socialist theory, especially the Marxist variety, was for a long time hostile to the Jewish national movement. Marx, Engels, and their immediate disciples were preoccupied with the problems of class and class struggle; a systematic study of national movements was undertaken only later on, toward the turn of the century, especially in countries where these issues were of particular importance and urgency, as in pre–World War II Austria. Marx and Engels

---

[2] *Der staatsfeindliche Zionismus* (Hamburg, 1922), pp. 62–63.

shared the view of their liberal contemporaries that cultural, economic, and social progress was gradually over-
coming national exclusivity and that the world (or Europe
at any rate) was moving toward internationalism. Unlike
the liberals, they did not believe that all national movements were equal; some were downright reactionary. It all
depended on whether a particular national movement
served or impeded the cause of revolution. About East
European Jewry they were ignorant, and as for the Jews
in the West they again shared the liberal belief that assimilation would solve the problem. The young Marx did
publish an essay on the Jewish question, but it is of greater
interest to the student of metaphysics than to the student
of history. Not for a moment did he believe in the existence
of a Jewish people; for Moses Hess's Zionism he had nothing but contempt. The idea that Judaism and the Jews as
a collective had a future must have appeared to him as an
aberration typical of the loose thinking of someone too
stupid to understand the implications of his own doctrine.
Judaism for Marx was a totally negative phenomenon,
something to be got rid of as quickly and as radically as
possible. As far as he personally was concerned, his Jewish
origin must have appeared an unfortunate accident of
birth and a matter of considerable embarrassment. But
this was by no means an original or specifically "Marxist" attitude. Many of his antisocialist contemporaries
reacted in exactly the same way. The liberals, too, were convinced that a man's national origin was not of great importance. They were first and foremost citizens of the
world and only secondarily German, Austrian, or Russian
nationals. Socialists of a later day held the same view, and
in this respect there was no substantial difference between
revolutionaries and reformists: Léon Blum and Eduard
Bernstein, Rosa Luxemburg and Leon Trotsky thought
of themselves above all as members of the international
socialist movement.

Only toward the end of the nineteenth century did the
Jewish issue assume greater importance in socialist thought
and policy, partly as the result of the spread of anti-Semitism. There were many Jews in the leadership of the European and American socialist parties; some delegations
at the meetings of the Socialist International before 1914

were almost exclusively Jewish. But with the rise of nationalist and anti-Semitic currents their position became more difficult and they grew more conscious (and self-conscious) of their Jewish origin. This did not, however, affect their basic conviction that the coming socialist revolution would solve the Jewish question wherever it existed, and that meanwhile everyone had to participate actively in the struggle for the liberation of the working class in his country of origin. In Western Europe early Zionism was regarded by socialists as a romantic, utopian, reactionary aberration. Bernard Lazare, a French Jewish socialist intellectual, was almost alone in sympathizing with the new movement. In Eastern Europe, too, not only Zionism but even less ambitious forms of Jewish nationalism such as bundism, with its demand for cultural-national autonomy, were emphatically rejected by the leading socialists. For Plekhanov and the men of his generation the bundists were merely "Zionists suffering from seasickness." The ideological rationale for socialist anti-Zionism was provided by Karl Kautsky, for many years the most respected interpreter of Marxist doctrine for West and East European socialists alike.

According to Kautsky the traits derived from the primitive races of man tended to disappear as economic evolution progressed; the Jews were a mixed race, but so were the non-Jews.[3] In the past the Jews had been an exclusive hereditary caste of urban merchants, financiers, intellectuals, and a small number of artisans, who from generation to generation bequeathed certain traits peculiar to these strata. But with the advance of industrial capitalism, the barriers were gradually broken down, the Jews obtained equal rights, and many of them were absorbed by the peoples among whom they lived. Anti-Semitism, or "the Jewish peril," was given a new lease on life by the reaction of the petty bourgeoisie against liberalism. There were two forms of defense against this pressure: proletarian solidarity and Jewish solidarity. Among the Jews of Eastern Europe, for specific economic and social reasons,

---

[3] *Rasse und Judentum* (Berlin, 1914); quoted here from the revised English translation, *Are the Jews a Race?* (London, 1926), pp. 89 ff.

the call for national solidarity, i.e., Zionism, had found a considerable echo, but it had no future. Where could space be found for a Jewish state, since all regions in the civilized world had been preempted? How were the Jews to be induced to work in agriculture? How was a powerful industry to be developed in Palestine? All theoretical considerations apart, Kautsky thus saw in 1914 insurmountable obstacles on the road to a realization of the Zionist aim.

His views had not basically changed when he returned to the subject after the war. He was impressed by the idealism of the Jewish pioneers in Palestine and their achievements, which must convince anyone who had doubted Jewish energy and resolution.[4] But Zionist enthusiasm was not likely to persist. He predicted that Jewish *Luftmenschen* and intellectuals would again congregate in the cities and the Palestinian proletariat would become more class-conscious. As a result Jewish capitalists would lose interest, and without capital the process of rebuilding would come to a halt. At best, Jews in Palestine would come to outnumber the Arabs, and the new Jewish state, although not embracing the great mass of world Jewry, would nevertheless be predominantly Jewish in character. But this was not at all likely, for the political conditions were rapidly becoming worse: "Whatever Zionism does not attain within the next few years, it will never attain at all."[5] Zionism, to summarize Kautsky's view, was not a progressive, but a reactionary movement; it aimed not at following the line of necessary evolution but at putting a spoke in the wheel of progress. It denied the right of self-determination of nations and proclaimed instead the doctrine of historical rights.

At this point Kautsky deviated from the views of Marx and Engels, who attached little importance to national self-determination; they frequently referred with contempt to "lousy little peoples" whose interests were to be ignored in the higher interest of history. Thus America's war against Mexico was progressive because it had been waged in the interest of history, and Germany's annexa-

---

[4] Ibid., p. 202.
[5] Ibid., p. 207.

tion of Schleswig was justified in the name of civilization against barbarism, of progress against the status quo. The fact that Herzl and Nordau intended to carry Western civilization to the East would not necessarily have shocked liberals of a later day. They would have rejected Zionism for reasons of realpolitik, because it appeared too late on the international scene and was not strong enough to accomplish its self-proclaimed task.

Kautsky was sure that the Palestinian adventure would end in tragedy. The Jewish would not become more numerous than the Arabs, nor would they succeed in convincing the Arabs that Jewish rule could be to their advantage. "Jewish colonization in Palestine must collapse as soon as the Anglo-French hegemony over Asia Minor (including Egypt) collapses, and this is merely a question of time, perhaps of the very near future."[6] There was no longer any doubt about the final victory of the "Arabian" [sic] people; the only question was whether they would reach it by peaceful concessions or by a period of savage guerrilla warfare and bloody insurrections. The poor, weak Jewish settlers in Palestine would be the chief sufferers in this battle, "the least able to defend themselves, as well as least capable to escape."[7] All one could hope for therefore was that the number of victims would not be great:

> But the dangers to the Jews who are lured to Palestine by a Messianic aspiration do not exhaust all the baleful effects of Zionism. It is perhaps far worse that Zionism is wasting the fortunes and resources of the Jews in a wrong direction, at a moment when their true destinies are being decided on an entirely different arena, for which decision it would be necessary for them to concentrate all their forces.[8]

Kautsky was referring to Eastern Europe, where the fate of eight to ten million Jews was to be decided. Since emigration could not help them, their destiny was intimately linked with the prospects of revolution. Zionism weakened them in this effort by encouraging ambitions which amounted to desertion of the colors.

---

[6] Ibid., p. 211.
[7] Ibid., p. 212.
[8] Ibid., p. 213.

What of the more distant prospect? Not liberalism, but only a victorious proletariat could bring complete emancipation. Then the Jews would be absorbed, would cease to exist as such. This was not to be deplored; the disappearance of the ghetto would not give rise to melancholy longings. Being city dwellers the Jews had the qualities most required for the progress of humanity; in Western Europe, though few in number, they had produced Spinoza, Heine, Lassalle, Marx; but these spiritual giants became effective only after they had burst the fetters of Judaism. Their work lay outside the sphere of Judaism, within the realm of modern culture, often in conscious opposition to Judaism.

> The Jews have become an eminently revolutionary factor [Kautsky wrote], while Judaism has become a reactionary factor. It is like a weight of lead attached to the feet of the Jews who eagerly seek to progress. The sooner [this social ghetto] disappears, the better it will be not only for society, but also for the Jews themselves.[9]

The disappearance of the Jews would not be a tragedy like the disappearance of the American Indians or the Tasmanians. For it would not be a decline into degradation but an ascent to an immense field of activity making possible the creation of a new and higher type of man. "The Wandering Jew will thus at last find a haven of rest. He will continue to live in the memory of man as man's greatest sufferer, as he who has been dealt with most severely by mankind, to whom he has given most."

Kautsky's views have been given at some length because they remain the most consistent and systematic exposition of the Marxist arguments against Zionism. The critics of a later day, Communist, Trotskyite, or New Left, base their arguments in all essentials on his, occasionally with differences of detail and emphasis.

In turn, the Zionist response to the Marxist critique can be summarized as follows: Marxism has been mistaken in underrating the importance of nationalism in recent history. National antagonisms have not declined in importance, even in countries in which communism has

---

9 Ibid., p. 246.

prevailed. The Marxist analysis (like the liberal analysis) may be correct sub specie aeternatis; history may move in the direction of one world, with equality for all races, nations, and peoples. But Zionism is not concerned with these distant prospects; it emerged precisely because, in contrast to the liberal and Marxist analysis, it assumed that the Jewish question would not disappear in the foreseeable future. On the contrary, it was likely to become much more acute. The appeal to the Jews to participate in the revolutionary struggle in their homeland was no doubt well meant, but even on the assumption that the interests of the Jews and the revolution were identical, it was not practical politics.

The Polish, German, or Austrian working class neither needed nor wanted the Jews as allies; they wanted to get rid of them, or, at best regarded them as an embarrassment in their political struggle. Jews have played a leading part in the early phases of all socialist and communist parties, but almost everywhere they have been squeezed out. Among the founders and early leaders of the German Communist party there was a majority of Jews; the year before Hitler came to power there was not a single one among the hundred Communist deputies in the Reichstag. Events have taken a similar course in the Soviet Union. This was not necessarily a disaster in Zionist eyes, but it certainly underlined the argument that the position of the Jews in the revolutionary movement was highly problematical. A New Left critic of Zionism wrote in 1970 that subsequent events have shown that Trotsky and Zinoviev, Kamenev and Radek had been right, not the Zionists. Since all these Bolshevik leaders fell victim to Stalinism, the argument is not exactly convincing.[10] With anti-Semitism on the rise, the Jews in Europe were condemned to be passive onlookers, not active participants in the revolutionary struggle.

The Marxist critics did not foresee the victory of fascism and the extermination of the majority of European Jewry. It had been argued that the temporary victory of the counterrevolution, despite its appalling consequences,

---

[10] *Zur Kritik der zionistischen Theorie und Praxis* (Frankfurt: Resistentia, 1970), p. 39.

did not necessarily refute the socialist thesis about the ultimate absorption and assimilation of the Jews in their native countries. But since Marxist analysis and prediction have been belied by recent history, there is no assurance that it will be borne out by future developments. The Marxist-Leninist thesis is based on the assumption that Communist regimes would successfully tackle the Jewish problem and that as a result the Jews as a group would disappear. But if there were no Jews left in Communist Poland in 1970, this happened not as the result of the emergence of a "new and higher type of man," as Kautsky predicted, but in a manner reminiscent of the exodus from Spain in the fifteenth century. The Jews have been difficult to absorb for capitalist and Communist societies alike; was it the "reactionary character of Judaism" that was responsible for this, or the fact that the Jews are an "eminently revolutionary factor" and thus likely to disturb the peace of postrevolutionary regimes? The possibility of Jewish assimilation in a truly internationalist society such as Lenin envisaged cannot be excluded, but such a society does not exist; the Soviet Union and the other Communist countries have moved steadily away from the internationalist ideal toward a new form of nationalist socialism. In these conditions total assimilation has become difficult if not impossible.

Present difficulties quite apart, Zionists claim that recent history has shown that the Marxist concept of nationalism, of the nation-state in general and of anti-Semitism in particular, is at best grossly oversimplified. According to Marx and his disciples, such as Kautsky, the Jew was the representative of modern capitalism, or to be precise, commercial capitalism, and having lost this function was bound to disappear. But this concept never made much sense in Eastern Europe, where the majority of Jews were concentrated, nor does it provide an explanation for pre- and postcapitalist anti-Semitism.

The Austrian Marxists, who faced the nationality problem in an acute form, were aware of the weakness of this aspect of Marxist theory and provided in the works of Otto Bauer and Karl Renner a more sophisticated analysis. Where Kautsky had originally regarded a common language as the decisive criterion for the existence of a nation (later he added a second criterion: territory), Otto Bauer defined a nation as a community of fate, culture, and character: "An aggregate of people bound into a community of character by a community of fate."[11] The Jews were still a nation, especially those in Eastern Europe, but everywhere they were in the process of ceasing to be one. As an "absolute minority," one lacking a common territory, they were, unlike the Czechs, doomed as a nation, bound to be absorbed into the cultural community of the European nations.[12] While not rejecting Jewish national culture and opposing compulsory assimilation, Bauer thought it would be wrong for the Jews to insist on national autonomy because this would retard the inevitable historical process.

This remained the attitude of the Jewish leaders and theoreticians of Austro-Marxism and the advent of fascism did not make them change their mind. Friedrich Adler wrote in 1949 that he and his father (one of the founders of the Social Democratic party) had always considered the complete assimilation of the Jews both desirable and possible. Even the bestialities of Hitler had not shaken him in his belief that Jewish nationalism was bound to generate reactionary tendencies, namely the resurrection of a language which had been dead for almost two thousand years and the rebirth of an antiquated religion.[13] The non-Jewish leaders of Austro-Marxism took, on occasion, a more lenient view of Zionism. Karl Renner developed a highly complicated concept of nonterritorial autonomy as the only feasible way to safeguard the interests of minorities in a multinational state. He did not include the Jews in this scheme, but unlike Bauer did not expressio verbis exclude them. Both bundists and Zionists welcomed Renner's scheme and adapted it for their own purposes. According to Pernerstorfer, another Austrian socialist leader, it was up to the Jews to decide whether they were a nation or not. There was no doubt that they had the right to national existence; whether the practical difficul-

---

[11] *Die Nationalitätenfrage und die Sozialdemokratie* (Vienna, 1907), p. 135.
[12] Ibid., pp. 366 ff.
[13] Quoted in *Leo Bäck Year Book*, 10 (London, 1965): 275.

ties on the road to national autonomy could be overcome was another question. Pernerstorfer thought that the Jews in Eastern Europe would survive in the long run only if they got an independent state.[14]

Such individual voices apart, the attitude of international social democracy toward Zionism remained hostile until the First World War. *Neue Zeit*, the theoretical organ of the German socialists, dismissed Herzl's *Judenstaat* as utopian and unworthy of serious consideration, a beautiful cloak in which a nation no longer alive was to appear on the historical stage for the last time, to disappear after that forever.[15] A few years later another (Jewish) contributor explained Zionism as the reaction of the Jewish bourgeoisie to modern anti-Semitism. Social democracy was not against Zionism in principle, he argued, but since the (bourgeois) Zionists were trying to achieve their aim not by a liberation struggle but by bargaining with Turkey, and since they were moreover preaching class solidarity and national separatism and did not reject religion, international socialism could not support them.[16] In English socialist circles Zionism was condemned as reactionary through and through, with Russian-Jewish émigrés such as Theodore Rothstein taking a leading part in denouncing the movement.[17] On occasion more sympathetic voices were heard; an English socialist journal promised that once the class struggle was won, the Jews too would find a place in the sun to shape their own national destiny. But on the whole English socialists did not pay much attention to the issue. French socialists were even less interested, but certainly not favorably inclined. After the publication in *Revue Socialiste* of a pro-Zionist article commenting on the Kishinev massacre, an editorial note dismissed as a myth the belief in Palestine as the home of all Jews. Zionism was psychologically understandable as a reaction to cruel persecution, but born of despair and

[14] Rudolf Springer [Karl Renner], *Der Kampf der österreichischen Nation um den Staat* (Leipzig, 1902), passim; E. Pernerstorfer, "Zur Judenfrage," *Der Jude* (1916–17), p. 308.

[15] *Neue Zeit*, 15 (1896–97): 186; 16 (1897–98): 600.

[16] Ibid., 19 (1900–1901): 324 ff.

[17] *Justice*, October 21, 1899; quoted in E. Silberner, *Sozialisten zur Judenfrage* (Berlin, 1962), p. 262.

based on a myth, it was, like all other forms of nationalism, reactionary and reprehensible.[18] Before 1914 the only
major exception to this wholesale rejection of Zionism on
the part of the left was the circle of the *Sozialistische Mo-
natshefte*, a revisionist journal edited by Josef Bloch in
Berlin which pursued an independent line on this as on
many other issues.

After the First World War many socialists modified
their attitude. Kautsky and the Marxist fundamentalists
remained opposed, and the attacks emanating from these
circles were harsh in both form and content. Zionism, according to a pamphlet by Alexander Szanto (to provide
a fairly typical example), was a harmful illusion, and the
sooner it was liquidated the better for the Jews. There was
no earthly chance that they would ever become a majority
in Palestine. Zionism was reactionary and chauvinistic;
far from contributing to the solution of the Jewish problem, it was trying to sabotage the absorption of the Jews
in their native countries. In Central and Western Europe
assimilation was about to be completed, Szanto wrote in
1930: "Anti-Semitism is merely engaged in rearguard actions."[19] Time was working against Zionism, but while
it did its mischief it was the duty of every socialist to combat it, and not to be neutral. For Zionism was not a marginal phenomenon, it was a cancerous disease. "Whoever
is not against it is for it."

There was however no longer a consensus on these lines
in socialist ranks. Vandervelde, one of the most respected
figures of the Second International and for many years its
chairman, visited Palestine in the 1920s; subsequently he
wrote with sympathy about the work of the Labor Zionists.
Other leading Social Democrats, including Louis de
Brouckere, Vincent Auriol, Camille Huysmans, George
Lansbury, Arthur Henderson, and Rudolf Breitscheid
joined, in 1928, a Socialist Committee for Working Palestine. The right of the Jewish people to a national home
in Palestine was recognized in various resolutions of international socialist congresses between 1917 and 1920. Jean

---

[18] Quoted ibid., pp. 89–90.
[19] *Der Zionismus—eine nationalistische und reaktionäre Utopie*
(Berlin, 1930), pp. 52–53.

Longuet, (Karl Marx's grandson), one of the leaders of French socialism, declared in 1918 that the idea of a Jewish national home in Palestine deserved the support of international social democracy. His colleague Léon Blum even became one of the non-Zionist members of the Jewish Agency in 1929. After the Second World War many Marxists, such as Harold Laski, admitted that their views on the Jewish question had been mistaken and accepted the necessity of a Jewish state.

Of symptomatic interest were the changes in the attitude of leading socialists of the older generation, such as Axelrod and Eduard Bernstein, who had earlier sharply opposed Zionism. Axelrod declared in 1917 that he was now in favor of the realization of the aims of Zionism. Bernstein, father of the reformist trend in German social democracy, also joined the pro-Palestine socialist committee in 1928. Before 1914 he, too, had favored the denationalization of the Jews, who, he said, no longer had any specific mission. He conceded that East European Jews might have to emigrate, but a rescue action on their behalf was not to be coupled with the idea of a Jewish state, which in any case would face insurmountable obstacles. That assimilation was desirable was as axiomatic for Bernstein as it was for Kautsky, his chief antagonist; there was in their view no justification for any specific Jewish solidarity or national separatism. Zionism was obnoxious and reactionary because it impeded assimilation.[20] After the war Bernstein admitted that he had underrated the importance and persistence of anti-Semitism. He declared that he felt too much a German to become a Zionist, but added that he followed the activities of Zionism with sympathy; it had inspired its followers to great creative achievements. Poale Zion was an active member of the Second International, much to the dismay of anti-Zionists like Szanto. But by and large Zionism remained a marginal issue for European social democracy; most of the Social Democratic leaders did not believe in the success of the Palestinian experiment, for both ideological and practical

---

[20] *Neue Zeit*, 2 (1891–92): 236–37; J. Moses, ed., *Die Lösung der Judenfrage* (Berlin, 1907), passim; *Neue Zeit*, 32 (1913–14), quoted in Silberner, *Sozialisten zur Judenfrage*.

reasons, though after 1918 their tone was on the whole sorrowful rather than angry. Those who had any firsthand knowledge of the Jewish problem were now more aware than previously that the issues involved were much more intricate than they had originally believed. By the late 1920s most socialists had realized that even if Zionism was mistaken, the Second International and its affiliated parties had no ready alternative answer to the Jewish problem. By 1945 most socialists recognized the right of the Jewish people to a national home.

Communism, claiming that it did have a solution, was not beset by such doubts. Lenin's rejection of Jewish nationalism was based on the writings of Kautsky and Otto Bauer, whom he frequently quoted. In some respects he went beyond them, asserting that nationalism even in its most justified and innocuous form was incompatible with Marxism. Even the demand for national cultural autonomy ("the most refined and therefore the most pernicious kind of nationalism") was thoroughly harmful; it satisfied the ideals of the nationalist petty bourgeois and was in absolute contradiction with the internationalism of the proletariat.[21] Marxists had to fight against any form of national oppression, but it did not follow that the proletariat had to support the national development of every nation. On the contrary, Marxism had to warn the masses against any nationalist illusions and to welcome every type of assimilation unless based on coercion. The Jews of the West had already achieved the highest degree of assimilation in the civilized countries. In Galicia and Russia they were not a nation either, but had remained a caste, not through any fault of their own but through that of the anti-Semites.[22] Jewish national culture was the slogan of rabbis and the bourgeois, and its advocates were therefore enemies of the proletariat.

Stalin, writing an elaboration of Lenin's view in 1913, defined a nation as a historically evolved, stable community of language, territory, economic life, and mental constitution expressed in a community of culture. According to this definition the Jews were of course not a nation;

---

[21] *Sochineniya*, 2d Russian ed., 17: 118.
[22] Ibid., p. 141.

they had no continuous territory of their own serving as a political framework and a national market. Only 3 or 4 percent of them were connected with agriculture, the remainder were city dwellers scattered all over Russia, not constituting a majority in any single province. What kind of a nation was this, Stalin asked, that consisted of Georgian, Daghestan, Russian, American Jews and so on? What kind of race, whose members lived in different parts of the world, spoke different languages, never saw each other, and never acted in concert? This was not a real living nation; it was something mystical, amorphous, nebulous, out of this world. The demand for national cultural autonomy was therefore ridiculous; autonomy was demanded on behalf of a nation whose existence was yet to be proved and whose future had not been recognized. All the Jews had in common was their religion, their common origin, and a few remaining national characteristics. But no one could seriously maintain that petrified religious rites and vanishing psychological traits were stronger than their socioeconomic and cultural surroundings, which were inevitably leading to assimilation.[23] The Bolsheviks sincerely intended to solve the Jewish question in Russia by giving full freedom to all Jews; assimilation was to be actively furthered. The oppressed Jews of Russia and Galicia were to become equal citizens of the new socialist society.

A detailed survey of the Jewish policy of the Communist party of the Soviet Union lies outside the range of the present study. In brief, after the revolution a "Jewish commissariat" was established to deal with the specific problem of the Jewish population. Dimanshtein, its head, promised that a Palestine would be built in Moscow by making the masses productive, and by organizing Jewish agricultural communes. Later on, greater emphasis was put on the industrialization of the Jewish population. They could maintain their own cultural institutions such as schools, clubs, newspapers, and theaters; Hebrew was banned but Yiddish could be freely used during the twenties and thirties. In the Ukraine and the Crimea predominantly Jewish areas even received regional autonomy

---

[23] *Marxism and the National Question* (New York, n.d.), pp. 6 ff.

and in March 1928 it was decided to set aside a special area in the Far East, Birobidzhan, for Jewish settlement. It was announced that by 1937 at least 150,000 Jews would be living there. There was tremendous enthusiasm among Jewish Communists abroad. Otto Heller wrote:

> The Jews have gone into the Siberian forests. If you ask them about Palestine, they laugh. The Palestine dream will long have receded into history when in Biro Bidzhan there will be motor cars, railways and steamers, huge factories belching forth their smoke. . . . These settlers are founding a home in the taigas of Siberia not only for themselves but for millions of their people.[24]

Kalinin, president of the Soviet Union, predicted that in ten years Birobidzhan would be the cultural center of the Jewish masses. Even staunch anti-Communists iike Haim Zhitlovsky, one of the theoreticians of Jewish socialism, and Lestchinsky, a Jewish sociologist, were deeply impressed; Birobidzhan would be a Jewish republic, a center of genuine Jewish socialist culture.

The dream of a Siberian Palestine did not last. Only a few thousand Jews came, and most of them turned back within a few months. Forty years after its foundation, Birobidzhan was a drab provincial region with about 25,000 Jewish inhabitants, a small percentage of the total population. No one, least of all the Soviet authorities and the Jewish Communists, wanted to be reminded of the affair. Partly it was the result of insufficient and incompetent planning, but basically it was not the fault of the authorities; Soviet Jews had no desire to build a second Zion on the shores of the Amur.

Despite the failure of Birobidzhan there was much sympathy in the West for the Soviet Union, the only country in which Jews were believed to be secure and in which the Jewish question was said to have been solved. These were the years of the world economic crisis, of the rise of fascist and anti-Semitic movements all over Europe. What in comparison had Zionism to offer? Its bankruptcy "was

---

[24] Quoted in J. Leftwich, *What Will Happen to the Jews?* (London, 1936), pp. 137, 149.

final and irrevocable," Otto Heller wrote in 1931 in a much-discussed book.

> In Western Europe the assimilation of the Jewish bourgeoisie, as well as of the lower middle class and the workers, was an irresistible process. In the East, under socialism, the Jewish question had been solved once and for all: Next year in Jerusalem? This question was answered by history long ago. The Jewish proletarians and the starving artisans of Eastern Europe pose a very different question: next year in a socialist society? What is Jerusalem to the Jewish proletarian? Next year in Jerusalem? Next year in the Crimea! Next year in Biro Bidzhan![25]

Heller's *Downfall of Judaism* presented the Stalinist case; its argument was borrowed by and large from Kautsky, though for other reasons the "renegade" Kautsky was by that time no longer in the good books of the Bolsheviks. Heller differed from Kautsky in adopting a more virulent tone. Zionism was a phenomenon frequently observed among a dying people; shortly before their demise they suddenly feel a new lease on life, only to expire the more quickly. Zionism was a product of the petty-bourgeois stratum in European Jewry, a counterrevolutionary movement. It was a historical mistake, an impossibility, since it tried to detach the Jewish question from the problem of commodity production with which the fate of Jewry was indissolubly connected. It was an anachronism, contradicting not just the laws of historical development but common sense.[26] Heller freely used Kautsky's similes without acknowledging their origin; Zionism was the last appearance of Ahasuerus, the eternal Jew on the historical scene. He had reached the end of the road; Judaism was doomed because it had lost its privileged, monopolistic position in capitalist society. At the same time the social conditions for a revival of anti-Semitism had disappeared. "Zionism, the last, most desperate and most wretched kind of nationalism, was thus breathing its last."

It was a persuasive theme, and, if its ideological premises

---

[25] *Der Untergang des Judentums* (Vienna, 1931), pp. 173–74.
[26] Ibid., pp. 21–22.

were accepted, logical and consistent despite its shrillness
and arrogance. But the book had one major flaw: it ignored the writing on the wall. When it appeared in the
bookstores Hitler's brownshirts were already marching
through the cities of Germany. Two years later anti-Semitism in its most rabid form had seized Germany and continued to expand all over Europe despite the confident
announcement that anti-Semitism had lost its "social foundations." A few years later Heller and many other Jewish
Communists lost their lives in Nazi extermination camps
or in one of the Soviet prisons from which there was no
return.

The case of Otto Heller is of symptomatic interest; the
views he expressed were shared by thousands of young
Jewish Communists all over Europe who were firmly convinced that communism and no other movement was
capable of solving the Jewish question. Nor was this belief
limited to committed party members; a growing number
of fellow travelers were influenced by it and Hitler's seizure
of power only strengthened them in their conviction.

When Heller's book appeared in 1931 Europe was still
relatively quiet, the situation of European Jewry seemingly secure. Six years later, when William Zukerman published *The Jew in Revolt*, there could no longer be any
doubt about the impending catastrophe. *The Jew in Revolt* is an ambitious analysis of the Jewish situation at a
time of crisis and suggests remedies. In the sharpest terms
the author condemns the schemes for emigration from
Nazi Germany, for the German Jews were deeply rooted
in German soil and bound to their country by a thousand
spiritual ties:

> It is a gross slander on the German Jews whose love for
> the fatherland is proverbial, to represent them all as be-
> ing ready to rush in panicky haste from it in a mass
> exodus at the first approach of misfortune. . . . After all,
> the Jews are not the only victims of persecution in Ger-
> many today. Why not a wholesale exodus of German
> Communists, Socialists, Pacifists, Liberals and Catholics?
> . . . The Jewish acceptance of the Jewish exodus plan
> from Germany is at the same time the voluntary ac-
> ceptance of the entire Nazi point of view with regard to
> the Jews. It is a complete Jewish capitulation to the racial

theory of Hitlerism. . . . It is playing the Nazi game in a manner which Hitler himself probably never dared to hope that the Jews would do.[27]

Zukerman believed that the main responsibility for the contemptible plan for emigration fell on the Zionist bourgeoisie:

> Fanatical Zionist theoreticians have been even more busy than the Nazis in preparing schemes and plans . . . Zionist financiers have actually raised huge sums of money for its organization and have started it on the road to success. The fact is that, inasmuch as the exodus plan has now become a popular solution for the Jewish problem, it is due more to a number of Zionist zealots and to a few big Zionist financiers than to the Fascists. Of all the paradoxes of our time, this one will probably go down into history as the most curious of all.[28]

But the author had no doubt that the plot for mass emigration would fail:

> In spite of the brutal Nazi persecution, the bulk of German Jews will remain in Germany, and they will be there long, long after Hitler is gone, when even his name is a mere legend in German history. . . . They bear the Cross of their suffering with dignity and fortitude, as behoves an ancient people which has seen martyrdom and knows that tyranny, no matter how powerful temporarily, cannot forever turn back the wheels of history. . . . They know that even if Hitler be all-powerful now and his regime successfully established for years to come, this is no reason why Jews should willingly accept his gospel of the Ghetto and exile.

The picture as Zukerman saw it was not all black, for there was one country where the Jewish problem had been solved. What struck him most forcibly in Russia was both the economic transformation of Russian Jewry and the mental change that had come with it.

---

[27] *The Jew in Revolt* (London, 1937), pp. 121–23.
[28] Ibid., pp. 112–13.

> Gone is the almost pathological desire of every Jewish
> parent to bring up his offspring as doctors or lawyers:
> Although the universities and higher schools of learning
> are open to the Jews as in no other country, there is no
> rush of a disorderly mob of Jewish youth into them. . . .
> Jews are positively the best factory workers in Russia
> and are sought after in every great plant.

The Soviet Union had been virtually freed of the scourge
of Jew hatred, the very meaning of the word "anti-Semitism" was being rapidly forgotten. The Soviet Union had
solved the Jewish problem "economically, politically, and
even psychologically. Whatever larger successes the Soviet
regime may or may not have to its credit, it has certainly
evolved a perfect solution of the Jewish problem."[29] Zukerman concluded this eloquent account by proclaiming
that the golden age of liberalism was at an end, that there
was only one road open to the Jews, whether he approved of everything going on in the Soviet Union or not:
as a Jew he could do no hing but follow the road shown
by Moscow for the solution of the Jewish problem. This
was a moral necessity. The great revolt of the Jews not
only against capitalism but also against themselves was
morally cleansing: "Whatever its social or political danger
to the Jews may be, morally it atones for everything.
Spiritually, the social-revolutionary movement is saving
the Jews for the world."[30]

These extensive quotations are necessary to convey the
full flavor of Zukerman's case; again it should be said that
such views were by no means the monopoly of an outsider. They were shared by liberals who had succumbed
to despair, even by some Jewish communal leaders and
rabbis. For this was the time when belief in the Soviet
Union was at its height: Stalin had stamped out unemployment and illiteracy, he had liquidated neurosis,
crime, juvenile delinquency, and alcoholism. He had produced a new type of man and in the process anti-Semitism was rapidly disappearing. The appeal to the Jews of
Germany not to be seduced by the siren song of the Zion-

---

[29] Ibid., pp. 131, 236.
[30] Ibid., p. 255.

ists but to stay in their native country was not exclusively
Communist either; it was shared, for instance, by the
bundists, from whom Zukerman may have received some
of his original inspiration.

The Communist critique of Zionism had its heyday in
the 1930s but later lost much of its appeal, and not just
because Birobidzhan had failed to offer a serious alternative to Palestine. It was above all the growing discrepancy
between Bolshevik theory and practice which made the
Communist case unconvincing. Lenin had no doubt been
sincere in his belief that mankind was inexorably moving
toward internationalism. It could have been argued that
however much the Jews resented the demand to give up
their national identity, the price asked was not too high if
in return they received complete equality before the law,
and if eventually all nations were to undergo cultural assimilation. But events in the Soviet Union were taking a
very different course from what Lenin had anticipated. In
the 1930s patriotism returned with a vengeance, the national heroes of Russian history were restored to a place of
honor, nationalism became a factor of growing importance in Soviet domestic policy. This left the Jews in a
vulnerable position; they were still expected to give up
their national identity and to become assimilated, but it
was no longer clear whether they should try to become Russians, Ukrainians, or Turkmen, or whether to be Soviet
citizens tout court. If so they would be the first and
only Soviet citizens, in the same sense that the German
Jews had been almost the only liberals and republicans in
the Weimar period, a position both unenviable and, in the
long run, untenable. Assimilation might have worked
within generations as a result of intermarriage and the
absence of Jewish education, if the Jews had been left in
peace. But they were singled out for attack in Stalin's last
years, and again later under his successors; their fate in
Czechoslovakia and Poland was no happier. They were
denounced as cosmopolitans and nationalists at one and
the same time. Such attacks, far from solving the Jewish
problem, helped to perpetuate it.

The Soviet attitude toward Zionism has remained consistently hostile. Originally it was rejected as a tool of
British imperialism. Later on, Moscow's alliance with the

Arabs made a firm anti-Israeli policy imperative. But there is every reason to assume that the Soviet attitude would have been negative even if considerations of foreign policy had not been involved. It would have been unthinkable to permit substantial numbers of Soviet Jews to emigrate to Palestine since this would have been tantamount to an open admission of the failure of the Soviet nationalities policy. Thus the Jewish problem in the Soviet Union has remained unsolved; while assimilation is still the aim, the conditions for making this policy a success do not exist. Consequently, the appeal of Soviet communism has declined among Jews both within Russia and outside. Of the many Jewish Communists in the West who gave enthusiastic support to the Soviet cause in the 1920s and '30s, few did not leave the party in disappointment. The official Communist case against Zionism, once advocated with so much ardor and conviction, no longer presents a serious ideological challenge.

Whatever Trotsky's quarrel with the old-guard Bolsheviks, he did not disagree with their policy toward the Jews. Like them he regarded Zionism as a wholly reactionary phenomenon. He showed little interest in the problem and while he commented on a great many issues in world politics at one time or another, he hardly ever dealt with Jewish affairs. One of the few exceptions was an article in *Iskra* in 1904 in which he called Herzl a shameless adventurer and referred to the "hysterical sobbings" of Zionism. Toward the end of his life he slightly modified his position. Recent experience had taught him, he said in an interview in 1937, that his old hopes for assimilation had been overoptimistic. Perhaps the Jews did need a territory of their own after all, even under socialism. But it would probably not be Palestine, and in any case the whole problem would hardly find a solution under capitalism.[31]

Some of Trotsky's disciples took a greater interest, and while they made no significant theoretical contribution (their views, too, were based on Kautsky), their opinions have a certain historical relevance, for they later influenced

---

[31] *Forward* (Yiddish), January 28, 1937; see also "On the Jewish Question," *Fourth International*, December 1945.

the New Left in its anti-Zionist outlook.[32] The chief Trotskyite ideologist on Zionism and the Jewish question was the Belgian A. Leon, a former member of a socialist-Zionist youth movement. Unlike most other Marxists who dealt with the problem, he was familiar with the writings of the theoreticians of Labor Zionism. Having reached the conclusion that Zionism, not excluding its extreme left wing, was incurably reactionary in character, Leon invested considerable efforts in refuting it: Other national movements in Europe had been closely linked with the ascending phase of capitalism, whereas the Jewish national movement appeared on the scene only after the process of the formation of nations was approaching its end. Far from being a result of the development of productive forces, Zionism reflected the petrifaction of capitalism. Capitalist decay was the basis for the growth of Zionism, but at the same time it was the reason for the impossibility of its realization.[33] Judaism had been indispensable in precapitalist society but capitalism had destroyed the social bases on which Jews had for centuries maintained themselves.

There is little in this that could not be found in earlier Marxist writers, not even the farfetched thesis that economic developments in Europe compelled the Jewish bourgeoisie to create a national state in order to develop its productive forces. This is more or less what Borokhov had predicted, though in contrast to Borokhov, Leon regarded it as a regressive development; for the Jewish question could be solved only after the victory of world revolution. Once world revolution had prevailed, once capitalism was overthrown, the national problem would lose its acuteness. For national-cultural and linguistic antagonisms were only manifestations of the economic antagonisms created by capitalism. Leon seems not to have been particularly concerned about the advent of fascism, for the "very exacerbation of anti-Semitism prepares the road for

---

[32] See for instance N. Weinstock, *Le Sionisme contre Israël* (Paris, 1968).

[33] *Conception materialiste de la question juive* (Paris, 1946). Quotations are from the English edition, *The Jewish Question. A Marxist Interpretation* (Mexico City, 1950), pp. 210 ff.

its disappearance"; fascism he predicted would accelerate the proletarianization of the middle classes.[34] Leon was arrested by the Germans a year or two after these lines were written and died like millions of other Jews in a Nazi extermination camp.

It is difficult to take seriously the vulgar-Marxist theses of Leon's present-day disciples in the United States, France, and Germany about the history of the Jewish people, anti-Semitism and Zionism. According to their theories the Jews who originally migrated from Palestine were forced to by economic causes. It would be interesting to know why elsewhere in the Near East economic factors had other effects. The Jews (it is further argued) were persecuted in the Middle Ages because they engaged in usury; wherever they had other occupations, there were no pogroms. But the Jews in Spain and southern Italy were expelled despite the fact that usury was not widespread among them, nor have the pogroms of 1096 (the First Crusade) anything to do with the social structure of the Jews of Western Europe. The idea that Zionism reflects the need of the Jewish bourgeoisie to have a market of its own is childish. The "money Jews" (as Herzl called them) wanted nothing of the sort, least of all in a backward province of the Ottoman Empire. When Herzl tried to gain their support they poked fun at him and threw him out. The annual budget of the world Zionist movement after Herzl's death amounted to some $10,000; even in the 1930s it was no more than about $1.5 million. A single Jewish community, Berlin, spent more each year on social welfare than the Jewish Agency for building Palestine; this figure should suffice inasmuch as the "class interests" of Jewish haute finance are concerned.

Herzl and Nordau are attacked by the New Left for having been "inveterate pessimists," for having maintained the "inevitability of anti-Semitism." But even Nordau, the most alarmist of all Zionist leaders, was in retrospect too optimistic, claiming in many speeches and articles before the First World War that it was unthinkable that whole Jewish communities would be destroyed as they were in the Middle Ages. More recently the Trotskyite

---

[34] Ibid., pp. 222, 228.

critics of Israel have claimed that Israel provoked the war
of 1967 because it could not overcome its economic crisis.
It could be argued with equal logic that Mark Rudd and
Miss Dohrn joined the Weathermen because they did not
receive enough pocket money at home. The New Left
critique of Zionism and Israel reminds one of Marx's
famous dictum that all great events in history appear
twice, the second time as a farce: after Kautsky—Otto
Heller and Zukerman, and forty years later yet another
generation of critics. Perhaps Marx was mistaken: some
events keep repeating themselves—the third time as the
theater of the absurd.

Zionists paid little attention to the views of Leon and
other Trotskyite ideologists, for wherever they differed
from Kautsky and the Bolsheviks they offered (to put it
mildly) no startling new insights. Even in West Germany
where the New Left devoted time to the study and critique
of Zionism it did not go much beyond traditional arguments of anti-Zionism such as had been voiced before
the First World War by the German patriotic Anti-Zionist Committee.[35] Shorn of ideological underpinnings, it
always amounted to proving that Arab nationalism was
progressive whereas Jewish nationalism was evil. More attention was devoted by the Zionists to the strictures of
Isaac Deutscher, perhaps because, unlike the Trotskyite
and New Left writers, he was a well-known literary figure
who reached a wide public and who, because of his background, was bound to know more about the subject than
they did. Deutscher too regarded Zionism as a profoundly
reactionary movement, but he admitted that the Bolsheviks had taken an overoptimistic view of the chances of
solving the Jewish problem. At one stage in his career he
engaged in public heart-searching, writing in 1954 that he
had abandoned his anti-Zionism which had been based
on his confidence in the European labor movement: "If
instead of arguing against Zionism in the 1920s and 1930s
I had urged European Jews to go to Palestine I might
have helped to save some of the lives that were later extinguished in Hitler's gas chambers."[36] The Jewish state,

---

[35] *Zur Kritik der zionistischen Theorie und Praxis*, p. 7.
[36] *The Non-Jewish Jew* (London, 1968), pp. 111–12.

he wrote in a moment of weakness, had become a "historical necessity and a living reality." But he still believed that basically Zionism was a reactionary force and it did not therefore come as a surprise when, after the Six-Day War and shortly before his own death, Deutscher made a bitter attack on Israel in which he argued (as he had done forty years earlier) that Arab nationalism was progressive while Jewish nationalism was reactionary, that Israel represented neoimperialism in the Middle East, preached chauvinism, etc.[37] Zionism had worked from the outset for a purely Jewish state; Marxists should not allow their emotions and the memories of Auschwitz to drive them to support the wrong cause.

Deutscher's instinctive rejection of the Jewish national movement went deeper and was in a way quite unconnected with the conflict between Israel and the Arabs. All the Jewish geniuses throughout recent centuries, he wrote in his credo, the great revolutionaries of modern thought such as Spinoza, Heine, Marx, Rosa Luxemburg, Trotsky, and Freud, had been heretics; they all found Jewry too narrow, too archaic, and too constricting. It is interesting to compare this list of non-Jewish Jews with Kautsky's (Spinoza, Heine, Lassalle, Marx), and with Otto Bauer's (Spinoza, Ricardo, Disraeli, Marx, Lassalle, Heine). They all looked for ideals and fulfillment beyond Judaism. They had in common their rootlessness and their vulnerability; they were the natural protagonists of cosmopolitanism, the advocates not of nation-states but of internationalism. It was the paradoxical consummation of the Jewish tragedy that the decay of bourgeois Europe had compelled the Jew to embrace the nation-state.[38]

The composition of Deutscher's hall of fame is open to dispute and it seems a little farfetched to equate Freud's and Heine's attitude toward their fellow Jews with Trotsky's and Rosa Luxemburg's. These two failed precisely because they were "rootless Jews" and did not realize the depth of national feeling in Germany and Russia which made it illusory to pursue an internationalist policy. Trotsky wrote in his autobiography that nationalist passions

---

[37] Ibid., pp. 126 ff.
[38] Ibid., p. 26.

and prejudices were incomprehensible to him from his
earliest childhood, that they produced in him a feeling of
loathing and moral nausea. Rosa Luxemburg complained
to a friend (Mathilde Wurm) in 1917: "Why do you come
with your special Jewish sorrows? I feel just as sorry for
the wretched Indian victim in Putamayo, the Negroes in
Africa. . . . I cannot find a special corner in my heart for
the ghetto." This in a way was an understatement of her
position, because like some other Jewish revolutionaries
she showed symptoms of that familiar phenomenon, Jewish self-hatred. It is difficult to imagine that Lenin, an internationalist second to none, would have referred with
such dismay to "special Russian sorrows." Deutscher,
theoretically at least, was aware of the dilemma; after all
he does mention the vulnerability of the cosmopolitan
Jew. But he had no clear answer for the perplexed Jewish
revolutionaries of his own time. Deutscher's opposition to
Zionism is based in the last resort on the liberal critique
of the Jewish national movement. The erstwhile follower of
the Galician Rabbi of Ger emerges as a modern, socialist
"protest rabbi"[39] unshaken in his belief that the world
is moving away from national sovereignty and the nation-state toward internationalism, and that the message
of the world of tomorrow, the message of universal human
emancipation, is the one which Jews should retrieve, not
their misplaced enthusiasm for parochial nationalism. Here
the belief in a specific Jewish spiritual mission is replaced
by a purely secular credo. But the message of internationalism is not pronounced with the same measure of conviction as in the works of the socialists before 1914. It was
easier then to be optimistic in this respect than after 1945.
Deutscher must have felt that his strictures against the
evils of nationalism might conceivably influence some
Jews, but he cannot have been confident about their effect
on the Russians, the Chinese, and other nations, "socialist"
or nonsocialist. It was easier to denounce Zionism than to
point to an alternative, for the prospects of the non-Jewish
Jew acting as pioneer and apostle of internationalism in

---

[39] This refers to a group of German rabbis who publicly dis-
sociated themselves from Herzel after the appearance of *The
Jewish State* and were called by the Zionists *Protest Rabbiner*.

an intensely nationalist world were clearly not very promising.

Marxists agree with the liberal critics of Zionism in regarding assimilation as desirable, and rejecting Zionism for trying to impede this inevitable process. Such a vision does not lack consistency; it certainly entails fewer complications that the Zionist endeavor. Its main weakness is that it does not provide clear answers for the present and the foreseeable future. The Marxist appeal to Jewish toilers and intellectuals to share in the class struggle in their native countries was not practical politics in Germany in 1933, and it has encountered obstacles to a greater or a lesser degree everywhere. Zionists concede that it was a historical misfortune that the Jewish national movement appeared so late on the historical scene; the emergence of a Jewish state in the nineteenth century would have created fewer problems. They will accept the view that the nation-state is not the final goal of human history but only a transitional stage. But while it lasts, what are the Jews to do in those countries in which assimilation is just not possible?

To this vital question there has been no convincing answer by the Marxist critics of Zionism. They could argue, as some did, that the problems of individual nations have to be subordinated to the higher interests of the world revolution, and that seen from this vantage point, the Jewish problem was not the most important. The Jews are expendable; other nations too have come and gone in history. Persecution, the slaughter of millions of Jews, is a regrettable episode, but the revolutionary is concerned with the future of all mankind; what does the future of a small people matter in the global context? Zionists were unlikely to be impressed by this argument for more than one reason. Those advocating abstract internationalist principles are usually influenced by the interests of the nations to which they belong. Furthermore, Zionism rejects as unreasonable the demand that the Jews should subordinate their national aspirations to the higher interest of the future ideal world state—which may (or may not) come into existence one day, and may (or may not) be superior to the present order.

Zionism no doubt can be subjected to trenchant criticism

from different points of view. But as a national movement and a weltanschauung its validity can neither be proved nor refuted; it is as legitimate, or illegitimate, as other national movements—or nations. And as far as anti-Semitism is concerned Zionism has a strong case; its analysis has been more fully confirmed by recent history than the predictions of its critics.

The Problems of Israeli Socialism

Ben Halpern

BEN HALPERN—professor of Near Eastern and
Judaic Studies at Brandeis University, author of
The Idea of the Jewish State, and an editor of
Midstream.

David Ben-Gurion, in one of his sardonic moods, once
said he no longer called himself a Zionist in view of what
those Zionists who remained in exile by choice had made of
the name. He added that he no longer called himself a socialist in view of the corruption of *that* name by fifty years
of the Soviet regime in his native Russia. Coming from
Ben-Gurion, the disavowal of both socialism and Zionism
had an effect of irony, if not paradox, for it amounted to a
personal revisionism, turning inside out the man's whole life,
as well as the whole history of Israel. By now we are quite
accustomed to a similar judgment from other quarters. For
many on the left today it is a mere commonplace, hardly
carrying a thin edge of sarcasm, to say that Israel is, of
course, not socialist.

This, about a country where the land and most other basic
natural resources are, in the main, nationally owned and
publicly administered; where almost half of the economy is
nationally or publicly owned and managed; where the private sector generates a smaller share of net national product and employment than anywhere outside the Communist bloc; where the labor federation, one big union for the
whole country and for all branches of the economy, or-
ganizes (without the aid of legal compulsion) about 90
percent of the workers; where, consequently, the labor
unions and not private employers are second to the government in determining economic and social policy; and where

there has never been any government since the birth of the nation which was not dominated by labor parties, with labor ministers continuously in control of the army, the police, the treasury, the school system, the foreign office, and housing and development.

Now, for old-line Stalinists none of these facts need present any conceptual difficulty. For them a socialist is whoever Moscow infallibly declares to be a socialist; and that decision is based, with accuracy and precision, on the foreign policy interests of the USSR.

One of the virtues claimed for the New Left—and maybe possessed by it in some respects—is its casual disregard for the tags, slogans, and doctrinaire conceptions of the Old Left. To be called a socialist by virtue of total subordination to Moscow does not in itself guarantee high marks among the radical young. Nevertheless, the name "socialist" is a generally good one in politically awakened young circles today; and generally these are disposed to deny that label, or question its application, to Israel.

In part this is owing, if not to Israel's freedom from Russian domination, then to its current dependence on American support: America being, of course, quite dogmatically labeled as "imperialist." In part also it is a consequence of the highly unorthodox character of Israeli socialism which, in spite of the elastic minds of the young, is too original, too free, and too spontaneous for many on the New Left, as well as the Old, to grasp.

A few relatively well-informed critics deny Israel's right to be called socialist after a close study of its current trends, rather than its professed ideals and basic structure. They are aware that in its first years Israel had perhaps the most egalitarian income distribution of any civilized people in the world; and, according to this criterion of social justice, it was far more socialist than the Soviet Union, to say nothing of the capitalist world. The Israeli economic growth rate, unsurpassed in the free world, is probably equal to the best performance of the regimented socialisms, and it is maintained under a democratic system of free association, without politically enforced production quotas. But in the past decade or more, Israel's growth has been bought—not by suppressing freedom, but by permitting inequalities rapidly approaching those of advanced industrial countries; and it has offered (without notable success) to sell publicly owned enterprises or assets to private investors.

Whatever Israel may once have been, these critics reject the claim that what it now is or is becoming should be accepted as an example of socialism. A fair discussion of the question therefore requires that we consider Israel's past and future, as well as its present condition.

Whether Israel is called socialist or something else is, in itself, a matter of indifference. The most original founding father of the Israeli ethos, the venerable A. D. Gordon, always used to repudiate indignantly the name "socialist." Yet the values he preached and practiced and which were taken up into the marrow of Israeli society were both authentic products of the humanistic socialism of nineteenth-century Europe and a direct evocation of its ultimate source, Jewish prophetic messianism. Other primary architects of Israeli ideology and social structure, from Nahman Syrkin and Ber Borochov, Berl Katzenelson and Yitzhak Tabenkin, Yitzhak Ben-Zvi and David Ben-Gurion, to Meir Yaari and Pinhas Lavon, drew extensively from the social democratic (Marxist), social revolutionary, populist, anarchist, and syndicalist traditions of their times. They were also pacifists, vegetarians, feminists, and religious socialists.

What they had in common was that, either with a sense of liberation or still struggling against powerful inhibitions, each of them rebelled against his own particular socialist tradition on one central point: What would constitute the true process of liberation for the Jewish people? The primary intuition of the Jewish nationalist radicals of the 1880s, 1905, and the period after World War I was that neither liberal nor socialist revolutions would solve the basic Jewish social, cultural, and political problems or the economic anomalies which, as socialists, they conceived to underlie all the rest. Only the creation on a new and normal economic base of a free Jewish society, in its own land and with its own authentic culture and political sovereignty, could truly liberate the Jews.

This intuition was directly grounded in critical facts of their immediate situation. They noted that not only Russian reactionaries but workers, and even revolutionary intellectuals, conducted or condoned pogroms. They noted that industrialization, which according to Marx should turn peas-

ants, artisans, and the petty bourgeoisie of preindustrial
society into proletarians, did not have this effect upon
Jews. Industrialization did, indeed, destroy their old class
status in Eastern Europe, but it failed to give them a new
one. They were simply ejected by the dialectic of history
from the stable social structure. Instead of factory-employed
proletarians, they became a rootless mass of middlemen
without fixed commerce or a source of sweated labor in the
most insecure and declining parts of the economy: small
artisan shops or sweatshops that scratched out a bare subsistence on subcontracts from mass-producing consumer
goods industries. Inexorable economic pressure, the mount-
ing congestion and bitter poverty of the ghetto, as well as
acute political and social oppression, drove them to emigration, the only door to hope and freedom.

How these facts were faced was the primary element that
differentiated Jewish socialists in early twentieth-century
Eastern Europe. One type recognized the facts, but with
indifference. If Jews did not become true proletarians, or
if they escaped by emigration, it did not really matter, since
the revolution did not depend on them. Proletarianized Russian and Polish peasants would carry on the class struggle
and consummate the destruction of the regime. Jewish revolutionaries, intellectuals and men of the masses, who might
be personally motivated by their Jewish oppression to join
the good fight, were helpful auxiliaries and catalysts of the
revolution; but they were not historically essential. As for
the Jewish problem, that relic of outmoded religious prejudice, it would disappear with the natural disappearance
of the Jews into the humane cosmopolitan harmony of the
classless society.

Men who thought like this did not care to be bothered
with the Jewish problem. Their Marxian dialectic—which
took little interest in nations generally and then only in
large nation-states forming major politico-economic units of
historical geography—dismissed the unproletarian Jews and
their problems as irrelevant. Yet some of them found a
fruitful field of activity among Jewish workers, the first to
organize successfully, and notably the most activist, in the
Russian movement. Other socialist leaders were themselves
too Jewish to ignore Jewish interests so lightly.

These men founded the Bund and, having created a separate Jewish labor organization, had to give some consideration, however reluctant, to their difficulties of doctrine. While responsible for the success of certain tactics which were adopted among social democrats generally, the bundists went no further in regard to the Jewish problem than to defend, first, their separate organization, and second, the principle of Jewish cultural autonomy. For this purpose they hardly needed theoretical innovations, since they could simply apply the doctrines of Austrian Social Democrats like Otto Bauer and Karl Renner to the Jewish situation. But the cardinal question—the anomalous Jewish economic situation and all its implications—they largely ignored.

It was precisely this question that Labor Zionists took seriously, concentrating their major efforts on specific theoretical and practical solutions. Some, especially those not bound by the modish Marxist categories, tried to overcome the basic anomaly directly by resettling themselves as the farmer-worker class of a new Jewish society in the historic homeland. This exposed them to attack as utopians by Marxists and other anti-Zionist radicals. Labor Zionists who were Marxists had to rebut the charge of utopianism by developing a class analysis which proved the historic necessity or inevitability of the return to Zion as a resolution of the anomalies of the Jewish diaspora. In any case, Labor Zionists, whether Marxist or "utopian" socialists, agreed that the Jewish anomaly would never be resolved until either the organized voluntary effort of Jewish radicals or the necessary dialectic processes of Jewish history would lead to a free Jewish society based on a normal economy in Palestine.

Within the twentieth-century Marxist movement theoretical innovations were usually the consequence of a need to adapt general theory to particular situations, especially to particular national situations. Bernstein's revisionism arose in Germany and Austria in order to deal with the clear evidence that advanced industrialization, together with an apparent chance for democracy, produced neither total proletarization nor a polarized war of workers against owners. The strongest theoretical reactions against this revisionism, based on a new Marxist theory of imperialism and a strategy of mass uprisings directed by politically aware cadres of full-time revolutionists, came from Rosa Luxemburg and

V. I. Lenin. As spokesmen of relatively backward and despotic Eastern European societies, they preached the "Russian method" of 1905 as a general Marxist line. In our own time, special situations in places like China, Indochina, Cuba, and Algeria have added to a widely accepted canon of Marxist theoretics. In the same way, Labor Zionism, in its Borochovist version (which found some adherents in the Finnish and Armenian Social Democratic parties as well), recast Marxism in a shape appropriate to the objective Jewish situation. It is the only school of Marxism to have done so.

But one of the anomalies of the Jewish position was that objectively appropriate theories left no room for a solution in terms of the local situation of the Jewish masses. Only by transcending it and creating a revolutionary new situation *elsewhere* could a solution be achieved. What was required was a revolution in geography as well as history. This meant that diaspora activities of Jewish radicals directed toward the economic distress of Jewish workers were mere palliatives, while those directed toward the general social revolution were unrelated to the dialectic of Jewish history.

Yet it is important to note that this implication of the Labor Zionists' attitude toward Jewish ghetto life, which according to their opponents made them inherently a defeatist force in the revolutionary struggle *in situ*, did not lead them to desist from immediate political and trade-union activity in the diaspora. In the face of pogroms and the ferocious oppressiveness of the tsarist regime, or the Austro-Hungarian-Polish quasi-parliamentary equivalent, active Jewish self-defense and participation in the general progressive movements were an unquestioned imperative, a command of vital, immediate self-interest and honor. Some developed the theory that consolidating and strengthening the diaspora Jewish community was a prerequisite for successful concentration in the Jewish homeland, and toward this end they often favored the independent action of Jewish political parties. Other Labor Zionists, who in a "utopian" spirit believed in immediate migration to Zion or whose analysis denied that the Jewish social structure could be satisfactorily stabilized in the diaspora, often preferred to work through, or at least with, the general radical parties.

The skepticism of Labor Zionists about the possibilities of diaspora Jewries has proved to be basically justified. Corrections that might have to be made in the light of more than a half century of experience relate to details, and not, as in the case of opposing viewpoints, to fundamental positions. The "anomalous" economic position of the Jews in the diaspora was not reduced to normal either by social revolution or by assimilation into free Western societies. Rather than being effectively proletarianized, the Jews tended to become a professional, managerial, and bureaucratic elite or part of the bourgeoisie.

The Jewish problem disappeared neither in the revolutionary or the free democratic societies. In certain situations it produced the kind of social pressure that leaves Jews no freedom (nor, as we well know, even the chance of survival) except through emigration. Backward agrarian societies like Poland, Romania, Hungary, and, one may add, Turkey, Algeria, Tunisia, Libya, Egypt, and Iraq have striven for economic modernization following their national liberation in a climate of chauvinist fanaticism. In that sitnation, such countries had no room for Jewish middlemen —any more than liberated African nations now have for East Asians, or the Libyans and Egyptians or the Turks had for other "foreign" elements like Italians and Frenchmen, Armenians and Greeks, who were thrown out and/or expropriated. The same basic situation, intensified by the greater power of the chauvinist majority, applied to Jews in certain industrialized or industrializing empires, where strong sacral-feudal-autocratic traditions persisted even after the Russian, German, and Austrian revolutions deposed their monarchs. Acute or chronic oppression left these Jews no hope for freedom, except the escape hatch of emigration. When that was not open, tragedy, quick or enduring, befell the Jews. For our generation, this is a matter of immediate experience as well as of recent history.

The Labor Zionist analysis is basically justified for the advanced industrial democracies as well. The "anomaly" persists—Jews are conspicuously not proletarianized—and its effects remain even if Jews suffer neither direct oppression nor a distant pressure to emigrate. In the quasi-revolution of America's greening, the Jews play no historically essential role, no matter how significant a number of the bodies and how prominent a share of the blown minds they provide for violent confrontations. The envisioned collapse of America and the dawning of an Aquarian age provide no solutions for the nagging subacute infections of anomalous Jewishness; and even the Wagnerian death and transfiguration scenes—the *Juden-dämmerung*, the acts of self-abnegation and outright self-betrayal—they are required to play out leave them still anomalous Jews and Jewish anomalies throughout the brief, unhappy course of their New Left revolutionism.

Intellectually, therefore, the premises of Labor Zionism were largely borne out. In practice, as is well known, the Labor Zionists built major parts of Israeli society and left their mark on its whole structure. But one must note at once that the specific ideas with which they came to Palestine, whether as utopians or Marxists, were not decisive for the forms in which the social system of Israel arose and has continued to reshape itself to this day.

The non-Marxist radicals among them regarded themselves simply as volunteers for whatever tasks the creation of a normal Jewish society required. In the words of Joseph Trumpeldor, they offered themselves as "iron bars" to be fashioned into whatever instruments were necessary. Primarily and immediately they felt this meant to take up a personal lifelong mission of serving as a rural labor class in the new plantation settlements that the Zionists had begun to establish.

The Marxist contingent, repudiating such idealistic utopianism, had two ideological openings for immediate work in Palestine. The task of directing to its objectively inevitable goal the flow of emigrants generated by diaspora anomalies gave them one field of political activity: the Zionist congress and the Zionist administration which partially regulated immigration to Palestine. And since Zionist organs were actively engaged in this task, some socialist Zionists argued that it was essential to fight for proletarian interests within that arena. The other field, accepted even by those who repudiated work in the Zionist arena as "class collaboration," was the organization of Jewish—and also Arab—workers already living in Palestine and "neighboring lands." The Marxist theorists within Labor Zionism conceived of the native Jewish populations of the whole Ottoman Empire as a class base for socialist Zionist organization.

But in spite of the best ideological intentions and the most dedicated commitment of both the idealist and Marxist camps, their actual achievements did not occur in the fields or ways their theories demanded. The young radical idealists did not succeed in establishing a solid base of Jewish workers in the Zionist plantation villages, and the young Marxists had no great success in organizing the class struggle among native Ottoman Jews.

What happened to the socialist Zionists was the common lot of all successful socialists. Their ideologies addressed themselves with precision to the strategy of revolution, but their theories outlined no more than vague visions of the tasks that came after victory. Moreover, the socialist Zionist won his revolution against the diaspora system virtually on the day he uprooted himself and emigrated to Palestine. On that day he also took up a new and critical battle: building a normal Jewish society on socialist lines and preventing a replica of the diaspora from arising in Zion. But while he had at his command a theory to analyze the old system and a strategy to overthrow it, his approach to this new task was based on no more than sheer utopian commitment to communal brotherhood.

For the early twentieth-century Zionists communal brotherhood was no mere abstraction, no mere sentimental illusion or shallow fashion. It was a real bond forged in the small underground units of Zionist-socialist self-defense and in the revolution of 1905. After the First World War, this communal brotherhood was cultivated among them through the intense collective eroticism of the youth movement counterculture in Central and Eastern Europe. From the beginning of the century to the Second World War, successive generations of socialist Zionists—traumatized by pogroms and massacres, wars, and expulsions—came together as small bands of brothers. Even before coming to Palestine, they chose, as a matter of principle as well as by force of circumstance, to live outside the old society.

And especially since conditions in Palestine made it possible for the new society to be built with little or no significant relation to the old, this fraternal dedication of Labor Zionists was an advantage of the highest order. There were vital tasks, like protection of settlements against marauders and cultivation of new lands in remote areas, for which such commandos of young volunteers, bound to each other in total comradeship, proved best suited. Not only did they achieve success in high-risk areas for the whole Zionist enterprise, but they also created institutions, in the image of their own brotherhood, which became the norm for a large and dominant segment of the new Jewish society in Zion. But precisely this functional success required abandoning simple for complex, naïve for sophisticated, principles of organization.

Before the First World War, socialist Zionists had already established the basic model of the Israeli commune, in its mobile and settled forms, and with its multiple defensive, agricultural, social, and political functions. What was then a mere model, exemplified by small bands of select comrades, grew after the war into a swelling mass organization, the Histadrut.

Young socialist Zionists, though a small part of the Jews who settled in Palestine before 1914, formed a major part of the immigrants who succeeded (often without British or official Zionist authorization, and across frontiers still blazing with war and revolution) in entering Zion immediately after the First World War and up to the Second World War. The accepted model for most of the firstcomers was the communal rural settlements established before and during the war. The young pioneer settlers also consciously emulated the mobile socialist militia, Hashomer, of prewar days: a body of professionals committed to all the political and social tasks (including, for some, a prospective military uprising and, at the same time, permanent settlement on the frontiers) which the national liberation of the Jews might require. But the Zionist Organization lacked the means to settle on the land more than a small portion of the aspiring communal farmers. The others found provisional work as road gangs or construction workers or farmhands in the booming towns and villages, and most then settled permanently as urban workers in the trades they learned on these jobs. Still, they retained the ethos of their original commitment and built its communal principles, as far as possible, into the new institutions they created in the city:

above all into the organization that contained them all, the Histadrut.

Beginning with some four thousand workers in December 1920, the Histadrut grew rapidly. Almost at once it came to comprise a majority, and soon the overwhelming majority, of Jewish workers in Palestine. Over this mass the leaders, recruited to a major extent from the leadership of the kibbutzim, exercised a powerful influence. Initially this extraordinary influence of the communal attitude was guaranteed by the predominant role of the kibbutzim in recruiting and training worker immigrants in the diaspora.

The main instrument of the British mandate in Palestine for controlling Jewish immigration according to the criterion of "economic absorptive capacity" was restrictive quotas for the admission of labor. As the quota was based on a guarantee of a sort by the Zionist Organization that the workers would be employed, the "immigration certificates" were allocated to the Zionists for distribution. They, in turn, distributed these permits to enter Palestine according to criteria they considered would best serve the "upbuilding of the national home": preference usually went to Hebrew-speaking young candidates aged eighteen to thirty-five who had been trained abroad as agricultural workers.

Such training was provided mainly by emissaries of the several socialist Zionist parties, drawn largely from kibbutzim in Palestine. The communal system, where all labor was done collectively and all were totally responsible for the needs of each, permitted the detachment of workers for public service, including long service abroad—a luxury that no worker who was the sole support of his dependents could ordinarily permit himself. The kibbutzim committed themselves thoroughly to the project of training immigrants abroad, for this was their method for recruiting new members for their growing settlement federations. Of those they trained, only a small minority became kibbutz members permanently; but most of those who did not still experienced a deep crucial attachment to the kibbutzim and communal ideals they represented.

By the mid-thirties a good half or more of the Jewish workers in Palestine had been recruited and trained before immigration by the kibbutz emissaries. A main instrument had been the diaspora Zionist youth movements, each attached to one of the kibbutz federations. In such movements as Hashomer Hatzair and Gordonia a deeply intimate bond of comradeship and ideological loyalty was forged, uniting peer groups of labor immigrants in a tight cohesion with each other and with the leadership and policies of the several kibbutz federations. Only a minor proportion, 3 to 7 percent, of the Palestine Jewish community belonged at any one time to kibbutzim. But the proportion who at one time or another had lived in kibbutzim was far larger, while, as mentioned, half or more of the workers had been trained primarily under kibbutz leadership before coming to Palestine.

A major segment of the Palestine Jewish workers, then, were kibbutzniks in principle, who only by chance failed to become permanent kibbutz members. Not only they but many others without this background looked to the kibbutzim as the ideal embodiment of socialist Zionist principles, and learned to refer the problems of their own urban, noncommunal way of life to this model. Upon this base there arose not only the extraordinarily high representation of kibbutz members in the Histadrut leadership (and today in Israel's parliament, government, and above all in the elite corps of the armed services and the officer cadres); but it was also the foundation upon which near-communal principles and models of organization were built into the Histadrut structure.

The Histadrut is, first of all, an all-purpose labor organization, and not a simple federation of trade unions. Its functions approximate the total responsibility of the kibbutzim for their members. In the society of Israel it forms in many respects a distinct subcommunity; one which comprises over a third and serves more than half of the population and, in many ways, has dominated the life of the whole society. Ninety percent of the workers (a term which in Israel includes many of the self-employed) and about 60 percent of the whole population are served by the Histadrut. While its trade-union section is the primary power for setting wages and working conditions for all Israel's employees, the Histadrut is also a major investor and entrepreneur, especially strong in agriculture, transport, and heavy industry. It employs in labor cooperatives and labor-controlled corporations about one-fourth of Israel's capital and manpower. It maintains the largest medical service organization in Israel, caring, among other client members, for all immigrants brought in by the World Zionist Organization. From the first it considered cultural as well as ideological activities on behalf of the labor community to be among its functions; and before the rise of the state it controlled a comprehensive labor school system throughout the country. It was also the major coordinating body which, together with the Zionist Organization on one hand and the kibbutz federations on the other, organized and for a long time controlled the Haganah, the Zionist defense force, as well as the recruitment, training, and settlement of new immigrants. Placing new workers in jobs and making jobs for workers was always a major reason for the large-scale extension of Histadrut enterprise into new fields of investment and development. To this day, Histadrut institutions exercise the strongest power in precisely those remote areas of Israel where private investors are reluctant to risk their capital.

The egalitarianism, as well as the all-encompassing mutual responsibility, of the kibbutzim is also a Histadrut principle. This still remains a powerful influence, in spite of rapidly rising pressures to apply differential incentive pay and merit increases as a way of stimulating greater labor productivity. So, too, the democratic centralist principles of organization characteristic of the kibbutzim also still characterize the Histadrut (and the labor parties of Israel), in spite of growing tendencies for devolution of authority and federalism of structure.

Despite a massive change in conditions, the structural principles of Israeli labor parties and organizations remain appropriate to the small-group cohesiveness upon which not only the individual kibbutzim but the kibbutz federations and the whole institutional labyrinth of Israel's labor community were built. Generally speaking, socialism implies relations between men more like those of a family—or an army—than of a contractual association. Both rights and duties, as in a family, are without limit, yet functional positions (especially in a socialist organization with significant political, historic objectives) are firmly defined. Role functions—as of parent and child, leader and follower—are carried out with a rigor arising

out of devotion. These principles, firmly implanted by
youth movement training, were applied not only in the
simple, cogenial setting of the communal settlement (especially of the kvutzah or small commune) but throughout
the structure of Israel's highly complex labor community.

Like the IWW, the Histadrut is built on the "one big
union" principle. All its constituent parts—the trade unions,
the corporate and cooperative enterprises, the manifold service organizations—operate, formally at least, under the
control of the central Histadrut government. In the choice
of this government—concretely, that is, of the Histadrut
convention—all members, whatever subordinate body they
belong to, participate through individual, general, equal,
secret proportional elections. (Representation is based
on party lists submitted to the electorate.) The convention
elects a smaller council which chooses the directorate and
executive officers of the whole organization. Authority is
therefore exercised from the top down, from the center out.
Histadrut dues (including compulsory payments for medical and other insurance) are paid directly to this center,
which then allocates funds to the unions and other agencies, whose budgets it approves. Collective bargaining demands of the unions, like settlement projects sponsored by
the agricultural federations or investment policies projected
by the corporations, are in principle determined centrally
or subject to veto or revision centrally. The officers of many
types of subordinate organizations are subject to approval
by the central directorate. These features, in general, are
also characteristic of the structure of the several labor parties and—in spirit, but to a much lesser degree, in fact—
of the federations of kibbutzim and the agricultural settlement federation.

Together with this formal centralism, which in a growing
society could easily degenerate into mere bureaucratism,
Israel's labor community is also characterized by an extraordinary degree of pluralism, as is the whole Israeli community. The multiplicity of totally demanding associations
that built Israeli society arose from and also perpetuated
the individual commitment from which the whole project
began. The aim of Histadrut leaders was to unite the entire
class of workers under a common program and discipline;
but the intimate bonds of comradeship underlying the party

and settlement structures precluded such a merger of idea and organization. The particular form of socialist Zionism in each brotherhood involved lives too deeply to allow easy compromise. (It was on the basis of such comradeship that separate political parties, especially on the left, arose.) Thus the actual control of the kibbutz movement and of the other agricultural labor settlements (as well as of the urban producers' cooperatives, for somewhat different reasons) always remained in the hands of close-knit groups of their own members. Their effective loyalties were primarily directed (insofar as they went beyond the face-to-face group at all) to their own particular federation of settlements and only secondarily to the general Histadrut.

An exception to the rule of pluralism and federalism underlying the formal centralism of Histadrut government was the trade unions. Precisely these organs of economic class struggle were the most centrally governed field of Histadrut activity. It is an exception that proves another rule already alluded to: that the Histadrut was built on the basic principle of individual, voluntary, and, one may add, total commitment

For a suspicion of trade-union "economism" and narrow craft self-interest was a heritage of Labor Zionism from its socialist, revolutionary origins in Europe. In Zion the trade-union mentality not only seemed a possible menace to revolutionary class consciousness; it also stood in the way of the broad and flexible commitment of individual workers to any and every task Zionism required. The organizational device that might prevent degeneration of the Histadrut into a protector of special interests, a tendency capable of weedlike growth even among class-conscious workers, was an effective, and not merely formal, centralization of trade unionism in "one big union." The logical correlate of centralism is the availability for all required tasks, under whatever conditions are necessary, of all the individual recruits under the immediate discipline of the central command. This ideal—which in other fields of Histadrut activity was realized mainly by its formally subordinate but actually autonomous constituent organizations— was implemented centrally and directly, with considerable success, in regard to the Histadrut trade unions.

Having arisen spontaneously, this unique Histadrut style

of labor organization soon appeared to some of its advocates—and with considerable reason—as in independent
variant of socialism with its own dialectic and strategy, distinct from the other recognized schools. Without committing themselves to a fixed theoretical statement of this view
(for these men—notably Berl Katzenelson and, in his own
rather crude way, David Ben-Gurion—were self-consciously antidoctrinaire), they felt they had found a formula
which by its own organic expansion would convert a potent
germ cell of socialism within the small Jewish community in
Palestine into a full-scale Jewish socialist society. And in
time this society would comprise the Jewish community as
well as the main body of Jews in the world. The labor camp
of the Histadrut would grow "from class to nation," as
Ben-Gurion put it, owing to the inherent advantages—
economic, cultural, social, and political—of the Histadrut
way over all other purported methods of achieving the Zionist aim; owing indeed to the indispensability of the Histadrut method for any ultimate success of Zionism. And
from time to time, though it was a matter of less interest,
one would hear in these circles that Labor Zionism had
found a revolutionary strategy for building socialism that
could find wide application throughout the world.

The immediate arena, however, was the world Jewish
community, and in particular the Zionist movement and
the growing Jewish society in Palestine. Here the Labor
Zionists enjoyed wide sympathy from the beginning, though
certainly not the dominant power they now exercise in Israel. They carried out functions recognized among Zionists
as critical in building the Jewish national home; and especially the "utopians" among them took on the farmer-
worker-guardsman role in a spirit directly derived from the
populism inherent in Zionist nationalism. The Zionist movement was full of nonsocialist types, from Theodore Herzl to
Louis D. Brandeis, who believed in a cooperativist method
of "social engineering"; Franz Oppenheimer, the foremost
twentieth-century exponent of such views, was himself a
leading German Zionist. The widespread use of cooperative methods by Labor Zionists thus enjoyed general Zionist support not simply because they were effective in specific
tasks vital to building the national home, but because of a
certain affinity for such ideas in the Zionist movement as a

whole. As settlers on land purchased (or "redeemed") by the Jewish National Fund in Palestine—land that was to be an eternal possession of the Jewish people—the Labor Zionists were associated with a sentimental and popular symbolism anchored in religious tradition. But neither their class-struggle doctrines nor their collectivist experiments were favorably regarded by other Zionists, and even their militant views on political tactics, in the early years of the mandate, made them a suspect minority in the eyes of the Zionist establishment.

Within a decade from the beginning of the mandate, the Labor Zionists rose to the dominance in the Zionist movement that they have retained in the state of Israel to this day. The base of their strength was the massive immigration of workers and the success of the Histadrut in organizing them into a relatively compact economic force and political coalition. No other section of the Palestine Jewish community possessed a party as large as the Mapai or such effective channels for cooperating with cognate parties as Mapai had through the Histadrut. By the thirties, labor—in particular, Mapai—dominated world Zionism, primarily through its dominant position in the political and economic structure of the Palestine Jewish community. The socialist Zionists cemented this position by their alliance with progressive general Zionists of Chaim Weizmann's school.

One might add that the influence of Labor Zionist ideas and models of organization extended to political opponents, who paid the socialists the compliment of imitation. From the twenties on, Israel's "clericalist" parties were strongly affected by this influence; and their labor factions, which in the thirties became dominant in Orthodox nationalist politics, not only built kibbutzim and cooperatives following Labor Zionist models, but used the Histadrut medical services and aligned themselves with the policies of the Histadrut trade-union section. The radical nationalist right in Israel had some of its roots in militant nationalist circles of the Labor Zionist camp, a phenomenon not unknown elsewhere; but it is a less commonplace feature that there were rightist nationalist kibbutzim—or (to take a revealing trifle) that when the problem of seating first arose in the Knesset, the militant nationalists refused to be seated on the right in accordance with standard practice in Europe. The antilabor bourgeois parties in Israel sometimes take a line (for example, in favor of nationalization) more usually associated with socialist parties—for in the Israeli context, nationalization of Histadrut service organizations would represent a step back toward nonsocialism.

Looking ahead to the rise of the state and the immigration of hundreds of thousands of Jews, Israeli socialists expected to integrate these masses into the institutions that had grown up out of earlier worker immigration; they were sanguine that the socialist establishment of the labor class would soon become the socialist society of the whole people. But living under a socialist establishment, and not merely making revolutions to establish it, produced problems not foreseen in theory.

One such development is the much-publicized "crisis" of the kibbutzim. It is a crisis that can only be understood in the context of the prior expectations of kibbutz leaders. Precisely in the last period of the mandate the kibbutzim proved to be a major instrument for absorbing Jewish refugees, and in particular the illegal immigrants. It was then that the collectives rose to a peak of 7 percent of the whole Palestine Jewish population and proved their capacity to integrate unselected and unprepared masses, including refugee children and recruits from Muslim countries like Morocco and Turkey, India and Iraq. Histadrut leaders anticipated a major role for kibbutzim in absorbing far larger numbers of such immigrants once the Jewish state was successfully established.

These anticipations, as everyone knows, were not fulfilled. The postwar immigrants rejected integration into the kibbutzim. This was true of the European displaced persons, whether escaping concentration camps or the barracks life of a Russian kolkhoz, and of the massive immigration from Arab countries. After the regimented oppression they were escaping the collectivism of a kibbutz seemed hard for European Jews to accept, while Jews from the Middle East brought with them traditional forms of family cohesiveness not compatible with the complete individual commitment required by a kibbutz.

If events after 1948 reduced the role of the kibbutz federations, they increased enormously the potential role of the socialist Zionists in the new institutions of the state. The labor parties were now responsible not only for their own Histadrut institutions or the Zionist-organized parts of the Palestinian Jewish economy, but also for sovereign authority exercised in every activity subject to government. In the past the kibbutz principles had become diluted when they were extended through the Histadrut network into environments radically different from those of the outpost rural settlements. Or at times the kibbutz principles had been transformed in accordance with new requirements. Now the extension of Labor Zionist responsibility to control of the state similarly required unforeseen adaptations and new departures. These processes could be noted in the post-1948 kibbutzim as well.

Not the kibbutz federations but the staffs of the World Zionist Organization, the Histadrut, and the government were now the direct instrumentalities through which immigrants were integrated into appropriate institutional settings (other than those who from the first had found their way into the Israeli social structure privately). And while kibbutz members remained disproportionately prominent in the leadership and staffs of these institutions, they had to operate in circumstances far removed from those of communal settlements.

At first the favored method for settling the new, mostly Middle Eastern or North African immigrants who crowded the reception camps was to establish them on the broad stretches of sketchily cultivated land abandoned by the Arabs on Israel's new frontiers. Since the newcomers rejected the kibbutz, the model chosen was the Israeli moshav: a type of small leaseholders' producers cooperative in which the family rather than the commune formed the economic unit. Veteran Israelis who had preferred this style of life had retained the full-scale cooperative purchasing and sales methods, the town-meeting democracy, the voluntaristic commitment to national tasks, together with the ideological self-awareness, of the other socialist Zionists. But precisely these were hard to inculcate among the new immigrants settling in moshavim.

In a short time the new immigrant moshavim became a major success of Israeli agricultural planning and social absorption, a worthy model for other modernizing countries that had to deal with similar traditionalist populations;

but they did not reproduce the total individual commitment or the same forms of pluralistic yet centralist democracy of the earlier settlers. The Histadrut was compelled to exempt the newcomers from full loyalty to its cooperative sales and purchasing networks. The Zionist organization and the government, responsible for remarkable technical achievements in social and agrotechnical planning (especially in regard to soil and water use), had for the sake of stability to accept forms of village governance that defeated major social aims. The villages had to be segregated according to group compatibility instead of being merged to form a single Jewish ethnic body; and in setting up autonomous village councils, the government, Zionist, and Histadrut functionaries (as well as the several parties) had to rely on traditionalist types of leadership instead of creating the ideological brotherhoods they had in mind. The veteran Israeli leaders themselves, instead of serving as true instructors according to plan, too often were reduced to acting as mere administrators.

Both the paucity of resources and the settlers' preferences soon necessitated a further readjustment of central settlement planning. Projects for settling outlying regions of Israel began to be planned in terms of development towns instead of border villages. Such new settlement cities were strongholds of Mapai and the Histadrut far more than the older, central cities. The Histadrut, through its corporate employers and welfare services, shared with the government primary responsibility for building them. But in an urban setting the socialist Zionist ethos finds expression in forms less intimate and more formal, less voluntaristic or disciplined and more mechanical and restricted than is possible in rural settlements. This was especially true of the large majority of Israelis, both veterans and newcomers, who lived in the cities and towns of Israel's densely settled older regions.

In urban areas the primary person-to-person approach of the old Histadrut group of socialist Zionists to the Israeli mass is through the trade unions, Histadrut services, and the labor parties. Far-reaching adjustments in the aims as well as methods of these institutions were forced upon the old Histadrut fellowship by the needs and demands of this large new clientele.

Major changes have also taken place in the functions and structure of the trade unions since the founding of Israel. As with the growth of the cities they bulked ever larger in the Histadrut, the trade unions had pressed successfully for more autonomy within the centralist structure—and this had begun even before the creation of Israel. The mass influx after 1948 of unskilled, unemployed immigrants made protection of established wage and living standards a vital task. Backed now by the state, the unions, who almost alone had upheld conditions of decent employment and worker protection, established a degree of job security and wage guarantee unrivaled in the free world. This security on a rising standard was steadily extended to the new "second Israel" as the immigrants acquired skills and, moving out of the care of public agencies, came into the ranks of organized labor with tenure of employment; and in those years, the generality of Histadrut coverage was also extended to include (no longer separately organized) Arab workers and formerly separatist workers of right-wing party affiliations.

The unions, increasing their autonomy within the Histadrut, came under strongly heightened pressures from new members with special interests and diverse backgrounds who did not easily, let alone voluntarily, accept the discipline of central, ideologically justified policies. Many of these workers reflected the sense of ethnic grievance of Middle Eastern or North African Jewish immigrants. Their continuing segregation was in good part a response to their own demands; but, together with their inadequate educational achievement, it led to their de facto restriction to low-skill, low-paid employment or to subsistence on sadly inadequate welfare grants for those marginal groups who remained unemployable or only partly (hence insecurely) employed. Within the unions, such grievances led to wildcat strikes and the organization of ad hoc action committees defying central Histadrut discipline—a development also increasingly evident among high-skill trades and professions, with right-wing leanings among the members, who had shown reluctance to become associated with the Histadrut. Some of these welfare dependents, who generally also had communal grievances, were recruited to parties hostile to the socialist establishment, and on occasion severe problems followed

In dealing with these questions the socialist Zionist establishment is confronted with difficulties as well as opportunities arising from the fact that it can now act also—or only—through state agencies. If the class has not become the nation, it has become responsible for, and the dominant force in, the whole nation. This presents possibilities for indoctrination and allocation of socialist Zionist obligations, universally applied: to all schoolchildren, or young people of the age for active service, or all members of cooperative societies registered under pertinent laws, and so on. The temptation to use the methods of legal enforcement could undermine the voluntarism of Israel's socialist commitment; or because of the universality of certain functions (like education or welfare—and especially medical—services), it could undermine the pluralistic, autonomous basis for Israel's cooperative (including collective) sectors.

The state (and now also the Histadrut) is built on a broader party base than the old socialist Zionist network; it includes opposition parties on the right. Not only are coalition requirements often broader than those once needed for governing the Histadrut (where the dominance of the kibbutz elite was accepted as a consensus item); the objective requirements of the state often lead to methods which were formerly rejected, on socialist grounds, when Labor Zionists had tasks of much narrower scope. If, for example, Israel had until recently no real unemployment insurance scheme and its direct welfare payments remain relatively tiny, it is because of the principled insistence of the workers that they need work, not the dole. Another aspect of the same phenomenon was the ability of Histadrut institutions, until 1948, to insist on 51 percent control of voting shares in enterprises for which they solicited private investment. Today when the government owns one-fifth of the economy and nearly all land is publicly owned, and when a main source of capital even for private enterprise is the public purse, the socialist government is ready to sell national assets to private investors in order to attract desperately needed capital. We have already mentioned that it is a right-wing demand that the state (where the rightists' share of power is greater) nationalize such

Histadrut bases of power as its cooperative medical service.

The underlying cause of the doubts voiced about Israel's socialism—when these are founded on relatively objective considerations and not derived from mere anti-Israel partisanship—is that if it is a socialism, it is an *achieved* socialism; and a socialism, moreover, achieved within conditions of freedom and of immediate involvement in the problems of a free, industrial society. The initial socialist Zionist successes, the kibbutzim and the whole Histadrut complex, were based on the ideological commitment of a relatively select group who, nevertheless, assumed major responsibilities within their own society. Because they were relatively isolated, they were close knit, disciplined, and voluntarily committed; and because they were vitally functional in their environment, they did not shrivel and decay or survive in calcified encapsulation, but grew and exerted influence and developed in continuing transformations.

With the rise of the state, the relative isolation of the socialist Zionist sector of Palestine Jewry was thoroughly overcome. The Histadrut camp, opening its doors to every element of the Israeli working community and to all the disparate tendencies of Israel's population, also took cognizance of the entire range of Israel's problems, going beyond the working class. Not a "proletarian dictatorship" or a regimented cadre of party activists but a functioning pluralistic democracy was the instrument with which Israeli socialism approached the tasks of government: economic development, cultural advance, social integration—all in the most difficult conceivable circumstances of political and military encirclement and national emergency.

For Israeli socialism, until then building its own unique cosmos on thoroughly new principles within but essentially apart from the old world, the rise of the state precipitated a confrontation with all the standard problems of advanced industrial as well as backward but developing societies. The old ideologies and institutions, remote as they were from issues like national budget management and full-scale social and economic planning, nevertheless provided attitudes and skills that permitted notably rapid and

flexible adjustments to some standard problems. Israeli
methods of dealing with penal problems (probation), un-
equal educational opportunities, and the integration of diverse communities within a common Jewish peoplehood
have been rapidly evolved and vigorously applied. But this
has meant taking up positions familiar to other socialist
movements in free societies though sometimes inherently
repugnant to the traditional Israeli socialist ethos, as, for
instance, recognizing that work relief alone cannot take
care of all welfare needs in a rapidly changing society; or
that rapid development requires a policy toward investment which may contradict the established national or
public dominance in vital economic functions (often more
in principle than in fact, because private investors are still
reluctant to take Israeli risks).

If Israel presents a confusing picture to outside observers it is because problems like these, such as can only
arise in a successful socialism which is at the same time a
free democracy, are being faced seriously. There is no
guaranteed outcome in any free exercise of such responsibility. An achieved state of society and a solidified establishment which evaded such responsibility or renounced
such freedom might perhaps be easier for some to recognize as socialist. But one may doubt whether such socialism would be worth having—or, in Israel's case, could
survive.

The Kibbutz: An Experiment in Microsocialism[1]

Haim Barkai

HAIM BARKAI—Senior lecturer in economics at the Hebrew University of Jerusalem.

INTRODUCTION

Kibbutzim are familiar landmarks in Israel. The 230 or so kibbutz settlements established since 1909 have put their imprint on the geography of the country. Their impact on the ideology and politics of Zionism and on the evolving institutional and social structure of the Jewish community in Palestine, and later of Israel, was even more significant. The world fame of the kibbutz, not to mention its standing as a household word in Israel, bears ample evidence to the extraordinary position which the kibbutz as a socioeconomic entity and the "kibbutznik," as a symbol of identification and sometimes degradation, have acquired over the years.

This position of eminence was reached and maintained even though each kibbutz is a rather small community, and the kibbutz movement as a whole has always been a minority phenomenon. The average size of a kibbutz is about four hundred in population and two hundred in membership. Only three kibbutzim have a population of one thousand or more. Total population grew from about five to six hundred in the early twenties to close to a hundred thousand in the early seventies, probably the

[1] Several statements in this article are based on data and quantitative analysis prepared for my study, "The Growth Patterns of the Kibbutz Economy," at the Falk Institute of Economic Research in Israel. The study is financed by this institute and the Twentieth Century Fund.

69

largest number of people ever to live in collective communities, but still a small fraction of the Jewish, and necessarily of the total population.[2] By 1927 when the existing kibbutzim were already stable entities, kibbutz population was about 2.5 percent of the total. In 1970 it was about 3.6 percent, after reaching a peak of somewhat less than 6 percent of total Jewish population in the late thirties.

Population and membership grew rapidly by any standard. Even if we take 1927, and not 1921, as the base year, these figures imply an annual average growth rate of about 10 percent for the forty-five years ending in 1971. Population growth decelerated considerably in the fifties and sixties, when it was close to 1.5 percent—still a significant growth rate if compared to growth rates of rural communities in industrial societies, which are usually negative.

Though the principles of the collective do not permit the use of differential material benefits as a stimulus to workers, kibbutzim are among the more efficient production units in the country. This allows the kibbutz population to enjoy a living standard about equal to the

---

[2] Deganiah Aleph was settled by ten people who decided to run the settlement on semicollective principles in 1910, which is usually identified as the formal foundation date of the kibbutz movement. Deganiah's first decade, was, however, a period of trial and error involving very small numbers—membership and population were never larger than about twenty. By 1920 it was a going concern and served as a prototype of a collective community to the thousands of Jewish pioneers who immigrated to Palestine immediately after World War I.

Several hundred of these young people, who came mainly from postrevolutionary Russia and were inspired by the ideology of Zionism and the vision of socialism, joined in 1920 to form the Work Legion. The Legion, which was run on semi-collective principles, accepted a contract from the Public Works Department for the building of several roads. After fusion with another group of pre–World War I immigrants to Palestine it defined as one of the tasks of the "workers' commonwealth," which it hoped to establish, the establishment of large collective settlements. The settlement of Ein Harod in 1921, with several hundred members, the establishment of several other smaller collective settlements between 1918 and 1921, and Deganiah's reorganization as a full collective, suggest that the early twenties is a more reasonable foundation date of the kibbutz movement.

average living standard in Israel. It also means that kibbutz consumption levels put kibbutz population in the upper third of the Israeli population by consumption levels. Annual growth rates of about 5 and 4 percent of income and consumption per capita, respectively, in the fifties and in the sixties, underline the dynamics of this process. This rapidly rising trend means that toward the end of the seventies kibbutz (and Israeli) living standards will be close to the present consumption levels of western and north European populations.

That the kibbutz is a collective in the full sense of the term makes these facts of unique significance. A sketch of its structure and government may indicate the functioning of this intricate organism, which is guided by socialist principles in the running of production and in the distribution of income. The flow chart attempts to convey the most essential elements of kibbutz structure and linkages in formal terms.

The democratic nature of the kibbutz is underlined by the position of the general assembly at the top of the organizational chart, although the growing complexities of production and distribution as a result of growth induced the kibbutzim to give up their innocent belief in direct control of every aspect of communal life by all members meeting in the general assembly. The initial attempt at direct control has given way to a more indirect technique with an elaborate network of offices, committees, and functions, as outlined in the chart.

The general assembly, which meets weekly on Saturday nights, is the central deliberative organ and ultimate source of power. A council composed of twenty to thirty people is, in the larger kibbutzim, empowered to discuss in depth most of the subjects which come to the general assembly, make its recommendation to the former, or take a final decision (subject to appeal).[3] The secretariat (which meets every week) is composed of the main office-

---

[3] Acceptance of candidates for membership, a delicate subject, is usually voted by the general assembly without long deliberation, on the basis of the recommendation of the council. In the council each candidature is given a more thorough hearing.

Kibbutz Structure and Government

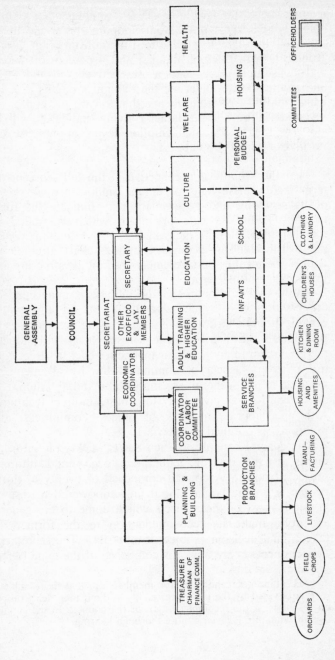

holders, the general secretary, the economic coordinator, the labor coordinator, the treasurer, the coordinator of education, and several lay members. It is the main decision-making organ. Most of the details are studied and decided by the host of special subsidiary committees, such as the economic and labor, housing, welfare, education, and culture committees.

A cardinal role of these committees, which are as close to the grass roots as possible, is in selecting members to offices and managerial functions. The economic committee nominates branch coordinators, the labor committee decides on the composition of the personnel in every production or service branch, the education committee decides who will be the school principal and, say, who is going to be in charge of the baby and infant houses.

This elaborate system of committees and managerial function means that a significant part of the adult population serves on the governing bodies of the community. If we add to branch coordinators and take duplication into consideration, the number of members so serving can reach 80 to 100 in a kibbutz of average size, or 40 to 50 percent of members at a given time. And since as a matter of principle rotation is practiced, almost everyone at some time serves on one of the governing and managing organs. Thus, if any system of running communal affairs can be identified as a system of self-government, the kibbutz can.

The specific contribution of the kibbutzim to human experience is undoubtedly their attempt to apply socialist principles to everyday practice within communities based on voluntary membership. This has led them to adopt a set of rules of action and behavior, which can be summarized as follows:

1. All kibbutz property is commonly owned—the legal title is that of the collective.

Assets which serve in production are operated by the community. Some of the assets which serve for consumption purposes are also run and used on a communal basis. Others are distributed for personal use.

2. The kibbutz abides by the principle of "self-labor." Hired labor should not be employed.

3. Kibbutz manpower is at the community's disposal.

The allocation of time to work, study, and leisure, and
the allocation of labor between alternative employments
in production or in service branches, is determined by the
relevant organs of the community.

4. The kibbutz maintains equality in the distribution of
real income. This involves a severance of the link between an individual's contribution to production and his
real income.

These tenets set rules for the running of the production
sector where kibbutz income is earned, and for the distribution of real income among the members of the community. Let us first visualize the workings of the production sector and then the problems of consumption.

THE PRODUCTION SECTOR

Production and the provision of services are organized
as separate units—"branches," in kibbutz parlance. Each
branch is run by its permanent team headed by a branch
coordinator. If seasonal work is required, the permanent
staff is reinforced by temporary personnel. Land, equipment, and buildings are put at the disposal of the branches
as required. This means that the production and service
branches compete with each other for scarce resources—
land, capital equipment, unskilled and skilled labor, and
entrepreneurial talent. The function of the branches as the
elementary cells of the economic structure is underlined
by their identification as distinct reporting and accounting
units, which allows checking of their performance.

A permanent team is a group of experienced members
who are allocated to a specific branch for a period of several years. This informal group includes from four to ten
people.[4] The running of a branch is informal. The branch
meeting exists, though its responsibilities are not specifically defined. The branch coordinator in many cases simply
emerges from among the members, though formally
branch coordinators are nominated by the economic
committee for production branches, and by the relevant
committee for service branches.

---

[4] But the permanent team in a manufacturing enterprise, which
is one of several branches in many kibbutzim, may be larger, as
elaborated below.

The permanent team shares responsibilities for the day-to-day running of the branch. It usually also initiates the adoption of new techniques which may involve changes in equipment and product mix. More extensive development plans are first studied by the permanent team before being submitted for approval by the relevant committees, the secretariat, and finally the general assembly, if need be.

Motivation at the grass roots, which means at every production and service branch, is the sine qua non of kibbutz viability, both on the entrepreneurial and managerial plane and on the more humble plane of the man on the job—the tractor driver, or the man working in the dining room. The continuous growth and success of the kibbutz in terms of accepted indicators indicates that so far this problem has been solved. How this has been done, and particularly what social and institutional setup encourages a maximum effort by individuals, is probably the most important aspect of our subject.

The question of how the kibbutz succeeds is more easily raised than convincingly resolved. We do know what is *not* the answer. Differential material benefits, a major means for motivating individual performance in the nonkibbutz world, are ruled out by ideology and in practice. Still nonmaterial benefits, which are also relevant in the non-kibbutz world, are not excluded. Respect and esteem for a good day's work and for success in entrepreneurial functions is undoubtedly important in motivating individuals toward work and responsibility in the kibbutz. And displeasure with people shirking work is, in a closely knit community such as even the largest kibbutz, a powerful sanction.[5]

The expression "attitude toward work," which kibbutz parlance has turned into a Hebrew idiom, conveys in a nutshell that self-discipline counts most—self-discipline

---

[5] It is important to stress that in the late sixties 95 percent of the kibbutzim had a total population of 800 or less. Kibbutz members in such communities know each other very well indeed. This is less true of the handful of settlements which have a population of 1,000 to 1,500. Still, even there, direct personal contacts are strong by the standards of the nonkibbutz environment.

sustained by the socialist maxim "From each according to his ability" and by the puritan concept of "human fulfillment" through work. These notions, which require each individual to make the greatest effort for the "good" of the community even though he cannot expect to be rewarded personally, require relatively great powers of abstraction among the members. This is not to say that community "disapproval," which is mainly informal, fulfills no function in maintaining work discipline. Necessarily, however, it is of minor relevance.[6] Personal effort in a kibbutz depends ultimately on ideology and thus on the intellectual ability of members to understand, absorb, and turn into motive power a complicated set of abstractions.

Self-discipline sustained by ideology explains the behavior of the individual. The kibbutz itself is another matter. There must be rules for operating the components and performance criteria to ensure optimal allocation of manpower and other resources among competing production and service branches. One may therefore ask: What are the rules which guide the operation of each production unit? And what are the principles of coordination among the units that make up the production sector of the kibbutz? Finally, how do these mesh with operations of the personal service sector?

Consider the problems faced by a given production branch—say, the dairy. It uses labor, capital equipment—which in this particular case includes the herd of cows, cow sheds, the milking parlor, and foodstuffs—to produce milk. How do the people in charge of this branch decide how much to produce, and on what basis do they determine the factor combination—that is, the size of the various inputs to be used, such as labor, feeding stuff, and fixed equipment?[7] And it is not only factor combination

---

[6] A formal decision asking an individual to leave a kibbutz— the strongest sanction possible—is very rare. The annual number of such expulsions for the entire movement is probably not more than ten. A motion of censure put to the general assembly, also considered a very strict measure, is rather exceptional.

[7] Note that even in this case the equipment-labor ratio is not predetermined by existing production techniques. It is always possible to change the eight-hour milking shift, usual in Israel, to

in the short and long run which has to be determined. The size of the operation, which means the size of output—and in the long run this applies both to the possible extension and feasible contraction of production and even the phasing out of a branch—has to be determined.

The general rule for production branches is obvious—size and composition of output and input combination should be set to ensure that the difference between sale proceeds and (alternative) costs is maximized. This maximum net income condition is conceptually identical to the conventional rule for efficient production applied by a competitive firm. Yet under kibbutz conditions its application involves a peculiar problem related to the use of labor. The nature of this may become clear if we specify more closely the relevant variables and parameters.

Since the output of every kibbutz is small in relation to the size of the market, product prices are a given datum. The size of the sales proceeds of each branch thus depends on exogenous data—prices and the quantity produced, which is a decision variable. On the cost side kibbutzim are too small to affect input prices—the prices of raw materials, water, machinery—so that only the quantities of these inputs are variables, the determination of which is part of the problem.

This condition applies neither to kibbutz labor nor to land. The latter carries a nominal rent, and wages are obviously not paid to kibbutz labor, so that prices for these two major inputs are not exogenous market parameters. Yet, though there is no formal charge for the use of labor and land to any of the branches, the use of them is evidently not "free" to the kibbutz, and therefore is not free to its branches. The scarcity condition (which is actually what the dismal science of economics is all about) is not imposed by the conventional market constraint of price, but constitutes a quantity constraint on the kibbutz. The employment of labor and the allocation of land to any production and service branch—given a feasible full employment situation—inevitably has an alternative cost

---

a twelve-hour milking shift, usual in western Europe. This would reduce the labor intensity of the operation and correspondingly reduce output. The number of feeding units and the type of machinery could also be changed quickly.

in terms of the diversion of these resources from employment in other existing or projected branches.

The land endowment of each kibbutz is a given quantity.[8] The size of the labor force in the short run is a given datum too. In the longer run, though, its size does change —it rose slowly in the fifties and sixties. Yet, whatever the determinants of the long-run supply of kibbutz (self-) labor, a wage rate as such is not one of the determinants of its (limited) size at any point of time.[9]

Though the quantity constraints on labor and on land complicate somewhat the formal specification of the kibbutz model, this is merely a technical complication which can be dealt with analytically. On the basis of information concerning the technical relationships in production and service branches (production functions), exogenous price data of factors and of products, institutionally specified demands for personal services and amenities, and finally the quantity constraints on labor and land, it is possible to deduce the optimal solution for each kibbutz of the size of its outputs and the allocation of its inputs. This solution involves the setting of "shadow" prices for land and labor,[10] which represent the alternative cost of land and labor from the point of view of the kibbutz.

Thus, given the prices for all factors, including shadow prices of factors which "belong" to the kibbutz, and product prices, each production branch is requested to follow

---

[8] Institutional constraints in the form of landholding not directly related to kibbutzim mean in practice that the size of the land endowment of a kibbutz is a datum.

[9] Though the wage rate as such is not a determinant of kibbutz labor, per capita income is undoubtedly one of the factors which determine the size of membership and thus the size of kibbutz labor force. Per capita income and even income per worker and wages are, however, not identical in a kibbutz.

[10] A formal presentation of the model of the kibbutz production sector, in the short run, the analytical technique of deriving the optimal solution, and the nature of this solution in terms of factor allocation, output mix, and the corresponding shadow prices of land and of labor, is Haim Barkai, "Rules for Operating the Kibbutz Production Sector," *Proceedings of the Israeli Academy of Sciences and Humanities* 4 (1971); 281–96 (in Hebrew). The extension of the model to include the operations of the personal service sector, as implied in the statements made in the text, is conceptually straightforward.

a simple rule: it should produce a product mix and use a factor combination which maximizes the difference between sales proceeds and the alternative cost of factors *inclusive of labor and land.* If the rule of maximizing this difference—defined as "net branch income"—is followed by every production unit, net kibbutz income will be the highest feasible under the given set of technological, market, and ideological constraints.[11]

Note that if the supply of labor is given by the size of kibbutz membership, the shadow price of labor deduced from the equilibrium conditions reflects ideological constraints. This optimum position, which specifies the quantities of factors bought in the market, the allocation of these and of the kibbutz's own factors between competing branches, and the product mix, is consistent with the cardinal tenet of "self-labor."

Modern techniques of analysis and data processing make an optimum solution along such lines not only conceptually meaningful but practically feasible. Since the short-run labor supply is a known quantity, it is evidently easier to reach an equilibrium solution for shorter periods. Yet the approach is flexible enough to allow solutions for the longer run. The crucial difference between the long run and the

---

[11] Calculations of branch profitability, introduced early in kibbutz history, were supposed to serve as a yardstick for the evaluation of performance. Yet since wages as such were operationally meaningless, and also due to ideological considerations, the yardstick for performance which has been specified and used was the "labor day." This has been defined as the difference between the value of sales and the cost of raw materials and of depreciation divided by the number of labor days worked in the specific branch. Since this yardstick implicitly attributes the whole added value to labor (which is consistent with labor theory of value assumptions), the ranking in terms of labor days of the most capital-intensive and land-intensive branches was always first. This suggested prima facie, even in the thirties and forties, that the extension of farming and animal husbandry and the elimination of labor-intensive branches like vegetable growing is the optimal policy for kibbutzim. Restrictions on the size of land and on the financing of fixed capital stock prevented this from being carried out in practice. This underlined the inadequacy of the labor-day criterion as a basis for decisions concerning the structure of the kibbutz production sector. Its failure as a tool for efficient management is evidently due to its abstraction from two cardinal economic constraints—the land endowment and the cost of capital.

short run is the specification of the long-run supply function of labor. This cannot be expected to be a fixed quantity; kibbutzim have gained and expect to gain population
and labor through natural increase and inflow, and have
been losing population and labor through outflow. Inflow
and outflow probably depend on internal factors such as
expected living standards, and on exogenous factors such
as the size and country of origin of immigration, the
state of the economy, and last but not least, the ideological
ramifications of the political situation. Birthrates, hence
natural increase, may also partly depend on these factors.

This difference in the nature of the supply functions
means that the long-run shadow price of labor may be
different from the short-run price. Specifically, in response
to rapid technological change and the expected growth of
capital stock, on the one hand, and an expected small
expansion of kibbutz population and labor force, on the
other, the long-run shadow price of labor is expected to
rise. This suggests the adoption of policies for the phasing
out of labor-intensive branches and operations, hence for
far-reaching changes in the branch mix of the production
sector and a restructuring of demand and reorganization
of the personal service sector. In practice this was the most
important feature of the evolving pattern of the kibbutz in
the sixties. The rapid extension of manufacturing, the introduction of (partial) self-service in dining halls, and
the tendency to shift from the local kibbutz school to the
district school are obvious examples.

"Self-Labor"—Principle and Practice

The equilibrium setup of kibbutz production in terms of
factor allocation and product depends crucially, as we
have seen, on the size of its labor force. The consistency
of the optimum output mix and input structure with
ideology depends therefore on the application in practice
of the self-labor principle. This means that the kibbutz
labor force should consist of members and candidates to
membership, older kibbutz children, and groups of
"temporaries."[12] The common denominator of these three

---

[12] Temporaries are Hachshara (preparatory) groups which get
their social and economic training and are meant to serve as

groups is the absence of a wage nexus between the individuals who belong to them and the kibbutz. This constraint on the actual size of the labor force is operational only as long as the ideological barrier against employment of hired labor is not breached. The barrier is more easily maintained the smaller the economic incentives to rupture it.

Our analytical framework suggests the context in which economic forces can generate powerful pressures to hire labor. The equilibrium solution which specifies the optimum for the kibbutz in terms of factor allocation and product mix involves also, as we have noted, the determination of the shadow price of kibbutz labor. Now suppose that this price, which actually represents the productivity of labor (at the margin), is higher than relevant market wage rates. Then the kibbutz can evidently increase its income, hence per capita income of kibbutz population, by hiring labor. And obviously the greater the gap between the shadow price of labor and market wages, the greater the temptation to breach the ideological barrier which separates the kibbutz production sector from the general labor market.[13]

---

nuclei for a new kibbutz, and youth groups who spend their holidays doing part-time seasonal work. The temporaries are a minor component of population—in the sixties they were about 10 to 12 percent of the total population—and a significantly smaller component of the labor force.

[13] An equilibrium configuration which involves a positive difference between the shadow price of labor and market wages, hence lower per capita income than feasible, is prima facie not optimal from the point of view of the kibbutz. Yet since an equilibrium setup of this nature is the result of the limit on the supply of labor imposed by the principle of "self-labor," it is undoubtedly optimal since it ensures the highest per capita income consistent with ideological tenets. This suggests at once that the loss of per capita income—the difference between the equilibrium level of (per capita) income if the principle is observed and the equilibrium level of income if it is breached—offers a measure of the (minimum) cost of abiding by this principle of socialist ideology.

Since the self-labor principle does not apply to the economy, its maintenance by kibbutzim reduces not only their per capita (material) income, but also that of the economy as a whole. Now, if maximum per capita income is an accepted goal, which for Israel's economy it undoubtedly is, the strict application of the self-labor rule by kibbutzim has a negative effect, though a minor one, on the economy as a whole.

In the twenties and thirties, and for most of the kibbutzim in the forties, this was not a realistic possibility.
The shadow price of kibbutz labor was very low and this
obviated any incentive to employ nonkibbutz labor.
Disguised unemployment was the rule rather than the
exception for most kibbutzim before the Second World
War boom which began in Palestine in 1941. The situation was changing in the later forties and from the early
fifties onward almost all the kibbutzim in existence for,
say, ten years, had labor shortages. In terms of price
relatives this suggests a gap between the shadow price of
kibbutz labor and market wage rates of unskilled and
semiskilled farm and factory labor. Since not many new
kibbutzim were established after 1951, most of the kibbutzim passed into the phase of labor shortage by the
end of the fifties. Thus the economic incentive to breach
the rule of self-labor effected more and more kibbutzim;
by the middle sixties the dilemma of whether to engage
hired labor was facing practically every kibbutz.

The advent of the kibbutz industrial revolution since
the middle fifties has had an important bearing on this
issue. Even small-scale manufacturing enterprises require
at a minimum ten to fifteen people for one shift. A two-
shift operation, usually required for efficiency, means that
such a manufacturing enterprise needs about 15 to 20
percent of the labor force at the disposal of a kibbutz of
average size. Efficiency in some lines of production, such
as plywood manufacturing, plastics, and food, requires
plants engaging at least forty to fifty workers in a shift;
even a kibbutz with a population of eight hundred would
be hard-pressed to supply so much labor. Kibbutzim are
therefore inevitably caught in the dilemma—to reject a
promising line of manufacturing or to engage hired labor.
When the latter option is adopted it is initially considered
as only a stopgap.

The general economic situation in the fifties also had
some bearing on the issue. In the wake of mass immigration, unemployment was a major problem, and most
severe among new immigrants. Public opinion and government applied moral pressure on kibbutzim, which were
short of labor, to forgo—temporarily, as it was put then—
their principle of self-labor.

These factors succeeded in breaching the ideological fence, that separated the kibbutz from the economy's labor market. By 1954 kibbutzim employed probably 2,500 hired workers, about 8 percent of total kibbutz employment. Because of rapidly rising kibbutz labor productivity and an accelerating process of industrialization, the economic incentive to engage more hired workers grew significantly in the latter part of the fifties and sixties; yet the movement succeeded in containing the trend. The number of hired workers in the later sixties was about 5,500 to 5,800, about 8.5 to 9.2 percent of the total.

This slight erosion of the principle of self-labor is due mainly to manufacturing, where the intensity with which hired labor is employed is of a different order of magnitude than in other production and service branches. In 1969 more than 50 percent of the employees in kibbutz manufacturing enterprises were hired workers, compared to 14 percent in farming and 4 percent in personal service branches.[14]

This "nonfailure" on the employment front—as kibbutz people would prefer to describe the containment of forces pushing toward a rise in the proportion of hired workers in kibbutz employment—prevented the irrevocable erosion of self-labor principles. Staving off what might have been a fatal blow to the kibbutz as a form of social organization induced the introduction of labor-saving techniques at a rapid pace in the production sector and also in the personal service sector, which demands a considerable slice of kibbutz labor force.

INCOME DISTRIBUTION—THE PRINCIPLE OF EQUALITY

To sever the link between an individual's contribution to production and the personal benefits he receives is the key to turning the socialist principle of equality into everyday reality. Equality is interpreted to mean "to every-

---

[14] Several large enterprises are by now only partly owned by kibbutzim: they have been organized as limited liability companies in which the other partners hold 50 percent or less of the share capital. Partnerships with nonkibbutz interests have been established for several reasons, including the "legalizing" of the hiring of labor. Whether this offers only a formal escape from the dilemma is, of course, open to dispute.

one according to his needs within the means of the community." The qualification added to Marx's well-known phrase expresses the scarcity constraint, which is always present and was especially in evidence during the heroic days of the twenties when real income was sometimes not much above starvation levels.

The needs concept, we may note, has been specified in terms of individual choice, so that the kibbutz technique of income distribution, as it has been evolving over fifty years, must satisfy three conditions: allowing for differences in the tastes of individuals, adapting living standards to real income, and ensuring equality in a nonmechanical sense. One obvious way to meet these not necessarily consistent conditions is to adopt a technique which supplies goods and services "free," so to speak, to members, yet maintains overall budgetary control.

Communal dining, a common practice in the twenties, even among temporary work groups, was initially introduced more in response to exogenous conditions than to ideological motivations, and seems perfect for the purpose. Its consistency with collective living is obvious. The communal dining hall has evolved as the focus of kibbutz life, operationally and symbolically—the central location and architectural eminence of kibbutz dining rooms underline this. A felicitous aspect of communal dining is the feasibility of realizing the principle of equality without overt rationing and its unsympathetic trappings. It can be practiced while allowing a limited, though growing, variety, which means some freedom of consumer's choice.[15]

As far as food is concerned, and this is a major item of the consumption basket,[16] equality in the kibbutz is not only preached but practiced. Now, if "collective consump-

---

[15] Variety was quite limited in the thirties. (In the twenties when kibbutzim were poor as mice it was practically nonexistent.) Though the variety of food offered at each meal is limited, a choice between two main dishes is now always possible. The range of choice has been growing, in effect growing with income.

[16] Food was undoubtedly the dominant item of expenditure in the twenties and thirties, when it claimed about two-thirds of total consumption expenditure; in the early fifties it was still more than half. In the later fifties and the sixties the ratio fell rapidly and by the end of the sixties it was 30 percent. Food is still the largest single item in the consumption basket.

tion" (kibbutz parlance for this technique of distributing real income) could be practiced generally, you would have an optimal solution from the point of view of equality, on the one hand, and budgetary control, on the other. All the other components of consumption—housing and furniture, clothing and footwear, health and education, holidays and sundries like cigarettes—would be distributed by a technique similar to that used for food.

And indeed collective consumption on a free-for-all basis—which means that rationing is not applied at the individual level—is applied to the distribution of other consumer goods and services. At the opposite pole from food, they include items that industrial societies have by now made into public goods—the so-called welfare-state items. Health care, which is unlimited, is an obvious example, and so are retirement benefits.[17] Items such as maternity leave and the equivalent of full life insurance, both of which are ultimate goals of the welfare state, are, because of the very nature of the kibbutz, part and parcel of its way of life. They were devised and introduced in the twenties and thirties, which means that they anticipated later developments in western and northern Europe.

Child care and education until the age of eighteen are also "free" communal services.[18] The principle of equality

---

[17] Since accounts of individual income are not run in the first place and membership endows everybody with the right to every good or service offered by the community, the "drawing of a pension" in the technical sense of the term is meaningless. The technical significance of retirement, expressed in reduction of required working time, is restricted to the production facet. Otherwise everything is the same; the kibbutz provides the most comprehensive old-age insurance feasible.

The kibbutz insures everyone with Kupath-Holim—the Histadruth health service. Yet since health care is literally unlimited, the kibbutz covers from its own funds anything which does not come under this scheme. Kibbutzim participate in the old-age insurance scheme run by the National Insurance Institute. They pay the dues, and are paid the benefits due to each of their members after the retirement age, which is sixty-five. The pensions paid by the National Insurance scheme are only a minor component of the cost to the kibbutz of its own scheme.

[18] Children, defined to include the under-nineteen age bracket, live in almost all the kibbutzim separately, in "children's houses." Nurseries, kindergarten, and twelve years of elementary and secondary schooling make up the kibbutz educational system, which

of the sexes, requiring equal treatment in every type of work from household jobs to those in production branches, induced what is now called "collective education." The kibbutz system of child care, one of its most characteristic features, had to be devised consistently with this constraint.

The technique of "free" distribution has, however, never been applied to the whole range of goods and services. Clothing and footwear, cigarettes and toiletries, housing and furniture and (some) household equipment, and also "holiday money" are allocated to individuals by means of rationing techniques.

Clothing and footwear, for example, are individually chosen. Even if a standard costume, similar to the monastic habit, were adopted as the only outfit used by kibbutz members, there would still be problems of size. And since the kibbutz was never conceived as a monastic order, individual taste has always been of considerable significance in regard to dress and footwear. Initially, kibbutzim attempted to run the clothing store on a nonindividual basis, but this was in the twenties and early thirties, when expenditure on clothing, footwear, and similar items was minimal owing to low incomes. They soon restricted the nonindividual basis, though with some ideological misgivings, to working clothes and linen.[19]

---

also includes facilities for extracurricular studies for children with talents in the arts. Every child is given full opportunity to develop its intellectual and artistic potential without much reference to budgetary constraints.

The extension of this rule to the realm of higher education is not finally settled. In practice, most kibbutzim allow education at one of Israel's universities to everybody after returning from military service.

The comprehensive system of education, which even now offers more years of schooling than the eleven years required by law; its flexibility in response to the individual's special needs; and also the small size of the kibbutzim causing low student-teacher ratios—these make education expensive for the kibbutz and require a higher share of disposable income than in the country as a whole—which is also true of health, accident and old-age care.

[19] In practice this meant that working clothes, linen, and similar items did not carry a personal identification number, while other clothes did. After laundering, these items were handed out in the weekly clothing pack on a nonpersonal, random basis.

It should not come as a surprise that it was the women who initiated and continued to lead the trend toward individual choice of clothing. By the end of the thirties kibbutzim adopted an allocation mechanism by which each individual was allocated a specified clothing basket composed of several items, which allowed some choice of items within prescribed limits. This device, called the "personal budget," was applied to footwear, cigarettes, and holiday money, (which was very small, even by the standards of the thirties and forties). The clothing and footwear budgets were run much like the point systems perfected during World War II, and cigarettes and toiletries were rationed. These several "budgets" were kept separate.[20] Thus, not only does the community control how much is consumed but to a large degree also what is consumed.

Housing also illustrates the intricate problems involved in the application of the rule of equality to real life. Since in most kibbutzim children live in their own houses, the rule that requires similar housing conditions for all can be, so it seems, easily applied by allocating similar space to each family. Yet differences in size and quality of housing units, which reflect mainly their time of construction, exclude the possibility of an equal distribution of housing services to adults at any point of time. Some members live in better, often much better apartments.

Since housing is a major component of living standards and equal distribution of housing services is impossible, special allocative devices had to be devised, namely a code for allocation of housing and consumer durables based on a principle of "potential" equality. Priorities, measured in points give major weight to length of service in the settlement (and in the kibbutz movement) and to age.[21] Special factors such as health may apply too. Mem-

---

[20] The itemization not only puts cigarettes, toiletries, stationery and stamps, furnishings, minor food items like tea, coffee, and biscuits, holiday money, footwear, and clothing into separate compartments. It specifies even the number of shirts, trousers, jackets, and overcoats in the clothing budget.

[21] For kibbutz-born members length of service is age minus eighteen years. Note, however, that this has operational significance for adults only. Children of families joining a kibbutz are integrated at once within their age group, which means that they benefit immediately from every service and amenity given to it.

bers' rank in points determines their housing standards
and the composition and quality of consumer durables put
at their disposal.

Equality with respect to housing and consumer durables
does not mean equal consumer benefits at every point of
time. Equal rights to a given level of real consumption
to everyone of the same point ranking is only slightly
related to potential though not actual contribution to production, through length of service.

THE PERSONAL BUDGET CONTROVERSY

The kibbutz could not have survived without efficiently
running its production sector. Productivity gains, impressive even compared to the Israeli economy as a whole,
ensured rapidly rising disposable income which, from the
middle fifties onward, was high enough to approach affluence in European terms. But these high and rising incomes
brought into question some traditional techniques for distributing income, the personal budget technique in particular.

This issue took shape in the middle forties. In the sixties
it was put squarely on the agenda of the movement in
response to suggestions, support for which has been
gathering momentum, to scrap the personal budget technique of distributing nonfood and nonwelfare-state items
and to substitute a "comprehensive budget." This gave
rise to a controversy of great significance to the future of
the kibbutz.

Those who favor the comprehensive budget maintain
that the personal budget, which essentially involves physical rationing, is outdated and wasteful.[22] A ration system
could be run efficiently, they maintain, only when communities were small and homogeneous in background and

---

[22] Formal definitions of the two techniques:

Personal budget.—The same amount of money is allocated to
each member to cover his needs in a specific consumption category shifting of unused balances between categories is not permitted.

Comprehensive budget.—The same amount of money is allocated to each member to cover his needs for all categories in the
comprehensive budget. Shifting of balances between categories in
the comprehensive budget is permitted.

age group, and when choice of goods was limited. As long as incomes were low, food and the welfare-state items, all distributed on a "free" basis and warrantedly given high priority, swallowed up most of the consumption expenditures, leaving little for clothing and the other highly individual items.

The poverty constraint was, however, disappearing in the forties, and even more rapidly in the fifties and sixties. A continuous rise in real income allowed more than proportional growth in expenditures on personalized items and thus more consumer choice. The detailed itemization imposed by the personal budget limits the freedom of individuals unnecessarily. It causes waste: first, communal and individual preferences may conflict; second, a rationing system encourages people to exhaust their annual rations in all categories.

The tokens (or balances) in the comprehensive budget can be used for goods and services at nonsubsidized prices from the kibbutz store, or can be converted to money for off-kibbutz purchases.

The comprehensive budget system divides kibbutz income in three categories. The first is goods and services distributed on a "free" basis: food, maintenance of children and education, cultural activities, retirement benefits, etc. The second is housing and furniture, allocated as in the past on a point system. The third is the remaining consumption items, which make up the comprehensive budget.[23]

In spite of advantages that seem obvious to outsiders this proposal has met strong opposition and was the sub-

---

That the first clear-cut definition of the terms is so recent is instructive in itself. See Hakibbutz Haartzi Hashomer Hatzair (Social Department), *On Consumption; A Collection of Records, Interviews, and Articles* (January 1971, in Hebrew).

[23] The "free distribution" category accounted for 60 to 65 percent of total consumption expenditures in the sixties; housing services, 20 to 25 percent; comprehensive budget category, 15 to 20 percent.

The "free distribution" category accounted for close to 70 percent in the fifties and about 75 to 80 percent in the forties and thirties. Expenditures on food were about 25 to 30 percent in the sixties, 35 to 40 percent in the forties, and probably about 50 and 60 to 65 percent in the thirties and twenties respectively.

ject of heated debate in the sixties. Two of the three major kibbutz federations have failed to adopt the proposal, and at present it is applied only in a minority of kibbutz settlements.

The traditionalists do not agree that the comprehensive budget has only technical significance. They find substitution of individual for communal choice to be objectionable. The comprehensive budget applies to 15 to 20 percent of total consumption expenditure today, they argue, but this share has been growing rapidly and will continue to grow. Essentially, the traditionalists reject the comprehensive budget because they consider it a retreat from the principles of collective consumption. They maintain that the pure model of collective consumption envisages free distribution of every commodity and service—for example, an allowance for holiday money should be allocated to be spent only off the kibbutz. Admitting that growing affluence allows for more variety, and more personal choice the traditionalists suggest extending the range of "free" items. They note that some items, such as toiletries, were once rationed but are now free goods.

The traditionalist argument would be stronger if they favored adding clothing and footwear to the "free" list. But the obvious temptation to individual members to build up a sizable wardrobe makes this impossible. The traditionalists can therefore only suggest more flexibility in the clothing and footwear budget to allow choice within a detailed list of similar items ("clothing groups," in kibbutz parlance). This practice, in fact, is followed in most kibbutzim and will be for a long time unless the comprehensive budget is accepted. The more individualistic attitude of the younger generation, bred by growing affluence and probably changing attitudes toward ideology, as well as a better understanding of the inevitable waste involved in every rationing system, may yet tilt the balance toward reform.

INDUSTRIALIZATION

Industrialization, which began in the early forties and grew in the fifties and sixties, sets another challenge to the kibbutz. The rapid progress of kibbutz industrialization is one of the best indicators of the spirit of enterprise, as well as of the relative ease with which labor and other resources can be shifted. To sever the link between living standards and occupation is to reduce a major source of friction, which in the nonkibbutz environment reduces labor mobility. This has eased the existing massive shift into manufacturing—which will probably gather further momentum in the seventies. The massive transition to manufacturing, which has been the major contributor to raising kibbutz productivity and has enabled kibbutzim to keep pace with Israel's rapidly rising living standards, poses major problems to the kibbutz.

The main problems of establishing a manufacturing enterprise in a kibbutz are of size and of division of labor. Even a small factory requires a permanent labor force of fifteen, or usually closer to twenty to twenty-five people; and manufacturing—in contrast to repair shops, which were always an integral element of the kibbutz production sector—requires that most personnel do routine jobs. It also requires a smaller number of highly trained, motivated, and talented personnel in managerial and entrepreneurial capacities.

The kibbutz production sector consists of a great number of production units, most of them farming branches run by small teams of permanent workers. The team of even a large branch in one of the larger settlements is five or six, at most ten people.[24] The small size of the work team has made it possible to run the branches nonformally. There has never been a clear-cut separation between white-collar functions and manual work. The branch coordinator, who is formally responsible for running the branch and who spends the majority of his time on managerial functions, usually takes an active part in doing the job itself, while the other members of the team take a hand in managerial and even entrepreneurial functions

---

[24] Seasonal work, if necessary, is handled by reinforcing the permanent work teams with kibbutz labor not permanently allocated to the branch. In the summer, when seasonal reinforcement is particularly required, it is the part-time work of the fourteen-to-eighteen age group of kibbutz children and of youth groups spending the summer in kibbutzim which makes it possible to meet the demand for labor.

which allow some play to their initiative, and prepare
them in due course for the top job in this or another
branch.

This informal way of running the production sector—
which evolves naturally in farming—is the most perfect
form of worker's management. In contrast to the Yugoslav
variant of worker's management, which has recently been
given much publicity, it did not begin with a predesigned
and complicated set of rules and regulations. It evolved,
rather, in response to practical requirements, and it has
proved itself in practice for fifty years.

But this informal way of doing things, which allows
such freedom to the individual in carrying out his tasks,
has to give way in manufacturing establishments. The
production line, which means routine jobs, also means
that every operator becomes dependent on the one preceding him, which calls for greater specialization and
stricter coordination. The greater expertise demanded from
technical and entrepreneurial personnel forces a sharper
dividing line between manual and managerial jobs, which
can lead to the formation of a relatively closed managerial
elite which excludes members with little natural talent for
leadership and business. The very size of the labor force
and the elaborate division of labor can create a psychological barrier between managerial personnel and those permanently engaged in routine jobs, with the substitution of
formal work discipline for the traditional informal ways
based on self-discipline.[25]

The crucial issue is whether the presumption of equality,
the basic premise of kibbutz life, can withstand developments in manufacturing enterprises which are more and
more run on the basis of a growing inequality in know-
how, expertise, and responsibility. One escape from this
impasse is to promise, formally or implicitly, that everybody with reasonable capabilities will be drawn into
expert or managerial functions. Training in an institute of

---

[25] The fact that in some kibbutz manufacturing enterprises
members are required to clock in and out when entering and leaving the plant—though this has no meaning in terms of material re-
ward—may indicate how things are moving. The more these
manufacturing enterprises grow, the greater the problems of work
discipline, which in turn requires stricter regulation.

higher education and future employment in a technical capacity offers promise for the younger generation. But vertical mobility cannot apply to everybody: in particular, not to the elderly, the age group of fifty-plus, the efficient utilization of whose labor power is usually an important factor in deciding to establish a manufacturing enterprise in the first place.

Availability of openings in other production or service branches—rotation of jobs and forestalling the formation of an entrenched group of functionaries—is another escape valve for people with routine jobs. Such rotation, however, is more difficult within the manufacturing field. The immediate cost of rotating, say, the chief engineer of a plant to a six-month stint in the dining hall may seem prohibitive. There follows a conflict between long-run considerations in favor of rotation and calculations of short-run costs.

Most of the problem would disappear if further expansion of manufacturing were stopped. This would reduce the number of hired workers to a negligible figure, avoiding any further erosion of the self-labor principle, and ease such problems as identification with the work place and conflict between management and unskilled workers. But slowing the pace of the industrial revolution might well doom the kibbutz movement, whose success as a form of social organization would have been impossible if it had failed to organize production efficiently. One of the main determinants of this efficiency has been the ability of the kibbutzim to identify growth sectors and to adapt their production potential to the more promising products.[26] Hence the industrialization drive, which means in practice that kibbutzim have been voting with their feet in favor of further industrialization.[27] Since Israel is rapidly developing a versatile industrialized economy and since a successful attempt to maintain high productivity gains in farming means further reduction in labor inputs,

---

[26] These are expressed quantitatively by comparatively high factor labor and capital productivities at the margin, and by the 4 to 5 percent annual average total productivity gains of the last two decades.

[27] Employment in manufacturing has grown by 65 to 70 percent since 1960 and by 250 percent since 1950.

the kibbutz movement has no option, so it seems, but to industrialize further, if it is not to become a kind of "natural reserve." The challenge facing it in the seventies is that of adapting its social framework to the requirements of manufacturing industry while maintaining its socialist principles.

INTERKIBBUTZ EQUALITY

Though we have referred to the kibbutz movement as a whole, we have actually been considering only the workings of the individual kibbutz. This presumes that each kibbutz is a separate entity in terms of production and distribution. And indeed, this is one of the most important principles of the Israeli collective movement, adopted only after a sharp debate in 1922. It has never been questioned since.[28]

The principles of collective production and of equality in the distribution of real income apply only within each kibbutz. Relationships with other entities, whether kibbutzim or nonkibbutz units, are purely commercial. Thus, while in theory and practice a kibbutz is a socialist community, it operates in a nonsocialist environment. It therefore has to accept the rules of a market economy for extrakibbutz relationships, raising problems, for example, of hired labor and of interkibbutz relations.

-----

[28] The debate referred to a practical problem: whether Ein Harod, which had been established in 1921 by the Work Legion, should have complete financial independence or whether its current expenditures should be controlled by the national executive of the Work Legion. The policy of centralization was strongly supported by leading members of the Work Legion but was opposed by the majority of members of Ein Harod. The debate caused a split in the Work Legion when the majority in Ein Harod opted for decentralization, which meant that all the operational decisions on the running of the settlement would be taken by the members of the settlement only. Self-rule of each settlement was adopted in practice by all kibbutzim, setting the pattern for the movement as we know it today.

The debate between those who favored central control and those who objected to it was strongly affected by the concurrent controversy in the Soviet Union. Many of the leading personalities in favor of centralization returned to the Soviet Union in 1925.

Although kibbutzim are separate legal and economic entities, each one belongs to one of three kibbutz federations, and they identify spiritually with the movement as a whole. The movement formally and informally controls a vital lever of kibbutz life—the inflow of manpower from the nonkibbutz environment. The harmony of outlook, which is so important to the strength of the kibbutz movement, could be severely affected if there were significant material differences between kibbutz settlements. Such differences, though technically possible because of decentralization, have not been permitted by a movement which has made equality into a basic tenet. Interkibbutz mobility is a practical check on tendencies for too large divergences of living standards—if these were not ruled out by ideological considerations in the first place.

Though differences do exist, it has been an accepted impression that they are minor. Estimates for the fifties and sixties based on per capita income and on consumption expenditures support the impression that intrakibbutz inequality was small.[29] Nor are these results a matter of chance. Since practically every kibbutz settlement started after 1921 and since most of them are not yet twenty-five years old, control of the endowment of real resources—the basic capital and land endowments—is a major factor in equality. And indeed, the policy of the Jewish Agency's Settlement Department, in charge of settlement activities during the period, has always been guided by the principle of equality, interpreted to mean that the allocation of means of production must be on a per capita basis. Each unit settled on land has accordingly been allocated an "equal" endowment, which varied in composition according to technical requirements but should be expected to allow the same income per family.

---

[29] These estimates employed the "Lorenz" and "D" measures of inequality, which can take values between 0 and 1 for absolute equality and absolute inequality respectively. None of the Lorenz measures for per capita consumption for the years 1954–65 was higher than 0.01. The values of the D index were 0.05–0.06.

The corresponding measures for interkibbutz inequality of disposable income per capita were higher. The highest Lorenz measure was 0.16 and the highest D measure, 0.11. The time series of the measure showed some trend of growing inequality in income, but no trend in consumption.

To carry out the principle is a tricky matter indeed, due to differences in location, natural conditions, successes and failures of marketing projections, and possible differences in the most important production resource—the human factor.[30] However, great homogeneity of the human factor among kibbutzim is an important social characteristic of the movement, and this has helped maintain the remarkable interkibbutz equality of living standards.

Industrialization may, however, have a significant effect on interkibbutz equality. Since most kibbutzim venture into industry at a late stage of their development, the equal endowment rule applies to a much smaller extent. One factory may succeed where another fails. The availability of a small cadre of trained personnel at an early stage of manufacturing can make the difference between success and failure. And since manufacturing is rapidly becoming the major branch, great differences in performance and hence in per capita income may result. Whether the kibbutz movement could reduce these large differences by income redistribution is an open question.[31] Industrialization, which is a major factor in pulling kibbutzim out of relative autarky and strengthening contact with nonkibbutz elements of Israel's economy and society, also offers a strong challenge to interkibbutz equality.

---

[30] Israeli experience has shown the great significance of the latter. Considerable differences in performance, hence in family income, have appeared within five to ten years in cooperative settlements, though each family was allocated an identical land and capital stock endowment.

[31] Interkibbutz taxation is progressive, yet the sums involved, which are used to finance the central organization of the kibbutz federations, are too small to effect significantly differences in income.

The main and most promising way in which the kibbutz movement attempts to work towards interkibbutz equality is by a manpower tax imposed on the older and more prosperous settlements. The "men" acquired in this way by the central kibbutz authorities are usually highly trained and experienced personnel; they are allocated for periods such as a year, and sometimes even more, to help train working and managerial personnel of the younger and less experienced kibbutzim. They do that by living in the new settlement and usually apply the "do it yourself" technique. This interkibbutz free "manpower service" is undoubtedly a major factor in assuring greater interkibbutz equality in the long run.

THE SIGNIFICANCE OF SURVIVAL

One may be tempted to ask what the success or rather nonfailure of the kibbutz movement proves.[32] We should state first what it cannot prove. Since it has accepted the rules of the game of a market economy, this daring social experiment cannot give guidance on democratically controlled socialist economy—it has not attempted to. But it has shown that a socialist form of organization on the microeconomic and microsocial planes is viable. One may ask whether viability depends on the relatively small size of kibbutz communities.[33]

The facts should suggest even to skeptics that substitution of a collective personality for an individual ego is not inconsistent with remarkable economic performance, whatever the standard of comparison. The inevitable delay in decision making which involves "democracy in action" and in practice means a system of rule by committee, as well as some waste due to the fact that the budget constraint is not applied on the individual plane, is compensated for by purely economic advantages made possible by the nature of the kibbutz:[34] the most important of these are probably economies of scale, much greater inbuilt facilities for internal factor mobility, and last but not least, easier access to training and learning which induces rapid improvement in the quality of the most important production factor—human labor.

It would be misleading to evaluate the kibbutz only as a socialist entity. Though it does attempt to carry socialism into effect on the microplane, its ideology and practice

---

[32] This expression was used by Martin Buber when referring to the kibbutz movement in a lecture he gave in 1945. It still seems apt today.

[33] We may note in passing the fierce debate which was raging in 1921, before the settlement of Ein Harod, whether a kibbutz of 150 people is a viable proposition.

[34] These points were made by opponents of the kibbutz in the running debate on its viability which was at its height in the late twenties and early thirties. The economic difficulties of kibbutzim at the time supported those who maintained that the absence of personal incentive is a necessary consequence of a collective way of life, and that red tape and the neglect of collective property are inevitable in a collective.

have always been closely related to Zionist ideology and
practice. The fusion of Zionism and socialism has been
the very essence of the commune's conceptual framework
and its practice.

If a working definition of Zionism is the reestablishment
of a Jewish national entity in its historical homeland, the
resettlement of Eretz Israel (the Land of Israel) has been
identified as the necessary condition of this process. This
approach won the day after a lengthy debate between
supporters of "practical work" in Eretz Israel and those
who saw in the establishment of a Jewish state in Palestine a practical proposition as early as the twenties.[35]

Though not the only form of social organization of the
Jewish settlement movement, the kibbutz was in its vanguard. Ever since the establishment of Deganiah and
particularly after 1921 when the theory of establishing a
large and growing kibbutz community came into being,
the Zionist idea of settlement and the socialist idea of
building it as a collective were fused into one. The concept of socialist Zionism in its purest form meant the establishment of a kibbutz in Palestine. The identification of the
several generations of kibbutzniks with the kibbutz as idea
and institution draws on both national aspirations and socialist fulfilment. It would be hard to imagine a movement
of a hundred thousand people living in socialist communities, which are part and parcel of an industrial society,
were it not for the national factor which pulled people
into the kibbutz and induced them to stay on.

In turn, it goes without saying that national aspirations
could not have made kibbutzim a practical proposition
but for the availability of a highly educated social strata
which could think in terms of the rarefied abstractions
required to make a kibbutz tick. This condition probably
excludes the adaptation of the kibbutz to the social environment of developing countries. If the kibbutz as a
form of social organization is practical anywhere, it is in
the highly industrialized societies in the West. Workers
who can think in highly abstract terms and who look for

---

[35] The Zionist labor movement was always in favor of the
constructive approach, sometimes called "another acre and another
cow."

ideals no longer embedded in material realities only, are undoubtedly available in these societies. The establishment of some communities might be an omen of things to come. For kibbutzim to materialize in the West, candidates must realize that they will stand or fall according to whether they solve the problems of production.

Images of Israel: A Personal View

Ronald Sanders

RONALD SANDERS—author of *Israel: The View from Masada* and *The Downtown Jews*, associate editor of *Midstream*.

In recent years the gap has widened between what Israel is and what many Americans imagine it to be. Jews even more than Gentiles have helped to create this gap. American Jews who have prospered greatly over the past quarter of a century and who have made large financial contributions to aid Israel's growth are often likely to take a proprietary air toward that country and to represent it in their own image to themselves and to America at large. The struggles and achievements of the Israelis are transformed by such Americans into mere vicarious projections of American middle-class self-satisfaction, entitlement to which is bought by an annual check to the Jewish National Fund and a trip to Israel itself once every three years or so. Viewed this way, the Jewish state tends to look like a Levantine Miami Beach, a huge Dan Hotel sprawled along the eastern shore of the Mediterranean Sea, in which Jews have shown a special ability to rise to heights of success in the military trades similar to that which their American cousins have shown in other forms of business. It takes on the aspect of a fortified Middle Eastern frontier for an American Jewish suburbia gone militant, which serves to fend off the onslaughts of less fortunate, non-Western ethnic groups and the expansionist ambitions of Russian communism at one and the same time. If some of the more radical-minded sons and daughters of middle-class American Jews often take a dim view of Israel, this is not necessarily because what they

think they see there is in any way different from what their
parents think they see.

The "image" of Israel thus presented to many young
Americans today is strikingly different from the one that
presented itself to my generation when it was young, at
the time the Jewish state was founded. In May 1948, I
was going to a Brooklyn public high school with a student
body that was largely Jewish and middle class. On the
whole, we leaned somewhat to the left in our politics—
which ranged anywhere from New Deal to Stalinist—and
at the same time we regarded the creation of the state of
Israel as a major step in the general worldwide progress
of social justice after the defeat of fascism. Neither before
nor since, even among Jews, has the identification of the
idea of Jewish statehood with the aspirations of the left
been so easily achieved as it was in our case; but the
time was perfectly ripe for it then. We had been weaned
during a war against an immense force of evil which had
proclaimed socialism and the Jews to be its two worst
enemies and had sought to exterminate both. Indeed, Hitler had often sought to identify Judaism and socialism as
one and the same. The Jewish people had thus been presented to the world as the objective representative of anti-
fascism in its purest form. We, the first generation to grow
up in the wake of that disaster, often accepted this identification proudly. Those of us who were Jewish and leaned
toward the left politically considered ourselves to be, as
Jews, the embodiment of the cause of social justice, an
honor we claimed by the mere fact of our existence, much
as blacks have done in more recent years.

Not that this kind of identification, which has often
appeared with variations throughout the lively relationship between the Jews and the left, has always pointed in
the direction of Jewish statehood. The Jewish Workers'
Federation, or Bund, for example, which flourished in
Russia and then Poland from the turn of the century to
the Second World War, was founded upon a mystique
which identified its vision of a Jewish national culture—
based mainly on the Yiddish language—with the aspirations of Marxian social democracy, but which was vehemently anti-Zionist at the same time. In those classic days
of Marxist theorizing, it was still possible to argue that

Zionism—even Labor Zionism—offered a mere "utopian" solution both to the Jewish question and to social problems in general. Good Marxists stayed home to deal with the problems of existing society instead of retreating into wildernesses to found new societies, and bundists were more concerned about being good Marxists than Labor Zionists were. Years later Martin Buber in effect was to reply to the bundist argument by proclaiming proudly, in his *Paths in Utopia*, that the central socialist institutions of Israel—above all, the kibbutz—did indeed belong to that tradition which Marx had labeled "utopian." But what, asked Buber, was wrong with this? Had Marx provided the last word on which were the "correct" forms of socialism and which were not? On the other side of the coin, Lenin had called the bundists into question by referring to them, in Plekhanov's wisecrack, as Zionists afraid of seasickness. By my time, these questions had all been rendered obsolete by history. Bundists and Zionists—as well as Jewish Communists—had fought side by side in the Warsaw ghetto during its last days. Of the various principles of Jewish and potentially socialist self-assertion represented by the ghetto fighters, only Zionism had survived the Holocaust; bundism had been swept away with the masses of East European Jewry that had formed its moral base, and Jewish communism had emerged a mere fossil that would increasingly seem a contradiction in terms.

For my generation, then, the founding of the state of Israel in 1948 represented a simultaneous realization of two ideals: Jewish liberation and social democracy. Jewish liberation, either in its assimilationist or culturally autonomist forms, had proved impossible for the traditional Jewish communities of central Europe; and if new possibilities for Jewish life had since opened up in Western Europe and America, bitter experience nevertheless had proven that the only secure future, culturally as well as physically, for the Jewish people as a whole lay in the continuing existence of an autonomous community in which at least some of the Jews of the world—in particular, those who had either been rejected or not taken in anywhere else—could live and sink roots into a land of their own. Whether one went to Israel or not, its presence in the world was to be proof for all time that justice in human history could not be subjugated by some genocidal fascist urge. As for the socialist side of the story, its history in Europe had demonstrated that the doctrinal justifications of old were as nothing alongside the moral claims that successful practice could make. Whatever the dialectically "correct" approach to the land question, the fact remained that Israel as well as the Soviet Union had created a system of agricultural collectives, and there could be no doubt which of the two methods of collectivization answered to a genuinely democratic definition of socialism. In this, as in other matters, Israel proved to be a vital laboratory for the question of how the aims of socialism could be achieved on a purely voluntaristic basis; for Israel was, and still is, one of the most socialist of the liberal democracies of the world.

I should confess that, for my own part, the impact of this generational experience of Israel contributed to making me into a bearer of a certain Jewish–social democratic mystique similar to that of the traditional Labor Zionists. Like them, I consider it to be far from accidental that the Jewish state is also a great experiment in social democracy. Indeed I believe, as they do, that a viable Jewish state could not have been created in any other terms in the twentieth century. I have never been, strictly speaking, an orthodox Labor Zionist, and never belonged to any ideologically committed organization; but the experience of 1948 had certainly conditioned me to become the kind of fellow traveler to Zionist socialism that I did indeed become in the 1960s. I had done some research in the history of bundism and of the Yiddish-speaking labor movement in New York, and thus was already caught up in the romance of finding affinities between the Jewish spirit and the essence of social democracy when I first visited Israel in the summer of 1961. Was I going to have to strain hard to find confirmation of my beliefs? Then, before I had been in the country a week, I was picked up in a bus riding through the Galilee by a pair of kibbutzniks, a married couple in their thirties, who invited me to stay in their kibbutz for a few days. I got off the bus with them and worked there a week and a half. I had tramped and worked on farms a little in America, too, but never with the sense of naturalness and casual ease

that I experienced this time in Israel. Egalitarianism filled
the air wherever I went like the glow of that powerful Middle Eastern sun. I was under the spell of my own pre-
dilections, to be sure, but reality helped confirm my feeling that I was in one of the great socialist democracies of
the world.

It was in the fall of 1961, right after that trip, that I
read the works of Moses Hess and became one of his
followers. It is significant, I think, that posterity has tended
to split this nineteenth-century German-Jewish social
theorist in two parts. He is well known as an early socialist
thinker to many people of the left who are not aware of
his Zionist side at all. On the other hand, many a bourgeois textbook in Jewish history celebrates the author of
Rome and Jerusalem as a "precursor of modern Zionism"
without mentioning his personal associations with men
like Marx, Engels, and Lassalle, or his lifelong involvement in the European socialist movement. It is as if the
partisan of each side of him has been embarrassed by the
other; but Hess was very much a totality, and this is what
is particularly interesting about him. Although inclined to
reject "the Mosaic religion" in which he had been born
along with religion in general during his "Young Hege-
lian" days, he did not subsequently follow Marx and
Engels toward philosophical materialism so far as to
rid his own socialist vision of a strong element of idealism which, years later, was able to accommodate the
revival of a mystical Jewish nationalism. Good Spinozist
that he was, he came to view his socialism and his Jewish
nationalism as two modes of a single substance. He became convinced that there was no difference between the
spirit of Judaism and the spirit of social democracy; that,
as he wrote in one of his letters, "der Geist des Judentums ist ein sozialdemokratischer von Haus aus." He therefore believed that a Jewish national revival would be the
historic event which would introduce the era of social
democracy to mankind—but that this could take place only
when the bulk of European Jewry had broken away from
the scenes of their past physical and continuing moral
bondage and returned to the ancestral homeland of the
Jewish people.

I found Hess's formulations not only quite appealing,

but also illuminating of a good deal of subsequent history. His relationship with Marx—his rejection of Marx's more hard-edged radicalism, and Marx's disparagement both of Hess's gentle idealism and of his persistent Jewish leanings (he tauntingly called Hess "the communist rabbi")— seemed to me to foreshadow quite accurately the subsequent relationship between radical Marxists and the "Jewish" Jews in the socialist movement, particularly in Russia. I had always noticed the large Jewish presence in the history of socialism, particularly in Central and Eastern Europe, but it was only after reading Hess that I saw a certain pattern: the radical Marxists, such as the Bolsheviks, tended to be less congenial to any kind of Jewish national or autonomist consciousness than were the more liberal, "revisionist" wings of the socialist movement. The history of the Bund's relationship to the Russian social democratic movement provides the classic instance of this pattern. In time, it was social democratic Menshevism that provided a better atmosphere for Jewish consciousness of any kind, and that included greater numbers of Jews in its ranks, than the more radical Bolshevism did. The Menshevik synthesis died on Russian soil, of course; but it has been revived in Israel.

I therefore believe that Israel is not merely a social democratic country, but one that has played and continues to play a special role in the history of social democracy, much as the Jewish social democrats of Europe did in the late nineteenth and early twentieth centuries. In Europe right down to the Nazi terror, and in Israel today, Jews have been among the foremost bearers of social democracy in the eyes of the world, the principal carriers both of its virtues and of its failings, and the attitude toward Jews and toward Israel has very often been a rather accurate barometer of the attitude toward social democracy. Hitler hated Jews at least as much as he hated all genuine socialism, and Stalin—and his successors—have been as zealous to stamp out all forms of Jewish cultural autonomy as they have been to suppress any manifestations on Russian soil of a more liberal approach to the socialist future than their own. It is therefore not surprising that the newest partisans of authoritarian radicalism, the New Left, have generally been hostile to Israel; they reject it as decisively as their elitism and their pipe-bombs reject the values of social democracy.

There is, in fact, a wholesale rejection of traditional values involved in the antagonism of the New Left toward social democracy in general and Israel in particular. Israel is in many ways the end product of a long history of European aspirations and conflicts which reached its climax in the conflagrations of the 1940s. Socialism and the Jewish question were both peculiarly European matters, very much involved in one another and in the agonies which brought about the Second World War. Then that war brought the European era of world history to an end, in effect, and out of the ashes of the old European civilization there arose a state which was both Jewish and socialist—a postfinal solution to both questions—and which planted itself on the soil of the Middle East. This is where the ironies begin. As the last European nation-state, created out of sufferings at the hands of the established powers more extreme than those experienced by any other European nationality, Israel now finds herself surrounded by hostile non-European neighbors who claim no responsibility for Jewish suffering in the recent past and who see the Jewish state as something that has been imposed upon their soil by the established powers of the West. In a stroke, the old victim has become someone whom many point to as the victimizer. Furthermore, Israel has come forth into an era when social democratic values have gone out of fashion. Born ideologically in an era when the values of productivity were as preeminent as the problems of production were, Israel had made *work* into an almost religious ideal. But the values of productivity have not been accorded much importance by spokesmen of the third-world ideology, for whom a principle of psychological authenticity that comes from being a member of an oppressed race has very often replaced the principle of creating wealth through work as a moral claim to emancipation. Ironically, the Jews of Europe had answered to this standard long before it became current, but at the time Zionism was founded they were still living within a system of values which had induced even Marx to claim rights for the proletariat on the basis of its productivity rather than its sufferings; and so the pioneers of Israel sought to validate all their claims by showing to themselves and to the world how hard and usefully they could work. Unfortunately, in the moment of their greatest success, much of the world around them ceased to admire that kind of performance.

The young people of the New Left are in many ways true offspring of the post-European era. They not only reject much of the old European civilization that they never have been a part of anyway, they also often revile it as a long history of the oppression of non-European peoples. They tend to see many of its most cherished values as merely the guises of tyranny. As children of the era of affluence, of the culture of postproductivity, they tend to see all the moral claims of wealth-creating work as self-centered bourgeois exploitation. The productive and economic successes of the kibbutzim, or of the Histadrut enterprises, are for young Jews of the New Left the same thing as the business successes of their fathers. This is why even the most socialist aspects of Israel seem to them —as they seem to their fathers much of the time—scarcely different from the most capitalist aspects of America. It is also why a regime headed by some self-centered sheikh who rides quickly in his air-conditioned Cadillac past the needy masses of his country can somehow seem to them less antithetical to their progressive principles than egalitarian Israel does. For them, Israel is Western, hence imperialist; it is productive, hence capitalist; it is social democratic, hence reactionary; and it is Jewish, hence racist. They are inclined to look upon it as a kind of Toynbeean fossil, not of Syriac civilization, but of a now equally extinct European civilization, which has been artificially grafted onto Middle Eastern soil—much as, in the eyes of their anti-Semitic predecessors of remote and recent times, the Jewish community once seemed to have been grafted artificially onto European soil.

Israel is thus a country whose identity gets to be tangled up in people's prejudices about it, whether for or against. This tends to be true of revolutionary societies in general. Foreign visitors to the Soviet Union or to the United States also seem quite unable to return from their trips merely describing what they saw, as they might after traveling to most other countries; they feel impelled to argue a case. But Israel may be the most argued-about country in the world at this moment. When I returned from my first trip to Israel I was convinced that it had provided the twentieth century with all kinds of definitive solutions—to the Jewish question, to the problems of socialism, to the alienated condition of modern man—and I argued and sermonized about all this both in conversation and in print. Then when I went back there for longer looks—living there for a year in 1963–64, then again for much of 1966—I became mildly disillusioned, and critical of conventionalized images I had set up the first time around. Yes, the kibbutz was still a great socialist enterprise and the most successful experiment in the creation of agricultural communes in the world, but it now also looked a little tired and stagnant, bypassed by the mainstream of Israeli social and economic development in the many years after it had ceased to be the spearhead of that development. Yes, Israel was still the most egalitarian country in the world, but some Israelis were now clearly a bit more equal than others, particularly if they were Russian Jews rather than German Jews, Ashkenazim rather than oriental Jews, or Jews rather than Arabs. Yes, Israeli sabras were far less alienated in Tel Aviv than their parents had been in the capitals of the world, but there now seemed to be a touch of restlessness—classically Jewish or universally modern—about them too. Yes, settling in Israel was a successful resolution to all kinds of Jewish problems, but not to mine or to that of a great many others. Israel still seemed to me one of the most vital facts in the world today—above all for Jews, but also significantly for socialists and for mankind in general—but it was no longer the Absolute Principle of my summer of 1961, to be argued vehemently for or against in terms that were virtually abstract. It was still quite unique and charged with moral considerations, but it was also more like a country, which is a good thing for any country to be.

I really believe that both Israel's proponents and its detractors in America and elsewhere should become better acquainted than they ever have—or than most of ﹍them are ever likely to be—with the ways in which thousands of ordinary people live in Israel. Socialists should also be concerned with this, for socialism is a humanism, after all, and the humanization that has taken place in Israel after its age of pioneers, gods, and heroes is an especially appealing sight from the socialist point of view. A story famous in Israel tells of how Chaim Nachman Bialik, the foremost poet of the modern Hebrew revival, heard the news one day of a robbery committed in Tel Aviv by a Jew, and said—this was many years ago—"Thank God, we are a nation at last." It remains true that a nation is not only a community that carries on great dialogues with History, but also one in which people rob, cheat, get drunk, goof off, look for a good time, make love, have children, get sick, get fed up, gripe about their work, and struggle merely to make a living most of the time; and, despite rhetorical images to the contrary, Israel answers to all these criteria.

I have often felt that American visitors to Israel— politicians, big contributors, Zionist youth, and Weathermen, all alike—should be required to include in their itinerary a bus trip to a village on the Mediterranean coast which I shall call Ramat Rivka. Ramat Rivka is a settlement village made up primarily of "new" immigrants who have arrived in Israel from the mid-fifties onwards, mainly from Romania and Morocco, and their children. It is a community of the sort of ordinary Israeli workers that few American tourists get to meet—for though many Americans visit kibbutzim, it should be understood that kibbutzniks, in their failures as in their achievements, really are a class apart, a laboring elite of a special kind that is quite different from a normal proletariat. The residents of Ramat Rivka work primarily for a living rather than for some high principle. Some of them hold minor clerical positions or own small businesses; a greater number work in service occupations or are manual laborers. Some have achieved a bit of prosperity in a solidly lower-middle-class kind of way; others are still quite poor. When I first entered Ramat Rivka in the winter of 1964 and found myself on a dirt street lined by two rows of somewhat battered one-story stucco houses, down which was coming a horse-drawn cart driven by an old Jewish worker with a huge beard and a creased, sun-cured face, I was sure that I had suddenly been afforded a vivid glimpse of what a nineteenth-century Russian-Jewish shtetl must have looked like, an image straight from the world of Sholom Aleichem. Then when I turned another corner and saw two women, creased but not old, their heads completely covered in kerchiefs, their bodies draped in long, flowing, colorful but dirty and ragged dresses, I thought I had made a mistake and that I had in fact entered an Arab village. But these were Jewish women from North Africa.

I knew a girl who lived in Ramat Rivka and worked as a nurse in a nearby hospital. She was the elder of two sisters born in Casablanca to a mother who was still only nineteen years old when her husband died and left her a widow with the children. The mother was from a middle-class family, but after the fashion of her society she had never been taught to read, and so she became quite dependent upon the kindnesses of her relatives after her husband's death. For a time she lived with her daughters in the home of her late husband's well-to-do brother, but his proprietary air became too much for them, and about 1955 the girls, then in their teens, were at their own urging sent to Israel under the auspices of Youth Aliyah. A few years later, once the girls had begun earning a living, their mother came to Israel to join them, and the three had settled down in a small apartment in a *shikkun*—a housing development—that stood at one end of Ramat Rivka. A year or so before I met the family, the younger daughter had gotten married. She lived with her husband, who had emigrated from Romania with his parents as a boy and who was now the proprietor of a small garage, and their infant son, in a one-story house a few minutes' walk from where her mother and elder sister lived. They usually saw one another every day.

The mother worked as a cleaning woman from time to time, but her chief source of support was her elder daughter Shulamit, who paid the rent and a good deal more out of the modest salary she received as a nurse. Shulamit was devoted to her nursing duties and worked quite hard, on a schedule of three ten-day stretches a month, each separated from the other by a two-day "weekend," and each one comprising a different eight-hour shift—8 A.M. to 4 P.M., then 4 P.M. to midnight, then midnight to 8 A.M. This schedule made it hard for Shulamit to keep up with the normal distribution of day, night, and weekend by which other people live, but it did not keep her from leading an active social life. She had innumerable relatives to visit in Ramat Rivka alone, for her mother was one of three sisters who had had several children each, and they all had settled in this village, where they lived and passed the time in one another's houses with an ease and an air of being perfectly at home that made it seem as though they had been in this place for generations.

I particularly remember the Saturday nights in Ramat Rivka when I strung along on some of these family visits. In general throughout Israel, sunset on Saturday afternoon has something of the quality of a starting gun being fired, when people who have held themselves in restraint all day in observance of the Sabbath suddenly take to the streets for a good time. This is when the cafés and movie houses open all over the country; and Ramat Rivka's single movie and single café were no exception. But few people there seemed to go to these; what they above all seemed to want to do was stroll about in the center of town, amidst swelling crowds that flowed into the gutters and made it impossible for the occasional motorcycle or automobile that came along to pass with any ease. Families with baby carriages ambled about, gazing at or exchanging greetings with other families, with or without baby carriages, heading either nowhere in particular or to the house of a relative, where the tables would be decked out with plates of sunflower seeds and of pastries, pots of tea and bottles of sweet cherry brandy, lying ready to nourish conversation or even a good deal of pleasant communal staring at the ceiling into the night.

This life was warm and intimate, pleasant but also provincial and in some ways austere. Shulamit was deeply attached to it, but there was also another life which drew her strongly, and to which she went as much as possible, in Tel Aviv, which was about an hour's bus ride away, and in Jerusalem, where she would stay overnight with friends. There she entered a world of theaters, shops, bookstores, cosmopolitan cafés, and friends who were studying or had studied at the university and were doing interesting things. In that world, Shulamit reverted a little to being Jeanette from Casablanca—for this had been her name before she took a Hebrew one for herself as a ward of Youth Aliyah

—winner of a French prize in elementary school, ardent reader of classic novels, and the proud owner of a collection of Livres de Poche which stood against one wall of the relatively bare little apartment that she shared with her mother. This Shulamit was even inclined to have "airs" as far as some of her neighbors were concerned, and she did indeed tend to hold her nose rather high whenever she made her way in some bright new dress bought in a Tel Aviv shop past the ragged women and barefoot children who always crowded around the front doorstep and in the hallways of the building in which she lived. Not that her attitude kept her from being a good neighbor when the occasion warranted it. I was at her house one evening when the infant daughter of a couple living upstairs was found dead in her sleep, smothered in her own pillow while no one had been home watching her. The husband, as was his wont from time to time, was off somewhere on a drinking bout and had not been seen for two or three days. His wife was illiterate and completely helpless in most situations, all the more so in this one. Shulamit simply took over, and did everything that had to be done with a vigor and a competence that astonished me. She never failed to help the more unfortunate people around her when she was called upon to do so; but she looked down her nose at them all the same.

When I knew Shulamit, I was in the fullest throes of my reaction to the discovery that Israel was not the utopia I had originally imagined it to be. In those years just before oriental and Ashkenazi Jews found themselves fighting side by side in June 1967 and discovered that they understood one another better than they had realized, it was common for critics of the Israeli establishment—both in and out of the country—to talk about the problem of "the two communities" of Israeli Jews. I had become an ardent critic on this issue, and I was proud of my friendship with members of the oriental community. But it was hardly something to be proud of, for it was not sincere; traditional sort of ideologue that I had gotten to be where Israel was concerned, it was based more upon a spirit of polemical one-upmanship than upon any genuine emotion. I kept trying to conceive of Shulamit as a pawn for my moral crusades. I used to try to persuade her that the problems and contradictions of her life were due to her being a victim of social injustice, although she usually found that my arguments had little to do with her own experience. I used to tell her that she should change her life, get a university education, settle in Tel Aviv and Jerusalem, and thereby prove that no limits could be imposed upon her; she would reply that she was too attached to her family to leave Ramat Rivka. Then, as images of a Jewish "third world" passed through my head, I would hold forth poetically about the people of her village, saying that they were the salt of the earth; she would say that some of them were nicer than others, but that they were on the whole rather ignorant and provincial. I would then try out my point that she, like all oriental Jews, was being unjustly held down by the Ashkenazi establishment; but she would reply that the Ashkenazim were still, on the whole, better educated than the oriental Jews, and that they therefore should be the ones running the country at the present time.

In other words, no matter what I said, she would not allow me to turn her life into the set of abstract arguments I was inclined to make of it. Without even being aware that she was doing so, she kept hinting in her responses at more things in heaven and in earth than were dreamed of in my ideology. It was a good lesson for me, not only about Israel but life in general. I should already have learned it by then; hadn't I worked in factories while still a student and discovered that the proletariat were far more complex in person than my social theories about them were? How much more true this was of a whole country! Countless Americans have gone to Europe and stood by in utter frustration as they listened to intellectuals there turn their country into a set of abstract arguments. In talking about America there, I have often found myself presenting "the other side of the story" even when discussing issues on which I am vehemently critical at home. For after all, even when we are most at odds with America, the fact remains that it is the locus of our lives and not a bloodless abstraction posed merely for the benefit of some Left Bank ideologue's spleen. We are as manifold and as contradictory as reality itself—and so is Israel, which has suffered more in recent years than even America from the abstractifying treatment it receives at the hand of ideologues. That is why I would, if I could, require anyone who is about to begin an argument about Israel, whether in praise or in condemnation, to take a trip to Ramat Rivka before he says another word.

Reflections of an Israeli Intellectual

T. R. Fyvel Talks to Amos Oz

AMOS OZ—member of Kibbutz Huldah, a leading younger Israeli novelist, author of *Somewhere Else* and *My Michael*.

FYVEL: Mr. Oz, I wish my knowledge of the latest trends in Israeli writing were less fragmentary, because as you know, translations are few.

OZ: Few, and often inadequate. For instance, they have not conveyed the crucial distinction in Israeli writing since the Six-Day War between war reportage and what we in Israel call victory literature telling us how marvelously we fought and defeated the Arabs, and on the other hand the more profound new works of prose and poetry which all appear strikingly pessimistic, more than before.

FYVEL: Pessimistic about the general human situation, which would today not be unusual, or about the specific Israeli situation?

OZ: About both—quite a few of our younger prose writers have used the situation in Israel with its strains between the communities and uncertainties about the future as a symbol of the general human situation of today.

FYVEL: How would these writings compare with European war literature?

OZ: Their sensibility is very similar. That is, you would not find much naturalistic war literature in contemporary Hebrew writing, but more of an allegorical use of the basic facts of war and fighting or the symbolical use of these elements—I think of the surprising sudden appearance of the crusader theme in several pieces of writing. One example is in a famous and controversial poem by Dalia Rabikowich called "Horns of Hittin"—the battlefield above Lake Tiberias where Saladin defeated the crusaders.

In her poem, she describes the crusaders as handsome, attractive, picturesque, brave, cruel, and very naïve. Her sympathies are divided. Aesthetically she admires the beauty of the crusaders with their golden helmets, beautiful horses, and fine habits; but morally, and that's the troubling thing in the poem, she identifies herself with the Muslims and justifies Saladin's victory on the grounds of the naïve cruelty in the crusader outlook.

FYVEL: Was this poem meant to raise direct questions about the rightness of the Israeli cause?

OZ: It was meant more to express an ambiguous experience, an ambiguous feeling, although it was, of course, immediately taken up as an ideological challenge. This is one problem for an Israeli writer.

FYVEL: You are on record as saying that compared to Jewish writers elsewhere, the young Israeli writers of today are handicapped by the lack of a usable past. Is this your strong view?

OZ: My strong feeling. To take my own case, my father was born in Odessa in Russia and my mother in Rovno, which was then Polish but is today also in Soviet Russia. Now, my parents often told me about the ideological difficulties of Jewish life in anti-Semitic surroundings— after all, we Jews invented the whole idea of "alienation" —and they sometimes talked nostalgically about the landscapes of their childhood. But they would never tell me what these places and their homes were really like; what everyday life felt like, what the street, the house, the dining-room table looked like. As a novelist, I'm worried by this complete lack of knowledge because I don't think we Israelis can write about ourselves, not with any depth, as if we'd simply emerged from the sea. This is why in the prose works of the new Israeli writers you find foreign-born older people appearing as secondary characters, as cardboard heroes or caricatures or as targets for protest, but you find little understanding of the outlook and motives of the elder generation.

FYVEL: Is this so unusual? Take Saul Bellow's novel *Herzog*, which I believe was widely read in Israel. The hero, Herzog, is a professor of philosophy in New York while his father was a little Jewish bootlegger up in Canada— a gap surely almost as wide as between young Israelis and their foreign-born parents.

OZ: There is a crucial difference. Moses Elkanah Herzog, as Bellow describes him, is completely cut off from the world of his father, and his own sufferings and alienation are completely different, and yet he knows all about the life of his father, the Canadian bootlegger. He knows and understands the miseries his father endured far better than a young Israeli writer could understand his antecedents because the young Israeli would have been brought up to forget—as in the famous dialogue, where a visitor asks an Israeli: "Why did you come here?" and the Israeli says, "I came here to forget." "To forget what?" "I forgot."

FYVEL: So what I think you are saying in effect is that Herzog can sympathize with his father, the unsuccessful bootlegger, because he sees in that wretched figure an intelligent Jew imprisoned by fate, while the young Israelis simply don't know enough about the fate their Jewish parents endured.

OZ: They were brought up not to know enough, and not to sympathize with what they did not know.

FYVEL: Well, I still think this generation gap is not as unique to Israel as you imagine, though admittedly it must have a special quality for the young Israelis who find themselves today in a state of siege, relied on to defend a country which was handed down to them like a legacy. Have they begun to question just how they were put into this position?

OZ: Recently, yes! Before the Six-Day War, Zionism was as natural for the young Israelis as air and water and the landscape. It was there. It was obvious. Since then, paradoxically because of the ease of the victory, we have also become aware of Zionist paradoxes.

The old Zionists wanted one secure shelter for Jews in this cruel world—I need not stress how insecure Israel is today. The Zionists also argued that we needed one piece of land as the homeland for scattered and persecuted Jews. Now it is argued that we need more Jews for the piece of land we hold, turning the argument upside down. It makes one question the whole inward-looking, romantic, nineteenth-century Zionist theories with which we are burdened.

FYVEL: Perhaps you yourself are too sweeping in dismissing a whole non-Israeli past. Alas, Zionism wasn't just a matter of theory. As you know, my father in Vienna in 1895, at the age of nineteen, became a lifelong Zionist as a result of the Dreyfus affair. He felt then that there was no future for Jews in a hostile central Europe.

I would say that in the half century from Dreyfus in 1895 to the climax at Auschwitz in 1945, nearly every event in European Jewish history seemed to prove the Zionist thesis—it was not the only truth but was one truth.

OZ: Certainly. I quite agree.

FYVEL: As I see it, this period ended with the Holocaust and the founding of the state of Israel; then came an interval of perhaps ten years and then a new era began in which Israel became less secure while Western Jews progressed in every direction. So as I—from my longer experience—would put it, there was a period when what you call nineteenth-century Zionist theories seemed to apply, and now a second period when they appear no longer applicable. Yet you feel you still have to cope with the old theories.

OZ: I can accept all of this because my whole adult life, and that of my generation, has fallen into this second period. Many of us, I speak of the intellectual minority, are questioning Zionist principles again and, I assume, trying to reinterpret Zionism to see what is gone and what remains meaningful. Really, this comes down to facing up to two great challenges. The first, as you said, is that the Jews in the West have advanced so much.

FYVEL: Well, one could almost say that the typical English-speaking Jew today is not the businessman but the Ph.D.

Oz: Quite so, and therefore some Israelis who go abroad to Western Europe or America must be a bit shocked. Many of us were brought up on the old stereotype image of Diaspora Jews as being small merchants and lost people in small towns in Eastern Europe, altogether a dying nation.

Now we are shocked to discover that the Jews in the West have become a leading intellectual minority and in their intellectual achievements are obviously superior to the Israelis. This is quite an experience for us, leading to further questioning of the accepted formulas we were brought up with.

Fyvel: Taking your personal case as example, does such self-questioning lead to new positive conclusions?

Oz: In a way, yes. We come to realize that survival, mere physical and national survival, heroic as it is in the case of Israel, is in itself also not enough; nor are we Israelis superior to other Jews simply because we have built up and successfully defended a country. We also realize that the very achievement of the state of Israel has made the old territorial Zionism anachronistic.

What remains valid? I believe that for Jews in Israel, just as for Jews abroad, the most relevant question is that of our identity. What is it all about? Why should it be preserved, and how? For the Jews in Israel it is easy to see how the questions of security and identity have become mixed up. But Soviet Jews have been made aware very brutally again that they have a Jewish identity. In the United States, such things as Negro anti-Semitism and Jewish masochism on the New Left have made Jewish identity again a question uneasily talked about. In this context, in reformulating this quest for a Jewish identity in the spirit of my own time, I am a Zionist.

But this brings me to the second challenge. I was brought up with the accepted formula that the confrontation I saw was between the Jewish *nation* and the Arab *population*. If this formula was ever true, nowadays it is far from reality. I accept the fact that within this small piece of land called Israel or Palestine, today there are *two national entities*—not just two populations, not two communities, but two national entities: the Palestine

Arabs like the Israelis are searching for their identity. Any approach to a solution must take this fact as its starting point.

FYVEL: As a young Israeli novelist, can you imagine how the world must look to your counterpart—to an intelligent young Palestinian Arab?

OZ: Very troubling indeed. I can largely understand his sense of injury and the psychological wound he bears over the loss of his country for reasons he finds hard to grasp. I am sure even an educated young Arab knows as good as nothing about Zionism as a reaction to European anti-Semitism. Even Hitler's killing of six million Jews is a remote and abstract event to him; or in any case it was a massacre committed by Europeans while the Arabs themselves were under European rule, and therefore a matter for Europeans to make good. Oh yes, I can define his viewpoint very well. What troubles me is that so few young Arabs can see my viewpoint; that of an Israeli grown up here in the country. I don't ask that they should sympathize with my viewpoint or even understand its background, but simply that they should know it!

FYVEL: At one time Zionism enjoyed much romantic international support, but today it seems strikingly the turn of the Palestine Arabs. As the kibbutz girl with a rifle was at one time a piece of British journalist folklore, so today it is the Fatah guerrilla in his camouflage suit. In particular, what do you think of the attitude of the New Left whose leaders, Cohn-Bendit, Tariq Ali, and all, say that Arabs are good, Arabs are right—and Israel is wrong and must be liquidated.

OZ: The whole thing seems to me such a gross and romantic oversimplification that it takes one back to the Middle Ages and the wars of religion!

General Dayan sits in an office while the Fatah leader Yassir Arafat lives in a cave; therefore Yassir Arafat is necessarily right and Dayan wrong. Dayan is a general and Arafat is not, therefore Dayan is wrong. Israel is supported by the United States, and as we all know the United States (and never the Soviet Union) represents evil on earth, and therefore Israel is wrong and the Arabs right.

The Arabs are alleged to be colored people whereas the Israelis, in the mythical picture the New Left has of them, are all European and white, therefore they are wrong and the Arabs right. This oversimplification is not politics —it is mythology.

FYVEL: All the same, do you think these attacks harm Israel's case?

OZ: Of course these Communist and New Left attacks— usually word for word the same—hurt us among public opinion abroad, but they also confuse the Arabs themselves. At one moment they talk in high-flown revolutionary terms about the need to liberate both Jews and Arabs from the yoke of Zionist colonialism and the next moment, when there is a fire in the Aqsa Mosque, they forget all these phrases and talk pure Muslim racialism. Our conflict just isn't that simple.

FYVEL: To turn from these outside factors, when you spoke of solving the conflict on the basis of recognizing that two national entities live in the area called Israel or Palestine, I take it you envisage the creation of an Arab and a Jewish state. Can I also take it that you see this as not just leaving the Arabs sitting in the hills, but that the area allotted to the Arab state must be generous, with access to the sea, as viable as possible?

OZ: The territorial partition would have to reflect, generally speaking, the present ethnographic reality.

FYVEL: All this also implies separating the conflict between Israelis and Palestinian Arabs from the secondary conflict between Israel and the Arab states; and of course one can argue convincingly that way that Egypt and Israel really have no major strategic interest dividing them. But in the present terrible deadlock, how do you see the steps to disentangle these conflicts?

OZ: As tremendously difficult. As I don't need to tell you, we also have our extreme elements who grow stronger the more bombs Fatah throws. On the Arab side, the relationship between a Palestinian state and Hashemite (Bedouin) Jordan is also complicated to work out. In the case of Egypt, well, I have served on the Suez front and know there are thousands of Russians on the other side planning war against me. I am sure the Russians see it as in their absolute interest to keep the conflict hot, which is why I don't believe in big-power talks—but do you want me to go into political detail?

FYVEL: No, you're a novelist not a politician, so let's skip such detail. Let's assume that by some marvelous compromises an Israeli and a Palestinian Arab state can be created. Now here we come to the crux. As long ago as 1936, the Peel Commission said almost what you say about two separate national entities living in one country, and so advocated partition. Now, in 1938, when I was your age, no, rather younger, I published a book called *No Ease in Zion*, written rather in the aftermath of the Peel partition proposals, where I said that however one partitioned Palestine, any Jewish state would have a sizable Arab minority. Therefore any Jewish state would, in population, be a mixed state, and I said that the Zionists must make the development of such a mixed state their official policy.

Was it feasible? Well, thirty years have passed and we have become far more skeptical about mixed societies. Do you think that after thirty years my arguments are still valid or that too much has changed?

OZ: The answer has two parts. As far as your arguments for equal civil, educational, and economic rights for Arab minorities—great or small as in the state of Israel—are concerned, I am completely with you. I think what you said thirty years ago is still completely relevant. But this is only half the story.

I don't think the most liberal mixing can take the place of a national solution of the Israeli-Arab conflict—I don't mean the solution of a binational state but of two national states for two national entities. Of course there can be no exact demographic division, but there is a gap like an abyss, I would say, between a Palestinian Arab minority in Israel who enjoy all civil rights, economic advantages, and cultural facilities and a minority who enjoy this while they have behind them the existence of an independent Palestinian state so that they can live and feel as Arabs!

After all, I do not agree with the concept of Uri-Avneri and his group of a completely non-Zionist Israel. I retain my links with Jews elsewhere, as I think the Palestinian Arabs should feel part of the Arab world. Merely stopping all Jewish immigration will not bring us a single Arab convert.

FYVEL: I think I see your theoretical picture of an Israeli or predominantly Israeli state and of a separate Palestinian Arab state, but do you think the latter is viable?

OZ: Technically, I imagine it would probably integrate in some way with Jordan, that is, with the Palestinians, rather than with the East Bank bedouin, assuming their natural leadership. But look, I do admit that in the late twentieth century, creating yet another separate little state, a Palestine Arab state, may be a nuisance or even economic nonsense, because such a state could never be economically really independent.

But then, half the 120 members of the United Nations are states which cannot be economically or logically justified. Yet they were created in order to satisfy a deep emotional longing for the attributes of independence. The Palestine Arabs likewise have this longing and it should be satisfied.

FYVEL: Let me get this straight—do you think that if such an Arab state existed, the position of say Arab students at the University of Jerusalem would be notably different?

OZ: If Arab students can join such a university not as members of a tolerated minority in Israel, nor even just as welcomed guests, but as foreign students who are coming to attend a university in a neighboring country, and who are expected to remain fully Arab in outlook, as in the case of visiting students anywhere, I think this would be quite a different situation for them. It would, of course, also change the university.

FYVEL: One more point—do you see any prospect of your ideas finding any echo on the Arab side?

OZ: It would be tempting to say that discussing the idea is at least worth trying, but I can say more than that. I believe an influential group of Palestine Arabs would tend toward a solution based on the recognition of two national entities. I have some evidence of this.

FYVEL: A last question—do you think there is any immediate prospect of progress toward such a solution?

OZ: One can, one should discuss the question, but I admit practical progress may still lie well in the future. And for the present . . . when I return with my family from Oxford to Israel I shall have to do my reserve army service. This might be an opportunity to think of the future while experiencing the present just as it is.

Israel: The Two Kinds of Jews

Nissim Rejwan

NISSIM REJWAN—born and educated in Baghdad, came to Israel in 1951, formerly editor of the Arab-language daily *Al-Yaum*, now Senior Research Fellow at the Shiloah Middle East Center, free lance journalist.

According to a recent survey conducted by the Israeli Ministry of Education and Culture, 18,000 Jewish youths between the ages of fourteen and seventeen are neither working nor studying. The survey, which relates to the year 1969, also reveals that this large army of idle young men and women constitute 9.3 percent of a total of 207,-000 youths belonging to that age-group. (Of the rest, 65.9 percent were studying, 18 percent were working, and 6.6 percent were working and studying.)

If we take into consideration the fact that no less than 70 percent of all Israeli Jews of the fourteen-to-seventeen age-group are today Afro-Asians (a term which in Israeli statistical jargon denotes either Jews born in the Middle East and North Africa or their direct descendants), and that for many years now an almost total identity has existed in Israeli society between "deprived" and "Afro-Asian," one conclusion becomes clear: practically all the 18,000 young idlers to whom the Education Ministry survey refers are children of families hailing from the countries of the Middle East and North Africa.

It is from the ranks of these marginal youths that most of the young delinquents hail—the youth gangs who wantonly rioted in the development town Sderot, wrecking shop windows and molesting passersby; the underprivileged young men and women from the slum areas of

125

Ramat Hasharon who make life unbearable for the inhabitants of the nearby Neve Sharett, a new and relatively luxurious quarter built for new immigrants hailing largely from Eastern Europe; the youths who daily invade Tel Aviv nightclubs and discotheques and refuse to pay their entrance fees. It is from these ranks, too, that the Israeli "Black Panthers" come—a relatively small and so far rather insignificant group which a year or so ago suddenly began to make the headlines of the Israeli press.

One way of tracing the wide and rather persistent socioeconomic gap separating the two main ethnic-cultural divisions of Israel's Jewish population—the Europeans and the Middle Easterners—is by considering the manner in which the mass immigration from the Orient was received back in the early years of the state. From the very beginning, it appears, the overwhelmingly East European leadership had strong forebodings about the prospect of flooding the country with "Levantines." In his autobiographical fragment *Level Sunlight* Maurice Samuel offers a glimpse of the fierce internal controversies surrounding Israel's decision to launch the operation known as *kibbutz galuyoth,* the ingathering of the exiles.

Though these debates never quite came to the surface, the gist of the argument of those who opposed the operation was that it was dangerous to bring to the country "those masses that issued from a medieval world and needed long preparation for the new environment." Large numbers of the immigrants, Samuel reports, "had no feeling whatsoever for the Jewish State, and knew nothing of the spirit that had built the country for them." But that was not all:

> Many had . . . acquired the deep-seated conviction that government, any government, was something sinister, something to be circumvented. For them a state was an evil thing, plotting evil against the individual. Or else, if they came from the East, they could not conceive of the existence of government officials who were not licensed thieves. . . .

Even the security argument was not enough. Samuel relates how, in the midst of the operation *kibbutz galu-*

yoth, Prime Minister Ben-Gurion "cried out that the country was in danger of Levantinization because the flood of primitive, panicky Oriental Jews was not matched by a comparable flow of volunteer Jews from the trained West." Considering, however, that Ben-Gurion was the architect and the first advocate of the operation, Samuel comments wryly: "But the Arabs were beaten precisely because they were Levantinized; and if there was no prospect of a compensating contribution from the West, the tide of Eastern immigration into Israel should have been controlled as far as it could be, and not whipped up artificially. . . ."[1]

From then on the story is fairly well known. The new mass immigration profoundly changed the face of the Jewish community. Producing a socially mixed population, this immigration suddenly created an enormous heterogeneity in a society that formerly had been rather selective and homogeneous. There were two other ways in which this change was expressed. Unlike the old settlers, the new immigrants were not grounded in an ideology; and, again unlike the old population, the majority of these newcomers hailed from Muslim countries, thus substantially strengthening the cultural element of the Middle Eastern Jews in Israel. The situation was further complicated by the fact that the Middle Easterners found themselves suddenly plunged into a different way of life, different techniques, new kinds of social and political relations, and a novel set of sociocultural values. The shock and the estrangement between this type of new immigrant and the European old settler were thus mutual.

The bearing of this state of affairs on subsequent developments on Israel's communal front was obvious. Sociologists have long remarked on the fact that we all acquire our sense of self from the response of others to us. A child who constantly encounters such remarks as "You are inferior, you are bad, you are incompetent" will internalize these attitudes and finally conform to them. In intergroup relations, similarly, there are powerful pressures that tend to make members of an outgroup into the type of person the ingroup's stereotyped image makes them out to be. If, for instance, on the ground that its members

---

[1] *Level Sunlight* (New York, 1953), pp. 64–68.

are "inferior," a group is given poor schools, poor jobs, few opportunities for self-respect and self-appreciation, and little chance of advancement, the dominant ingroup soon proves its belief to be correct: it has created the conditions for the confirmation and reinforcement of its own prejudice.

But there is another, "brighter" side to the same coin. For while a pattern of discrimination is a firm structure, with several mutually reinforcing supports, the vicious circle described here is not always unbreakable. In the case of the above child, for instance, a powerful counterimage supplied by a loving mother, a sympathetic teacher, a friend, or a successful person from his own group with whom he has identified can be very effective in restoring to the child his self-confidence and self-respect, and ultimately a wholly different "looking-glass image." In the case of a denigrated outgroup, too, the same sort of reverse process, though much slower, not only can take place, but can do so from ostensibly very modest, almost unnoticeable beginnings.

Despite their small number and relative insignificance, the Black Panthers' emergence on the Israeli scene can be considered a sign of the times and of things to come. For some time now, a handful of Israeli observers and students of the communal-ethnic problem have been warning against the authorities' prevalent view of the whole issue of immigrant integration—especially where Jews from the Middle East and North Africa are concerned.

What, precisely, are the premises on which the exclusively East European "power elite" of Israel based its policy of immigrant absorption? How did Israel go about the task of making those hundreds of thousands of Afro-Asian Jews who began to flood the country in the early years of the state part and parcel of the new emergent Israeli society?

The answer to this question is far from easy. The term *mizug galuyyot*, which translated literally means "mixing the exiles," has generally served as an expression of the Israeli ideal of immigrant absorption. Yet *mizug galuyyot* is a rather problematic term, overcharged with emotion, sociologically devoid of real content, and culturally somewhat arbitrary and ill conceived. In actual practice, moreover, it often seemed to denote little more than "remolding" the oriental immigrant, "bringing him up to our own level," and making of him something that he is not. The result has been *de*culturation, marginalization, and educational and cultural deprivation.

This, obviously, was not what was needed to bring ethnic harmony to a society that was a mosaic of cultures, ways of life, and attitudes. What, then, ought to have been the goal in the ethnic sphere? On the face of it, "integration" sounds a far more reasonable, humane, and attainable ideal than *mizug galuyyot*. However, it too presents certain difficulties. Ethnic integration can be defined as a situation in which the members of a society, regardless of their color, religion, or ethnic origin, move freely among one another, sharing the same opportunities and the same privileges and facilities on an equal basis. Thus defined, the term carries to some degree a connotation of assimilation: the loss of separating group identities, *with differentiation only on an individual basis.*

The main difficulty posed by integration, as defined above—which in itself may be taken to be a desirable and attainable ideal for Israeli society—is its seeming emphasis on *individual* absorption. Now the idea of individual absorption, or assimilation, is based on a theory that the sciences of man have long discarded—namely, the theory of "social individualism." This theory teaches, in brief, that society is made up of isolated individuals who depend mainly upon their own talents for the positions they achieve in society.

"Individual assimilation," which means the absorption into the prevailing sociocultural structure—individually and one by one—of certain "qualified" members of the outgroup, is thus tantamount to a rejection of outgroup cultures. It says in effect: "You can be one of us only if (1) you surrender your group affiliation and (2) you become like us."

This is the surest way to marginalize members of the outgroup; it has also been a tool for social inequality and discrimination, especially in the case of societies, such as Israel, where the rights, attainments, and privileges of an individual rest largely on the status achieved by the group to which he belongs rather than on his purely individual attributes.

Thus, although the ultimate goal of Israeli society has generally been considered to be integration, this goal could not be attained by the process of individual assimilation suggested by the ideal itself. Before we can behave as an "integrated society" we must first try to create the right framework in which such integration can take place. This may well prove to be a transition period toward full integration, but without it it would be impossible to reach that goal in a healthy, orderly, and humane manner.

This framework must be based on tolerance and mutual acceptance and appreciation between ingroups and outgroups, rather than narrow ethnocentrism and mutual suspicion and contempt. This is the way of what is variously called "cultural pluralism," "democratic pluralism," or just plain "pluralism." Now "pluralism" has been defined as a system of society in which membership in distinctive ethnic, religious, or cultural groups is accepted and even applauded. Pluralistic societies pride themselves on the freedom granted to diverse groups to preserve their different cultural heritages, speak different languages, and develop their own independent associations.

Pluralism, in this sense, means participation—and participation can be meaningful only in the sense of political and institutional power. In a multiethnic society like Israel the balance—or imbalance—of power among the ethnic interest groups holds the key to social integration—or lack of it—in that society. In other words, integration becomes meaningful only if a balance of communal power prevails. If imbalance prevails, if most or all of the power lies with one ethnic or communal group to the deprivation of other groups, then this spells absence of integration. The emergence of a Black Panther movement in Israel, no matter on how small a scale, is only one indication among many that the time-honored policy of *mizug galuyyot* has failed, and that a new and far more radical path must be followed if the country is really to attain even a small measure of communal-political power balance.

To sum up: A share in the decision-making processes of the larger society is the channel to effective participation and the attainment of a desirable position in that society. Acquisition of power enables a group to progress; progress, similarly, brings with it positions of, and access to, power—through education, high-level occupation, and wealth. Power and progress constitute two elements in a cycle that can affect minority groups beneficially; whereas powerlessness and lack of progress constitute the elements in a vicious cycle that can affect these groups adversely. Either cycle has important psychological, social, and political consequences, especially in a society that calls itself pluralistic and democratic.

Powerlessness and lack of progress—these, plainly, are the two elements of the vicious circle whose workings in the ethnic field in Israel have been so marked during the past twenty years or so, and one of whose net results has been the emergence of the Black Panthers. The question that now poses itself is: Can the circle be reversed? Can it be made to take on a beneficent character instead of its present adverse one? It is plain that such a development cannot be realized unless the disadvantaged communities can gain real power—power that would enable them to make the progress necessary for obtaining more power, more progress, and so on. However, with political power in Israel divided so neatly, and conveniently, between the existing parties—which also possess the necessary means to maintain it—the prospects of such a development look bleak indeed.

In Israel today there is a curious diversity of views on the country's communal problem. Three-and-a-half years of intermittent war and visible economic prosperity have had two undeniable effects on the situation—a very considerable increase in social solidarity between the various Jewish communities on the one hand, and a sharp turn for the better in the material conditions of the Middle East-ern–Sephardic element. In the realm of attitudes the result of these changes has been a fairly pervasive optimism concerning both the actual situation and the future prospects of communal integration. Although an accurate estimate of attitudes is beyond the scope of this article, I believe the situation in this sphere until recently could be summed up as follows:

1. On the official ingroup level there was, until very

recently, near unanimity that the communal problem had been solved once and for all. According to this estimate, the Middle Eastern element had both proved its mettle and attained its socioeconomic aspirations. As far as the cultural aspect is concerned, it was felt that the Middle Easterners, and especially the native-born among them, were not only willing but actually eager to embrace the emerging general culture, which is neither Western nor Eastern but a unique amalgam produced by the unique position that Israel holds in Jewry and the world community as a whole.

2. On the popular level both the Middle Easterners and the Europeans, especially of the second generation, seemed likewise satisfied that the process of integration was nearing a successful end. Culturally, native-born Israelis, children of Jewish immigrants both from Europe and from Middle Eastern and North African countries, share the same interests, like the same Mediterranean dishes, enjoy the same music, hum the same hippie songs, and share the same pride in their society's cultural and military superiority over its neighbors.

It hardly needs pointing out that, in themselves, these changes in attitudes could have very far-reaching effects on the communal situation. Reinforced by a corresponding change in the material standards of the Middle Easterners, however, they could signify the onset of a truly revolutionary change in the situation, a veritable breakthrough. However, there was another side to the coin—a different set of factors that were bound to militate against the prospects of such communal harmony. These factors resided largely in the socioeconcomic and educational spheres, rather than the strictly cultural, and may be summarized in four closely interrelated phenomena.

To start with, though the material standards of the Middle Easterners have risen considerably, those of the Europeans have gone up even more substantially, thus making the socioeconomic gap between the two communal divisions even wider.

Secondly, while economic prosperity and its results have been most visible in the cities and the larger towns with "mixed" populations, development towns, border immigrant settlements, and largely "communal" villages with overwhelmingly oriental populations have not benefited from the boom in any comparable manner. In these areas, generally inhabited by Jews of North African, Yemenite, or Kurdish origins, discontent and bitterness have tended to increase, especially among the young generation. Though the general material standard may have improved, the disproportionate rise in the general level of life in the cities and in neighboring veteran settlements and kibbutzim has tended to accentuate intercommunal differences.

The third factor relates to education. The educational gap —which needless to say parallels the communal division —is still extremely wide. As far as primary education is concerned, while all Israeli children are obliged to go through nine years of education, their educational level on leaving school is often disastrously uneven. The pattern here is all too familiar: the economically underprivileged Middle Eastern parent produces the culturally deprived child.

In secondary education, the situation is even more precarious for the average oriental pupil: having finished his primary schooling with a low standard of attainment he can hardly be expected to cope with more advanced lessons—and even this assumes that his family can carry the financial burden of sending him to a secondary school.

As to higher education, it would be sufficient to recall that while the Middle Eastern element now constitutes well over half of the population—and while children of oriental origin make up some 70 percent of the country's kindergarten population—the percentage of Middle Eastern and North African students at Israeli institutions of higher learning is less than fifteen. However, even these statistics are somewhat deceptive, since in any given academic year most of the oriental students are first-year students, of whom a considerable proportion eventually drop out either because of lack of attainment, failure to adapt themselves, or lack of means.

The fourth and last factor tending to work against communal integration and harmony is the virtual monopoly of positions of power and influence by the Europeans, and the consequent "European" aspect that the country and its institutions continue to present to the world at large. Apart from the erroneous image of Israel that it

tends to create outside—at a time when the state is accused of being an alien element in the region—this state
of affairs also tends to alienate the Middle Eastern element inside Israel, leads to its partial marginalization,
and increases its general dissatisfaction with the prevailing situation.

The problem of communal integration, which at certain
periods during the past two decades seemed to threaten
the very fabric of Israel's sociocultural life, now boils down
to a largely economic issue and considerations of political
representation and cultural "status." If the seventies are
to be different from the sixties—if intercommunal harmony is to prevail—the key now lies almost entirely with
Israel's economic policy planners and budget drawers. A
substantial rise in material standards among the Middle
Easterners in the coming few years, greater participation
in the country's political life both at home and abroad—
these can bring about a radical change in the communal
situation.

II

CONFLICT IN THE MIDDLE EAST

The Myth of Zionist "Original Sin": A Few Historical Notes

Joseph Neyer

JOSEPH NEYER—professor of Philosophy at Rutgers University, author of articles in professional journals on social and political philosophy.

In current discussion concerning rights and wrongs in the Middle East conflict, advocates of the Arab position usually go back to the events of the early part of this century, from which the basic premises of their argument are said to be derived. These events are clothed in the hazy image of an early "Zionist aggression" which is used to justify the Arabs since that time.

For instance, in discussions of the war of 1948, Arab propaganda frequently takes the position that the invasion of Palestine by five Arab states was in effect a rescue operation to save the areas of Palestine allocated by the United Nations Partition Resolution of 1947 to the projected Arab Palestine state from Zionist incursion.[1] Then the advocate of Israel's position may assemble the evidence to support the proposition that the Jews of Palestine had accepted the provisions of the Resolution of 1947 and that the hostilities of 1947–49 were initiated by the Arabs;[2]

---

[1] For instance, Fayez A. Sayegh, "A Palestinian View," *Time Bomb in the Middle East* (New York: Friendship Press, 1969).

[2] Maxime Rodinson, *Israel and the Arabs*, trans. Michael Peel (Harmondsworth: Penguin, 1968), p. 37; Christopher Sykes, *Crossroads to Israel* (Cleveland and New York: World, 1965), pp. 332 ff.

On April 16, 1948, Jamal Husseini, spokesman for the Arab Higher Committee of Palestine, told the UN Security Council, "The representatives of the Jewish Agency told us yesterday that

the Arab rejoinder here frequently is that, whatever may
be the details of what was a very confusing situation, the
Jews were the aggressors, since, if there had been no development of a Jewish community since 1917, there would
have been no war of 1948. A similar logic leads to the
doctrine that any attack by terrorists from across the borders upon Israeli agricultural settlements is "defense"; any
effort by Israel to reply to such an attack by destroying
the nest of the terrorists is "aggression." An understanding
of this semantical situation and its background sheds light
upon discussions in the United Nations that might otherwise appear bizarre.

The year 1917 is regarded in Arab propaganda as the
beginning of a fundamental wrong that must be righted
if human history is to unfold in a normal way, and if words
are again to have their ordinary meanings. It is the date to
which the Arabs appear to want to return and to start
history afresh. Thus the Covenant of the Palestine Liberation Organization, as amended in 1968, reads, "Jews who
were living permanently in Palestine before the beginning
of the Zionist invasion will be considered Palestinians."
Among the resolutions of the Palestine Council, the legis-
lative body of the PLO, one finds the affirmation "that the
aggression against the Arab nation began with the Zionist
invasion of Palestine in 1917."[3] It may be concluded,

---

they were not the attackers, that the Arabs had begun the fighting. We did not deny this. We told the whole world that we were
going to fight."

[3] Although the 1964 Palestine National Covenant was translated officially into English, the covenant as amended in 1968 has
received no official translation, so far as the writer is aware. The
1968 covenant is much more radical in the prospects its offers the
Jewish population. Whereas the earlier document could be interpreted as allowing Jews who were in the land as late as 1948 to
remain, the covenant of 1968 moves the date back to 1917. Several
English translations of the amended document have appeared. I
have used the translation in the *New York University Journal of
International Law and Politics*, 3, no. 1 (Spring 1970). The translation (by Y. Karmi) of each article of the covenant is followed
by commentary of Yohoshafat Harkabi. The quotation in the
present text which dates the "Zionist invasion" as 1917 is taken
from Harkabi's commentary on Article VI. The reference is to the
section on the resolutions of the Congress (1968) entitled "The
International Palestinian Struggle," p. 51.

then, that in the "democratic state" projected by Fatah, only Jews who lived in Palestine in 1917 and, presumably, their descendants will be found among those "Muslims, Christians, and Jews" who will participate as "free and equal" citizens.

Let us return, then, to 1917, the year of the Balfour Declaration, and the years that immediately preceded and followed, and consider the realities behind the moral judgment that is made today. Were the Jews wrong in working to establish their own communities in Palestine? What right had they to do so? In responding to the question, there is no intention of dealing with the niceties of international law or with the pretensions to precision of a certain type of moral methodology. Rather, the concern is to recall some of the facts of the situation which should be kept in mind, if the moral response of common sense is to be relevant.

It is necessary to recall, in the first place, that before the First World War the whole area that is now divided into the states of Saudi Arabia, Jordan, Syria, Iraq, Lebanon, and Israel—this vast underpopulated area of west Asia (as the Indians refer to it)—was governed by Turkey. The present divisions did not exist, nor did most of their present names. After the Romans suppressed the last Jewish rebellion in 135 A.D., Judaea was renamed Syria Palestina. However, in the 1,700 years before the First World War, Palestine was not to be found on a political or national (or ethnic) map of the world. Whether under Roman, Byzantine, Arab, or Turkish rule, its inhabitants, who had suffered many invasions, were never conscious of themselves as a national unit.[4] "We have to recognize," says historian James Parkes, "that the mass of the [Palestinian] population [before 1914] had no real feeling of belonging to any wider unit than their vil-

---

[4] See George Antonius, _The Arab Awakening_ (London: Hamish Hamilton, 1945), p. 15, n. 1, where the author informs us that the term "Syria" is used by him to include "the whole country of that name, which is now split up into the mandate territories of [French] Syria and the Lebanon, and [British] Palestine and Transjordan." This work, often referred to as the "classic of Arab nationalism," was first published in 1938.

lage, clan or possibly confederation of clans."[5] The language spoken was mainly Arabic, but the persons usually referred to as Arabs were the desert bedouin nomads and, occasionally, the effendi landed aristocracy, who might thus refer to their supposed descent from the noble families of the conquering tribes that came out of the Arabian peninsula in the seventh and eighth centuries.

The modern Zionist movement began during the Turkish administration, long before the Balfour Declaration of 1917. Jews, "lovers of Zion" they called themselves, began to trickle in during the 1880s. And during the years of this century before World War I came the second aliyah, Ben-Gurion's generation, who with their sons created the "foundations." These pioneers found a land that was arid, desolate, and forsaken—spoiled by years of misuse by men and goats. The warfare between tribes and villages right into the second half of the nineteenth century had surpassed the excesses of violence that had characterized early feudal Europe, and this warfare had had its effect of spoliation upon the land and its inhabitants. There were, of course, oases of cultivated and civilized life among the landowner effendis who lived in the towns.

The Muslim peasant stock the lovers of Zion found in the land were mainly composed of former Jews and Christians who had become Muslim during the period after the

---

[5] *A History of Palestine from 135* A.D. *to Modern Times* (New York: Oxford University Press, 1949), p. 248.

It is not argued here that the novelty of Palestinian nationalism is reason for denying its reality or its legitimacy. Nor should it be denied that its beginnings can be found early in the century. In fact, the Jews were among the first to recognize it. At the Conference of Lausanne, called by the Palestine Conciliation Commission in April 1949, representatives of Palestinian refugee groups appeared unexpectedly and asked for a hearing. The delegates of the Arab states refused to meet with them, but they established friendly contact with the delegation of Israel. See Walter Eytan, *The First Ten Years* (New York: Simon and Schuster, 1958), pp. 57–58.

Until late in the 1950s insofar as there was thought to be a "clash of nationalisms," this was regarded as involving Jewish and Arab nationalism—not "Palestinian." This is confirmed by examining the change in the language of Arab "information" materials in this country.

Arab conquest.[6] But Jews who were self-consciously Jews had always remained a part of the population. The Palestine Jews had always sustained relations with the Jews of the diaspora, who had been spiritually nourished by the Palestine centers of learning. The Jews of the diaspora had always maintained a stream of immigrants, albeit sometimes thin, to the Holy Land. They had always in their daily prayers expressed their yearning for the return. "Modern Zionism" was a continuation and intensification of a process that had been going on since the dispersion in 135 A.D., with an infusion of Western European humanist ideas on the possibility of man's re-creation of himself by himself.[7]

Now what was the character of the "Zionist invasion" that is supposed to have followed the Balfour Declaration? The image conjured up is that of hordes of East European Jews landing on the shores of Palestine armed with weapons requisite for driving out the native Arabs and creating lebensraum for themselves. Many serious young Arabs, as well as young Americans, now seem to believe something like this took place.

If there was an invasion it was of a bizarre kind, because its effect was an increase, not a decrease, in the Arab population. If we consider the land that was to become mandated Palestine west of the Jordan River,[8] the

[6] Parkes, op. cit., p. 24.

[7] There was also the difference that modern Zionism has always been shaped, in part, by the pressures of a rescue operation, a feature that began not in 1933 with the genocidal ambitions of Hitler but with the anti-Semitism and the pogroms of late nineteenth-century East Europe. Perhaps what was novel was not the pogroms but the technological revolution which made possible an immediate international awareness of and reaction to them. The intense international commitment toward the rescue of fellow Jews was always there—motivated by a moral tradition and by guilt at one's own escape. It is felt most keenly by those who have been nearest the peril.

[8] In 1922 Winston Churchill as colonial secretary succeeded in having the provisions regarding the Jewish homeland withheld from application to the mandated area east of the Jordan in order to create the emirate of Transjordan for Abdullah, grandfather of the present King Hussein. This area was more than two-thirds of the territory included in the League of Nations mandate. The Jews regarded this as the first of the "partitions" to which they assented in return for peace.

population consisted in 1919 of about 580,000 Arabs and 65,000 Jews. From 1919 to 1936, the period in which the basic social substance of the Jewish community was established through immigration, the Arab population increased to 968,000, thus exceeding in absolute numbers the increase of the Jewish population during the same period. The Arab increase was largely a response to opportunities created by the industry, agriculture, improvement of living conditions, and medicine established by the Jewish immigrants.[9] Not only did the rate of natural increase rise steadily, but, in the period between the Balfour Declaration and the United Nations Partition Resolution of 1947, Palestine became a land of Arab immigration.[10]

The Jewish socialist pioneers drained the swamplands and marshes, eliminated malaria, and irrigated the rocky soil that nobody had been able to live on for many years. The land was purchased from the Arabs at high prices with money collected mainly from the impoverished people of East Europe, who were looking for an escape from the ghettos and for an opportunity to recreate themselves through communal labor. Owing to carefully developed policies on the part of the mandatory government and the Jewish Agency, remarkably few Arab tenant farmers were displaced by land purchases, and substitute locations were usually found for these.[11] The number of Arabs displaced by land purchase was negligible compared to the number of Arabs who became landless as a consequence of foreclosure by Arab creditors. And the mufti of Jerusalem admitted in testimony before the Royal Commission that

---

[9] J. C. Hurwitz, *The Struggle for Palestine* (New York: W. W. Norton, 1950), pp. 28–29.

[10] Parkes, op. cit., pp. 320–21; *Palestine Royal Commission Report* (London: His Majesty's Stationery Office, 1937), chap. 10. For large Arab immigration during Second World War years, see UNRWA *Reviews*, Information Paper No. 6 (Beirut, September 1962). The early "lovers of Zion" began the stimulation of Arab immigration. Some writers have come out with the conclusion that in 1942, 75 percent of the Arab population were either immigrants or descendants of immigrants into Palestine during the preceding one hundred years, mainly after 1882. Ernst Frankenstein, *Justice for My People* (New York: Dial Press, 1944), p. 130.

[11] *Palestine Royal Commission Report*, pp. 240–41.

there had never been any forced sale of land by Arabs to Jews.[12]

The complaints about the "land problem" were made mainly in the towns for purposes of external consumption. When the fellahin (peasants) participated in violence against the Jews, it was usually because their religious fanaticism was played upon by such personages as the Mufti.[13] And the traditions of violence and the taking of booty were in, most Arab lands, old and honorable. Thus, when Arab nationalist violence developed, it combined the novelties of European ideas with a variety of impulses that were older and more "primitive"[14]—including, incidentally, the concern of the Arab religious authorities and squirearchy that their establishment not be disturbed by the example of more progressive and democratic designs for living.

Let us examine some of the international documents which purported to sanction the plans and projects of the Jews in Palestine. Most of the Jews of the world rejoiced over the Balfour Declaration in November 1917. It is easy to agree that this unilateral declaration[15] was an act of pretentious imperialism on the part of Great Britain, for what right had she to "view with favor the establish-

---

[12] Sykes, op. cit., p. 163.

[13] "It was often true that attacks on Jewish settlements were not made by Arab neighbors who might have been supposed to have seen before their eyes the effect of the supposed theft of their land. The attacks were from other villages, and from the mercenaries of the Mufti, and occasionally from Bedouins; and in many cases the Jews were warned and even protected by their Arab neighbors." Parkes, op. cit., pp. 321–22.

[14] Readers of T. E. Lawrence will recall that booty was the cement that held together the following of the Hashemite princes as they came up from the south to molest the Turks during World War I. There was nothing dishonorable in the pursuit of booty, which appear to be a constant trait of certain modes of quasi-nomadic life—modes destined to pass away with or without the presence of Israel.

[15] See Leonard Stein, *The Balfour Declaration* (New York: Simon and Schuster, 1961), pp. 587–601, for an account of the slow and grudging quasi-official "endorsements" that came from the other big powers. This reluctance came not so much from an opposition to Zionism as it did from an unwillingness to allow Britain to take the lead.

ment in Palestine of a National home for the Jewish people"? And what legal or moral consequence follows from such "favor"? The central committee of the Poale Zion (Workers of Zion) party, meeting early in December 1917, referred to the declaration as "one of the attempts of world imperialism to exploit liberation movements for its own ends."[16]

The ingredients that went into the making of the declaration were plural and complicated. The realpolitik of today's political science tends to rule out of consideration that the Protestant biblical background of the British statesmen of 1917 prepared them to understand the reality of the concept of the return, and it tends to forget that these men were romantics as well as realists. Such political science places its emphasis on British concern about the Suez Canal and keeping the French in bounds in the Middle East. What was probably crucial in the decision to take this step was the British exaggerated estimate of the power of world Jewry to help or hinder the World War I struggle, especially in America and Russia.[17]

This was exactly the kind of "imperialist" motive that guided Great Britain in the promises it made in 1915–16 to the Sherif Hussein of Mecca, great-grandfather of the present king of Jordan, through the correspondence between Hussein and Sir Henry MacMahon, high commissioner in Egypt. With Turkey in the war on the side of the Central Powers, Hussein was trading an Arab revolt against Turkey for British material support and promises of Arab liberation. Whether Palestine was within the territory explicitly excluded from the projected Arab state or states, according to the MacMahon correspondence, has been debated at length. The trouble is that the excluded territory was depicted in words without the aid of maps, and it must be appreciated that Palestine was only 1 percent of the land area to be liberated.[18]

The Balfour Declaration of 1917 was important to the Jewish people because it was the first official recognition

---

[16] Aharon Cohen, *Israel and the Arab World* (New York: Funk & Wagnalls, 1970), pp. 125–26.

[17] Stein, op. cit. p. 347.

[18] For two opposing views, see Antonius, op. cit., chaps. 7–9, and Stein, op. cit., pp. 249–51, 267–69.

of Zionist aims. A political agency with authority and power had at last said to the representatives of a community still in the dream stage, "We recognize you as someone to reckon with." But it is possible to argue that this unilateral statement had no moral meaning for the rest of the world.

The same limitation cannot be placed upon the import of the mandate of the League of Nations, which was confirmed on July 24, 1922, and which gave to the mandatory, Great Britain, the responsibility "for placing the country under such political, administrative and economic conditions as will secure the establishment of the Jewish National Home . . . and also for safeguarding the civil and religious rights of all the inhabitants of Palestine" (Article 2). It placed upon the administration of Palestine the commitment to facilitate Jewish immigration and to encourage "close settlement by Jews upon the land, including Statelands and wastelands not required for public purposes" (Article 6). The mandate had the authority of the only international agency in existence at the time which was prepared to make decisions concerning the vast land area that was formerly administered by Turkey, the "sick old man of Europe." That authority made the decision to devote 1 percent of the land area liberated to the development of a Jewish homeland.[19] On the basis of the promises of that decision, a part of the Jewish community invested their lives in the land. The only authoritative international voice of the time was telling the Jews to go ahead and see what they could make of this arid land. Two generations later, can this international judgment and promise be said to be morally irrelevant?

Of course one can always raise the question what that judgment was based on. Obviously, whatever imperialist designs may or may not have been operating in the minds of some members of the League, they were aware that they were contributing to the solution of a pressing humanitarian and national problem—the "Jewish problem." They felt they had good grounds for choosing this particu-

---

[19] The ratio of 1 to 100 gives an inadequate idea of the smallness of Palestine in relation to Arab land, since it does not take into account Egypt and the rest of North Africa, which in those days did not necessarily refer to themselves as "Arab."

lar piece of underpopulated geography, which, since 135
A.D., had always had its destinies shaped by forces from
outside the land. Further, as stated in the preamble to the
mandate, "recognition has . . . been given to the historical connection of the Jewish people with Palestine
and to the grounds for reconstituting their national home
in that country."

Now from the point of view of humanism and socialism, can the justification of a political movement involving a substantial immigration be derived, at least in part,
from so tenuous, so metaphysical, so theological a notion
as *historical connection* with the land to which immigration is proposed? The answer from the point of view of
present values is perhaps negative. But there is a somewhat different question for present-day humanism to consider. It is a fact that most people who thought about the
matter during the nineteenth century and up to the time
of the mandate—and this includes Jews, European non-
Jews, and Arabs—attributed a unique importance to the
historical connection of the Jews to the Holy Land; from
this fact, does it follow that we today can have a moral
respect for a commitment that was made partly on the
basis of that historical connection? The answer, I suggest,
is yes.

No "original sin" was committed in 1917, or 1922, that
could justify an uncompromising and genocidal Arab intransigence and refusal to seek reasonable and humanist
solutions in 1948 or 1967 or today. As Mr. Gromyko said
to the General Assembly of the United Nations at a time
when, in the face of the Arab hostilities of 1948, the
USSR stood firm for UN authority and for partition, "In
analyzing the various plans for the future of Palestine,
it is essential . . . to bear in mind the indisputable fact
that the population of Palestine consists of two peoples,
the Arabs and the Jews. Both have historical roots in
Palestine."

It may appear surprising, in view of more recent expressions of Arab views in the United Nations, to speak of
Arab understanding of Jewish aspirations at the end of
World War I. Those were optimistic times, when Britishers
like Sir Mark Sykes and T. E. Lawrence could work
simultaneously for independent Arab and Armenian states

and for Zionism, and could bring the representatives of each together to reinforce one another's aims. Lawrence was present at the first meeting of the Emir Faisal[20] and Chaim Weizmann, leader of the Zionist movement, at the Transjordanian desert encampment of Faisal's army, in June 1918. Weizmann gives a graphic account of the meeting in his memoirs: "Time was to prove . . . that the Emir was in earnest when he said he was eager to see the Jews and Arabs working in harmony during the peace conference which was to come."[21]

The agreement between the Emir Faisal and Weizmann, drawn up by Lawrence before the Peace Conference on January 3, 1919, contained a number of articles which offer a reply to those who hold that the Arabs at the time were in no position to understand what the Zionists had in mind. Article 2 speaks of boundaries "between the Arab State and Palestine." Article 3 endorses the Balfour Declaration. Article 4 refers to the encouragement of Jewish immigration "on a large scale." Article 5 speaks of the assistance that the Zionists will provide for the development of "the natural resources and economic possibilities" of the Arab state.[22]

Below his signature Faisal indicated a reservation, that he would not be bound by the agreement unless "the Arabs are established" in accordance with demands that were being addressed at the time to the British foreign secretary. That this reservation made the document not binding is true, but not altogether to the point. For the document is significant as expressing an important Arab point

---

[20] One of the sons of Sherif Hussein of Mecca and the first king of Iraq. As leader of the military revolt, he had attained a position which entitled him to speak for the Arabs, if anyone could. This is not to deny that there were Syrians who regarded themselves as more "civilized" than the southerners and who were fearful of the increased prestige of the Hashemite family. See George Antonius's account of the Committee of Seven who addressed the British government on this subject from the safety of Cairo (op. cit., pp. 270 ff.).

[21] Chaim Weizmann, *Trial and Error* (London: published by Harper & Brothers for East and West Library, 1949), p. 293.

[22] *The Israel-Arab Reader*—a documentary history of the Middle East conflict, edited with an introduction and comments by Walter Laqueur (New York: Bantam, 1969), a convenient source of such documents.

of view of that period. It is not here urged that it would have been difficult to find Arabs who opposed that point of view. On the other hand, the Faisal-Weizmann agreement is not an isolated manifestation of the spirit which it expressed, nor is it the first.

For instance, as far back as 1911, Zionists were holding meetings with Arab members of the Turkish Parliament in Constantinople; the political program they discussed was based on the understanding that when the Arabs achieved the political decentralization of the Arab provinces, the Jews would be given Palestine as one of the autonomous areas in return for assistance in the economic development of all the provinces.[23] Conversations along these lines were also going on between Arabs and Jews in Palestine during World War I.[24] A representative of the Zionist Organization attended the first all-Arab congress, in Paris in July 1913, as an observer; Arab speeches at the congress explicitly recognized the historic connection of the Jewish people with Palestine, and welcomed Jewish immigration.[25]

When the Syrians presented their case to the peace conference in Paris after World War I, they asked only for a federation with Palestine, despite the fact that they had regarded Palestine as southern Syria.

> We have suffered too much from sufferings resembling theirs [the Jews], not to throw open wide to them the doors of Palestine. All those among them who are oppressed in certain retrograde countries are welcome. Let them settle in Palestine, but in an autonomous Palestine, connected with Syria by the sole bond of federation. Will not a Palestine enjoying wide internal autonomy be for them a sufficient guarantee? If they form the majority then, they will be the rulers.[26]

---

[23] Cohen, op. cit., p. 85.
[24] Ibid., pp. 30–31.
[25] Ibid., pp. 96–97.
[26] David Hunter Miller, *My Diary at the Conference of Paris* (New York, 1924), meeting of the Supreme Council of February 13, 1919, 14:414. (Quoted in Frankenstein, op. cit., p. 93.) Miller was legal adviser to the U.S. mission in Paris. He collaborated with Sir Cecil Hurst in preparing the initial draft of the League of the Nations Covenant.

During World War I, Jews and Arabs in Palestine experienced great suffering, both from material deprivations and from oppression on the part of the Turks, who were trying to root out subversion on the home front; the two subject peoples came to each other's assistance and saved each other from starvation in different parts of the country. An Arab-Jewish gathering was held in Jerusalem in December 1915 to foster rapprochement; as the idea spread to other parts of the country, it was discouraged by the Turkish authorities. The Turkish commander in Jerusalem was dismissed for his part in fostering such activities[27]—intimations of coming events under the mandate, in which British imperialism was to play a similar role in discouraging cooperation between the two peoples.

If one studies the daily relations of Arabs and Jews under the mandate, the picture that emerges is not what is suggested by present-day images. For example, the diaries of Colonel Kisch, who occupied the position of chairman of the Palestine Executive from 1923 to 1931, reveal a continuity of efforts on the part of progressive Arabs and Jews to work out a productive life together.[28] These efforts were often frustrated by the encouragement the British administration gave the uncompromising and reactionary sector of Palestine Arab politics, headed and symbolized by Haj Amin el-Husseini. "There was in Palestine," says Christopher Sykes, "a small educated class which included men who had enjoyed high office under the Turkish Sultan, and this class, small as it was, was also much too big to allow of any possibility that Palestine could be politically transformed without danger of strife."[29] When the chips were down, this was the class with which British imperialism cast its lot.

The political gangsterism of Haj Amin,[30] who occupied the offices of mufti of Jerusalem and president of the Supreme Muslim Council, began in the twenties and reached

---

[27] Cohen, op. cit., pp. 116–17.

[28] F. H. Kisch, *Palestine Diary* (London: Victor Gollancz, 1938).

[29] Op. cit., p. 26.

[30] See Colonel Richard Meinertzhagen, *Middle East Diary 1917–1956* (New York: Thomas Yoseloff, 1959), especially pp. 55–56, for the role played by British officers in encouraging Arab vio-

its height during the "disturbances" of 1936–39, when the number of Arabs murdered by Arabs exceeded the number of Jews murdered by Arabs. Any challenge on the part of Arabs to the power of the mufti was likely to result in assassination or intimidation to the point of flight from the country. The victims included wealthy Arab "notables" as well as progressive elements, but in the majority of cases they represented sectors of the Arab population that were prepared to look for modes of accommodation with the Jewish population. The late thirties was the period of England's appeasement of the Axis. It is understandable that in Palestine this political style led to seeking out the bully in the situation—indeed, the one most likely to go over to the Axis if not adequately appeased —and attempting to come to terms with him.[31]

There is no intention of entering into the long and complicated story of the deterioration of the mandate administration. The point is that when the role of British imperialism is understood, the growing polarization between Arabs and Jews in the late thirties and forties is altogether compatible with the view supported above that what took place after 1917 was no rape of the land, no "Zionist invasion"; and it was not regarded as such by the Arabs at the time.

These days the image of the "Zionist invasion" is reinforced with other vilifying images of which the most fre-

---

lence. The *Diary* is a rich source of material bearing upon the role of the British administration in sabotaging the purposes of the mandate. Meinertzhagen served as chief political officer in Palestine and Syria from 1919 to 1920 and as military adviser to the Middle East Department of the Colonial Office from 1921 to 1924. He tells us that he had been an anti-Semite, and his experiences in the Middle East made him pro-Zionist. (The name is of Danish origin, not German Jewish.) Other writers show some disdain for the pro-Zionist bias in his writings. The fact is, he was unique. Should one rule out as information sources the books of other British officers who served in the Middle East, simply because they have Arab sympathies?

[31] The mufti's power became so great that even while in exile as a consequence of collaboration with the Nazis, political decisions of Palestine Arabs were referred to him. See Joseph B. Schechtman, *The Mufti and the Fuehrer* (New York: Thomas Yoseloff, 1955).

quently used is probably Israeli "expansionism," taken as a confirmation of the "original sin"—supposedly issuing from the same state of depravity. According to Arab mythology, the official Zionist program is graphically illustrated by a map in the entrance of the Israeli Parliament building; here, the future domain of Israel is purportedly shown to stretch from the Nile to the Euphrates. When Egyptian officers, prisoners taken in 1967, were invited to inspect the building and found no such map, they insisted that it had been temporarily concealed from view.

The simplest argument against this image of Israeli "expansionism" is the plain fact that for some years before June 1967, Israel sought some kind of dependable big-power guarantee of nonaggression in the Middle East. She could get no favorable response from the big powers, who always feared that a movement in this direction would offend the sensibilities of the Arabs. The demand of the Arabs has always been for the freedom to make another try at a Tel Aviv rendezvous—with the idea held in reserve of a rescue by the United Nations and the big powers from the unhappy consequences of such an attempt. In 1950, the United States, Britain, and France committed themselves to the Tripartite Declaration, in accordance with which they would prevent changes by force on Israel's borders. It did not take long, however, before Israel was given to understand that the declaration had withered away. And in the days before the hostilities of June 1967, the governments of France and England made this withering quite explicit, in case there was any misunderstanding.

As Communist leader Moshe Sneh said at the celebrated informal parley of distinguished Israelis and notable Palestinian Arab leaders in Jerusalem on August 28, 1968:

> The Israel government's offer to transform the demarcation lines [armistice lines of 1949] into permanent frontiers held good for 20 years right up to June 5 of last year, when the Six Day War broke out. And I can assure you that as late as the morning of June 6, if any Arab ruler had come forward and said "let's sign a peace treaty on the Rhodes demarcation lines", not a single Israeli Minister or politician would have refused. Every

Israeli I know, and that goes for the Herut leaders [extreme nationalists and right wing] too, would have jumped at the opportunity.[32]

Perhaps the most effective rebuttal to the charge of Israeli expansionism came soon after the 1967 hostilities from an Arab, Cecil Hourani, for ten years an intimate adviser to President Bourguiba of Tunisia. In his article "The Moment of Truth,"[33] Mr. Hourani makes the point that each time the Arabs tried to destroy Israel, enlargement of Israel's territory followed in the course of her self-defense.

> Another consequence of our unwillingness to accept as real what we do not like is that *when reality catches up with us, it is always too late.* At every debacle we regret that we did not accept a situation which no longer exists. In 1948 we regretted that we had not accepted the 1947 U.N. plea for partition. In May 1967 we were trying to go back to pre-Suez. Today we would be happy—and are actually demanding the U.N.—to go back to things as they were before 5 June. From every defeat we reap new regret and a new nostalgia, but never seem to learn a new lesson.

Mr. Hourani suggests that the Arab objective should have been the containment of Israel "rather than its conquest and destruction." This pattern of losing the advantages of the position one has by pushing for totalistic goals began at the close of the mandate period when, for instance, the Arab governments rejected the British White Paper of 1939, "which was in our favor."

The myth of Zionism's original sin and the image of an inevitably expansionist Israel are basic components of a systematic ideology (or mythology) which purports to exhibit the diabolical nature of Zionist Israel and thus justifies the intransigent enmity of the Arabs. What are the causes of this intransigence and irreconcilability? Without

---

[32] Reported in *Israel Magazine*, January 8, 1968.

[33] First published in Arabic as a supplement to the Lebanese *el Nahar*, probably the best daily paper in the Arab world. Translated into English in *Encounter*, November 1967.

pretending to give a complete answer, a few suggestions may be offered.

In the first place the modern migration of substantial numbers of Jews to Palestine occurred during a period when great changes were bound to come to the Middle East—with or without immigrants. Depending on one's outlook, these changes may be referred to as modernization, industrialization, Westernization, or democratization. One may bewail the loss of the ancient styles of life, but the Jews are hardly responsible for the changes in social structure that are disturbing all of Asia and Africa. Nor are they responsible for the fact that the Arabs have found it particularly difficult to decide how much of the older forms they must give up in order to have the supposed benefits of modernity. But there they are—the Jews —with their own unique synthesis of the old and the new, in forms of life that are sometimes unsettling and disturbing.

The inevitable social changes necessarily hurt certain social classes, which perceive themselves as threatened with social and material dislocation, or loss of power and privilege. In Palestine, the Jews arrived in time to serve as scapegoat for all the resentments associated with the pains of social development, not only in Palestine, but eventually in the entire Middle East. The good old days remembered dimly by the descendants of the old squirearchy—the absentee landlords who sold part of their land to the Jews and then contributed their tithe to the development of extremist Arab parties—those good old days are associated with a time before so many Jews came into the land. All that is required to recapture those days, it seems, is to roll back history, only a half century.

The conflict between Arabs and Jews is not the only conflict in the Middle East. Disunity, competition, and rivalry among Arabs exist not only among states, but among guerrilla groups, which have various ideological leanings and various patrons among the states. This intra-Arab competition and distrust not only make it difficult for them to conduct war, but to make peace, since any Arab movement toward peace can be exploited by rivals in the Arabs' competition for power. As for class conflict among Arabs in the Marxist sense, it has largely still to be developed, although it exists with intensity on an ideological level among the competing states and guerrilla groups. The relationship of Zionism and Israel to the intra-Arab opposition has shifted. During the mandate period and until the late fifties the important opposition to Zionism came from those who feared that its success would contribute to the global diffusion of socialism and communism;[34] but today Israel is said to be the obstacle to the success of the progressive forces in the Middle East. It is true that conservative regimes have succeeded in channeling the revolutionary energies of the Middle East into the traditional antagonism toward Israel. Large sums of money go from the oil kingdoms and sheikhdoms to the guerrilla groups, and thus these regimes avoid becoming themselves a target of the kind of terrorism from outside which they have experienced. But it is hardly the fault of Israel that most of the guerrilla groups (not all) have accepted this misalliance and have decided that the destruction of Israel must precede social revolution.

Arab irreconcilability to Israel is fostered by the professionalization of contemporary politics, especially the politics of revolution. For the revolutionary has chosen not only a type of "work," but, more important, a mode of life in which his associates, his life-style, his self-identity are determined—not to speak of his economic security. Whole careers and lives are built into al-Fatah. And it is not easy for an educated and idealistic young man in the Middle East to find a career that will bring him the sense of mission and self-fulfillment that he can find in a Fatah public-relations office at a time when the ancient forms of community are breaking down. The Palestine Liberation Organization has written into its covenant a provision for the continuation of responsibilities for its "fighters" after the battle is won (Article 30), thus assuring them a lasting vocation.

---

[34] Fayez A. Sayegh, *Communism in Israel*, Arab Information Center, Information Papers, no. 4 (New York, May 1958). Here Israel is pictured for cold-war-conscious Americans as the center of communist subversion in the Middle East. The shift to the image of Israel as the obstacle to progress is associated with changes in the strategy of external powers, and this essay purposefully avoids this area of consideration.

However, in considering the causes of Arab intransigence, it should not be overlooked that the Arabs have real grievances against Western imperialism, which, in view of Arab history and character structure, have contributed to the rise of a tradition of violence and irreconcilability. This aspect, as it affects Israel, is epitomized in the reservation which Faisal appended to his agreement of 1919 with Weizmann, in which he declared that his readiness to seek harmony with the Jews would be conditioned by the receptivity of the Western powers to Arab aspirations. Without going into the complicated details of the promises made, the expectations aroused, and the frustrations delivered, it is enough to recall that Iraq, Syria, and Lebanon required years of struggle to achieve their independence from France and England. Syria and Lebanon had to wait until the end of the Second World War. Of course, the Jews of Palestine were not responsible for European treatment of the Arabs, and in the end they had to fight their own war against British imperialism. But their immigration was associated with the projects of imperialism, and they provided a convenient scapegoat for frustrations outside Palestine.

Finally, in explaining Arab intransigence, it is necessary to refer to the kind of social-psychological considerations developed by Gil Carl AlRoy in a recent article.[35] Islam, he points out, is a religion associated with political domination and martial prowess. By the eighteenth century the deterioration of Islamic hegemony in the face of Western Christendom created a malaise among Arabs which was hardly assuaged by the paternalistic efforts of Western Christians to assist in the "Arab awakening" of the mid-nineteenth century. Further, the immigration into Palestine which began at the turn of the century had two bad features: it came out of the West, and it was composed of Jews who had mastered some of the powerful magic of the West. Now despite recent Arab efforts to por-

---

[35] "Patterns of Hostility," *Attitudes Toward Jewish Statehood in the Arab World* (New York: American Academic Association for Peace in the Middle East, 1971), pp. 42–60. With minor change of statement and emphasis, AlRoy's analysis is followed in this paragraph.

tray the history of Arab-Jewish relations prior to this century as idyllic and pacific, the fact is that the absence of bloodshed has been somewhat exaggerated; insofar as there was peace, it was based upon Arab domination and the Jew's knowing his place in the Islamic order of things. For so unmartial a character as the Jew now to win military victories over the Arab is an absurd nightmare, or a situation created by the temporary reign of the devil. Hence a mythology develops to "make the outrage of Jewish statehood temporarily bearable," and it is of such a nature as to strengthen Arab intransigence.

One does not make real peace with the devil. At most one makes "temporary arrangements," truces, or perhaps armistice agreements, the violation of which is hardly a cause for guilt. This does not mean that the state of irreconcilability must remain unchanged. It does mean that peace will not come as the consequence of flying junkets of members of the State Department. When it comes it will be more the consequence, for instance, of the "open bridges" policy initiated by that old "hawk" Moshe Dayan, who had the imagination to take the risks involved in large-scale visitations of Arabs from all over the Middle East, because he perceived that the increase of contacts between the peoples is the only conceivable beginning of peace. In 1970, 55,000 Arabs from outside Israel and occupied territory spent their vacations in the West Bank, and one doesn't go for a vacation to a land governed by a "Nazilike oppressor." In time, the discovery will be made that the Israeli, indeed the Zionists, are not the devil. And it will be perceived that the hopes of destroying Israel are doomed to fade.

Grounds for hope can be found in new Arab and Israeli generations who will know how to make contacts with each other. Fortunately for the Arab-Israeli impasse in our times, new generations now make their appearance about every five years. And there is taking place today what looks like the beginnings of fragile new forms of communication—outside establishment channels—between Arabs and Israelis, from which new and undreamed-of modes of thought and cooperation may emerge.

The Palestinian Refugees:
Resettlement, Repatriation, or Restoration?

Marie Syrkin

MARIE SYRKIN—Professor Emeritus of Humanities
at Brandeis University, editor of *Jewish Frontier*,
is the author of *Blessed Is the Match: The Story of
Jewish Resistance*, of *Golda Meir: A Biography*,
and other books.

The problem of the Arab refugees has long swelled beyond its original proportions. At first a relief problem resulting from an unsuccessful war, it has become since 1948
what the Arabs accurately describe as "the cornerstone of
the Arabs' struggle against Israel." Yet, though the plight
of the Arab refugees has aroused more global concern
than any of the immense refugee problems which have
plagued our unhappy time, objectively viewed it was the
one which admitted of the simplest solution and on whose
alleviation most United Nations funds have been expended.
Unlike millions of destitute refugees driven across con-
tinents—be it in Pakistan, Indochina, Biafra, or Eastern
Europe—the majority of the 600,000 Arabs who abandoned their villages in 1948 fled anywhere from four to
forty miles across the partition border to another part of
mandatory Palestine, where they have been maintained
by international funds for over two decades. Admittedly
the more than $500 million spent by UNWRA on the
bleak refugee camps has provided only minimal fare, lodging, and education, but the Arab states in pursuit of their
political objectives have refused all constructive proposals
for liquidating the camps prior to a general settlement of
the Arab-Israeli conflict. By this tactic they have created
a parody of the Jewish tragedy of the twentieth century.

157

In the Arab version, an Arab from Lydda or Haifa dwells in the "exile" of Hebron or Jericho, dreaming of his lost "Zion."

No matter how genuine nostalgia for a particular village may be, Israeli survivors of European death camps or oriental Jews expelled from North Africa or Iraq are bitterly offended by comparisons which they view as a deliberate travesty of Jewish fate. They will tell you that the loss of a hometown does not constitute national homelessness, that a way of life which requires no shift in landscape or ethnic environment does not comprise an alien diaspora, that the Palestinian Arabs, who enjoy one of the highest birthrates in the world, are not enduring genocide, and finally that dislocation is not deracination.

This impasse has been further complicated by the call of the Palestinian guerrillas for "restoration." The guerrillas in the refugee camps, who though sworn to the destruction of a member state of the United Nations are nevertheless maintained on UN relief rolls, punctuate their threats of annihilation with demands for repatriation— ironically based on Paragraph 11 of the 1948 UN resolution, which reads: "Refugees wishing to live at peace with their neighbors should be permitted to do so at the earliest practicable date."

The transformation of Arab refugees into Palestinian revanchists has obviously added a new dimension. As a movement of "national liberation" the Palestinians have captured the imagination of much of the left, who hail them as the Vietcong of the Middle East; their slogans and acts of terror arouse instant sympathy among the disciples of Fanon and devotees of the third world. Even those not automatically turned on by revolutionary jargon are troubled by the vision the commandos raise of a lost Palestinian homeland temporarily obscured by Zionist chicanery but now emerging into the light of day. The focus of the ideological debate has shifted. The Arab refugee, whose problems could presumably be solved by compensation, resettlement, or partial repatriation, has been replaced by a dispossessed Palestinian people whose aim is "liberation." The substitution of the burly Palestinian exile for the pathetic refugee has changed the terms of the argument and disposed of any solution except the elimination of Israel. Even the withdrawal of Israel to the 1967 borders would not lessen the force of the Palestinian's demand for his homeland. For while the Arab states reoccupied the territories they lost in 1967, the guerrillas would remain free to undo the evils of the partition resolution of 1947.

Though the immediate military impact of this scheme may be limited, the emergence of the commandos has undoubtedly born fruit on the propaganda front. A reappraisal of the Zionist idea appears to be taking place post facto. Judging from articles whose authors employ references to the history of the mandate, confidence in the moral validity of Israel's case has been shaken among people who formerly accepted the rise of Israel as the rectification of a historic wrong. Some are now disturbed not only by the endless warfare and its grim aftermath of human suffering but by the very existence of Israel. Despite all its wonders and achievements should it be there? In this context the wrongs of the Arab refugees of 1948 merge with the fresh problems generated by the Six-Day War of 1967, particularly that of Palestinian nationalism.

The origin of the problem cannot, therefore, be ignored. In 1948 did the Arabs flee, though free to remain, or were they ruthlessly driven out? Since the Arab case against Israel begins with the charge of expulsion, this question is still relevant.

I arrived in the six-week-old state of Israel in June 1948, when the Arab exodus was in full swing. One of my tasks was to draw up a report on the subject for the newly formed Israeli Bureau of Information. There were no documents and no studies. All that was available in those days was the fresh reactions of Jews and Arabs—as yet undoctored by policy. From my interviews with Arabs in villages which had accepted the authority of the state of Israel instead of fleeing to the enemy, and from my discussions with clergy of various denominations who had helplessly watched the departure of their flocks, the chief impression I got was one of astonished dismay on all sides. The Arabs agreed that the villagers who had fled could have stayed as they themselves had stayed, but the refugees had "listened to the mufti"; and the Christian clergy described scenes of ungovernable fear which no reassurance had been able to stem. One sturdy mother superior told me, "I said to them, 'Don't be afraid; I'll protect you,' but they ran." The Jews to whom I spoke were still bewildered by the spectacle of tens of thousands of Arabs leaving their homes and possessions and rushing in panic toward the sea or the mountains. The deserted Arab villages, the abandoned Arab quarters of Jaffa and Haifa, presented the same baffling picture. I heard many conflicting explanations: the Arab leaders had ordered the exodus; the British had instigated it; the Mufti's "atrocity propaganda" had backfired; the Irgun massacre at Deir Yassin had terrified the Arabs.

The two schools of thought—that the exodus was a deliberate part of Arab military strategy, and that it was an uncontrollable stampede which the Arab leadership strove unsuccessfully to check—were not contradictory. Apparently, what began as a calculated move degenerated into irrational frenzy. The development of the exodus as well as Arab statements indicate that the flight was at first stimulated by the Arab leadership to inflame the populace (since the Palestinian Arabs had shown little stomach for battle); to create an artificial Arab "refugee" problem which would elicit world sympathy to counterbalance the claims of Jewish refugees; and to prepare the ground for invasion by the Arab states who could then appear as the saviors of their brethren. An additional reason was no doubt the desire to evacuate Arab civilians from territory which the Arab states expected to bomb. But the smooth functioning of this scheme was impaired by the very completeness of its success. A planned evacuation turned into a hysterical stampede.

Wealthy Arabs began to leave Palestine shortly after the passage of the UN partition resolution and the outbreak of disturbances in December 1947, expecting to return after the Jews had been liquidated by the Arab states. As early as January 30, 1948, a Palestinian Arab newspaper (*As Shaab*) took occasion to chastise the first wave of refugees:

> The first group of our fifth column consists of those who abandoned their houses and business premises to go to live elsewhere. Many of these lived in great comfort and

luxury. At the first sign of trouble they took to their heels in order to escape sharing the burden of the struggle, whether directly or indirectly.

The departure of individual wealthy Arabs could, however, hardly be described as flight. The condition in which these Arabs left their homes, without bothering to remove even readily transportable valuables, indicated that they had complete confidence in the rapid success of the Arab invasion and were merely absenting themselves temporarily. They left neither in haste nor in fear; they merely locked the front door and drove off for what was to be a vacation at some distance from the local unpleasantness. And their departure was observed with understandable alarm by less moneyed Arabs unable to make similar traveling arrangements.

The first signs of a large-scale exodus were noted in March 1948 (though several hundred Arab children had been evacuated previously from Haifa to Syria as a routine safety measure). In the last week of March and the first week of April, thousands of Arabs started to trek from the Sharon coastal plain to the Arab-controlled hill regions. Many sold their poultry and flocks to Jewish friends before leaving.

This first wave of departure was viewed with a mixture of fear and regret by their Jewish neighbors, who wondered what evil it might portend. The obvious explanation seemed to be the imminence of a full-scale Arab attack with heavy aerial bombardment. Where Arab and Jewish farmers had been on friendly terms, there was a genuine desire to maintain relationships which boded well for the future. But the Arabs would not stay. Later it was learned that the Arab Higher Committee had ordered the evacuation of the coastal plain after the picking of the citrus crop. So calm and well organized was this phase of the exodus that the cooperation of Jewish settlement guards was enlisted to provide transportation through Jewish areas for women, children, and the aged. The evacuation of the Sharon is notable because it disposes of the Arab charge that the flight started as a result of the massacre at Deir Yassin by Jewish terrorists. The massacre (April 9) took place after the evacuation of the Sharon.

Another instance of evacuation by Arab command occurred in Tiberias. Since March there had been sporadic clashes in this sleepy, idyllic little town on the shores of the Lake of Galilee. Once Arab gangs infiltrated the Arab quarter and transformed it into a base against the Jewish residents, serious fighting broke out. On April 18, when the battle turned in favor of the small Jewish community of two thousand, the six thousand Arabs, obviously in obedience to a directive, suddenly began leaving in long convoys. The British, instead of aiding in the pacification of the town, provided transport.

The Jews of Tiberias were so startled by the unexpected departure of the Arabs that the Jewish Community Council of Tiberias issued a statement declaring: "We did not dispossess them; they themselves chose this course. But the day will come when the Arabs will return to their homes and property in this town. In the meantime, let no citizen touch their property." The months of savage warfare ahead were to change these kindly sentiments, but they are important historically as evidence of the original Jewish reaction to the Arab exodus.

Perhaps the clearest indication of why the Arabs fled is afforded by the events in Haifa. On April 22, after the breakdown of Arab resistance in Haifa, truce terms were offered by the Haganah which specifically guaranteed the right of Arabs to continue living in Haifa as equal citizens under the then-existing binational municipal council. The British let it be known that they considered the terms "reasonable." At first the Arabs agreed, but they changed their minds later in the day, explaining that they could not accept the terms for reasons beyond their control. Nor were the "reasons" far to seek. The Arab radio was broadcasting directives from the Arab Higher Executive ordering all Arabs to leave Haifa.

The reports of the British Chief of Police in Haifa, A. J. Bridmead, suggest how earnestly the Jews tried to persuade the Arabs to stay. On April 26, Bridmead wrote: "The situation in Haifa remains unchanged. Every effort is being made by the Jews to persuade the Arab populace to stay and carry on their normal lives, to get their shops and businesses open, to be assured that their lives and interests will be safe." In a supplementary report issued the same day, Bridmead repeated: "An appeal has been made to the Arabs by the Jews to reopen their shops and businesses in order to relieve the difficulties of feeding the Arab population. Evacuation was still going on yesterday and several trips were made by Z craft to Acre. Roads, too, were crowded. Arab leaders reiterated their determination to evacuate the entire Arab population, and they have been given the loan of 10 three-ton military trucks as from this morning to assist the evacuation." And on April 28, Superintendent Bridmead was still writing: "The Jews are still making every effort to persuade the Arab population to remain and settle back into their normal lives in the town."

But no assurances could stop the flight. Very quickly, the proposed strategic evacuation turned into a panic, as the 70,000 Haifa Arabs began to rush toward the port, seeking to "escape" by any craft available. Families crouched for days on the docks, refusing to move until some vessel took them to Acre. Unlike the quiet departure of the Arab gentry months earlier, this was a stampede in which people seem to have jumped suddenly from a dinner table, from bed, or from their work, driven by an impulse to flee.

An article in the London *Economist* (October 2, 1948) quoted a British eyewitness account:

During the subsequent days the Israeli authorities who were now in complete control of Haifa . . . urged all Arabs to remain in Haifa, and guaranteed them protection and security. So far as I know, most of the British civilian residents whose advice was asked by Arab friends told the latter they would be wise to stay. Various factors influenced their decision to seek safety in flight. There is but little doubt that far the most potent of these factors was the announcements made over the air by the Arab Higher Executive urging all Arabs in Haifa to quit. The reason given was that upon the final withdrawal of the British, combined armies of the Arab States would invade Palestine and drive the Jews into the sea, and it was clearly intimated that those Arabs who remained in Haifa and accepted Israeli protection would be regarded as renegades. At that time the Palestinian Arabs still had some confidence in the ability of the Arab League to implement the promises of its spokesmen.

The example of Haifa was found to have a profoundly disquieting effect on the whole Arab population of Palestine, and indeed the subsequent flight from Jaffa can be viewed as a natural corollary of the exodus organized by the Arab leadership in Haifa. As mass hysteria developed, many Arab villages were abandoned even before these were threatened by the progress of the war. After May 15, the process was accelerated. There are repeated instances of thousands of Arabs fleeing before a handful of Jewish troops.

In Safed, for instance, some 14,000 Arabs picked themselves up one night and fled from the 1,500 Orthodox Jews who lived in the winding, cobbled streets of the ancient town. One must see Safed to appreciate what this means, for the Arabs not only outnumbered the Jews but had every strategic advantage, occupying all the strongholds of the town, as well as dominant positions on the surrounding hills. The Jews were caught in a kind of narrow trough.

I came to Safed on a late Friday afternoon. Amid the debris of recent battle, the Jews of the town were dressing up for the sabbath. In the twilight, walking along the streets, one could already hear the chanting of prayers. Old men in round, furred hats and long cloaks were going to the synagogue. Women with lace shawls over their sheitels (wigs) sat in the doorways of their shelled homes. Up above, in the main street, soldiers were strolling along with their girls; Jewish refugees, just a week from the British detention camp of Cyprus, were seeking lodging in the abandoned houses; but below, in the old Jewish quarter, nothing had changed. "It is all in God's hands," the Orthodox Jews of Safed had declared in refusing to evacuate the town despite the urging of the British.

The Hotel Merkazit, where I stayed during my visit, had been completely riddled with bullets. Most of the windows were broken and many of the walls damaged. The place had obviously received a thorough shelling. But the aging, bearded innkeeper and his wife had stayed, despite their apparently hopeless position, exposed to heavy Arab fire on three sides.

Whatever the reason, the Arabs fled from Safed, as they had from Haifa, in the wake of their leaders.

It should be added that while it was not Haganah policy to encourage the exodus, some hostile villages threatening the road to Jerusalem were evacuated by individual Haganah commanders. The relief of Jerusalem, besieged by the Arab Legion (which had cut off the city's water supply), constituted one of the major struggles of the war. Consequently, a number of villages which served as bases for the enemy camped in the surrounding hills were forcibly cleared, and their inhabitants joined the exodus. But these were isolated instances, occurring late in the fighting, and involving numbers too small to affect the scope of the mass flight or to explain it.

To compound the confusion surrounding the flights from different towns and villages, the various Arab factions were not agreed about the tactics pursued by the Arab Higher Committee. In Baghdad, on July 25, 1948, a radio commentator criticized refugees who complained of the treatment they were receiving in the Arab states and who wished they had stayed in Palestine with the Jews. Such people should be shot as spies, he said, and he added: "The Jews will make you their slaves if you return to them; they will feed you only on bread and water; they will force you to sleep in the open, five on one blanket; they will take your wives and daughters from you. Prefer death to the Jews."

But dissident voices could also be heard from the outset; and as the strategy turned to a calamitous defeat and the manufactured refugee problem became a genuine one, the chorus of dissatisfaction grew louder. As early as March 30, 1948, a Palestinian Arab paper (*As Sarih*) wrote:

> The inhabitants of the large village of Sheikh Munis and of several other Arab villages in the neighborhood of Tel Aviv have brought a terrible disgrace on us all by quitting their villages bag and baggage. We cannot help comparing this disgraceful exodus with the firm stand of the Haganah in all localities situated in Arab territory or bordering on it. But what is the use of making comparisons; everyone knows that the Haganah gladly enters the battle while we always flee from it.

King Farouk of Egypt, in a broadcast to the Arab world on July 9, 1948, also expressed his dissatisfaction with "the Palestinian Arabs who ran away leaving their houses and lands behind, giving a chance for a large Jewish immigration and putting Palestine in danger of a Jewish majority."

In Damacus, too, the Arabic radio (August 3, 1948) had occasion to find fault with the refugees: "The Arabs of Palestine are responsible for the heavy losses of the armies in Palestine and the present unfavorable situation. They ran away in the face of a threat by a small minority and spent more time talking over their own affairs than fighting for their country."

But perhaps the most telling comment was made by the Near East Arabic radio broadcast on May 15, 1949, a year after the establishment of the Jewish state:

> If the Arab leaders had not spread the most horrible and frightening stories of Deir Yassin, the inhabitants of the Arab areas of Palestine would never have fled their homes and would not today be living in misery. The Arab leaders and the Arab press and radio announced on May 15 that the Jews were scared to death and would soon be thrown into the sea by the advancing armies; but it wasn't long before opinions had to be changed as the Jews scored nothing but victories and the Arabs suffered nothing but defeats.

A curter summation was offered five years later by the Jordan daily *Al-Difaá*: "The Arab governments told us, 'Get out so that we can get in.' So we got out, but they did not get in" (September 6, 1954).

Despite the evidence, the temptation to rewrite history is not confined to Arab propagandists. I. F. Stone, reexamining the Zionist case shortly after the 1967 war in the *New York Review of Books* (August 3, 1967), disposed of the argument that the refugees ran away voluntarily as a "myth." This might be accepted as a routine "progressive" view, except that in 1948 Stone had published an enthusiastic account of the young Jewish state, *This Is Israel*, in which he described the flight of the Arabs:

Ill-armed, outnumbered, however desperate their circumstances, the Jews stood fast. The Arabs very early began to run away. First the wealthiest families went; it was estimated that 20,000 of them left the country in the first two months of internal hostilities. By the end of January, the exodus was already so alarming that the Palestine Arab Higher Committee in alarm asked neighboring Arab countries to refuse visas to these refugees and to seal the borders against them. While the Arab guerrillas were moving in, the Arab civilian population was moving out.

Mr. Stone goes on to describe the "phenomenon" of the "sudden flight" of Arabs from Tiberias and Haifa. Not one word in Mr. Stone's firsthand, on-the-spot report suggests the use of force. On the contrary, every word supports what he twenty years later would dismiss as "myth."

That the Arab refugee chose to cast his lot with the Arab invaders of Israel is a matter of record. The aggression in which he joined in defiance of the partition resolution of the United Nations created new circumstances, and by no rational, legal, or moral standard could the fledgling state, unexpectedly victorious, be asked to welcome its enemies. There are, after all, some historical comparisons that are worth making.

Such champions of the Arabs as Soviet Russia and Communist China have been somewhat less than cordial to those of their citizens who sided with opponents, and the émigrés from those countries are less than eager to return, knowing the reception that would await them. It is even more instructive to recall the attitude of the American revolutionaries toward the Tories who fled the thirteen colonies and made cause with the British. The founding fathers, notably Benjamin Franklin, objected not only to their return but to the granting of compensation for their confiscated estates. So long as the young republic was in danger, Franklin, who conducted negotiations with the British in regard to the Tory refugees, refused to countenance their return. In 1789, he wrote of a group of loyalists who had settled in what was then British territory: "They have left us to live under the government of their

king in England and Nova Scotia. We do not miss them
nor wish their return." Though the loyalists were of the
same stock as the revolutionists and there was no scarcity
of land for them to return to, the Americans were not
disposed to trust their good faith: "I believe the opposition given by many to their re-establishing among us is
owing to a firm persuasion that there could be no reliance
on their oaths" (Benjamin Franklin, in a letter dated June
26, 1785).

I will not deny that after the War of Independence in
1948 I heard few expressions of regret from Israelis for
the departed Arabs. The months of bitter fighting in which
600,000 Jews repelled the onslaught of five Arab states had
changed earlier attitudes. Now the flight of the Arabs was
viewed by many Israelis as another in the series of "miracles" which had made possible the emergence of Israel,
for the tiny state had been obliged to offer refuge not only
to the survivors of Hitler's death camps but to oriental
Jews fleeing from persecution in Muslim lands. A kind of
unofficial population transfer took place. Somewhere between 500,000 and 600,000 Palestinian Arabs left; approximately the same number of destitute oriental Jews
came in from Arab countries in the Middle East and North
Africa.

The exact number of bona fide refugees has since become a matter of contention, with the numbers varying
according to who does the counting. In answer to the
present Arab claim of 2,000,000 refugees, Israel cites the
figures supplied in December 1946 by the government of
Palestine (the British) to UNSCOP. According to these
figures, the *total* number of Arabs in unpartitioned Palestine was 1,288,000; of these 500,000 resided in mandated
territory later annexed by Jordan; 100,000 lived in the
Gaza Strip, later annexed by Egypt; and 140,000 Arabs
remained in what became Israel. The total number of Arab
refugees, then, could not have exceeded 550,000. That in
May 1967 the total number of refugees on the UNRWA
relief rolls amounted to 1,344,576 can be explained by a
combination of factors: a high birthrate; a low death rate
(achieved by good sanitary conditions, along with a policy
of not reporting deaths so as not to lose ration cards);
the padding of relief rolls; and the registration of local

Arabs eager to enjoy a better diet than that available to the indigent in the Middle East.

UNRWA officials admit their relief rolls to be grossly inflated, and that the number of individuals receiving ration cards does not correspond to the number of bona fide refugees. At the close of 1948, for instance, Dr. Ralph Bunche, then acting UN mediator, estimated the number of refugees to be 500,000. But the UNRWA relief rolls for 1948 numbered 960,000. This disparity has been maintained to the present. The Arab host countries have consistently opposed the checking of the relief rolls for false or duplicate registrations; consequently, the accretion to the rolls of many thousands of Arabs who may have been authentic refugees from poverty in Jordan, Lebanon, or Syria, but not refugees from Palestine, has gone unchallenged.

The lot of the Arab refugee is miserable. Even though physical conditions in the camps maintained by UNRWA may compare favorably with the standard of living of the local population, no one will pretend that camp existence is normal. However, the refusal of the Arab countries since 1948 to permit the liquidation of the Arab refugee problem has been motivated by frankly political considerations. Arabs make no secret of the fact that "the refugees are the armament of the Arabs and Arab nationalism" (Egyptian government radio, Cairo, July 19, 1957). A resolution adopted at a conference of refugees in Syria in July 1957 makes Arab past and current policy crystal clear: "Any discussion aimed at a solution of the Palestine problem which will not be based on ensuring the refugees' right to annihilate Israel will be regarded as a desecration of the Arab people and an act of treason."

Those who share the Arab conviction that Israel should be destroyed have reason to applaud such declarations. It is hard, however, to understand those who accept the existence of the Jewish state yet urge the "repatriation" of what to all intents has become a hostile army.

Were the same criteria applied to the Palestinian Arabs as to other victims of postwar dislocation, resettlement would have been viewed as a satisfactory solution. Neutral students of the refugee problem have reached the same conclusion:

I hold the view that, political issues aside, the Arab refugee problem is by far the easiest postwar refugee problem to solve by integration. By faith, by language, by race and by social organization, they are indistinguishable from their fellows of their host countries. There is room for them, in Syria and Iraq. There is a developing demand for the kind of manpower they represent. More unusually still, there is the money to make this integration possible. The United Nations General Assembly, five years ago, voted a sum of 200 million dollars to provide, and here I quote the phrase, "homes and jobs" for the Arab refugees. That money remains unspent, not because these tragic people are strangers in a strange land, because they are not, not because there is no room for them to be established, because there is, but simply for political reasons which, I re-emphasize it is not my business to discuss.[1]

Only on the assumption that Israel must be obliterated did the Arab tactic acquire cogency. Otherwise, the resettlement of Palestinian Arabs among their kith and kin with full international assistance and Israeli compensation for abandoned properties would have seemed both reasonable and fair.

The 1967 war inevitably further complicated the refugee question. Some 300,000 Arabs, over one-third of them UNRWA camp dwellers, fled in the wake of the fighting, many before the arrival of the victorious Israeli troops. Though as in 1948 Arabs raised the charge of "mass expulsion," investigations by United Nations officials and foreign journalists proved the accusation groundless. The million Arabs who remained peaceably in their homes on the West Bank provided the best refutation. Those who crossed over to the East Bank did so for a variety of reasons. Some, remembering Hussein's premature injunctions to his people on the treatment of a conquered enemy ("Kill the Jews wherever you find them—kill them with your hands, with your nails and teeth"), expected no better from Israeli soldiers. Others feared that they would lose remittances from relatives working in Saudi Arabia

---

[1] From the report of Dr. Elfan Rees, Commission of the Churches on International Affairs and World Council of Churches' Adviser on Refugees (Geneva, 1957).

and other oil-rich states along the Persian Gulf if they remained under Israeli occupation. Still others preferred to live in an Arab state rather than under Israeli military government, no matter how benign. An interesting sidelight is provided by the fact that one-third of those given permission by the Israeli authorities to return to the West Bank failed to do so. Some 7,000 unused permits for Arab families remain. A further consideration may have been the assumption that Israeli authorities would finally conduct a census of bona fide refugees in the UNRWA camps. An Israeli census of the West Bank and Gaza in September 1967 disclosed a total of 443,000, though the UNRWA rolls counted 628,000.

The question at issue, however, is not the accuracy of the numbers but the nature of the ultimate solution, for whatever the figures the terms of the equation have been altered. To the humanitarian problem of the refugees has been added the more fundamental one of Palestinian nationalism emerging in the "exile" of the camps and developed in Beirut, Damascus, and Cairo.

The suffering of the Arabs who abandoned their homes and villages in 1948, and in lesser measure in 1967, is incontestable. But whether they were the victims of Israel or of the failure of Arab design to liquidate Israel, whether they fled or were driven, whether the Israelis were savage or generous victors, is no longer of the essence of the debate. A refugee problem, given the will, can be settled in the Middle East as elsewhere in the world; an irredenta with all the profound passions it arouses is another matter. Hence the continuing debate on the rights and wrongs of the Arab-Israeli conflict, particularly insofar as it presumes to question the continued existence of the Jewish state, must frankly face the new problem posed by the Palestinians.

Are we witnessing the synthetic creation of a Palestinian identity as a weapon in the anti-Israel arsenal? In the total evaluation of Arab and Jewish rights this question looms large. The Palestinian nationalist is a recent factor in the Arab-Jewish conflict, and one treated respectfully by Israeli commentators, many of whom argue that the origin of Palestinian nationalism is irrelevant to the issue. Supposing it did spring belatedly out of the head of Arab na-

tionalism merely as a hostile response to Israel? The lad
is alive and kicking and calling him bastard will not remove
him. But by the same token Israel is also there; if its ouster
is demanded on the grounds of illegitimacy, then the
counterclaims must be examined. Can the newcomer be
fed only at the expense of the Jewish state or is there room
elsewhere in the family domain for his natural development?

The question of origins is not merely academic. The al-
Fatah terrorist who attacks an El Al plane in Zurich justifies his act on the grounds that the first Zionist congress
took place in Switzerland in 1897, so ushering in the
"horror" of Zionism to the world scene. Commentators of
all shades of the political spectrum seek to determine
future policy according to their view of what actually
took place in the last fifty years or more. Obviously, if the
British sponsorship of the Zionist endeavor was a bad
business to begin with, at best an error of judgment as
Dean Acheson discreetly indicates in his memoirs, or at
worst a gross injustice as Toynbee would have it, then the
possible accommodations of the present must be made
with such history in mind. Any view of what should now
be done to achieve a peaceful settlement between Arab
and Jew is bound to be practically affected by a determination of the extent of the injury. A dispossessed Palestinian people, able to flourish only within the area of the
Jewish state, would require concessions from Israel sharply
different from those that might be made for the same number of dislocated refugees. That is why a discussion of
Palestinian nationalism is not a futile exercise. There is
little hope of devising a satisfactory territorial solution if
the existence of Israel is really predicated on the ruthless
dispossession of a people from its homeland—something
radically different from the dislocation or resettlement of
individuals as an aftermath of war.

The first point to be made is that the characterization
of Palestinian nationalism as "artificial" does not come
from Zionist adversaries but from classic Arab sources.
In the period before and after the issuance of the Balfour
Declaration Arab nationalists consistently protested the
use of the name "Palestine" or the adjective "Palestinian"
to demark them from other Arabs in the region. All the

declarations of the nascent Arab nationalist movement from 1880 on concentrated on "the unity of Syria" with no references to Palestine as other than "south Syria." Nothing could be more explicit than the statement of the General Syrian Congress in 1919: "We ask that there should be no separation of the southern part of Syria, known as Palestine, nor of the littoral western zone which includes Lebanon, from the Syrian country. We desire that the unity of the country should be guaranteed against partition under whatever circumstances." The Arab congress meeting in Jerusalem in 1919 formulated an Arab covenant whose first clause read: "The Arab lands are a complete and indivisible whole, and the divisions of whatever nature to which they have been subjected are not approved nor recognized by the Arab nation."

The extremist mufti of Jerusalem originally opposed the Palestine mandate on the grounds that it separated Palestine from Syria; he emphasized that there was no difference between Palestinian and Syrian Arabs in national characteristics or group life. As late as May 1947, Arab representatives reminded the United Nations in a formal statement that "Palestine was . . . part of the Province of Syria . . . Politically, the Arabs of Palestine were not independent in the sense of forming a separate political entity."

Before the creation of the Jewish state the whole thrust of Arab nationalism was directed against what its proponents viewed as the dismemberment of an ideal unitary Arab state. Even the setting up of several independent Arab states was viewed as a subtle thwarting of Arab nationalism. Nor was there a change after the establishment of Israel.

With an eye to the future, the Arab Ba'ath party, which describes itself as a "national, popular revolutionary movement fighting for Arab Unity, Freedom and Socialism," declared in its constitution (1951): "The Arabs form one nation. This nation has the natural right to live in a single state and to be free to direct its own destiny," and equated the battle against colonialism with the "struggle to gather all the Arabs in a single, independent Arab state." No mention of Palestine, except as usurped Syrian territory, tainted any of these formulations. Even Ahmed

Shukairy had no hesitation, as head of the Palestine Liberation Organization, in announcing to the Security Council that "it is common knowledge that Palestine is nothing but southern Syria" (May 31, 1956).

From the foregoing it is obvious that for Arabs "Palestine" was merely an inaccurate name for a sector of the Middle East and that this separate designation was the result of imperialist plotting against Arab independence. In contrast to its role in Jewish history and tradition, in Arab eyes Palestine was neither the cradle of a nation nor a holy land. Arab national passion was engaged by the concept of a greater Syria or an even larger united Arab state, not by this tiny segment which had become detached through the force majeure of foreign colonialism. In the lexicon of Arab nationalism the independent existence of a Palestine state, like the existence of an independent Lebanon, represented a violation of the Arab national will.

Historians have repeatedly pointed out that Palestine as a political unit ceased after the Roman conquest of the Jewish commonwealth, and that it was restored centuries later as a distinct political entity by the British mandate for the specific purpose of establishing a Jewish national home. Admittedly this fact of ancient history would have little relevance to the present if up to the Balfour Declaration there had developed an Arab diaspora, which like the Jewish diaspora, had an emotional fixation on Palestine. Nothing of the kind took place. Even when the desert Arabs revolted against Turkish rule during World War I, the Arabs in Palestine were so little concerned with independence that they continued to fight alongside the Turks till liberated by the Allies.

The concept of Palestine as a separate national entity arose among Arabs as a reaction to Zionism after the Balfour Declaration. It is worth noting in this connection that those Arab spokesmen who originally welcomed the setting up of a Jewish homeland in a small portion of the territories freed from Ottoman rule made no pretense that they viewed the abstraction of Palestine from the total area assigned to the Arabs as other than the loss of a given number of square kilometers. Emir Feisal signed his celebrated agreement with Dr. Weizmann (January 1919) in behalf of the "Arab Kingdom of Hedjaz," and in his letter to Felix Frankfurter, then a member of the Zionist delegation to the peace conference, the emir wrote a few months later (March 1, 1959): "We are working together for a revived Near East, and our two movements complete one another. The Jewish movement is national and not imperialist. Our movement is national and not imperialist, and there is room in Syria for us both."

The Arab guerrillas who justify their demand for bases in Lebanon as in Jordan and Syria with the argument that the Arabs are one nation and therefore have the right to use each other's territories interchangeably, operate completely within the tradition of orthodox Arab nationalism. Some sophisticated Arab spokesmen have become aware of the pitfalls presented by Arab avowals that they are all one people with no difference between Jordanian, Palestinian, and Syrian. The editor of the Amman weekly, *Amman al Masa* warned that such reasoning might make the notion of the resettlement of Arab refugees "respectable," since its advocates could justly claim that the refugees were merely being moved to another part of their Arab fatherland, whatever its name. Such considerations, however, do not trouble the guerrillas who move freely across the borders of the Arab states as citizens of the Arab nation.

The youth born in Lebanon or Jordan who is taught on the one hand that the Arabs are one people whose land was cut up by the imperialists, and on the other that his family was thrust out of a Palestinian Eden whose allurements increase with each decade of Israeli achievement, is not likely to be worried by logical niceties. Whatever the contradictions, current Arab strategy is not likely to renounce a successful technique. Nevertheless, in the face of the evidence no proponent of Arab nationalism would deny that the Palestinian variant is a very recent mutation.

Equally to the purpose is the fact that the absence of a distinct Palestinian nationalism provided a rationale for the Balfour Declaration. In their various negotiations with the Arabs in regard to the territory liberated from the Turks, the British were faced with demands for a greater Syria, a kingdom of Hedjaz, an Arab state, never for an independent Arab Palestine. The Arabs who opposed the Balfour Declaration and the mandate objected to a foreign intruder in their midst and to the diminution in any measure of their vast holdings. All this is human and understandable. Just as understandable on another level is the not ignoble calculation which allotted 1 percent of the huge area freed by the Allies for the establishment of a Jewish national home. Lord Balfour expressed the hope that the Arabs would recall that the great powers had liberated them from the "tyranny of a bestial conqueror" and had given them independent states. He trusted that "remembering all that, they will not grudge that small notch—for it is no more geographically, whatever it may be historically—that small notch in what are now Arab territories being given to the people who for all these hundreds of years have been separated from it."

It is necessary to repeat this statement because contemporary anti-Israel polemics—from the high-minded exhortations of Noam Chomsky to primitive rantings—maintain the fiction that the British and the Jews proceeded with a total disregard of an Arab presence in Palestine. The many pages devoted to analyzing the Sykes-Picot agreement, the McMahon letter, and the recommendations of the King-Crane Commission—all premandate documents—indicate that however proponents varied in the solutions they offered, every aspect of the Arab case was considered; it did not go by default as rewriters of history like to pretend. The King-Crane Commission, appointed by President Wilson to study the question of the Palestine mandate, brought in an outspokenly hostile report; it urged the abandonment of a Jewish national home and proposed instead that Palestine be included "in a united Syria state" for which the United States should hold the mandate. The very nature of the anti-Zionist opposition—American, British, and Arab—its indifference to Palestine except as part of an Arab whole, made the reasoning of pro-Zionists like Lord Balfour plausible. Their psychology may have been faulty; the Arabs did and do "grudge" the "little notch," but nothing could be more irresponsible than to foster the myth that Arab national feelings were ignored by the promulgators of the Balfour Declaration.

The same holds true for the Zionists. Those who lived to graduate from utopian visions to the hard bargaining tables of diplomacy were foolhardy innocents only in the extent of their hopes for Jewish-Arab cooperation in the Middle East. They were thoroughly aware that Palestine, though denuded and sparsely inhabited, had a native population. They came prepared with agricultural studies and demographic charts demonstrating that soil reclamation in Palestine would make room for more Arabs as well as Jews and would provide a better life for both. They were certain that the Arabs would prosper materially as the result of Jewish settlement, nor did they disregard the more delicate matter of Arab national feelings. Weizmann, a more reliable authority on this subject than romantic predecessors like Herzl, declared unequivocally that the Zionists assumed that the "*national* sentiments of the Palestinian Arabs would center, in Baghdad, Mecca and Damascus, and find their natural and complete satisfaction in the Arab kingdoms which resulted from the Peace Treaty settlement in the Near East."

The Zionists proved poor prophets—with one vital exception. Paradoxically, their coming did make more habitable room in Palestine. I refer of course to the period of Jewish settlement till the establishment of Israel—the period in which the Jews strove unsuccessfully to live in peace with their Arab fellow citizens. If peaceful Jewish colonization beginning at the turn of the century had resulted in the dispossession of the local population this would have been a more serious indictment of Zionist policy than the subsequent flight of refugees in later wars. No such dispossession took place. Since the current indictments of Israel include not only the urgent troubles of the present, but the "historic wrong" done the Arabs through their dispossession by Jewish settlers, this must be clearly established. Instead of diminishing, the Arab population increased spectacularly in the three decades after the Balfour Declaration. It grew from 565,000 in 1922 to 1,200,000 in 1947—an increase of 100 percent and striking evidence of the stimulus provided by the agricultural and industrial development of the country. During the same period Egypt showed an increase of 25 percent, while Transjordan, lopped off from Palestine in 1922 and also under a British mandate but closed to Jewish immigration, remained static.

Not only the local Arabs prospered because of the better sanitary and economic conditions created by Jewish labor. After the Balfour Declaration Palestine changed from a country of Arab emigration to one of Arab immigration. Arabs from the Hauran in Syria as well as other neighboring lands poured into Palestine to profit from the higher standard of living and fresh opportunities provided by the Zionist pioneers.

Up to World War I the picture of Palestine is one of a wasteland inhabited by impoverished, disease-ridden peasants in debt to absentee landlords in Beirut, Damascus, Cairo, or Kuwait. The transformation of the country comes when the sand dunes and marshes purchased by the Jewish National Fund from absentee landowners at fancy prices are reclaimed at an even greater expenditure of Jewish lives and labor. The Valley of Esdraelon, today one of the most fertile regions of Israel and the location of flourishing kibbutzim, was described by the high commissioner of Palestine for 1920–25 in the following words: "When I first saw it in 1920, it was a desolation. Four or five small, squalid villages, long distances apart from one another, could be seen on the summits of the low hills here and there. For the rest the country was uninhabitable. There was not a house or tree."

Not to exculpate the Jews but to defend British policy, the not overfriendly British secretary of state for the colonies Malcolm Macdonald, declared in the House of Commons (November 24, 1938): "The Arabs cannot say that the Jews are driving them out of the country. If not a single Jew had come to Palestine after 1918, I believe the Arab population of Palestine would still have been around 600,000 at which it had been stable under Turkish rule . . . It is not only the Jews who have benefitted from the Balfour Declaration. They can deny it as much as they like, but materially the Arabs have benefitted very greatly from the Balfour Declaration."

In the light of the grim present, a recital of former benefits rings hollow if not downright offensive. But this much emerges from the record. In 1948, the Jewish state, created through partition and in one-sixth of the territory originally envisaged by the Balfour Declaration, emerged without dispossessing a single Arab. Prestate Zionist settlement had brought Arabs into the country instead of driving them out, uninhabited land had been made habitable, and the abstraction from Arab sovereignty of the territory on which the Jewish state arose represented no 'blow to the goals of Arab nationalism as till then expressed. Had the account between Arabs and Jews been closed in 1948 with the acceptance by the Arabs of the compromise represented by the partition resolution, it would have been difficult to place the Arabs in the loser's column. The Jews had their tiny, much amputated state. The original area envisaged by the Balfour Declaration in 1917 had been approximately three percent of the former Turkish provinces but by the time of the mandate in 1922, the Promised Land had been whittled down to less than 0.8 percent through the truncation of the territory east of the Jordan for the purpose of establishing Transjordan. The Jewish state that emerged after the partition resolution shrunk further to one-half of 1 percent. In other words while six independent Arab states had emerged to enjoy sovereignty over 1,250,000 square miles, the Jewish state was ready to dwell in peace with its neighbors within its 8,000 square miles. But this balance could not be struck.

Now there were to be dispossessed Arabs who would continue to multiply but without flourishing, while the Jewish state would expend on war and defense the energy and tenacity that had formerly been expended on the desert. From this point on, the drama unfolds with the fatality of a self-fulfilling prophecy. As has already been indicated, all kinds of reasons have been offered for the wild flight of the Arabs from Israel in 1948: they were driven, they were terrified, they acted in obedience to the orders of the Arab High Command, etc. Whichever of these explanations is believed or dismissed, none makes adequate allowance for the swiftness and readiness with which the flight took place. People picked themselves up as though they were going from the Bronx to Brooklyn, not as though they were abandoning a homeland. Part of the speed was due to irrational panic, part to the assurance of return after victory, but it was undoubtedly abetted

by the subconscious or conscious feeling that flight to a
village on the West Bank or across the Jordan was no
exile. The Arab who moved a few miles was in the land
he had always known, though not in the same house. He
arrived as no stranger and any differences between himself and his neighbors were due to local antagonisms, not
national alienation. The West Bank which had been Palestine till its seizure by Abdullah in 1948, Jordan which
had been Palestine till 1922, offered the familiar landscape, language, and kin of the abandoned village.

TV interviews have familiarized us with the Arab refugee pointing from his hillside barrack toward his native
village in Israel. Sometimes an Arab student indignantly
claims to behold the house his family left behind. His
anger is understandable. Nobody enjoys seeing his property
used by others even if compensation is available. But the
very proximity of the abandoned neighborhood, while
tantalizing, is the true measure of how little national loss
the Arab from Palestine suffered. Even for so slight a
cause as a new subway or urban relocation people are
shifted larger distances and to stranger surroundings than
the changes endured by the majority of the Arab refugees.
Nasser had no qualms about dislodging whole villages for
his Aswan Dam despite the objections of the inhabitants,
and the ease with which the Soviet Union repeatedly
shifted huge numbers of its people to further some social
or political purpose is a matter of record. Only in the case
of the Arabs has village patriotism been raised to a
sacred cause.

Arab refugees left so readily not because of cowardice,
but because departure represented no fundamental wrench.
I refer to the aftermath of the 1948 fighting. Even in June
1967 the comparatively small number who crossed into
Jordan did so in the assurance that both banks of the Jordan were home regardless of the physical privations endured as a result of the war. The mobility of the Arabs
as refugees or guerrillas, within Jordan, Lebanon, and
Syria, indicates strikingly the strength of Arab nationalism
and the tenuous character of the Palestinian attachment
except as a political tactic against Israel.

What bearing has all this on the present? Guerrillas will
not be disarmed by documents irrefutably demonstrating

that they are really southern Syrians, or by British census figures which prove just as convincingly that Jewish settlers did not displace their Arab neighbors. The refugee camps, with their potential for violence, continue to exist. Under these circumstances, is any accommodation short of the destruction of Israel possible? Should the Arab states with the active aid of Russia succeed in destroying Israel, a harvest of horror will be reaped for generations, as after the "final solution" of the Germans. Should Israel win again—the probable result unless the Soviet Union openly intervenes—Arab rage will not be lessened. The prospect of Fortress Israel, besieged by hostile millions, will become a bitter parody of the vision of the Jewish state which animated its founders.

The answer to the apparent impasse is not a Palestine state in which Jews—if we take at face value the assurances given—will be relegated to the status of a steadily dwindling minority. And anyone who has read the fine print of such Arab proposals knows how even the promise that the Jews will be allowed to live is amplified by references to "Zionists," "foreigners," and "imperialist criminals" to whom amnesty would not extend. A small number of Arabic-speaking oriental Jews might qualify for citizenship under these generous provisions. That the Jews of Israel remain sceptical of al-Fatah may be taken for granted. In any case, even if they believed that they would be neither exterminated nor deported, Israelis would be hard to persuade that some moral imperative demands the snuffing out of their country.

As they see it, no development in the contemporary world has weakened the argument for a Jewish state. On the contrary, the wave of romantic internationalism which threatened to swamp Zionism as a form of parochial nationalism has long receded. Emergent nationalisms are burgeoning all over the globe with the full blessing of the anticolonial left. In the midst of this ardor for movements of national liberation it is difficult to convince survivors of the Hitler era that Jewish nationalism is the only heretical specimen. Remembering not only active persecution but the barred doors and closed immigration quotas of every land during the Holocaust, Israelis are unlikely to agree that the only people with no national need are

the Jews. Surveying the globe from European Poland to
Asian Iraq, they would reverse the order: no people is
still in such desperate need of national independence if
only to ensure physical, let alone cultural, survival.

Ideology aside, no Israeli of the pioneer generation will
take seriously charges that his coming displaced the Arabs.
His personal experience in the process of rebuilding the
country testifies otherwise. That is why more concern on
this score is to be found among some sabras—not because
the young are perverse or more ethically aware than their
ruggedly idealistic parents but because they have no memory of the country to which their elders came. Golda Meir
knows that her toil in malaria-ridden Merhavia made an
uninhabited spot livable, just as she knows that her
grandchildren in Revivim, a Negev kibbutz, are creating
another oasis in the desert. In human terms is this good
or bad? Every farmer and kibbutznik will indignantly echo
the question. A scientist at the Weizmann Institute may
less rhetorically point out that only a dozen Arabs lived
on the waste on which Rehovoth was founded in 1891.
Even a city dweller in Tel Aviv will remind you that Jews
built this bustling city on a sand dune; the only ones displaced were the camels who used to parade slowly along
the beach. All are united in the conviction that their coming enlarged the habitable area for both Arab and Jew.

The post-1948 inhabitant of a former Arab house in
Jaffa or Jerusalem must resort to a more modest rationale.
He cannot speak grandly of his creative role as a remaker
of land and bringer of light. If he is an oriental Jew he
may call to witness the house and possessions of which
the Arabs despoiled him when he fled from Iraq, Yemen,
or another of the Arab countries from which half a million destitute oriental Jews escaped to Israel in an informal population exchange. A Western Jew will use the
mundane terminology of realpolitik: what morality demands that foiled aggressors escape scot-free? Besides,
Israel is prepared to discuss compensation for abandoned
Arab property anytime the Arabs want to negotiate a
peace settlement.

Once peace negotiations are underway, the terms of
Israeli withdrawal from occupied territories will be formulated and the boundaries defined. Whatever terms are

agreed on, through peaceful negotiations, we may take it for granted that no solution predicated on the liquidation of Israel through inundation by a flood of refugees under the guise of repatriation, or on its political destruction through the establishment of what has euphemistically been called a "democratic Palestine" will come under consideration.

Israelis may well be pardoned if they view acclaim for a proposal to snuff out hard-won Jewish national independence as another brutal manifestation of anti-Jewish sentiment so profound that it measures both the individual Jew and the Jewish people by criteria applied to no other group. In a period when the former internationalism of the left has been abandoned for the championship of national liberation movements all over the globe, no matter how minuscule or freshly hatched, only Jewish statehood is assailed as parochial or chauvinistic. The same spokesmen who display a sensitive regard for any burgeoning nationalism deplore the Jewish will to national independence as a deviation from the prophetic vision of the brotherhood of man. This difference in standards—a tribal one for all the peoples of the earth, clearly marked with ethnic insignia, and a universal one, stained in vanishing ink, reserved for the Jews—is unacceptable to those beckoned to disappear whether into the mirage of a nonexistent and improbable "socialist federation" or in the sands of a so-called "democratic Palestine."

As far as Israel is concerned, "restoration" is a battle cry, not an arguable alternative. Nor is repatriation a viable solution. By 1971 Israel had an indigenous minority of 450,000 Arabs. Through natural increase the 140,000 Arabs who had not joined the Arab exodus in 1948 plus 50,000 Arabs who had returned under Israel's family reunion plan had become 14 percent of the population. Demographic studies indicate that in view of the much higher Arab birthrate the proportion of Arabs to Jews in Israel will continue markedly to increase. While Israel fully accepts its obligations to its Arab citizens, it cannot admit an influx of hostile Arabs into its small area. Justice no more requires that Israel be swamped by an Arab tide than that its inhabitants be physically driven into the sea —unless, of course, one subscribes to Cairo's reasoning:

"It is obvious that the return of one million Arabs will make them the majority of Israel's inhabitants. Then they will be able to impose their will on the Jews and expel them from Palestine" (official Egyptian Propaganda Ministry broadcast, September 1, 1960).

This leaves resettlement, primarily in those parts of Palestine—the West Bank or Jordan—where most of the refugees are situated, or in underpopulated Syria or Iraq. Gaza, seized by Egypt in 1948, presents an especially acute problem because Egypt kept the refugees immured, neither permitting them to cross into Egypt nor giving them citizenship. (Since 1967 Gaza Arabs have been allowed to work freely in Israel or to cross over to the West Bank.) It should be borne in mind that a large percentage of the Palestinians have become integrated into the economies of their place of residence and, as in Jordan where they are citizens, play leading political roles. By now the camps hold not only the children of the original UN wards but also their grandchildren, despite numerous plans for liquidating the camps, notably including the $200 million Johnston plan which the Arab states rejected. As recently as July 24, 1970, Abba Eban called for the convening of an "urgent international conference on Arab refugees," even "in advance of actual peace negotiations." International funds and practical programs are available. Israel, though she demands that the value of confiscated property of oriental Jews expelled from Arab lands be counted in the total bill, has repeatedly offered compensation for Arab homes and land in Israel. Despite the calculated acerbation of the refugee problem for over two decades, all its humanitarian and social issues can be resolved.

But that's not the sticking point. Golda Meir, with her gift for stripping a question to its essentials, once said that the refugee problem would be settled "when the Arabs love their children more than they hate us." As long as Arab leaders consider the camps dynamite with which to spring Israel, the refugees will fester idly. As long as a world which since World War I has witnessed the convulsive migrations and resettlements of forty million refugees in every part of the globe will encourage the view that the Arab psyche can flourish only in the precise area of Israel and not in a nearby Arab town or village indistinguishable in climate, culture, language, and religion from the one abandoned, Israel will blandly be urged to accede in its extinction.

Nor need violence be done to the Palestinian nationalism which has developed in recent years. A reasonable proposal would be to set up a Palestine entity on the West Bank and the East Bank of the Jordan. It is the place where most Arab refugees already live and the dominant role of the Palestinians in Jordan is an open secret. Such a Palestinian state could satisfy newborn Palestinian nationalism and in conditions of peace prosper economically in partnership with Israel. The proposal, however, serves as a reminder that the Palestine homeland is basically in Arab hands and does not have to be recovered on the corpse of Israel. Given an honest will to peace, the exact delineation of borders and compensation for abandoned property lend themselves to negotiation. But such negotiation, to be meaningful, must be preceded by the recognition that the new national need of the Palestinian and the ancient one of the Jew can be satisfied within the confines of historic Palestine without the destruction of either Jewish or Arab Palestine.

Nationalism, Internationalism, and the Jews: The Chimera of a Binational State

Michael Walzer

MICHAEL WALZER—professor of Government at Harvard University, author of *Revolution of the Saints* and *Obligations: Essays on Disobedience, War and Citizenship.*

> *There are people in the world so crazy as not to realize that this is normal human existence of the kind everybody should aim at.*
>
> —NADEZHDA MANDELSTAM

I

From the beginning, Zionists aimed at a kind of normality, and political Zionists at a very particular kind. They sought the normality of statehood: a people on its own land, with its own institutions and its own police and army, freed from the dangers of exile and persecution (though not from the dangers of war). The political Zionists were like those elders of Israel who came to Samuel and said, "Make us a king to judge us like all the nations." Theirs was not a utopian vision, though it was often expressed in prophetic language, and it was and is open to utopian criticism. Sometimes that criticism isn't very interesting. When the citizens of powerful states like our own disdain Jewish aspirations to statehood or suggest that Jews (especially) should seek nobler ends, they act like those upper-class radicals who are impatient with working-class materialism. It is not easy to respond to such people, though no elaborate argument is necessary. One should simply rehearse the recent history of the Jews, or try to indicate to them how their own security and dignity are intimately connected with the exercise of sovereignty in their name. There isn't anything else to say.

That is not the case with another, more important critique of Zionism, rooted in Jewish experience but shaped largely by socialist ideology. When Marx wrote that the workers have no country, his words were false with reference to the workers, but they were an accurate description of most of the world's Jews. And countrylessness bred socialist internationalism, much as Marx thought it would, though the psychological mechanisms were more complicated than any he suggested. Jews have always been among the most fervent internationalists in the socialist and communist movements. With a special eagerness (which marked them out even when they felt closest to their gentile comrades), they looked toward the world Marx described in the *Communist Manifesto*, where "national differences and antagonisms between peoples are already tending to disappear more and more." Free from conventional political loyalties, they also freed themselves from any sense of Jewish identity and imagined that they already were the future citizens of the world socialist republic. They denied, in effect, what the Zionists had always insisted upon: that the case of the Jews was exceptional, that exile was abnormal.

Whatever the virtues of their position, Hitler settled the argument, at least temporarily, against the Marxist critics of Zionism. He proved the exceptionalism of the Jews and established the need for a Jewish state, as a refuge, if for no other reason. After the Holocaust, statehood became an ethical imperative. Nor have events since that time made it any less important. Antagonisms between peoples are greater than they have ever been (for reasons I will try to suggest); there are as many ways as ever to be frightened and insecure; and the most radical and dangerous way is still to be countryless or stateless. Until the revolution is upon us, then, people will seek the protection of the nation-state, much as they will go to work week after week while waiting for the messiah.

I am inclined to think that the argument remains settled. Yet the patent insecurity of the state of Israel, the emergence of a countryless Palestinian people, and the development in Western Europe and the United States of a New

Left profoundly hostile to Zionism have led to a reopening of the argument. It has been reopened, however, in a peculiarly parochial form. This is so for three reasons. First, it now focuses on a group of Jews reunited in a small corner of the world and no longer on a community dispersed throughout the world. Secondly, the Palestinians, far from describing themselves as universal men of the future, have developed a more or less straightforward nationalist position. And finally, the New Left has made its peace with virtually every nationalism in the world except that of the Jews. So it is not being argued these days that no one can be secure in a world of competing nation-states, but only that the security of Israel's Jews and the aspirations of the Palestinians are incompatible with the existence of Israel. The existence of Egypt and Syria, let alone of France and Germany, is not at issue. Indeed, there are times when it seems that the sum total of the new "internationalism" is binationalism in old Palestine. At any rate, this is the centerpiece of the contemporary leftist critique of Zionism, and its one, rather curious virtue is that its achievement neither requires nor would contribute to a world revolution. So the Zionists have won this much at least: the Jewish question is at last recognized to be susceptible to a local solution.

II

The term "binationalism" does not single out a particular or coherent doctrine. There are at least three views of what the successor state to present-day Israel might look like, and they suggest very different ways of dealing with the nationalist feelings of Jews and Arabs. What they have in common is the formal repudiation of the nation-state, more particularly the Jewish nation-state, which is condemned for its exclusive, parochial, and discriminatory character. But it is hard to see how binationalism in any form can avoid having that same character, since there would necessarily be some third nationality with regard to which the binational state is exclusive, parochial, and discriminatory (in its immigration policy, for example, an abiding issue in the Middle East). First the various views must be set out in some order, roughly characterized at least, though I cannot attempt an analysis of the detailed positions of different political groups.

Because it figures in the programs of the Palestinian guerrillas, the "democratic secular state" is currently the most important, as it is the most mysterious, of the alternatives to Israeli statehood. The phrase suggests a set of arrangements whereby Jews and Arabs would share an equal citizenship under a unified sovereignty. But it does not provide, nor do those who use it, any specification of the precise character of the arrangements. What will be the official language of the new state? What history will be taught in its schools? What holidays will be celebrated? How will immigration policy be determined? If it is really to be democratic, such questions will presumably be settled by the majority; but given the nonexistence of the state, who will decide who is to be the majority? And what division of power will be worked out with the (equally unknown) minority? Both Jews and Arabs, of course, regard Jewish or Arab statehood as perfectly compatible with democracy and secularism, and they are right to do so, at least in theory. But then how would a democratic secular state differ from either a Jewish or an Arab state?

It is a great deal easier to imagine a democratic secular state called Israel than one called Palestine: such a state already exists in substance (despite the power of Orthodox Jews), while Arab political culture offers little hope for anything like it in the near future. Now that the deracinated, frenchified, neo-Marxist elite of the FLN has produced a state so profoundly Arab and Islamic (and undemocratic) as contemporary Algeria, what is there to expect from al-Fatah? Indeed, the guerrillas have always been perfectly open about their own nationalism, even while insisting on their democratic and secularist commitments. Thus Article 1 of their national covenant, endorsed by all the major groups: "Palestine is the homeland of the Palestinian Arab people and an integral part of the great Arab homeland, and the people of Palestine is a part of the Arab nation." Given the parallel and opposite commitments of virtually all Israeli Jews, it is hard to imagine a democratic secular state that did not begin with the departure of one or another of the two peoples. So

Israel begin, and so Palestine no doubt would begin, if
the dreams of al-Fatah came true. "Jews who were living
permanently in Palestine until the beginning of the Zionist
invasion will be considered Palestinians," according to
Article 6 of the covenant—which means that the great
majority of Israeli Jews would not find a homeland in the
new Palestine. The "democratic secular state" is clearly a
false binationalism.

The second alternative is probably the only true binationalism. It would provide for separate and equal national institutions within a framework of state sovereignty.
Religious, cultural, and social separatism would be permitted (whether on a territorial basis or in some other
way), economic cooperation encouraged, and political unity
maintained. This is the proposal that I will be referring to
most often in what follows, and yet as soon as one asks
how political power might be apportioned in such a state
and what this or that apportionment might mean, the problems of the second alternative begin to look rather like
the problems of the first. It remains true, however, that
the second is at least an honest and integral vision, the
first only a rhetorical mask.

The third alternative is to give up any sort of unified
sovereignty and opt for a federation of virtually autonomous "entities"—states, for all practical purposes, though
advocates of binationalism think the term opprobrious.
Here there are, so to speak, no problems at all, beyond
those that have to be faced every day right now. That is,
if one could draw the line between an Arab and a Jewish
entity, few people would object to making it a dotted line
and compromising in small or even in significant ways
the absolute independence of the two political systems.
Once a line is drawn and the rights of the people on either
side mutually recognized and guaranteed, all sorts of things
would be possible. But the mere advocacy of federalism
makes it no easier to draw the line. And sometimes that
advocacy serves as a substitute for the politically necessary defense of the two entities and, above all, of Israel,
the entity that already exists—which only makes it harder
to draw the line.

III

The second of these alternatives is the one we must consider, but since it involves the living together of peoples who have been at war for a quarter of a century, it may be useful to begin with a more general question. Why is it that national differences and antagonisms between peoples (not only between these two peoples) have not tended to disappear, as Marx thought they would? Surely it is not because of the failure of the left; it is more likely because of its success. For what the left has done, again and again—it ought to be a source of pride—is to mobilize oppressed and passive people. And, again and again, these people have turned out to be nationalists, in the most elemental and powerful sense of that word. Indeed, it is the masses who are the carriers of nationalism. When they enter the historical arena, they come with their language, religion, age-old customs, and above all, their shared memories of oppression at the hands of foreigners. Unlike the upper classes even of subject nations, they have not been touched by the great imperial cultures of the prerevolutionary era, Hapsburg, Romanov, Ottoman, or British. They do not make their appearance, as many European Marxists expected them to do, as russified Poles, germanized Czechs, or Anglo-Indians. They appear as Polish, Czech, and Indian nationalists, and they can be effectively organized for political action only in movements and parties that promise national liberation.

The nationalism of the oppressed is one of the major discoveries of the modern age. It forces us to look again at the multinationalism of the old empires, probably the true historical source of the Marxist vision. Within those empires profoundly different peoples—Greek and Turk, Hindu and Muslim, Arab and Kurd, Ibo and Hausa— lived side by side in adjacent, even in the same villages and towns. They did not always live in peace: there were communal riots, pogroms, semiofficial and spontaneous massacres—little enough, however, compared to all that has happened since. In all the new countries, there are old men—I have met both Jews and Arabs—who remember those days with a nostalgia I do not want to imitate. What

made multinationalism possible was the oppressive rule
of cosmopolitan and imperial elites, aliens within the communities they governed. The real crimes of imperialism
were the work of those elites. The various subject nations had little to do with them, except as victims, for they
had no share in political power.

Once, however, those nations were mobilized and organized, the common life of the villages rapidly became
impossible. Greek and Turkish peasants could live at peace
under the indifferent rule of Ottoman bureaucrats. But
they could not live at peace under Greek or Turkish officials acting in the name of the liberated Greek or Turkish nation. When political power was the issue between
them, only mass transfer of populations could avoid the
fury of mutual slaughter. The same story can be told of
India, and here there is a special poignancy. For Nehru's
provisional government was warned in 1947 that communal rioting and massacre on a scale never seen before
would follow the partition of the subcontinent, and it was
urged to provide every possible means of transportation to
carry people across the new border. But the warning was
ignored, at least partly because of the socialist convictions
of Nehru and the men around him. They thought communal hatred was an imperial contrivance; in its full fury
it was, in fact, the child of independence.

IV

The left has always underestimated both the intensity
and the value of national feelings, even when its parties
and movements were systematically exploiting them. The
value doesn't derive only from the fact that human beings
respond to oppression, and survive it, by nourishing and
cultivating their particular ethnic, racial, and religious identities. It is also and more importantly the case that they
cannot live in freedom without creating such identities.
Political freedom, the freedom of a community rather
than of an individual, may begin with the removal of imperial bureaucrats, but its full development involves the
sharing and shaping of a common life. To be sure, the
citizens of new states often find themselves, after independence, with little more than what Marx called "the illu-

sion of a common life." But their nationalism is nevertheless not an illusion, and whether liberation occurs just
once or again and again, what the people insist on each
time is the reality of a national history that includes them
and of the symbols and rituals of national unity. Their
self-government, when it comes, produces a political culture radically different from the cosmopolitanism of the
old elites, if only because it is the achievement of men and
women with whom the old elites never bothered to talk.

Precisely for this reason, national liberation is threatening to all those minority groups who find themselves
trapped within the boundaries of a new nation-state, face
to face with a community mobilized for action, eager to
affirm its collective identity. In the past such minorities
made their peace with imperial bureaucrats and were protected or ignored by them; now the minorities stand in the
way of national unity. If recent history is any evidence,
they will fare badly at the hand of newly liberated peoples
and their new and busy officialdom. So it is not enough to
call for the independence of this or that oppressed nation,
though that is surely the right thing to do. One's political
virtue is always tested by the nation that comes next. Each
act of liberation makes the next more necessary, if crime
and cruelty are to be avoided. The universal principle that
all men have a right to govern themselves points toward
the proliferation of what, from the standpoint of the old
empires (or of the world socialist republic), must look like
parochial and archaic communities: the return of peoples
long repressed.

The freedom of Iraq, then, requires the freedom of
Kurdistan; the freedom of Nigeria, Biafra; the freedom of
Pakistan, Bengal. Similarly, the freedom of Israel requires
that of Palestine; and conversely, for those leftists already
committed to Palestinian liberation, Palestine requires
Israel. There is no way of avoiding the logic of the process
—at least no honest way—unless one decides that one national or protonational group deserves to be subjected to
another.

But it *is* a dilemma that universalism should lead so inexorably to parochialism on a universal scale. And since
leftists did not expect the dilemma, it should not be surprising that so many of them have coped with it so badly,

choosing to support or not to support this or that national
group on the basis of the most arbitrary distinctions (pro-
gressive/reactionary) or practicing a kind of guilt by association (as if oppressed people did not search for allies
wherever they can find them). And then leftists are discovered simultaneously supporting secession here and the
slaughter of secessionists there, paying close attention to
this national liberation movement while pretending that
that one does not exist. No doubt there are ways of ra-
tionalizing such judgments or refusals of judgment, and
even expediential reasons to offer for them. But I can see
no secure or justified general position short of support for
every popularly based movement (though not for every
vanguard elite) that aims at national liberation. How can
one measure the value of one people's self-discovery and
nationalist self-assertion against another's? Leaving aside
the most perverse of measurements, which devalues one's
own people, and the next most perverse, which exalts only
one's own, surely the relevant measuring principle is equality. What is required is equal political recognition for all
those aspiring nations which accept the principle of equal
political recognition.

But if we apply this principle, we are forced to worry
about drawing lines between the new nations. For what
they aspire to is independence. They want to have a life of
their own, reasonably secure against the interventions of
foreign powers. There may, of course, be some other political arrangement than conventional statehood that would
make this possible: so advocates of binationalism (among
others) claim. But assuming that the immediate cause of
the liberation movement is the experience of sovereign
power in someone else's hands, the effort to collect it into
one's own hands is not merely understandable, it is morally
irresistible. Faced with a people responding to its own
fear and suffering, seeking immediate relief, whatever criticisms we might want to make of the state as an institution
have to be postponed—or redirected. Turn Norway and
Sweden into a binational state if you can; but set the
Biafrans free.

At such moments, it seems to me, ordinary decency requires the drawing of new lines on the map—an uninspir-
ing, often arbitrary and cruel business, but necessary never-

theless. Here is the maxim of a chastened humanism:
Good borders make good neighbors. And a good border,
in a time of growing national antagonism, is a line so
drawn that different peoples are on different sides. I don't
want to pretend that that is very much more than a minimal moral position. There is, in fact, no acceptable way of
getting everyone on the right side of the line, and there
remain individuals of all sorts for whom neither side and
possibly no side can be right (the position, once, of the
Jews): they will stay behind to test the quality of the new
nation. The need for good borders is not all that follows
from the recognition of nationalist feeling that I have been
urging. Having established boundaries, it remains to fight
for minority rights, equal protection, and all the liberal
safeguards within them, and then for economic and political cooperation across them.

But whatever we do, nation building in new states is
sure to be rough on groups marginal to the nation (and
too small or scattered to secede from the nation)—those
archetypal aliens of the third world, for example, Jews,
Levantines, Indians, and Chinese, or colonial settlers like
the French of Algeria. For them, very often, the roughness
can only be smoothed a little; it cannot be avoided. And
sometimes, it can only be smoothed by helping people to
leave who have to leave, like the Indians of Kenya and
Tanzania, the colons of North Africa, the Jews of the Arab
world. No doubt this is a defeat for socialist internationalism, as it is for ordinary liberalism, but the refusal to help
only leads to a worse defeat. Emigration is the private
equivalent of secession, and like secession it is a right that
requires more than theoretical vindication. It points toward
an immediate and pressing problem: emigrants from country X must become immigrants to country Y. There must
be a place to go; there must be havens for refugees. Israel
was set up to be such a haven, and in turning now more
directly to the question of binationalism, I want to focus
on that feature of the new state.

V

I have been talking about Jews and Arabs all along,
though I have used other names and attempted a more

general argument. Whatever may be unique in their two histories, their inability to live together is not unique. Yet the efforts to create a Jewish-Arab state go back many years, and in the 1930s and '40s were supported by men as committed to their own people as to the principles of internationalism. I cannot discuss the history of their efforts nor describe the reasons for their failure. But I can at least suggest one of the reasons by exploring the question of immigration policy, which is central to the debate even today. For here is the point where all the arguments about sovereignty come into sharpest focus.

All states have immigration policies and most states make distinctions in their treatment of different groups of possible immigrants. These distinctions are sometimes abhorrent, but by no means ncessarily so. It is even generally recognized in the international community that certain states have special responsibilities toward certain peoples. In the aftermath of World War I and of the Balkan settlement, for example, Greece received many refugees from present-day Turkey and treated them differently from other immigrants. It did so because they were Greeks, though they had never lived within the newly drawn borders of the Greek state. But they spoke Greek, worshiped according to the Greek Orthodox rite, thought of themselves as Greeks, and were not regarded as foreigners by the citizens of Greece. Similarly, after World War II, Poland received refugees from the east, as did Germany, and the preferential treatment accorded these peoples was never, so far as I know, called discriminatory. Now the question that faced and still faces advocates of a Jewish-Arab state is simply this: What people or peoples are to be given preferential treatment? But this question opens up every other: How will decisions about immigration policy be made? What group will constitute or come to constitute the majority of the population? And so on.

Contemporary advocates of binationalism almost always insist that the Israelis must repeal the Law of Return, which declares that Jews will receive preferential treatment. But surely this would compromise rather than fulfill the binational character of the successor state, for it would deny the existence of a *nation* of Jews capable, as Greeks, Poles, and Germans are capable, of rescuing and rehabili-

tating their fellow nationals. At any rate, there are very few
Jews ready to agree to that; nor were the foremost advocates of binationalism in the decade before Israeli independence—men like Martin Buber, Judah Magnes, and
the leaders of the left socialist parties—willing even to consider the end of Jewish aliyah. "Our Jewish destiny,"
wrote Buber in a letter to Gandhi, "is indissolubly bound
up with this possibility of gathering, and this in Palestine."
He writes here, in effect, as a spokesman of the Jewish
national liberation movement, for Jewish history had
made "gathering" the essential prerequisite of freedom.
After World War II, it seemed the prerequisite also of
survival, and that is a time Israeli Jews are not likely to
forget.

There was never any significant number of Arab leaders
ready to concede the Jewish right of return, though that
right will doubtless be asserted on behalf of the Palestinians, now scattered throughout the Middle East, if a Pales-
tianian state is ever established. And that is a right the
Palestinians have, as do the Jews. It is virtually inconceivable, however, that the two rights could be accommodated
within a single binational state. This is one of the hardest
of issues, and every other difficulty of binationalism bears
upon it and is exaggerated by it. The new parochialism
with its intense pride and exclusiveness, the deep mistrust
of foreigners, the actual memories of war, the uncertain
balance of power and the fear it breeds: all these barriers
to coexistence become enlarged and distorted beyond all
reason when what is at stake is literally the future population of the proposed union. If the "gathering" of Jews and
Palestinians is morally necessary, then two separate states,
respectful of each other's sovereignty, are also morally
necessary.

One might, of course, question the moral necessity, and
advocates of binationalism probably must do this at some
point, though recent advocates have tended to press their
skepticism only against the Jews. They argue that a binational state can and ought to be built upon the latent class
loyalties of workers from the two national groups. They
assume that such loyalties are morally superior to the
manifest commitment of Jewish workers to diaspora Jewry
(and I suppose, though the point is not stressed, of Pales-

tinian guerrillas to the "Arab nation"). Hence their
attacks upon the Law of Return. I am not sure how such
judgments are made, but I doubt very much that the Jews
of old Palestine would rank high on any available moral
scale had they turned their backs on the Jews of Hitler's
Europe and sought an alliance with the (virtually nonexistent) Arab left.

Probably the argument reflects a theory of history according to which class struggle must at some point super-
sede national conflict, and "objective material interests"
override national feeling. At some point—perhaps; but
surely not at this point. Those Jews who might plausibly
struggle alongside Arab workers are mostly immigrants
or refugees from Arab countries. If binationalism were a
lively option, they might well have stayed where they were.
If the liberation movements of North Africa had not aimed
so explicitly at creating Arab nation-states, they might
never have become immigrants at all. Having immigrated,
they are likely to associate their objective interests with
the state that offered them a place to go. They have already chosen nation over class, as has virtually everyone in
the third world—which is not to say that the class struggle
is at an end in Israel or anywhere else.

VI

The choice of brethren and comrades cannot be dictated by abstract theory. Instead, we must begin our
theories with the choices men actually make and have
made. The defense of national liberation and then of the
right to statehood represents such a beginning. It pays
attention to what people want, always a good thing to do,
and imperative, one would have thought, for the left. It is,
however, as I have stressed before, only a beginning. One
can still attack the internal character of this or that movement or new state (I have a list of movements and states
that need attacking) or call for radical forms of cooperation across party lines and international borders. It is even
possible to urge that the right to statehood be foregone, so
long as one continues to defend the right and the security
of all those peoples who choose to exercise it. There is
nothing wrong, that is, with attempts to convert the Jews—

or the Palestinians, Tanzanians, or Pakistanis—to socialist internationalism. That is an old and honorable leftist occupation.

But there is a great deal that is wrong with attempts, before the conversion of the Jews, to undermine the state of Israel or call its survival into question. Contemporary advocates of binationalism are at least sometimes engaged in just such an attempt. That is why their major propaganda effort focuses on the people of the United States and Western Europe rather than on Israelis and Palestinians: it is not aimed at those who must be convinced if binationalism is ever to work, but rather at Israel's international allies. And then binationalism must be opposed, not only because it would deny Jews the right of national liberation, but also because it would deny them the protection of a state at a time when there is less hope than ever before of surviving without that protection.

Nor will such efforts contribute to a peaceful settlement in the Middle East, for no settlement there is possible which does not provide the conditions of "normal human existence" for both Jews and Arabs. At this moment in history, those conditions are represented by the nation-state. To deny any people statehood is not simply to put forward a theoretical position; it is virtually to make war against them. And that will not contribute to binationalism, or federation, or world socialism, or whatever we might find hopeful in the future.

Self-Determination and the Palestinian Arabs

Julius Stone

The establishment of a Palestine Arab state had, of course, been proposed in the partition resolution of 1947, accepted on behalf of the future state of Israel, but violently thwarted by the invasion of Palestine in 1948 by six Arab states seeking to destroy the new state of Israel. After the armistice arrested the ensuing war, which even the Soviet (nominally Ukrainian) delegate at the 306th meeting of the United Nations Security Council on May 27, 1948, condemned as an "unlawful invasion," Jordan and Egypt were left in military occupation of substantial parts of the abortive Palestine Arab state on the West Bank of the Jordan, and the Gaza Strip, in addition to East Jerusalem. Had the Palestine Arab state not been thus aborted, the specific "nationhood" of its population, scarcely manifest at that time, would perhaps have grown with the responsibility and experience of statehood. But this did not happen.

So that it was to be two decades more, in the sixties, and perhaps not until after the 1967 war, before "Palestinianism" in a specific sense entered the international stage. The fact that this entry was made in an explosive context of political passion and physical violence should not conceal the long-term issues which it raises. Because of these

Copyright 1970 Julius Stone. This paper was presented to the Australian Society of Legal Philosophy and the Grotian Society (Australian Group) on September 3, 1970. It was written during the author's visit to the Hebrew University Truman Research Institute in the late spring of 1970.

issues, "Palestinianism" in all its aspects needs to be examined as dispassionately as possible.

The "Palestinian entity" notion was invoked by Arab states at Arab League meetings in 1959, in the context of struggles not only against Israel, but also among themselves, looking to a still projected dismemberment of that state. The supposed claims of such an "entity," putatively associated with claims of "Palestinian peoplehood," have now come, since the 1967 war, to be offered as a central factor to be reckoned with in the current Middle East conflict.[1] And at this level, of course, very substantial preliminary questions arise as to the relevance of such an "entity" to the merits of this conflict. The confusions surrounding these questions were illustrated by the General Assembly resolution of November 5, 1970. Among the aspects of this resolution which split the United Nations, and indeed the Arab world itself, and marshaled the support of only 57 out of 127 UN members, was its reference to "the Palestinians" as "an indispensable element" of a Middle East settlement.

The first question is about the genuineness of the supposed association of this evoked entity with a Palestinian "people," much less with a Palestinian "nation," in the sense of those symbols which today implies entitlement to political independence.[2] Even scholars rather sympathetic

---

[1] See S. Shamir, "The Attitude of Arab Intellectuals," *The Anatomy of Peace in the Middle East* (American Academics for Peace in the Middle East, 1969), pp. 5, 21. And see on the role of new elites among the Palestinians, Y. Harkabi, *The Position of the Palestinians on the Israel-Arab Conflict and Their National Covenant*, trans. Y. Karmi (Jerusalem, 1969).

[2] The ideologues and draftsmen of the Palestinian covenant struggled, not wholly successfully, to appropriate the Arabic term for "nation" to Pan-Arab nationalism (*qawmiyya*) and the term for "peoplehood" in relation to the several Arab independent countries (*Wataniyya*). See, e.g., Articles 1, 5, 8–9, 12–14, and the commentary in Harkabi, op. cit., 7, 9–11.

When this complexity is added to the emotive indeterminacies of the terms "nation" and "people" such questions become endlessly arguable, and consistency of argument very difficult to achieve. D. Peretz's recent short article, "Arab Palestine, Phoenix or Phantom?" *Foreign Affairs* 48 (1970): 322, contains the following indications:

On the one hand, there was "no distinctive Palestinian peo-

to Arab claims have pointed out that when the British White Paper of 1939 had apparently made an independent Arab state inevitable, "most of the country's Arab leaders slipped into lethargy and paralysis of action which was to last nearly thirty years."[3] So that whatever interpretation is given to the sporadic and mostly localized attacks of Arabs on Jews in 1920, 1929, and 1936–39, it remains a puzzle how and why a Palestinian Arab nationalism, had it already existed, could have remained inert and passive during the critical years which followed 1939. As late as 1948, the main role of the Palestinians during the attack by the Arab states on the new state of Israel was either to accept life under that new state or to leave their homes to seek shelter with the Arab states and their armies. Pending more persuasive historical studies, these facts seem to point to a movement merely stirred and manipulated, and then only sporadically, by forces outside Palestine.

If, however, we assume that, at any rate in 1960, or 1967 or 1970, the Palestine "entity" demand has acquired a genuine relation to Palestinian Arab "peoplehood," the second question would be what bearing this fact could have at this stage of history on the military and political facts or on the moral rights and wrongs of the present Arab-Israeli conflict. This bearing is not likely to be a simple one. The tensions between the Welsh and the English, and the Scots and the English, still continue after many centuries of English dominance. No serious body of

---

ple" in 1918 (p. 323); that an elite manifesting "Palestinian consciousness" emerged in the sixties, and that the terrorist groups "within the last two years" (since 1967) had created a new identity for the Palestinians, distinguishing "Palestinian refugees" and "Palestinian Arabs" (pp. 325–26); and that thirty years of Palestinian "lethargy and paralysis of action ensued, even after the 1939 White Paper" seemed to make a Palestinian Arab state inevitable. On the other hand, he assumes that Arab riots of as early as 1920 and 1929 manifested "nationalism" (p. 323); and he speaks of the "*re*-establishment of Arab Palestine in the 'sixties" (p. 326).

On the covenant, see also Harkabi, "The Palestinian National Covenant," *New York Journal of International Law and Politics* 5 (1970): 228, and Harkabi, *Position of the Palestinians*.

[3] See very recently Harkabi, *Position of the Palestinians*, pp. 323–24.

opinion sees the answers for modern Welsh or Scots nationalisms in the establishment of new sovereign states of Wales and Scotland, or the annihilation or extrusion of immigrant Englishmen.

It is this second hypothetical question that I wish here to explore. For the first question above I merely hypothesize that an affirmative answer can be given for the past decade, so as to open the way for exploring the second.

Insofar, then, as we assume that there has arisen recently a specific "Palestinian" consciousness associated with the idea of establishing "a Palestinian entity," it is obvious that this must be, in some sense, a factor in the present stage of the Middle East conflict. But by the same token of chronology, this factor could not now be a decisive one for judging the rights and wrongs of events which took place half a century or even a generation before, in 1917 or 1922 or 1948. A nationalism hypothetically just emergent cannot be treated as if it had emerged decades before, for the purpose of facilely overriding entitlements then fixed and acted upon. To ignore chronology in such a way would be an arbitrary reconstruction of events and rights of peoples, as these latter in historical fact presented themselves after World War I, to claim a share in the distribution of the territories of the defeated Turkish Empire.

In the distribution of those vast ex-Turkish territories, embracing the whole of the Near and Middle East, the principal claimants, in historical fact, were the Arab and the Jewish peoples. The Arabs were, of course, dispersed over the whole area, with a number of cultural and political centers, but no particular center in Palestine. As Peretz observes of that period, "there was no distinctive Palestine people, nor political entity," and "the land and its inhabitants were considered backwater regions of the less developed Ottoman Syrian provinces."[4] And James Parkes has done well to recall the fact that, even at the height of the imperium of the Arab and then later the Turkish conquerors of the whole area, Palestine was never exclusively Arab or Muslim any more then it was exclusively Jewish

---

[4] Ibid., p. 323.

or Christian, either in population or in cultural or religious concerns.

The departure or reentry of Jews and Christians particularly reflected the degrees of tolerance or persecution by successive local rulers. A part of the Jewish people, driven from Palestine by the fire and sword of successive invading empires, remained as dispersed communities throughout the Middle East, and new ones grew up in Europe and North Africa. A part, varying as indicated, remained in Palestine. But for all the Jewish people, wherever they were, Palestine remained into the modern era the steady focus of its religious and national life, just as it had been the center also of its political life in the earlier millennium of the kingdoms of David and Solomon, and later of the Hasmoneans.

In this perspective it is clear that Jewish nationalism and Arab nationalism, each embracing its own cluster of scattered populations, each sharing specific cultural, religious, traditional, and historical experiences deeply rooted in the Middle East region, came simultaneously as claimants, the former to a part, the latter to the whole, of the territories liberated by World War I from the Turkish sway. These were the claimants among whom the admittedly unsaintly dispensers of justice after World War I made the allocations which began the modern period. It is critical for clear thought and fair judgment, in terms of modern ideas of the self-determination of nations, to identify these two peoples who were claimants at the time. For it is fatal to the judgment of justice, and may be a source of grave wrong in any context, to misidentify the claimants among whom the distribution is to be made.

Though this general point is valid for all contexts, the issue arising from the assumed recent emergence of Palestinian peoplehood offers a striking example of it. The facile assertion that Israel came into existence on the basis of injustice to the Palestinian people proceeds on a gross error of this kind. In historical fact the Arab claimants after World War I embraced Arabs of the whole area of whom, as already seen, the Arabs in Palestine were merely a peripheral and in no way "distinctive" segment, whose interests as such were taken into account. So that now to present a "Palestinian entity" and people, assumedly emergent in the sixties, as an additional claimant against Israel is an unwarranted and somewhat dubious game with history as well as justice.

The distribution which emerged after World War I and was implemented in the succeeding decades included the following features:

First, despite all the extraneous great-power maneuverings, Jewish and Arab claims in this vast area came to the forum of justice together, and not (as is usually implied) by way of Jewish encroachment on an already vested and exclusive Arab domain.

Second, the allocation made to the Arabs, as implemented in the now-existing dozen and more Arab sovereignties, was a hundred times greater in area and hundreds of times richer in resources than the "Palestine" designated for the Jewish national home.

Third, by successive steps thereafter, this already tiny allocation to Jewish claims was further encroached upon. Part of it was cut away in 1922 (namely, 70,000 out of 96,000 square kilometers, including the more sparsely populated regions) to establish the state of Transjordan (later renamed Jordan). It was proposed to cut away further parts of it to establish the Palestine Arab state by the partition of 1947. Most of the areas designated for that Arab state were in fact seized and thereafter held until 1967 by Egypt and Transjordan in the course of their first armed attack against the state of Israel in 1948.

The contemporary fashion of shortcuts in thought has recently tried to tear the Palestine refugee question from this context of history, into which it is the more important to reset it. The leaders of this fashion, if we leave out Arab spokesmen themselves, have been from the New Left, for whom history is rather a blank book in which Manichean judgments are written in black-and-white characters which stir indignation with minimal expenditure of thought.

It has been the more urgent to point out that it twists and parodies both history and justice to present the Palestine issue as a struggle between the Jews of the world on the one hand, and the Arabs of Palestine on the other, in which the Jews seized the major share. The struggle was rather between the Arabs of the Middle East region (including some hundred thousands living in Palestine) and the Jews of the world, in which the Arabs took a lion's share from which in due course a dozen and more Arab states emerged. Neither at the time of distribution, nor for decades later, moreover, was there any identifiable Palestine Arab people, much less any center of Arab cultural or political life in Palestine. There were Arabs who had lived in Palestine for centuries, as there were Jews who had lived in Iraq, in Yemen, and other parts of the region for centuries; and all of these (as I shall show) were to pay a price for the inheritances gained by their respective nations.

The errors involved can be shown in an analogy. Suppose a distribution of disputed ancestral lands between Clan Smith and Clan Jones was accepted by them in 1920. Half a century later, one member of Clan Smith, born after the distribution, began to claim a separate additional allocation for himself by forcibly ousting Clan Jones from its allotted portion, aided and abetted by the well-endowed Clan Smith as a whole.

Such a claim has, on its face, the following fivefold perversity. First, that the challenge to the distribution made in 1920 is made in terms of claimants and attitudes which did not exist in 1920, but emerged (if at all) many years later. Second, that the after-born claimant, the sacrifice of whose interests made possible the distribution to his own clan as well as to the Jones clan, should now stake his claim not against his own (the Smith) clan, or even against both clans together in some due proportion, but exclusively against Clan Jones. Third, that this belated new claim is asserted even so far as to negate the entire entitlement of Clan Jones. Fourth, that it is pressed, indeed, to the point of demanding destruction of the whole basis of existence of Clan Jones. Fifth, and finally, that Clan Smith now aids and abets this attack against Clan Jones, while offering little contribution toward satisfying its own dissatisfied claimant member out of its own ample endowment.

In the aftermath of these allocations, of which the overwhelming part went to Arab peoples, about half-a-million

Arabs were led to leave their homes in Palestine[5] and no fewer Jews were forced to leave their homes and properties in various Arab countries. It is commonplace, alas, justice being rarely perfect, that some marginal interests among the major claimants usually suffer a degree of wrong in the course of even a just distribution. It is also well accepted that some duty of redress to such wronged marginal interests must rest on all who benefit from the overall distribution, in proportion to their benefits, and according to some rational division of responsibilities. And such wrong in the Middle East flowed from the initial territorial settlement in the area in a process as drawn out as that from which all the Arab states, as well as Israel, emerged. Thus, correctly seen, any injustice to the Arabs of Palestine flowed from the creation of the present Arab states no less than from the creation of the state of Israel.

Israel, in any case, accepted the responsibility to re-settle and rehabilitate fully half of the million displaced persons involved, namely, the Jews from Arab lands. She accepted, in addition, a similar responsibility for a significant number of displaced Arabs, and she offered, as a part of a settlement, to receive back an additional 100,000 of the Palestinian refugees. Arab states, with vastly greater areas and resources, have accepted no responsibility for any substantial resettling of displaced Arabs. They have sought rather to keep the "Arab refugee" question alive as a weapon for political use against Israel, sometimes, as with Egypt in Gaza, by confining the refugees in a virtual concentration area on the borders of Israel. (The over-tones of artificiality in the recent "entity" notion suggest,

---

[5] It should be noted that even the half-million figure for "Arab refugees" of the 1948–49 war is regarded as a gross exaggeration by David Ben-Gurion, who was Israel's prime minister at the relevant time: "The refugee issue is one of the biggest lies, even among our own people . . . I have all the figures. From the area of the State of Israel only 180,000 Arabs left in 1948. There were 300,000 Arabs altogether in Israel, and 120,000 remained . . . Forty thousand came back under the family reunion scheme" (interview, *JPW*, October 5, 1970, p. 9; and cf. also for a recent non-Jewish account, J. Douglas Young, President of the American Institute of Holy Land Studies, letter to *JPW*, October 5, 1970, p. 15).

in this perspective, that it may be a refurbished form of that older weapon.)

The context in which the burden of making amends to Arabs and Jews displaced in consequence of the post–World War I territorial distribution must be approached is that very distribution. In the upshot, as has been seen, more than a dozen independent Arab states emerged endowed with something like 99 percent of the area. Only 1 percent of the area, and even less of the resources, were designated in 1917 for a national home for the Jewish people. This distribution overwhelmingly favoring the Arabs still remains the decisive context for considering amends to be made for incidental wrongs to marginal groups of Arabs and Jews, whether from Palestine, Iraq, or elsewhere. The moral principle involved is clear: that marginal wrongs in the course of a distribution fail to be made good by those who benefited from the distribution in proportion to their benefit.

This does not exclude that the international community generally also has a role to play in rehabilitation and resettlement. With these, as with so many other displaced groups, the international community has its own interest in fostering reconciliation and easing tension.

These moral principles are applicable both to Jews and Arabs, whether we assume that the Arab refugees fled from Palestine as a result of intimidation by Israelis during the 1948 Arab invasion, or (as the Israelis assert) because they chose to join invaders in the hope and confidence of thereby both securing their personal safety and possessions, and, in some cases, of sharing in distribution of Israeli land and goods after a victorious Arab dismemberment of Israel. Even, indeed, on the interpretation more charitable to the Arab refugees, their grievances only take their place alongside those of the half-million Jewish refugees driven from Arab states where they had lived for centuries, stripped of possessions and compelled to flee to the only refuge open to them in the state of Israel. Any final share of responsibility imputed to Israel to aid the half-million Arab refugees, in view of her small share of the resources distributed after World War I, would certainly have to allow for the heavy burdens she assumed toward the half-million Jewish refugees from Arab countries.

In summary, then, I am saying that all these displaced persons, Jews and Arabs alike, were casualties of the same attempt at a just distribution of ex-Turkish territories after World War I. The duties of aiding and rehabilitating all these casualties rest in due proportion on Arab as well as Israeli beneficiaries. Israel unquestioningly assumed full responsibility for half the refugees involved. A certain number of the Arab refugees have also been absorbed into some Arab states, notably Lebanon and Jordan. But this sets into relief the default of the other Arab states. Egypt, for example, literally confined its displaced kindred in Gaza, left the responsibility for their subsistence to the United Nations agencies, and concerned itself mainly for twenty years with channeling the refugees' resentment against Israel, turning their misfortune into a kind of weapon to be used against that state.

This default in duties of justice and humanity has been gross, even when measured by the standards of older sovereign states. These states have not always themselves, of course, been paragons of the duties of humanity; but the record since World War II has shown a remarkable recognition of these duties, stimulated no doubt by international concern for stabilization of frontiers and reduction of tensions. According to Holborn's *World Refugees* (1960) the truncated West Germany, after World War II, absorbed and rehabilitated no less than 9,688,000 displaced persons (5,978,000 from Poland, 1,891,000 from Czechoslovakia, and the rest from several other European countries). Small Austria received 178,000 Hungarian refugees in the aftermath of the Hungarian revolution of 1956 (Elfan Rees, *Century of the Homeless Man* [International Conciliation, 1957]). Italy provided a home for 585,000 Italians displaced from territory ceded to Yugoslavia, and from various parts of Africa (*U.N. World Refugee Year Secretariat*). France gave permanent asylum to 1,372,000 refugees (including Algerian Muslims) displaced by emergence of new sovereign states in North Africa and Indochina (*The New York Times*, December 1961, November 1962). The Netherlands, tiny and

crowded, welcomed and settled 230,000 refugees from Indonesia (Kraak, *Repatriation of the Dutch from Indonesia*). Turkey resettled 150,000 Turks expelled by the
Communist regime in Bulgaria (Kostarisk, *Turkish Resettlement of Bulgarian Turks* [1957]).

The standards of civilized duty are even plainer when
circumstances permit exchanges of populations which will
ease majority-minority relations, and therefore international tensions across new frontiers, as with the Greco-
Turkish exchange of populations after World War I, or the
less orderly Hindu-Muslim exchanges on the partition of
India in 1948. In such cases (and the Arab-Israeli case
is such a case par excellence) the duties of humanity are
reinforced by the concern of the international community
to reduce tension and stabilize frontiers. The default of the
Arab states has usually been accompanied, significantly,
by the very opposite motives—of increasing tension with
Israel, and undermining the stability of the frontiers.

It will be said, no doubt, by many who support the
Arab cause that the claims of Palestinian Arabs do not
rest merely on their displacement but rest on other titles.

It may, for example, be said (and it is usually implied
even when it is not said) that, after all, Arab armies did
conquer Palestine in the seventh century, whereas (for
example) the Jews displaced from Iraq and Yemen were
never conquerors of Iraq or Yemen. This raises the rather
important question whether a military victory, in the
course of an imperialist ancestral incursion thirteen centuries before, is entitled to some real priority over an
Israeli victory in two wars of self-defense, in 1948 or in
1967, and if so, on what grounds?

Anyone, indeed, with an aptitude for moral speculation of this kind would probably also be interested in the
question whether any moral priority attaches to that thir-
teen-century-old Arab conquest as against the still older
Israelite conquest of the land from the Hittites and Philis-
tines in the thirteenth century B.C.E., or as against the undoubted governance of the land by a succession of Jewish
judges and kings for many centuries thereafter? And, if
he thought that there was such a priority, he would no
doubt wish to find grounds for this.

All this is not to suggest that I myself would want to rest judgment on any such arguments, or that I invite the reader to do so. Quite on the contrary. I am rather saying that if we are beguiled by titles based on ancient Arab conquest, we cannot consistently dismiss from history the even more ancient Jewish conquest. If, on the other hand, we are beguiled by more recent Arab conquest, then we must face the fact that, among other titles, the present state of Israel rests on its military ability in our own age to defeat open aggression from the Arab states of the region, more than once and against extremely heavy odds.

It is, of course, absurd to attribute moral value to conquest as such or to mere antiquity or mere modernity of conquest, whether by Jew or Arab. Title from ancient conquest, no longer supported by possession, has an extra measure of absurdity. For it would call for dismemberment of many existing states, whenever we find surviving descendants of their earliest known conquerors, so that their erstwhile lands can be restored. There would be an intriguing choice of claimants, to be sure, for the rightful title to displace the English in the United Kingdom! The fates of numerous states of the Americas, North, Central, and South, would need much pondering. On grounds of modernity of conquest, if that test is chosen, the facts also support the Israeli claim. If we regard both antiquity and modernity of conquest as indecisive, one must ask what other moral grounds there can be for questioning Israel's possession, based as this is on rightful entry under international law, and twice successfully sustained against external aggression in a land with which her people have three millennia of continuing national attachments.

Indeed, according to some advanced anticolonialist ideas of our age, it is the Arab claims in Palestine and not those of Israel which would be in need of justification. One might, for instance, apply to the Palestine question the thesis of the notable international law historian Charles Alexandrowicz concerning the "reversion to sovereignty" of peoples overrun by foreign dominators centuries ago. It would be easy, under this thesis, to see the sovereignty of Israel in its land as but the just restoration of its former independent life and polity, after liberation from colonizers planted in its homeland by former Arab and Turkish imperialist conquerors. For, according to this thesis, the people of an ancient civilization which controlled its own internal and external affairs centuries ago, and was then submerged by foreign conquest or other domination, must be regarded as still maintaining its sovereignty throughout. So that even in our own age, centuries later, when its polity is restored in its original land, it must be regarded not as a new sovereign state asking for recognition, but as an old state reverting as of right to its former sovereignty.[6]

This theory, deeply responsive as it obviously is to the spirit of decolonization, may be thought to express a principle of morals and justice, rather than of technical international law. On any basis, however, its application to the Arab-Israeli conflict is of deep interest. It is clear that in the territory now in dispute, there were for about seven centuries both an advanced Jewish civilization and statehood; that for six centuries thereafter, there was a predominantly Jewish population and autonomous government; and that despite a succession of cruel centuries marked by repeated imperialist invasions and conquests, and the accompanying suppressions, decimations, and dispersions of the Jewish people, it has remained until today the center of Jewish religious, cultural, and social concern.

It is clear, too, that no identifiable people now survives which can show any similar special relation to the centuries of Jewish statehood there. From this standpoint the Palestinian Arabs were but colonists under the wing of imperial conquerors;[7] colonists, moreover, who never established there any specific local civilization or any independent political life. So far are we from any self-evident

---

[6] C. H. Alexandrowicz, "New and Original States: The Issue of Reversion to Sovereignty," *International Affairs* 45 (1969): 465–80.

[7] The common Arab argument according to which the Arabs of Palestine are but the descendants of the original Jewish and Canaanite population scarcely merits serious consideration. It is well known among competent historians that following the Roman destruction of Jerusalem in 70 A.D., and even more after Hadrian's suppression of the Bar Cochba struggle for liberation half a century later, Palestine because virtually depopulated, its inhabitants being either massacred or exiled.

validity of Arab claims to Palestine, even in terms of advanced anticolonialist ideas.

If Arab title from conquest thus fails, what of the rights of majorities? It is commonly urged as decisive, on behalf of the Palestine Arabs, that there were, at any rate, more Arabs than Jews living in Palestine when it was designated in 1917 as a national home for the Jewish people.

A majority which controls a state often does, of course, assert a right to forbid access by others which might disturb its predominance. Conceivably one might extend some analogous right to a majority living in a country which has built a distinctive national life fully identified with that country, even though that country is not an independent state. But of course, as we have seen, the Arabs of Palestine did not show any such specific national distinctiveness at any relevant time. Arabs of Palestine have until only recently identified themselves with Haifa or Jerusalem or Nablus or Jericho rather than with Palestine as a country. And non-Jewish as well as Jewish commentators have reminded us that the population of Palestine since the Arab conquest has never been exclusively Arab or Muslim. Jews, Christians, and others have always remained present in numbers varying with the degree of oppression and hardship visited by the rulers on non-Muslims.

In terms of moral principle, moreover, the Arab claim to exclude Jews after World War I (and now by the Palestinian national covenant retrospectively to expel all who thereafter entered) based merely on their own majority numbers proves far too much. For by it, present Jewish majority predominance would give a similar right of exclusive control, and one reinforced by the undoubted existence of the nation and state of Israel, and its capacity to meet external aggression, not to speak of the international instruments and sanctions of two world organizations confirming its basis. Nor does it make much difference to think in terms of power to exclude new entries but not to exclude reentries. A great number, probably now approaching a majority of individuals who remain enrolled as "Palestinian refugees" with UNWRA, have never lived in that part of Palestine which is now Israel. The basis of their claims to "reenter" could not be any different from the right to "reenter" of the descendants of Jewish refugees driven from their Palestinian homeland by successive waves of conquerors, including Arab conquerors.

In historical fact, of course, the Arabs' argument on this head is somewhat weaker than this. They did succeed by pressure on the British mandatory in limiting reentry of Jews to the mandate-declared "Jewish national home." Tests of "economic absorptive capacity" were then imposed against the Jews, and restrictive estimates were made of this capacity which history has shown to be quite arbitrary. The state of Israel has already shown that many times more than those estimates can live and flourish in an area smaller than what was at the mandatory's disposal. The claim that Jews at the time could only enter by displacing Arabs is shown by the same token to have had little basis.

It is also clear that no Arab refugee problem resulted from Jewish reentry and settlement.[8] Right until the critical years of World War II, the mandatory power continued to hold a considerable reserve of public lands, access to which was barred to Jewish settlement. This, in turn, created a seller's market in land in which Palestinian Arabs were able (and very ready) to reap high profits from the urgent aspirations of Jews to restore to cultivation a homeland where they could live as of right. Indeed, it was common knowledge, noted by royal commissions, that this reactivation of the land by Jewish resettlement attracted substantial immigration from surrounding Arab countries, increasing rather than diminishing the local Arab population.

The problem of displaced Arabs, now featured as part of the hard core of the Arab-Israel problem, was thus not a product of the Jewish reentry after World War I, but a by-product of the Arab states' resort to military force

---

[8] It is significant in this regard that Article 5 of the covenant only admits as Arab citizens of the there proposed Arab Palestine, Arabs living permanently there until 1947, even though "the Zionist invasion" under Article 6 was officially dated from 1917. Even in the Arab version of history, then, it is assumed that no substantial number of Arabs were displaced before 1947.

in 1948, in order to destroy the state of Israel.[9] I have here treated it not simply on that basis, but (in broader perspective) as an incidental wrong arising from the distribution made between the Arab and Jewish peoples. And I have shown that it was a wrong, along with the parallel displacement of Jews from Arab lands, for which the Arab states and Israel together, in due proportion, have duties to make redress.

It also is difficult to see how the state of Israel (or any other state similarly placed), having repelled Arab aggression, could be expected to invite wholesale Arab return. "Adherence to the enemy" in time of war is mostly a capital offense even in highly civilized countries.[10] In this light Israel's offering to readmit and resettle 100,000 refugees (about 20 percent of the total), in addition to actually receiving back 28,000 returnees whose status it legalized, and maintaining a steady willingness to contribute to resettlement of the rest, may be regarded as a fair response.[11]

---

[9] The official Israel view is more dour than this. See, e.g., Foreign Minister Abba Eban, in *GAOR*, 8th Sess., 449th Plenary Meeting, September 29, 1953, p. 215: "Can Governments really create a vast human problem by their aggression, possess the full capacity to solve it, receive bountiful international aid towards its solution, and then, with all that accumulation of responsibility upon their hands, refuse to join in the acceptance of any permanent responsibility for the fate and future of their own kith and kin?"

[10] See recently Y. Harkabi et al., *Time Bomb in the Middle East* (1970), p. 20, quoting Walid al-Qamhawi, *Disaster in the Arab Fatherland*: "These factors, the collective fear, moral disintegration and chaos in every domain were what displaced the Arabs from Tiberias, Haifa, Jaffa and tens of cities and villages." Harkabi claims that the supposed massacre of Arabs at the village of Deir Yassin in April 1948, later alleged to have triggered the flight, was scarcely mentioned in the contemporary reporting and only began to be offered as an explanation many months later.

[11] See the UN Conciliation Commission General Progress Report, December 11, 1949, to October 23, 1950, *GAOR*, 5th Sess., Supp. 18 (A/1367 Rev. 1); and cf. *Israel and the United Nations* (1956), p. 151. Between 1952 and 1954 the release of all outstanding balances and safe custody articles of refugees in banks in Israel was agreed on and Israel also cooperated with the Conciliation Commission's experts in identifying and assessing refugees'

It is in no way inconsistent with what I have said that nostalgic love of their former homes in Haifa, Jaffa, or elsewhere must be very strong among many Palestinian refugees, especially where the "host" Arab country has not enabled them to strike new roots in the country of refuge. Nostalgia in itself is an attachment of the individual heart and imagination. It may or may not also reflect that kind of shared group consciousness, experience and culture which manifest a specific peoplehood. Whether an Arab from Haifa, in 1948, who chose to leave his home and his Jewish fellow citizens in obedience to the call of Arab armies advancing to destroy them now manifests but a painful individual nostalgia, or a real "national" insurgence, may be difficult to say. And this is not made easier by the fanatical campaigns of inculcation of hatred against Israel, especially among the refugees, mounted for a score of years by the Arab states.

I have already pointed out that, even if we assume that such a group consciousness did arise in the sixties, it would have no retroactive virtue to divest the modest entitlement allotted to Israel in the basic territorial distribution of nearly half a century before. Now I will take account of some other aspects of the assumed recent upsurgence of Palestinian consciousness.

In the light of history, the main evidence of a specifically Palestinian peoplehood appears to date from the first "Palestinian congress" convened in Jordan-occupied Jerusalem in May 1964, or perhaps (as already noted), from the agitation of the notion of a "Palestinian entity" at Arab League meetings of 1959, and from about the same time among refugees. If some kind of Palestinian peoplehood is now to be accepted as a present fact, it

---

land holdings (*GAOR*, 7th Sess., Agenda Item 67, p. 5; *Twelfth Progress Report of the Conciliation Commission, Supplementary Report*, p. 8). The Arab position has, of course, insisted from the start that no considerations of Israel's security could be taken into account as regards repatriation of all refugees. See Doc. A/1367 Rev. 1, cited above.

The UN Conciliation Commission's proposal circulated to the delegations at the meeting on August 15, 1949, was for "the repatriation of refugees in Israel-controlled territory and in the resettlement of those not repatriated in Arab countries or in the zone of Palestine not under Israel control."

would certainly become relevant to the present prospects of future peace both among the Arab states, and between them and Israel, and later sections will deal with the manner of this relevance.

It could not, however, justify the deliberate destruction by the Arab states' military aggression of 1948 of the Palestinian Arab state proposed under the partition plan of 1947 accepted by Israel, any more than it could justify their then design of destroying the state of Israel. Nor, for that matter, could such late emergence of a Palestinian peoplehood afford ground (even if the enterprise were otherwise plausible) for reversing, at the present expense of the state of Israel, all the consequences of such repeated Arab state aggression. The mills of history no doubt grind slowly; but they also sometimes grind exceedingly sure.

Further, after the full sincerity of the adult exile's nostalgia is accepted, honest moral judgment still has to reject the inculcation in the next generation, who do not share that nostalgia, of a lamentable substitute consisting of hatred and lust for "revenge," which we find a Nashashibi declaring to be dearer even than the "homeland" itself.[12] This would be a lamentable moral corruption and crippling of children even if there were (as I have shown there is not) any valid ground for targeting these passions against Jews and Israel, rather than elsewhere. Hatred and vengefulness are not to be confused with courage and fighting spirit. The Jews, whose courage and fighting spirit few now doubt, have in the past (including an all too recent past) suffered wrongs of humiliation, oppression and barbaric slaughter, and of expulsion from a multitude of lands, including their own ancient homeland of Israel.

Even the proudest "know-nothings" of a younger generation which hungers for universal justice must be aware of this massively cruel, unjust, and tragic story. Yet even all this never led the Jews in any part of their bitter exile

---

[12] Nasir ad-Din an-Nashashibi, *Return Ticket* (Beirut, 1962), quoted at length and discussed in both its positive and negative aspects in Harkabi, *Position of the Palestinians*, pp. 4–6. Cf. the similar point made about teachers and textbooks in UNRWA schools, Peretz, op. cit., pp. 322, 325.

to corrupt oncoming generations with such seething hate
and vengefulness for their authentic living oppressors.

It is difficult to escape the impression that an important
part of the present conflict arises from a desperate search
to find scapegoats for mistakes and failures. It should
perhaps be expected that the refugees as well as the Arab
states should seek to project onto Israel the blame for
their own failures of judgment and will and frustrated
rivalries. Side by side with Israel are a number of more
ghostly scapegoats—"imperialism," an Arab-Soviet golem
called "Nazi-Zionism," and (at critical moments) some
rather more tangible ones, like the United States and the
United Kingdom. What is more complex and interesting is
the difficulties of the Palestinians in fixing their group
identity and defining their homeland, at least in part due to
their reluctance to face the fact that it is probably Jordan
rather than Israel which deprives them of their claimed
rights.

The Palestine within the promise to the Jewish people
in 1917 embraced both Cisjordan and Transjordan. This
Palestine on both sides of the Jordan was within the mandate requested by Britain and granted by the League of
Nations in 1922. At that time, however, Transjordan
was, at Britain's insistence, and over the protests of Jewish
organizations, taken out of the mandate provision for the
establishment of a Jewish national home and allocated to
the creation within Palestine of the emirate of Transjordan. So that when Transjordan in due course became independent in 1946, the new state was in fact, and under
the name of Jordan still remains, the Arab state within
Palestine. What is now called the West Bank as well as
Gaza and Jerusalem remained within the provision for a
Jewish national home until, in 1948, the state of Israel
was established, and Jordan, in attacking that state, seized
the West Bank and Jerusalem, as Egypt seized Gaza. This
further expansion of its territory by Jordan, whatever
its international standing, could only reconfirm Jordan's
character as an Arab state within Palestine. If it was not
called the Palestine Arab state, this was either semantic
evasion or it was only an idiosyncrasy of the Hashemite

monarch, for neither of which Israel can be held responsible.

Transjordan, then, on its creation in 1922, either had the function of a Palestinian Arab state, or it had no function but that of creating another throne for a Hashemite to sit on. The latter function has certainly ceased to suffice when 60 percent of its people are (as they have been since 1948) Palestinians, and when Palestinian peoplehood is assumed to be a present reality, claimant for a homeland. The available solution, rationally speaking, is for Jordan, with or without the West Bank and Gaza, to be the Palestinian Arab state. This solution, however, King Hussein's bedouin-supported regime has obviously rejected, even during its military occupation and attempted annexation of the West Bank before 1967.

The turning of the self-determination demand into a demand for the dismantling of Israel, in which Jordan and other Arab states could be expected to join, thus has the supreme attraction for the Arab side of avoiding, or at least postponing, the day when the Palestinians and the Jordanian government must settle the real issue between themselves.[13] It also has the attraction of postponing problems arising from the divisive ambitions of Syria, Iraq, and Egypt in the ultimate fate of the West and the East Bank of the Jordan, which a Jordanian-Palestinian Arab settlement would bring to a head. The recurrent crises in Jordan (for instance in September 1970), when the real issue comes close to the surface, put this analysis beyond doubt.[14]

In this situation all the parties concerned, and especially the Palestinians in their relative weakness, find it easier to join in a common campaign of blame and hate against Israel than to face the rather clear issues between them-

---

[13] It is tempting, but of course inconclusive, to recall in this context the words of the noted "Adonis" that "Arab man wants to make history while he is in fact running away from it" (quoted by Shamir, op. cit., pp. 5, 12).

[14] According to the al-Fatah spokesman in Cairo on September 24, 1970, "the only solution to the Jordan crisis is for the King to abdicate and leave the country" (*The Australian*, September 25, 1970; and cf. conversely the account of the bedouin royalist position by the *Guardian* (London) correspondent, reprinted in *The Australian*, September 25, 1970).

selves which must precede an Arab-Israeli settlement. At the present stage, accusation is focused on the spurious charge (covering over the basic inter-Arab conflicts) that what blocks the emergence of "Palestinian" consciousness and the "Palestinian entity" into Palestinian statehood is a refusal by Israel to recognize the claims of the Palestinians. The noise of internal Arab conflict can then be muffled by a chorus of denunciation and demands for the destruction of the state of Israel as the first precondition of Palestinian self-fulfillment.

Some thoughtful and sincere Israelis also advocate that Israel should immediately declare its "recognition" of a "Palestinian Arab" right of self-determination, though (quite unlike the Arab advocates) they do not conceive this to require the dismantling of Israel. They rather take the ground that Israel's recognition could in some way assist the conditions of Palestinian political emancipation in Jordan and territory of the West Bank. I would myself tend toward a similar view, adding, however, that an Israel reaffirmation of this sort would serve to restress Israel's constant support for the self-determination principle during the decolonizing age just past, and also help to return the attention of Arab states and Palestinians from their spurious charges against Israel to the real issues which must first be adjusted among themselves.

Well-intentioned criticisms of Israel policy should stop short of suggesting that any Israeli initiative could be decisive. To go further is merely to reinforce the use of a spurious issue as a pretext for refusing to settle internal Arab differences, and for demanding the destruction of Israel as cover for the refusal.

Probably for most Arabs living under Israeli administration their main present concerns are to live their daily lives free from terrorist violence[15] and from the Israeli

---

[15] In March 1970 alone, 103 Gaza inhabitants were wounded and 7 killed by Arab terrorist attacks, 5 killings being deliberate murders. According to reports of August 1970, there had been 15 political murders by terrorists between mid-July and mid-August, "apparently trying to liquidate Arabs suspected of collaborating with the Israel authorities" (*The Australian*, August 13, 1970; *JPW*, August 3, 1970).

authorities' countermeasures, to avoid future Arab reprisals for collaboration with the Israelis, and (above all) not to be caught within the major violence of renewed general hostilities. They cooperate only to a notably small extent in terrorist violence, and the degree of violence which in turn the terrorist groups now find it necessary to use against even the strongly anti-Israel Gaza Arabs suggests that there may be a real degree of willingness to cooperate with the Israelis. Yet, of course, on the other hand, their uncertainty as to the future territorial settlement deters them from such cooperation with the Israelis as might expose them to the malice of a future Arab regime.

In great contrast to this, "Palestinians" living outside the administered territories lack, as the above account of Article 6 of the covenant indicates, these motives of restraint, and their leaders have indeed strong motives driving them toward irresponsibility, and thrive on the sharpening and widening of the conflict. They are rabidly opposed, as Article 21 testifies, to what is called "all plans that aim at the settlement of the Palestine issue," and indeed openly oppose any conceivable solution.[16]

This shows that in the territorial distribution of ex-Turkish lands after World War I, the rival claimants were the Jews of the world on the one hand, and the Arabs of the Middle East (including the Arabs living in Palestine) on the other. The Arabs in Palestine had then no specific identity as a separate people with an additional claim as such. Both those beneficiaries in the distribution of half a century ago, shared the duty to make good, in proportion to their benefits, any incidental wrongs which may have been done. This duty extended both to Arabs in Palestine and to Jews throughout the Arab countries, who were affected by the consequences of that distribution. We have seen that it was the Arab people which received (in the form of a dozen and more Arab States) the lion's share of the distribution, and yet that it was Israel which (despite

---

[16] See also, for some additional documentation, the shorter account in Julius Stone, "Peace and the Palestinians," *New York Journal of International Law and Politics*, Winter 1970.

that fact) assumed the full burdens of resettling and rehabilitating more than half the displaced persons concerned, including a substantial number of Arabs.

The growth of more specific Palestinian Arab consciousness in the last decade, even if this now represents a
peoplehood entitled to self-determination, cannot be projected back into time so as to invalidate a distribution of
decades before. And this is the more so since, in all but
name, there is an already existing Arab state in Palestine
through which this people can fulfill itself. The territory of
present Jordan was cut out of the Palestine in which establishment of a national home for the Jewish people was
originally promised, constituting two thirds of its area.
Jordan is a Palestinian Arab state not only in that sense,
but because more than sixty percent of its population are
"Palestinian Arabs" in the strictest sense.

The crux, therefore, of the "Palestinian question" lies
between the Palestinian Arabs and the Hashemite Kingdom of Jordan, with collateral concerns of some Arab
states. Israel's contribution to solving it, whether in relation to frontiers or otherwise, must necessarily await some
progress in the settlement of the essentially domestic Arab
questions.

For complex reasons, centered on the unwillingness of
the Palestinian Arab leaders and Arab states to face these
domestic Arab issues, they have attempted to conceal it by
presenting the existence of the state of Israel as the obstacle to fulfillment of the Palestinian Arab aspirations.
This spurious version of the issues is explicit in the Palestinian National Covenant as amended in 1968. Article 6
requires in effect the expulsion of about two million Jews
from Israel, and Article 21 rejects every solution that is a
substitute for "a complete liberation" of Palestine, as
well as "all plans which aim at the settlement of the Palestine issue or its internationalization."

The Arab states seem thus, for the moment, to have
locked themselves in by endorsing the claimed "vanguard"
role of the "Palestine liberation" groups, in diversion from
their own military setbacks. For this expediency has in
turn involved endorsement by these states of the falsifica-
tion of the issues by which the leaders of these groups have
tried to avoid (or at least defer) the real issue, which lies

between them and Jordan. The fact remains that it is Jordan which, both historically and demographically, holds the key to the solution of the Palestinian question; while the spurious version presents the issue as a demand for destruction of the state of Israel to which that state cannot be expected to agree. The Arab states are thus committed to military efforts going well beyond their own vital concerns, and all the means and channels of the search for peace are blocked.

This situation represents a fatal circle, not only of Arab defeat and frustration in war, but also of defeat and frustration of their long-term interests and those of the Palestinian Arabs, not to speak of the rest of the world, in any genuine movement toward peace in the region. Until some degree of "self-liberation" is achieved by the Arab states from the more impossible demands of the leadership of the "liberation" Palestine groups, no Israel initiative could release West Bank and Gaza Arabs from the pressures of Arab states and terrorists, or the Arab states from manipulation by the Palestinian leadership, so as to permit fruitful negotiation to begin. If there is hope of this, it must come from self-interested recognition by Jordan or Egypt or both, that the spurious history-reversing "aims" of the present Palestinian leadership cannot succeed.

The Failure of the Fedayeen

Carl Gershman

CARL GERSHMAN—young writer and political activist, executive director of the Youth Committee
for Peace and Democracy in the Middle East, and
Vice Chairman of the Young People's Socialist
League.

In September 1970 the "Palestinian revolution" experienced the most crushing defeat in its short history.
Ironically, the fedayeen[1] did not fall at the hands of Israel,
the object of their most profound hatred and the cause, as
they have said time and again, of all their difficulties. The
defeat was administered by Jordan's King Hussein, a
monarch of limited popularity who few thought could
withstand the challenge of the fedayeen.

Once the bitter fighting had subsided in Amman, Irbid,
Jerash, Es Salt, and other Jordanian cities, a myth was
perhaps laid to rest. It was the myth of the heroic invinci-
bility of the fedayeen. Like all myths, it came into being
because there were people who needed to believe in it. The
Arabs, who saw their regular armies humiliated in the
Six-Day War, accepted the myth because they needed
revolutionary heroes who would redeem Arab pride and
self-respect. In the Western world, most of those who
identified with the New Left embraced the myth because
they too needed revolutionary heroes, though for different
and more complex reasons. The fedayeen did all they could
to popularize the myth because without it the reality of

---

[1] "Fedayeen," which comes from the Arab root "sacrifice," is
the word used to designate all Arab irregulars fighting against
Israel.

their weakness would intrude to lower their morale, blemish their image, and weaken their support.

For three years following the Six-Day War, the fedayeen were granted a period of grace. Despite a remarkably unimpressive military record, their popularity soared. Their accounts of guerrilla exploits against Israel, while sometimes fabricated and often grossly exaggerated, were believed by people hungry for victory. Their movement quickly gained momentum and became a threat, not so much to Israel as to Hussein, who had collaborated with them against "the Zionist enemy."

As the influence of the fedayeen grew, they began to challenge the authority and the pride of the Jordanian army. "They behaved as though they were on conquered territory," a Jordanian officer said of the fedayeen soon after the civil war. "You can't imagine how many times I was stopped by Palestinian militiamen in the street and frisked and quizzed. They had no scruples about 'requisitioning' our cars, or even, sometimes, hurling insults at us."[2]

The fedayeen not only antagonized Hussein's army and created a threat to internal order in Jordan; they also fought among themselves. In the early days of September, as the civil war in Jordan was approaching its climax, conflicts broke out between al-Fatah and the Popular Front for the Liberation of Palestine (PFLP), two rival fedayeen groups. According to a report by Jon Kimche,[3] on September 6 a group of men attacked the offices of *al-Hadaf*, a Beirut weekly which is the unofficial organ of the PFLP, beating up its editor and destroying its press. Commenting on the attack two days later, a PFLP official charged that it had been carried out "not by the Nasserites or the supporters of King Hussein but by the evil criminal forces of al-Fatah bent on silencing the voice of truth and halting the activities of the freedom fighters." He referred to similar attacks in the past and concluded:

---

[2] Eric Rouleau, *Le Monde Weekly*, December 16, 1970.
[3] Jon Kimche, *New Middle East*, October 1970.

We shall carry on our struggle against the evil of Yasir
Arafat, Hussein, and Nasser until they are all removed
from the scene of Arab affairs. There is no force in the
world that can stop us from liberating Palestine and
liquidating Israel . . .

Estimates of the casualties suffered by the fedayeen
during the civil war vary from five hundred to several
thousand. But whatever the precise figure, it is clear that
they endured an incalculable loss in influence, prestige,
and momentum. By February 1971, according to Israeli
sources, the real military power of the fedayeen had declined to 30 percent of their active forces in mid-1970, as
continued harassment by Jordanian authorities and successive military defeats brought on mass desertions. At the
height of their activities along the Jordan River, the fedayeen were responsible for thirty operations a day. By
February the number of incidents was down to about five
a week, and most of these were shootings across the river.

Moreover, in the months following the civil war, Jordanian authorities reinforced their hold over the refugee
camps which had previously been centers of support for
Fatah. Gradually the fedayeen were driven out of the cities.
On April 6, following a new round of fighting in Amman
and Irbid, Hussein issued an ultimatum that the fedayeen
withdraw their men and weapons from the cities to rural
bases in the Jordan Valley. The withdrawal, which Fatah
second-in-command Salah Halaf called an "inevitable
necessity," began on the following day.

Financial contributions to the fedayeen declined along
with their prestige. At the Eighth Palestinian National
Congress held in Cairo during the first week of March
1971, Dr. Zuheir al-Alami, the head of the Palestine National Fund, submitted a budget report which showed a
deficit for the first time in the seven-year history of the
Palestine Liberation Organization (PLO), the political
umbrella of all the fedayeen groups. The report attributed the financial crisis to a decline in the popularity of
the fedayeen and to the failure of the Arab League states
to honor their commitments to the PLO.

Nor was the defeat of the fedayeen in Jordan the only
reason for their loss of popularity. On December 21,

1970, *Newsweek* magazine, which only a year before had done a glowing feature on "The Children of the Storm," quoted a disillusioned Palestinian intellectual as saying:

> We've backed the fedayeen for three years with all the money and affection we could muster and what did they accomplish? They picked fights with the Lebanese and Jordanian armies instead of enlisting their help. They brought death and destruction to Arab cities, but they never established a single base on the occupied west bank. Their military effectiveness against Israel has been negligible and their Arab politics abominable.

During the months of their decline, the fedayeen found it more necessary than ever to resort to their long-established practice of "exaggerations in propaganda."[4] Such exaggerations generally consist in reporting imaginary operations and claiming credit for any kind of accident that takes place in Israel. For example, on February 27, 1971, Damascus radio reported the following series of "operations":

> On February 25 an El Al Boeing collided with a truck at Lod airport. The same day an announcement said that an El Al Boeing would not take off because of damage. Thus *two* aircraft were out of commission.
> The same day the funeral took place of General (reserve) Ilan . . . Was he really killed in a road accident?
> In Tel Aviv fire broke out in a store in Ben Hillel Street.
> All these occurred on one day. Is there no hidden hand behind those occurrences?

That same "hidden hand" has been responsible for the "murder" of Prime Minister Levi Eshkol, the "wounding" of Defense Minister Moshe Dayan, and the "destruction" of General Rabin's garage along with countless military and oil installations, factories, planes, and trains. The fedayeen have not been unaware of the danger that such

---

[4] Abu Haled Hussein of the Popular Front general command has criticized the armed struggle command of the fedayeen for its inability to "stop exaggerations in propaganda" (*al-Anwar* [Beirut], February 15, 1970).

extraordinary claims can harm their movement. In February 1969 *al-Hurriya*, a Lebanese weekly, quoted a Fatah leader as saying:

> The purpose of the exaggeration is to placate the Arab masses, especially the Arab people surrounding Israel, by telling them there are fighters everywhere working for the liberation of Palestine . . . But when disappointment comes I believe that the enthusiasm of the Arab masses and their support for fedayeen action will decrease considerably.

This prediction has now become a reality.

Serious internal conflicts accompanied the political and military decline of the fedayeen. Soon after the civil war Mamduh Saidam, the head of Fatah's military branch el-Assifa, who reportedly holds rightist views, unsuccessfully attempted to purge two leftist leaders of Fatah's political wing, Faruk el-Kadumi and Salah Halaf, who were accused of surrendering to Hussein at the height of the fighting in September. Arafat himself was not challenged at the time, but in January, during a meeting of Fatah's forty-member revolutionary council, he narrowly survived a challenge from the leftist political wing led by el-Kadumi. Voted out of office in a secret ballot, Arafat saved himself by demanding an open vote.

The Eighth Palestinian National Congress was also marked by internal conflicts which are likely to grow worse. Brigadier Abdul-Razzak Yehia, commander-in-chief of the Palestine Liberation Army (PLA), called upon the PLO to dissolve the central committee headed by Arafat.[5] Charging that "national disasters" had taken

---

[5] T. E. Lawrence one remarked that "Arab unity is a madman's notion," and nothing illustrates this better than the structure of the fedayeen movement, which consists of some one hundred guerrilla groups, the eleven most powerful being part of the PLO, which is known as the "terminal station of all Palestinian trains." There is division within groups (as in the case of Fatah), between groups (Fatah and the PFLP, for example), and between the various superstructures of the PLO (the division between the PLA, which consists of eight thousand men stationed mostly in Syria, and the Central Committee, which oversees the eleven fedayeen groups, is an example). The guerrillas have said that this leads to "fruitful competition," but the real result has been

place under the current "dictatorial" leadership, Yehia
said that the political and military groups within the PLO
should be brought together under a new leadership. A
confrontation between Yehia and Arafat was avoided
when the congress adopted a previous resolution which
called for a "military merger" between the fedayeen
groups and the PLA "within the next three months."
Arafat, however, lost some ground as the resolution also
stated that "the commander of the merged armed forces
and its Chief of Staff will be appointed by the new political
leadership."

Fatah and the PLFP also clashed at the congress as
Arafat submitted a six-point "national merger plan" for
the eleven groups within the PLO. PFLP resisted this, wanting no limit on its independence. A compromise resolution
was adopted settling the dispute temporarily, but the conflict revealed a deeper division over the nature of the
battle against Israel, and this may plague the organization
in the future.

It appears that the fedayeen have become too weak to
prevent a political settlement between Egypt, Jordan, and
Israel. Concerned now primarily with their own survival, they may have to go along passively with steps toward such a settlement, though never, of course, agreeing
to give up their own struggle against Israel. This position is
taken by leading elements in Fatah and opposed by the
PFLP. On January 20, 1971, Cairo's semiofficial daily
al-Ahram stated that the central committee of the PLO
"has decided to support political activity by Arab states to
liquidate the results of Israel's aggression." *Al-Ahram*
quoted a PLO spokesman as saying that "this is in accord with Nasser's view that there is no contradiction be-

---

chaos. One practice common among the fedayeen is "the stealing
of announcements," whereby several guerrilla groups claim the
credit for an action carried out or just announced by one of their
rivals. Attempts have been made to eliminate the "unfruitful" aspects of such competition through an endless number of coordinating bodies and "central commands." Such bodies accomplish
little more than to reveal the weak and disorganized state of the
fedayeen movement. During the September civil war two new co-
ordinating bodies were created, the Unified Command in Jordan
and the Supreme Committee for Palestinian Affairs in Lebanon,
but unity remained as elusive as ever.

tween Egypt's acceptance of the Security Council Resolution and the U.S. initiative on the one hand and the right of the Resistance to carry on with armed struggle on the other." The following day the PLO central committee reiterated its oppositon to the UN Resolution, but it did not deny the validity to the claims made in *al-Ahram*.

The *al-Ahram* disclosure, which came as a surprise to many people, only brought into the open a private agreement that Nasser had worked out with Arafat in August 1970. At the time, Nasser had obtained Arafat's approval of Egyptian efforts to reach a political settlement in exchange for Nasser's guarantee that such a settlement would not compromise the fedayeen struggle against Israel. The agreement was not disclosed, though a marked improvement was noticed in Egyptian-fedayeen relations.[6] The skyjackings and the destruction of the hijacked planes carried out the following week by the PFLP showed its opposition to any political settlement.

Nasser kept the agreement secret, as he had promised Arafat, and the central committee of the PLO ceased its direct criticism of his government. Sadat's subsequent decision to make the agreement public reflects his own weakness since he obviously feels it necessary to gain Fatah's public approval of his policies. Divisions over the issue of a political settlement have by no means been settled within the PLO, and there is likely to be more internal conflict if the Jarring talks produce any results.

The *al-Ahram* disclosure does not mean that the fedayeen are now more "moderate," but only that they are not strong enough to act independently of Egypt. The disclosure also underlines an aspect of Egyptian policy that is often overlooked in the West. The Egyptian leaders see the "1967 problem" as distinct from the "1948 problem." The steps they have taken toward a political solution of the former does not mean that they have given up on "solving" the latter. Speaking to the fedayeen at the Eighth Congress, Sadat told them that "the liberation of the territories is what we have chosen *for this stage*. Revolutionary Arab thought must define the *stages* of a consistent

---

[6] "Improvement Seen in Relations Between Nasser and Guerrillas," *The New York Times*, August 30, 1970.

and diligent policy out of the necessity that all the various strategies used in the confrontation with the enemy should flow out of one grand strategy. This will assure the victory of the Arab will." (Italics added.) Writing in *al-Ahram* on February 26, 1971, its editor Mohammed Hassanein Heykal criticized those who want to eliminate Israel before forcing Israel to return to its 1967 borders. "Some of us," he wrote, "have erred in commencing the latter step before the former."

For the present, the Egyptians have brought the fedayeen into line with their policy of two stages, and it is unlikely that the guerrillas will give them trouble in the near future. The weakness of the fedayeen was demonstrated most clearly in May during Secretary of State Rogers's visit to Amman for talks with Hussein. The terrorists had called a three-hour general strike to protest the visit, but it failed to materialize. Before the civil war in Jordan, this could not have happened.

The chief irony of the fedayeen movement—that it claims to be the vanguard of the Arab world and an independent movement of Palestinian resistance, but has actually been profoundly dependent on, and often dominated by, one or another Arab state—is reflected in its development before the Six-Day War. The use of terror by the Arabs against Jewish communities in Palestine predates the founding of the state of Israel by more than a quarter of a century.[7] But the modern fedayeen movement was not officially founded until the spring of 1955 when Nasser organized his own "irregulars" who infiltrated into Israel from Gaza and Jordan. Yasir Arafat was in Cairo at the time where he had founded the Union of Palestinian Students in Egypt, but the group did not take part in the fedayeen raids, nor did it found an independent terrorist group of its own. In 1956 Arafat took a sabotage course for Egyptian army officers, but by the end of the year he

---

[7] The description of such terrorism as "revolutionary" is not new. The official Communist party line in 1929 characterized the slaughter of the Jews in Hebron as "the revolutionary uprising of the oppressed Arabian masses" (*Leon Trotsky on the Jewish Question,* [Merit, 1970], p. 18).

was thrown into prison because of his connections with the Muslim Brotherhood, a right-wing extremist organization hostile to Nasser.[8]

Arafat left Egypt for Kuwait where he spread his ideas about the need for an independent Palestinian movement, but again it was Nasser who took action. In March 1959 Nasser issued the slogan of "the Palestinian entity" in the hope of mobilizing Palestinian nationalism to undermine Hussein and to strengthen Nasser's leadership in the Arab world. Nasser's pan-Arab dream collapsed with the disintegration of the United Arab Republic in 1961, and the Palestinians, who had hoped that Nasser would lead a united Arab world against Israel, were greatly disillusioned.

In February 1964 a summit meeting of Arab leaders was convened in Cairo where it was decided to set up the Palestine Liberation Organization. Nasser hoped to regain his prestige by sponsoring an independent Palestinian organization. The First Palestinian National Congress met in May 1964 and the PLO was founded under the leadership of Ahmed Shukeiri. The organization was independent in name only, since Shukeiri was Nasser's accomplice; but its creation did succeed, unintentionally from Nasser's point of view, in accelerating the rise of Palestinian nationalism.

During these years Arafat remained underground. In 1959 he and a group of followers founded the Palestinian National Liberation Movement, which they shortened to Fatah by reversing the first letters of the original name. They also began circulating a small monthly publication called *Our Palestine* in which they called for a Palestinian fedayeen movement independent of inter-Arab disputes. The success of the Algerian revolution in 1962 was a major turning point in Fatah's development. They thought they had found a model for their own movement, and they certainly had found a friend. Arafat had known some of the Algerian leaders during his student days in Cairo, and in December 1962 he traveled to Algiers where he met with Ben-Bella, Boumedienne, and Mohammed Khidr, the secretary of the ruling party who was a friend of Arafat

---

[8] I am indebted to Ehud Yaari's excellent book *Strike Terror* (New York: Sabra Books, 1970) for much of my historical data.

and shared his inclination toward the Muslim Brotherhood. The Algerian leaders agreed to set up a training program for Fatah guerrillas and also gave the group office space in Algiers. The training program was a total failure since most of the recruits were students from West Germany (where Fatah had a cell) who simply returned to their studies after completing the program. Nevertheless, the political support Fatah received was very helpful since the Algerians now had great prestige in the Arab world.

The failure of the training program presented Fatah with the dilemma of having a strategy but not the men to implement it. They resolved the dilemma in the only way possible: by hiring mercenaries, most of whom were recruited from among criminal and other fringe elements living in the refugee camps. These men did not turn out to be the best of fighters. In 1965, its first year of operations, Fatah conducted thirty-five raids, most of which were frustrated by Jordanian and Lebanese border guards. The first raid, on January 1, 1965, was over even before it began, as some of the terrorists backed out and informed Lebanese authorities of the group's plans. Nevertheless, "Military Communiqué No. 1" was released to the Lebanese papers which made a major story out of the "raid" until it was discovered a few days later that the announcement was false.

Arafat, to his credit, understood that his organization might get by without military successes as long as it played up its operations with dramatic "communiqués" appealing to anti-Israel sentiments and firing hopes for a massive sabotage campaign against the Jewish states. The Fatah motto was "We shall strike our enemy in order to win our people"—which indicated that the raids were intended more for propagandistic effect than military value. Sensitive to the mind and emotions of his audience, Arafat adapted his tactics accordingly. "The Arab mind," he said, "is influenced by words more than by ideas, and by ideas more than by action." Thus he built his movement, only to learn some years later that in moments of crisis a military-political movement needs more than rhetoric.

Before the Six-Day War, Fatah failed to distinguish itself either in the fedayeen movement or in the Arab world. Though it formed an alliance in 1965 with the

Syrians, who were anxious to appear as "hawks" in their struggle for Arab leadership against the Egyptian "doves," Fatah was opposed by Egypt, Jordan, and Lebanon. These Arab states were particularly hostile to Fatah's stated objective, which was "to entangle the Arab nations in a war with Israel." This did not mean that they wanted peace with Israel. Rather, they wanted to direct their own affairs and not be drawn into a conflict by a third party without being fully prepared. The Fatah was also bitterly opposed within the fedayeen movement by leaders of the PFLP and Shukeiri who were close to Nasser. Its day was not to come until after the Six-Day War when, with the collapse of the Arab armies and the humiliation of the Arab states, it appeared as what was later called "a ray of light shooting in the dark."

The fedayeen, along with the rest of the Arab world, condemned the Israeli occupation of the West Bank and the Gaza Strip, but unlike other Arabs, they also welcomed it. For the occupation removed the Palestinians from Egyptian and Jordanian control, thereby giving the fedayeen an opportunity to increase their influence in the territories without interference from the Arab states. More importantly, as a result of the war, according to a PLO statement, "the great majority of the Palestinian people are no longer a refugee people. They have become an occupied people with full freedom to choose the right road." While Mao's prescription to guerrillas that they act like fish in the sea could not apply to the fedayeen before the war, when they had to operate among the hostile Israelis, it could apply now. With the occupation, they at last had the chance to prove they had learned how to swim.

Fatah's emergence as the leading fedayeen group was due in good part to its quick recovery from the 1967 war. While much of the Arab world was immobilized by shock and despair, Fatah quickly analyzed the new situation and on June 23, 1967, only two weeks after the cease-fire, it proclaimed the "transfer of headquarters to the occupied territories."

A Fatah manifesto issued on September 1, 1967, and secretly distributed in the West Bank, outlined the strategy the terrorists hoped to follow:

The legendary resistance of Algeria, which had suffered more than a million casualties, will guide us on our way. We must understand that the foreign occupation is the beginning of a revolutionary war of liberation. Let us take as our model the struggle of the Vietnamese people, who are performing miracles against the American invader. The Zionist occupation is nothing but the rise of a new crusade.

The tactics advocated included economic boycotts, the election of local committees to give unity and direction to the fight, and the establishment of secret resistance cells which would carry out sabotage activities against communication lines, cars, and supply depots.

Such was Fatah's strategy of resistance; its failure to implement it was as complete as the defeat of the Arab armies in the Six-Day War. Why did Fatah fail? For at least three reasons: its own weaknesses, the effectiveness of Israeli policies, and the lack of cooperation from the West Bank population. Yehoshafat Harkabi, the Israeli expert on Arab affairs, has described some of the internal weaknesses which prevented the Fatah from setting up cells on the West Bank:

> Even if the manpower element of Fedayeen improved as students began to volunteer, the general level, operationally and organizationally, was low. Fedayeen members knew that there was no death sentence in Israel and that by surrendering they could save their lives and risk only a prison sentence. Fedayeen members have been extraordinarily ready to collaborate with the Israeli authorities, even if afterwards at their public trials they posed as national heroes. . . .
>
> . . . The readiness of Fatah members to inform on each other was well known by the population, as they witnessed how one arrest led to the arrest of many. Sympathy towards Fedayeen actions remained mostly on the abstract level and has not been translated into action. The Fedayeen organizations seemed too weak and fragile, and their action too sporadic to inspire the confidence needed for swaying the [West Bank] public.[9]

---

[9] *Fedayeen Action and Arab Strategy*, Institute for Strategic Studies, Adelphi Paper no. 53 (London, December 1968), pp. 26–27.

The Israelis took advantage of these weaknesses, and through a dual strategy of effective counterinsurgency and a nonoppressive—in many ways, humane—occupation policy, they quickly and with surprising ease broke the back of "the resistance." The Fatah was so deeply infiltrated that in September 1967 a captured terrorist revealed that there were already thirty-seven Palestinians accused of spying for Israel who were imprisoned by the Fatah. By the end of the year almost a thousand terrorists had been arrested, and in January 1968 the rate of arrests increased while the number of sabotage operations carried out dropped to six.

The Israelis also employed a policy of selective counterinsurgency, demolishing the homes (but never taking the lives) of those who collaborated with the Fatah. Nor was the use of selective counterinsurgency the only factor restricting collaboration. One objective of the Fatah was to force the Israelis into taking repressive measures against all West Bank Palestinians in order to provoke a mass armed uprising. By contrast, it was in the Israeli interest for normal life to return as quickly as possible to the West Bank. The terrorists, therefore, were in effect making life miserable for the West Bank Palestinians when a better alternative was possible. They came to be regarded as outsiders (as indeed they were) who wanted to use the local population for their own ends. The West Bank Palestinians, caught in the middle of a bitter conflict and suffering most from a new outbreak of hostilities, rejected the terrorists and chose to make the best of the Israeli occupation.

Any occupation is unfortunate, but that by the Israelis has been, on the whole, benign. It is certainly an improvement over the Jordanian occupation which preceded it.[10] During the eighteen years of Jordanian control, 300,000 Arabs had left the West Bank to escape depressed economic conditions brought on by discriminatory Jordanian policies. During the first three years of Israeli ad-

---

[10] The Jordanians had occupied the West Bank from 1949 to 1967 in violation of the 1947 United Nations partition resolution which created an independent Palestinian state in the area.

ministration, unemployment dropped from 11 percent to 3 percent, and living standards improved as Israeli pounds worth more than twice the West Bank's annual income were poured into services and development. A policy of open bridges was maintained to enable the Palestinians to travel to Arab states and to Israel. Moreover, the Israelis did not interfere with local self-governnent. In October 1970 a group of leading French political figures inspected the occupied territories and found that the inhabitants "had their own civil service, police, radio and press. In Jerusalem, pro-Palestinian literature was freely distributed. The Israelis even provided Government help to enable the Arabs to put up their own war memorial for Arab victims." A *New Middle East* report (February 1971) corroborates the high level of free expression which obtains on the West Bank. Surveying two new West Bank publications, *al-Basheer* and *Alwan*, the magazine notes that "it is a remarkable phenomenon not yet grasped by outside observers that the Arabic press of the Israeli-administered West Bank is now the only genuinely free Palestinian press in existence."

Still, relative peace, prosperity, and a measure of democracy are not the same as independence. Hopefully, that right will be granted the Palestinians as part of a lasting peace settlement in the Middle East. But in the context of the postwar situation in 1967, it is understandable that the West Bank population should turn its back on the cries of the terrorists and abide the Israeli administration. The terrorists had failed their major test and, in the process, suffered severe casualties. By the beginning of 1968, Fatah headquarters were transferred from the West Bank to Jordan. As Fatah leader Hani el-Hassan summed up the brief attempt at popular revolution, "It was disastrous."

Fatah responded to this military defeat by intensifying its propaganda campaign. Under normal conditions, its actions would have spoken louder than its words, but the mood of the Arab public in the years following the Six-Day War was not normal. Filling a void in the Arab national consciousness, the terrorists seemed to represent the new Arab man ready to cast aside all that was old and scarred by failure. Their calls for liberation through guerrilla warfare transfixed the Arab public, particularly the youth, who joined up in increasing numbers to fight against Israel.

But a mood cannot sustain a movement, and were it not for changes in Egyptian and Jordanian policy with regard to Fatah, it is unlikely that the organization would have grown as rapidly as it did. Egypt's reversal of its past opposition to Fatah followed the guerrilla group's unsuccessful attempt to take over the PLO at the Fourth Palestinian National Congress in July 1968. At the time the growing fedayeen movement was divided along clearly identifiable lines. Fatah was a relatively conservative, non-ideological Islamic organization calling for an independent Palestinian movement and for a jihad or holy war against Israel. (New volunteers had to swear by the Koran as part of their initiation ceremony into Fatah.) The PFLP, a much smaller and predominantly Christian group led by George Habash, appealed to pan-Arabic nationalism as opposed to Islamic sentiments, and based its claim for leadership on its radical call for a social revolution in the Arab world. In late 1968 the Democratic Popular Front for the Liberation of Palestine (DPFLP), a still more "radical" group led by Na'if el-Hawatmeh, a Jordanian, split away from the PFLP. Two other groups, El-Sa'ika and the Arab Liberation Front, where formed as extensions of the Syrian and Iraqi Ba'ath parties respectively.

Thus the fedayeen groups were divided by ideological and religious factors as well as by considerations growing out of conflicts in the Arab world between the so-called "radical" and "reactionary" Arab states. In viewing this situation, Nasser saw the fedayeen as a threat to his leadership in the Arab world and also as a weapon that could be used against him by Syria and Iraq. He concluded that he could best exercise control over the fedayeen by supporting, and having the support of, Fatah, which was the most powerful among the guerrilla groups. Nasser's new stance was responsible for resolving the power struggle within the PLO in favor of Fatah. At the Fifth Palestinian National Congress held in February 1969, Nasser delivered the opening address and Arafat was easily elected Chairman of the PLO. Nasser assured the new PLO command that "Egypt puts all its means, without any restriction, at the service of the armed resistance." The irony of Arafat's victory is that while he called for an independent Palestinian movement, he resembled Shukeiri, the original PLO leader he had bitterly opposed, in that he ruled at the behest of Nasser.

Hussein's reasons for supporting the Fatah were more parochial than Nasser's. He was concerned exclusively with regaining control of the West Bank. Fearing that Israel might either annex the area or establish an independent government there, he supported the Fatah in the hope that it could arouse the West Bank population to rebel against Israel. Hussein and Arafat could agree on immediate tactics, if nothing else, and by late 1967 they had formed a tacit alliance.

Following Fatah's withdrawal from the West Bank, it established its new headquarters in the refugee town of Karameh in the Jordan Valley. From this base the terrorists carried out raids on Israeli settlements in the Beisan Valley. Israel warned Jordan to cease giving support to the terrorists, but to no avail. Small retaliatory attacks were carried out, and finally, on March 20, 1968, a major assault was made on Karameh. The Israeli force encountered Jordanian regular units in addition to the terrorists and lost 28 men, mostly as a result of Jordanian fire. The terrorists lost 170 men and were forced to move eastward to Es Salt, Jerash, and Irbid, against the protests of the PFLP. Despite the success of the Israeli raid, Fatah propaganda transformed the battle into a great victory, and Karameh became a rallying cry for the fedayeen.

In allying himself with Fatah, Hussein made a serious mistake. He had misread Isreali intentions with regard to the West Bank, and even if he had not, Fatah had already amply demonstrated its inability to arouse an armed rebellion. More serious was Hussein's underestimation of the appeal of Fatah's propaganda. Fatah continued to gain support within Jordan, first by taking over the refugee camps and then by establishing bases in the major cities. Its numbers grew rapidly, from 1,000 at the end of 1967 to 10,000 two years later. Though Fatah remained ineffective against Israel, suffering heavy casualties whenever it attempted large-scale raids, it became a power inside Jor-

dan. Arafat would probably have preferred to avoid an
open battle with Hussein, but events pushed inexorably
toward civil war.[11] In September 1970 the long-awaited
conflict broke out and a chapter in the history of the fedayeen was brought to a bloody conclusion.

It might be said that while the fedayeen have failed
politically and militarily, they have succeeded ideologically by radicalizing Arab consciousness. Yet except for the
small and still relatively insignificant Democratic Popular
Front for the Liberation of Palestine, little has been done
toward shaping a new consciousness that could be a precondition for social revolution. The fedayeen suffer from
a flaw that deeply affects the Arab states: their attention is
so firmly riveted upon Israel that they have ignored their
own internal problems.

By Arab standards the ultimate objective of the fedayeen is conventional. They want the destruction of Israel.
Where the guerrillas have departed from conventional
Arab thinking is in their strategy for achieving this objective. The more radical Arab states have taken the view
that disunity has been their main weakness in the fight
against Israel. "Unity is the road to liberating Palestine"
has been their motto. But Fatah reversed this motto, declaring that "the Liberation of Palestine is the road to
Unity." In so doing they ascribed all the difficulties of
the Arabs, from disunity to poverty, to the existence of
Israel. A series of Fatah pamphlets entitled "Revolution-

---

[11] Following the civil war, in an interview with Eric Rouleau of
Le Monde, Arafat indicated that the conflict came about as a result of irresponsible behavior on the part of some fedayeen and
was not part of a planned strategy to overthrow Hussein, as has
sometimes been claimed. Among the causes he listed for the
civil war were "revolutionary exhibitionism, which consisted of
making our presence known in uncalled-for ways, of needless
actions which were harmful to our cause. Why did some fedayeen
have to drive around the city streets in heavily armed cars? Why
did others, also armed, go around collecting funds?" and "the
disagreeable behavior of some fedayeen towards members of the
Jordanian Army, which fostered the psychological campaign against
the Palestinian revolution" (reprinted in *New Outlook*, December
1970).

ary Lessons and Trials" puts this position forward without qualification:

> The Zionist existence is the cause of *all* our problems in the Arab region and the cause for the defeat of our expectations of a new dawn for the Arab nation. The hopes and aspirations of the nation and the solution of our problems can, by no means, be achieved unless *all* efforts are concerted for the sake of liberating Palestine and fully confronting the challenge of the usurping enemy. The Zionist existence is the root of *all* our diseases and not one of their consequences. (Italics added.)

The explanation given for this view is that the existence of Israel arouses "complexes, fears and irrational anxiety among Arabs of the anticipated danger of the hated Zionist Occupation." There is also a conspiratorial element: all the Arabs' problems are "devised by Imperialism to immobilize the basic national issue so that Palestine will continue to be occupied . . ."

This view has recently been challenged by the "leftist" DPFLP, which has argued that in the absence of a profound social revolution the Arabs will never have the strength to defeat Israel. Yet by far the dominant fedayeen view is still that the existence of Israel is the consummate evil which must be destroyed before any other problem can be dealt with.

It is this position of the fedayeen that has made possible the alliance between them and the conservative Arab states. These states have never looked kindly on calls for Arab unity since they have correctly viewed them as attacks upon themselves. When Nasser has declared that "the unity of Purpose should precede unity of Ranks," or when Syrian and Iraqi radicals have proclaimed that "the road to Tel-Aviv leads through Amman," they have meant simply that the precondition for victory against Israel must be the overthrow of the "reactionary" Arab regimes. Understandably, conservative states such as Jordan, Kuwait, and Saudi Arabia have supported a policy which would permit the maintenance of the status quo.

But official position of the fedayeen, as stated in the

Palestinian national covenant, is consistent with that taken by the conservative states. According to Article 27 of the covenant, "The Palestine Liberation Organization will co-operate with all Arab states, each according to its capacities, and will maintain neutrality in their mutual relations in the light of, and on the basis of, the requirements of the battle of liberation, and will not interfere in the internal affairs of any Arab state." Internal Arab quarrels are meaningless and counterproductive since, as Article 14 states, "the destiny of the Arab nation, indeed the very Arab existence, depends upon the destiny of the Palestine issue."

The fixation on "the Palestine issue" has left the bulk of fedayeen ideology without any radical social content. Arafat's ideology, or nonideology, was spelled out in an interview with the Lebanese weekly *el-Siad:*

> What meaning do the left or the right have in the struggle for the liberation of my homeland? I want that homeland even if the devil be the one to liberate it for me. Am I in a position to reject the participation or assistance of any man? Can I be asked, for example, to refuse the financial aid of Saudi Arabia with the claim that it belongs to the right? After all, it is with the Saudians' money that I buy arms from China. . . . Everybody asks what our social views are. Aren't we still in the phase of national liberation?

Arafat's reference to financial assistance from Saudi Arabia is instructive, for the conservative Arab states have been among the most generous financiers of the fedayeen. One of their motives is pure self-interest. By keeping the Middle East conflict boiling, they can keep Egypt preoccupied with Israel and thus prevent Egyptian expansion into the Persian Gulf. And indeed, Egypt's inability to fight two wars was demonstrated by its withdrawal from Yemen soon after the Six-Day War. The conservative states, of course, are also motivated by their hatred of Israel, the single issue that unites right and left in the Arab world. The success of Fatah is partly explained by its ability to appeal to both sides, maintaining a sufficiently militant posture to satisfy the left and pleasing the right by remaining neutral in Arab affairs.

Fatah's deficiency in social ideas has been compensated for by, and is perhaps one cause of, its glorification of violence. In "Revolution and Violence: The Road to Victory," Fatah proclaims that "violence will purify the individuals from venom, redeem the colonized from their inferiority complex, and restore courage to the native." The source for such statements is Frantz Fanon's *The Wretched of the Earth*. Fanon, a psychoanalyst, was concerned with the psychological dimensions of colonialism and saw violence as a way to liberate the colonized peoples from deep-rooted feelings of weakness and self-contempt. Whatever the psychological validity of these ideas, their political significance must be judged by the context in which they are applied. In the case of the Algerian war of independence, which was Fanon's own cause, the political objective was to drive the French out of Algeria. This goal was both feasible and admirable. In the Middle East, however, the objective of the fedayeen is to drive the Israelis out of Israel. Though the fedayeen draw a parallel between the two situations, their objective is really closer to the demand that the French leave France.

The objective of the fedayeen flows logically from their analysis of the problem that must be solved. If the existence of Israel is the source of all the pain and suffering in the Arab world, if it is indeed the supreme evil responsible for all other evils, then Israel must cease to exist. In dealing with absolute evil there is no room for compromise, which is why the fedayeen have adamantly opposed proposals for an independent Palestinian state in the West Bank and the Gaza. Their objective, as they say, is "the extinction of a society," "the destruction of the factors sustaining the Zionist society in all their forms: industrial, agricultural, and financial," "the blotting out of the Zionist character of the occupied land, be it human or social." And they have come to realize that their objective is unique and cannot be achieved through conventional war but requires a special kind of war, a "people's war" against Israel:

For the aim of this war is not to impose our will on the enemy but to destroy him in order to take his place. In a conventional war there is no need to continue the war if the enemy submits to our will . . . while in a *people's war* there is no deterrent inhibition, for its aim is not to defeat the enemy but to extirpate him. A conventional war has limited aims which have to be observed, for the enemy must be allowed to exist so that we can impose our will on him, while in a *people's war*, destruction of the enemy is the first and last duty.

This statement was made in the Fatah's monthly publication *Palestinian Revolution* in June 1968, a month before the new Palestinian national covenant was issued. Article 6 of the covenant is consistent with the Fatah statement and remains the official position of all the guerrilla groups in the PLO. It reads: "Jews who were living permanently in Palestine until the beginning of the Zionist invasion will be considered Palestinians." In the resolutions of the Fourth Congress, "the beginning of the Zionist invasion" is described as 1917, and it is added that "the meaning of 'removal of the traces of the aggression' must be removal of the traces of the aggression which came into effect from the beginning of the Zionist invasion and not from the war of June 1967." Significantly, though Article 6 has been widely condemned as genocidal, since it demands the elimination from Israel of practically all its Jewish citizens, it has not been amended at any of the four congresses held since.

The fedayeen, however, have been deeply concerned with maintaining their image as freedom fighters, and they do not want to lose support in the international community by seeming to appear not as the victims but as the executioners. They remember the damage done by Shukeiri's indiscreet declaration before the Six-Day War that the Arabs would throw the Jews into the sea, and they do not want to repeat his error. Thus, when their position in the covenant was made public (it was left to an Israeli, Harkabi, to translate the covenant since the position in Article 6 was not intended for external use), they countered with the slogan of "the Democratic Palestinian state." Their objective could now be stated in positive terms: instead of calling for the destruction of Israel, their new demand was for the creation of a democratic secular state in which Muslims, Christians, and Jews could live at peace with one another. Until today they adhere to two positions, the private position stated in the covenant and the public one embodied in their new slogan.

The slogan created new problems as it solved some old ones, for its very use forced the fedayeen to analyze its meaning and implications. They could no longer avoid defining their objectives: what would they propose beyond the immediate goal of politicide? With what kind of a state would they replace Israel? Certainly an Arab state, yet what about the 2½ million Jews living in Israel? What would be done with them?

In an important symposium published in the Beirut newspaper *al-Anwar* (March 8, 1970), representatives of the six leading guerrilla groups could provide no clear answers to these questions. The spokesman for the Arab Liberation Front proposed that the future state be part of a unified Arab nation which would have an overwhelming Arab majority. Yet this raised the issue of pan-Arabism which (aside from the question of its feasibility) has generally been resisted by the fedayeen in favor of Palestinian nationalism. If pan-Arabism were permitted to take precedence over local distinctiveness, it would make plausible the view that the Palestinians could be absorbed anywhere in the Arab world. Thus, the "liberation" of Palestine would not be required for the realization of their national identity.

Others suggested that the problem of a large Jewish presence would not be an issue since the Jews would want to leave Palestine. The Fatah spokesman, for example, explained that the Jews came to Palestine only because they "were deceived by the Zionist movement and the world imperialist movement," and would leave after the defeat of these forces. The spokesman for el-Sa'ika offered an even more interesting explanation—the Jews have a yearning for their original homelands, especially the Jews from the Arab countries which had treated them so well! The Sa'ika spokesman saw another reason why the Jews would want to leave: "the Zionist efforts to transform them into a homogeneous, cohesive nation have failed." His error of judgment is one that is often made by people who have had little experience with democracy—he interprets the vigorous debate and political divisions in Israel

not as the necessary by-products of a healthy democracy
but as a sign of disintegration of the society.

The spokesman for the DPFLP said that the issue of
democracy would present no problems in the new state
even if the Jews remained. "When we speak of democracy,"
he said, "it must be clear that we do not mean a liberal
democracy in the manner of 'one man, one vote.' We
mean a people's democratic regime . . ." In other words,
"the people," meaning the Arabs or Arab leaders, would
determine policy regardless of the number of Jews living
in the state.

Shafiq al-Hut, head of the PLO office in Beirut, was
frank about the difficulties presented by the slogan. "If
the slogan of the Democratic State was intended only to
counter the claim that we wish to throw the Jews into the
sea," he said, "this is indeed an apt slogan and an effective
political and propaganda blow. But if we wish to regard it
as the ultimate strategy of the Palestinian and Arab liberation movement, then I believe it requires a long pause for
reflection . . ." He warned that their discussion about the
meaning of the slogan "may be the beginning of a long dispute . . ."

By the end of the symposium, all of the participants,
having been unable to arrive at an acceptable definition of
the slogan and fearing that debate could divide the fedayeen, agreed that it was premature to raise the question of
a democratic state.

The *al-Anwar* symposium, which provides interesting
insights into the way fedayeen leaders think, indicates that
they are not likely to redefine their views through discussion and debate. If their position does change in the
future, it will most likely be as a result of the pressure of
events. The failure of the fedayeen to act according to
their words or to achieve any of their objectives should
ultimately lead to a shift in thinking as ideology accommo-
dates to the weight of reality. The alternatives would be a
continuation of futile and suicidal behavior.

The fedayeen will not soon disappear. They serve a
function for the Arab states who use them in their battles
against each other as well as against Israel. And not only
does their existence keep "the Palestine issue" alive, it

gives the Arab leaders flexibility in dealing with Israel: the fedayeen sustain Arab militancy at times when it is convenient for the states to assume a moderate posture.

Whether the fedayeen, as presently constituted, can continue to be a legitimate voice of Palestinian nationalism is another matter. As a "liberation" movement they have been a complete failure. It is inconceivable that by itself their strategy of guerrilla warfare could succeed against Israel. Such a strategy requires a population sympathetic to the terrorists and hostile to the government, and there is no sign that the Israelis will rebel against themselves in the foreseeable future. It is not even certain that the fedayeen can "provide the Arab struggle with its finest legends and epics," the role assigned to them by Heykal, who has always stressed their psychological value while doubting their military capability. What is more likely is that the fedayeen, unable to act against Israel, will increasingly turn their violence against themselves in factional warfare and against those Palestinians who wish to make peace with Israel. They have frequently threatened to kill any Palestinian who agrees to "the idea of the fraudulent Palestinian entity" in the West Bank and the Gaza, and their practice of heaving grenades into buses carrying Gaza residents to jobs in Israel is well known. The internalization of violence follows the pattern set in the 1930s when Arab terror took a far greater number of Arab than Jewish lives. This senseless killing serves no "revolutionary" purpose but only increases the suffering of the Palestinians.

At the Eighth Palestinian National Congress held in March 1971 the fedayeen passed a resolution which provides a basis for explaining the weakness of their movement. The resolution, entitled "The Unity of Palestinians and Jordanian Masses," declares that "a national link and a territorial unity forged by history, culture and language tie Jordan with Palestine from the earliest period." The resolution goes on to describe the Palestinians and Jordanians as "one people," and it explains the previous emphasis on Palestinian distinctiveness as having been necessary only for "a specific historical phase."

The passage of this resolution does not mean that the fedayeen have taken a more moderate position. Rather,

it shows that they now feel it necessary to make explicit
their claim to Jordan since, as a result of their defeat by
Hussein, it can no longer be assumed that Jordan is theirs.
But the resolution reveals something more basic which
the fedayeen did not intend. If their home is Jordan, then
they are not a homeless people. Thus, the objective of
their conflict with Israel is not to regain a home but to en-
large their present homeland. With such an objective,
their claim that they are a movement of national survival
sounds empty, and their weakness becomes understandable since they do not have the strength one would expect of a national movement struggling to survive.

The irony is that the one nation in the Middle East
which does derive strength from being such a movement
is Israel. In a recent interview, Golda Meir discussed the
source of Israel's remarkable strength and tenacity: "We
have come back to our home. We intend to stay, and we
shall fight to the death to stay. We shall win because we
have a secret weapon; we have no alternative."

But the fedayeen do have alternatives. They can continue to struggle for Israel's destruction, or they can accept Israel's presence, whatever the pain this may cause,
and begin to work out a means for coexistence. One can
only hope that out of the failure of the fedayeen the alternative of peace will emerge.

Israeli Policy in the "Administered Territories"

Michael Bruno

MICHAEL BRUNO—associate professor of Economics
at the Hebrew University of Jerusalem and director
of the research department of the Bank of Israel.

By the evening of Saturday, June 10, 1967, when the
firing came to an end on the Golan Heights, Israel had accomplished its greatest military victory. It was against an
alignment of foes that for a period of twenty years, almost
without break, had threatened the existence of the small
state. Feelings in Israel ran high. Six days earlier a memorable Monday brought to an end a period of three weeks of
the most tense waiting that this nation had ever experienced.

Israel was just barely beginning to emerge from the
"Mitun" (mild recession), which was in fact a very severe
economic slump. It was now in a deep crisis, its leaders
divided and indecisive. In a brilliant series of moves, cul-
minating in the expulsion of the UN force and the closing
of the Straits of Tiran, Nasser had caught Israel in a state
of impotence. Not only did he openly challenge its leadership on what was always clearly known to be an Israeli
casus belli, he had amassed on Israel's southern Sinai
border the biggest armor and air force concentration that
the Middle East had seen since the days of El Alamein,
while one of his generals held virtual command over Jordan's army on Israel's eastern borders. There was the prospect of another 1948-type strangulation on all borders at
once, and with it the trauma of a "final solution" only a
bit more in the past. As for the world, it stood by and
waited.

Feelings on that Saturday ran high not only because of

the triumph of a nation that was reasserting its will to survive. The preceding six days had unfolded in a series of most unexpected events. Counter to subsequent rationalizations of events, the fighting started with no clearly defined Israeli strategic objectives. Major effort had been concentrated on foiling the impending Egyptian thrust from the Sinai and the Gaza Strip. Now, six days later, not only were the Egyptian air force and armor crushed completely, but the Israeli army had managed to reach as far as the Suez Canal. As a result of Hussein's folly in refusing to stop the firing that his soldiers had started in Jerusalem on the fateful Monday morning, two days later, after a bloody battle, the Old City was in Israeli hands. The West Bank capitulated step by step to Israeli units. What started as a local silencing of artillery in Jenin and Qalqilia, towns facing Israel's precariously narrow coastal strip, ended in a complete conquest of the West Bank by Thursday. Finally, and this time by design, after considerable vacillation among Israel's leaders (who feared Russian intervention), the mighty Syrian Golan stronghold was attacked. For many years it had made life unbearable for Israel's farmers in the valley below. Two days later, it too was completely in Israeli hands.

The euphoria was bound to be short-lived. The men were returning home and in a few days the list came out of those who would never return. Eight hundred dead and 2,500 wounded may seem a small number to an outsider, but to a nation of 2.5 million, where everybody knows everybody else and the picture of every soldier lost appears on the front pages, this is a high cost indeed (in relative terms, more than total U.S. losses in Vietnam). The much larger numbers of dead and wounded on the other side, and the thousands of new refugees, left a deep impress on Israel's homebound men. The published dialogues[1] of soldiers bear vivid witness.

Nor was there much of a breathing space after this war, unlike previous wars that Israel had had to fight. Nasser

---

[1] See *The Seventh Day: Soldiers' Talk About the Six-Day War* (London: André Deutsch, 1970). Recorded and edited by a group of young kibbutz members. Hebrew publication: Siach Lochamim, 1967.

resigned but immediately returned to power on a wave of popular sentiment. Russia was beginning the biggest air shipments of arms ever, more than compensating Egypt for its war losses—a step which in many ways has extended the war to this very day. Israel was waiting in vain for the "phone call" about peace talks from Nasser and Hussein. It never came. In the meantime Israel was holding territories three and a half times its own size in area (though the total length of its new cease-fire borders had actually decreased). Moreover, for the first time it was now, almost against its own will, the custodian of a million Palestinian Arabs, close to one-third of them refugees of the 1948 war, most of whom had been kept for twenty years in inhuman camps, hotbeds of hatred, by the Egyptian authorities in the Gaza Strip.

These "administered territories" have become a subject of much argument. "Security versus Peace" or "Territories for Peace" became the favorite Israeli Friday-evening debating topic, long before there was anybody on the other side to start a serious dialogue with. It was clear from the start that no mere words would induce Israel to give up the new border, itself only half an hour's drive from Jerusalem, in return for borders that might bring Arab artillery back within range of Israeli urban centers, or that might potentially cut Israel in two, or that might make it impossible to cultivate its most fertile northern land. And Israel certainly would not agree to a policy that would start the whole thing all over again from the south, this time at a more advanced level of war technology, in the hands of a more sophisticated foe. Blessings, however, are seldom unmixed and decisions hardly ever come in black or white. There is the long-run trade-off between political and military strength. Also at stake is a possible loss of either the Zionist or the deep-lying democratic character of Israel. So there was endless room for debate, even if most of it had to be only within Israel itself.

The territories after four years—are they still a pawn in Israeli hands, to be given up in return for real peace, however that might be defined, or are they, as in the eyes of the unsympathetic observer from outside (or extremists from within), another manifestation of imperial Zionist expansion, a fulfillment of the "greater Israel" dream?

The problem of the occupied territories presented itself as a sudden dilemma which was tackled in typical pragmatic Israeli ways. Even more than the war from which it was inherited, there was little in the way of a grand design or long-term strategy. The underlying frame of reference throughout most of the period was mainly the government's "decision not to decide" on long-term "maps." And the dominant reason for that was a reluctance to get into a premature yet heated internal debate while outside there was still no one to negotiate with. In regard to Jerusalem, the Golan Heights, and more recently the Sinai, some independent long-term assessment of strategy can be made, in each case for different reasons, but for our purposes these are the less interesting. Almost no clearly defined long-term political decisions have been taken with regard to the two highly populated areas, the West Bank and the Gaza Strip, both parts of pre-1948 Palestine.

East Jerusalem is the only territory which from the beginning was officially annexed by Israel in a formal reunification of the city. This part of the city, with its seventy thousand Arab inhabitants, is now to all intents and purposes part of Israel. Its population has participated in a municipal election, it enjoys Israeli public-health, social, and legal services, and it has a sizable Histadrut (trade-union) membership.

Regardless of whether (like most Israelis, including myself) one is sympathetic to this particular decision, the unification in itself is historically irreversible. This may cause difficulties in the future with Jordan (or a Palestinian state if it is formed). I believe, however, that there have been sufficient indications on both sides to show that some compromise might still be worked out that would leave a unified Jerusalem as the capital of Israel (e.g., an Arab flag and jurisdiction over the Muslim mosques, maintenance of an optional Arab state citizenship by the Arab population, an access road from Arab territory, etc.). Such compromise would no doubt be hotly contested both inside and outside Israel. Meanwhile the fact remains that after twenty years of Jordanian conquest during which the Old City was not open to worshipers of all religions and nations, since June 1967 no visitor, whether Muslim or Christian, has been refused access to the holy places.

Management of these sites is completely in the hands of the respective religious authorities. Israeli authorities have even often had to act as go-betweens in the feuds among Christian sects over rights in the Holy Sepulcher. This is not meant to imply that all Israel's policies in Jerusalem are free from blame, only that the overall record is positive.

The Golan Heights, a virtually empty mountain plateau, dominates much of Israel's northeast fertile farmland, the Lake of Galilee and the sources of the Jordan's water. Its major use in the hands of Syria was as a Russian-planned series of fortified attack bases from which Israeli kibbutzim and towns were continuously harassed and bombarded. This formidable array of concrete fortresses is still there for anybody to see. So strategic is this position it seems unlikely that it will ever be returned to Syrian hands, and Israel has in fact already indicated in deeds its intention to settle the Heights. No formal annexation has taken place, however, and it is understood that if Syria is ever willing to sign a peace treaty with Israel the exact border on the Heights might still be negotiable. Yet the chances of a major shift back seem remote.

The Sinai Peninsula, though in terms of area constituting some 90 percent of the total occupied territories, has virtually no population (some 25,000 bedouin nomads) and is of little immediate economic significance to either side. It matters as an ideal launching pad for attacks on Israel—or on Egypt, as the case may be. Unlike the Golan Heights, the Sinai is regarded by most Israelis as a temporary military base, most of which could be vacated and placed under Egyptian civilian administration in return for an unambiguous peace and clearly defined security safeguards (e.g., effective demilitarization, jointly policed), and on condition that Israel maintains control over Sharm el-Sheikh, its gateway to the East, and the coast strip leading to it. There are differences among military experts as to the strategic importance of also keeping part of northern Sinai, which now forms an ideal buffer against any incursion from the south.

There is a general presumption, in Israel at least, that if Egypt genuinely wants peace, Sharm el-Sheikh should be of no importance to her and a way could be found to bridge over the differences that at present still look exceedingly large. More than anything else, it is the extent of Russian involvement that will probably determine the fate of any agreement.

But when we come to the "Palestinian" territories, the West Bank and the Gaza Strip, the problems are decidedly more complex. It is here that Israel's long-term objectives have been least clearly defined, and it is here that the Israeli political parties in Israel are most divided. The only minimum common denominator seems to be some version of the labor alignment's so-called "oral tradition." This calls for maintenance of the Jordan River as a security border, i.e., a line beyond which no Arab armies would be allowed to cross, but it does not commit itself to any of the several political solutions for the West Bank. As for the Gaza Strip, there seems to be common agreement in Israel (apparently also shared by Egypt) that it would not go back to Egypt's jurisdiction, but at the same time that this does not necessarily imply future annexation by Israel.[2]

An underlying Israeli reluctance to make long-term decisions is an important element to note at the outset, since it provides one source of both the strengths and the weaknesses of the policies and developments to be discussed.

The West Bank and the Gaza Strip together have a population of close to a million, two-thirds of whom reside in the West Bank. While the latter largely consists of indigenous population and only a small number of 1948 refugees, Gaza is in a very special position, being predominantly a refugee-camp center (150,000–200,000 refugees, depending on the definition used). The two areas also differ greatly in income, population density, and employment levels, as well as in political-social structure.

Israeli administration of the territories has from the beginning taken a peculiar combined military-civilian

---

[2] One political solution that has sometimes been mentioned is to link Gaza with the West Bank, thus providing a sea outlet to the landlocked area, and tying the political future of the two regions together.

form. While ultimate responsibility for policy planning has rested with a ministerial committee at the government level, the actual administration is under the auspices of the regional military commander and in all civilian matters it directly reports to the various Israeli ministries (Finance, Agriculture, Industry, etc.). The agencies are manned primarily by local Arab officials, most of whom were previously employed by Jordan and Egypt. It is illuminating to note that of over 8,000 permanent employees of the administration in the territories during 1969–70, only 380 were citizens of Israel.

From the very beginning the military command set itself the goal of a quick normalization of life in the territories. This meant a return to pre-June 5 conditions with a minimum of intervention in daily life, an absence of outward Israeli presence (no flags or any other signs of an occupation authority), and an "open bridges" policy allowing a more or less free flow of commerce and visitors across the Jordan, as well as the "green border."[3]

The philosophy of indirect and almost invisible rule has evolved in stages, by giving successive flexible and pragmatic answers to local problems as they arose.[4] When the territories unexpectedly came into Israel's hands, there was no established policy for dealing with such problems. Responsibility for local decisions often rested with young, pragmatic officers who were open to new ideas and outside (including academic) advice. They saw it as their job to create a possible bridge between peoples who had been at war for so many years. They were also eager to show that, with normalization, there was something to be gained from applying Israel's experience for the improvement of life among its neighbors.

At least in the economy of the West Bank, the success of their policy is borne out by solid figures. At first the average standard of living in the West Bank went down some 10 to 20 percent from a prewar level of about $200 per capita annually, but by the end of 1968 this loss was recovered. By 1970 annual income was increasing at an

---

[3] The previous cease-fire line was colored green on the maps.
[4] This part of the story is well described in S. Teveth's *The Cursed Blessing* (London: Weidenfeld and Nicolson, 1969).

annual rate of 10 to 15 percent reaching around $250.[5] The absolute level is still very low, but the improvement is rapid. Unemployment among male workers has dropped to 2.7 percent (from 7.6 percent in 1967), in fact below the unemployment level in Israel itself. A combination of relief employment, employment in Israel (see below), opening up of trade with both Israel and Jordan, a rapid rise in agricultural output, and renewed local investment have all contributed to this remarkable recovery. Israel's agricultural experts, together with local ex-Jordan agricultural officials, have been active in transferring the lessons of modern agricultural and irrigation technology, the use of new seeds, fertilizers, and insecticides, as well as modern marketing methods. This program seems to enjoy full cooperation of the large farming population of the West Bank.

While the number of Israeli workers in the West Bank has been kept very small, there has been a rapidly increasing influx of workers from the occupied areas into the Israeli labor market. Until the end of 1967 there was a complete official ban on such movements, partly out of fear of being swamped by cheap Arab labor while Israel was still recovering from its prewar recession, but also out of strong ideological motives—a fear that like the Giv'-onites in biblical times, its modern-day neighbors would become Israel's "hewers of wood and carriers of water" while Israeli Jews themselves would fall back to being the managerial class, nonmanual workers and shopkeepers, as in the diaspora. This might set back one of the central purposes of socialist Zionism—that manual work should also be done by Jews.

But as with other matters, the real forces of the market proved stronger than ideology. The "green border" could no longer be closed to the movement of people. What started as West Bank workers sneaking across to the Israeli borderline Arab villages and the construction sites in West Jerusalem finally ended with a controlled but

---

[5] All these figures are at constant 1969 local prices, converted at the official exchange rate. All our statistical data are based on publications of Israel's Central Bureau of Statistics and the research department of the Bank of Israel.

rapidly increasing enrollment of Arab workers through regional labor exchanges especially set up for this purpose. In addition to controlling the flow, these exchanges have another function—to ensure that the workers are paid Israeli minimum wages and receive all social fringe bene- fits.[6] Needless to say, work conditions such as number of hours worked, free meals, and transportation also con- stitute a vast improvement over past conditions. By 1970 the number of workers in Israel from both territories reached some 30,000, thus constituting over 15 percent of total employment in the territories (and less than 2 percent of Israel's). About 50 percent were employed in the construction industry, the other half in agriculture, some services, and industry.

Although economic activity in the West Bank has itself picked up very rapidly and renewed confidence has been shown through investment in housing and in the small but growing manufacturing sector in the cities, the reliance on outside work does point to a certain weakness of this boom. For its continuation depends mainly on economic conditions within Israel, and if that dependence is to be minimized, greater emphasis will have to be put on local indigenous industry, something that is only just beginning.

These developments have not benefited all strata of the West Bank population equally. Income distribution, at the expense of the top white-collar and self-employed profes- sional class, has probably become more equitable than it was before June 1967. With the disappearance of the cen- tral Jordanese administration, some of the more highly placed officials have of necessity lost in social status and possibly also in income (though for most of the period they have continued to receive their salaries from Am- man). And with easier access to public medical and legal services, the private professionals, at least in East Jeru- salem, have no doubt also lost in relative terms.

Nor was the transition without problems on the Israeli side. From a fairly early stage the authorities had to be

[6] This takes the form of a net direct payment of a wage which is about 50 percent above what such workers have received with- in the territory, plus a considerable fringe benefit that employers have to put into a special equalization fund set up for this pur- pose and indirectly channeled back into the territories.

alert to the potential danger of Israeli economic domination of the territories. While the population of the two territories amounts to about a third of Israel's, total GNP is only 4 percent of Israel's. The difference in size of industries, and the relative efficiency of public utilities, transportation, etc., is quite pronounced. So it would be an easy matter for Egged, Israel's bus cooperative, to devour the many small and relatively backward bus companies operating in the territories. But such take-overs have been consistently resisted by the administration on grounds of its noninterference policy. So far the overwhelming dominance of Israel's economy has been held in restraint, though the danger does, of course, remain.

The successful normalization of economic life in the West Bank helps explain the fact that even during the most active period of Fatah guerrilla activity across the Jordan (1968–69), local collaboration with the guerrilla movement was rather limited and short-lived. The army authorities took pains to apply a strong hand only to the key trouble spots. For the Arab inhabitants of the West Bank are no quislings, nor were they ever expected to love the occupier, however liberal his policies might be. Yet the potential loss of economic advantages, plus the realization that when punitive actions were undertaken they were for the most part scrupulously selective, have contributed to the general atmosphere of guarded restraint and comparative quiet. And it should likewise be noted that in spite of initial Israeli apprehensions, the thousands of workers roaming throughout Israel have had almost no effect on the general feeling of security. They also have too much to lose.

So far we have talked about short-run trends and policies, ad hoc adjustments of a relatively liberal ruler. What about the long-run trends, political as well as economic? Has noninterference been prevalent also in politics? The answer here is much less clear-cut. For a time it looked as if Israel was taking steps toward democratization of political life in the territories, starting with free elections to municipal office, and possibly going beyond that. By and large, however, Israel has not only maintained a status quo in political organization but has also resisted any practical moves toward greater political self-determination in the West Bank. In spite of considerable liberal opposition from within Israel, the authorities have on several occasions refused to grant permission to local Arab leaders to form nuclei for a regional cooperation that might eventually lead to greater political autonomy. This unfortunate fact does not reflect hidden annexationist objectives but is rather connected with Israel's repeated stand in favor of Hussein against a Palestinian entity—a stand in no small measure tied to U.S. backing of Hussein in his successful showdown with the Fatah in his own kingdom.

Officially Israel has always maintained that there is room for only one Arab state on the Jordan, and that whether this predominantly "Palestinian" state chooses to be ruled by Hussein is not for Israel to decide. Unfortunately, however, Israel has also refused to make an official declaration recognizing the right of the Palestinians to self-determination and territory, be it on one or both banks of the Jordan. A number of prominent Israeli political leaders have on occasion come out openly in favor of such a declaration, and so has a recent gathering of young Labor party members, but this has not become official policy.

One sign of Israel's indecisiveness in this matter has been the cooling off of a long-approved plan to set up an Arab University in Ramallah, close to Jerusalem. Since its founding might be associated with internal anti-Hussein political activity (Hussein has openly opposed the university plan, because he believes it would hamper his chances of ever cementing the two banks together), Israel suddenly decided to postpone the university for the time being.

In my view this policy is very shortsighted. Maintaining the right of intervention in Jordan in case of a Syrian invasion (as in 1970) is one thing, for here Israel's long-run security was obviously at stake. But the alienation of moderate Palestinians by not responding to their own wishes for self-expression—and not because of any principle but because of a pro-Hussein policy—seems quite a different matter. In the long run Israel might here be acting against its own self-interest. Obviously, it is not for Israel to decide for the Palestinians on either of the two banks what their future should be, but it also seems imprudent to put all one's eggs in one basket, thus indirectly opting for only one political solution. Jordan and Hussein may very well survive, but so will Palestinian bitterness. And while Israel should not initiate political steps that might be interpreted as the setting up of a puppet state, its policy should be flexible enough to respond to those political aspirations of the West Bank population that do not seriously endanger Israeli security.

While the normalization policy in the West Bank has in most aspects been successful, the story in Gaza is a much less happy one. The underlying basic conditions have always been different. The standard of living in the past has been only about half that of the West Bank. As a result of the normalization policy, this too has now risen about 40 percent above the prewar level but is still extremely low in absolute terms. Unemployment, too, although substantially decreased, is still considerably above that of the West Bank (4.8 percent in 1970). Employment opportunities in Gaza are much more limited. It is densely populated, industry and construction activity are very sparse, and employment in Israel is much hampered due to sporadic terrorist activity against both the Israeli authorities and any elements in the population who have shown signs of "collaboration" by going to work in Israel.

The major problem of Gaza is that some two-thirds of the population, close to 200,000, are refugees from the 1948 war, mostly camp dwellers who have been kept there by the Egyptian authorities in cramped and unhealthy conditions. Although the West Bank, too, has some refugees (about 50,000 camp dwellers), they have on the whole been living in much better conditions.[7] What marks out the refugees is their camp existence. Years of confinement with hardly any work, living off rations and memories of a distant past, breed a herdlike mentality and burning hatred—witness the pre-June 1967 scenes of mass

---

[7] Studies carried out by Israeli researchers show relatively small difference between refugees and nonrefugees in either of the two areas taken by themselves, as measured by average living standards, housing, employment levels, etc. One of the problems of the Gaza Strip is that the whole area is economically depressed and densely populated.

hysteria and bloodthirsty posters. These effects will take a long time and will require a new environment to wear off.

A gradual solution of the refugee problem should, in principle, comprise two somewhat distinct elements. One is the "macro" aspect—an attempt to absorb and diffuse them economically and sociologically in a wider developing environment. They should be attracted out of the camps into, for example, the economy of the West Bank, with housing and jobs in the urban areas.[8]

This absorption should be done in a manner that will gradually eliminate the outward symptoms of the refugees' camp identity, and should alleviate the economic and social misery, as well as the political instability. But it cannot completely solve the "micro" problem, that of the individual attachment to property and lands lost over twenty years ago.[9] A physical return, whether morally right or wrong, is not practically or politically feasible—just as a physical return of a Syrian or Iraqi Jew to his former home would not be feasible. One should not correct a past injustice by committing a new one. The Syrian or Iraqi Jew has acquired a new "home" in the "macro" sense of the word, and the Arab refugee deserves the same. Moreover, full compensation for lost property should eventually be worked out, as part of a peace settlement.

Israel has repeatedly expressed its willingness to undertake such compensation (with outside help) as part of an agreement in which both refugees inside and outside the administered territories would be eligible, while at the same time compensation would also be paid for Jewish property lost in Arab states. While beginnings in this direction, as a sign of goodwill, could be made even before peace is achieved,[10] the official stand of a quid pro quo on the broader question can be defended. What is

---

[8] Agriculture cannot absorb but is more likely to provide a net outflow of labor in the coming years.

[9] A young child on being asked where he comes from would not mention the camp in which he himself was born, but rather the village or town in which his family resided before 1948: "Ana min Yafa," i.e., "I am from Jaffa."

[10] It has, for example, been suggested by a number of Israelis that a pilot project could be started with the Palestinian refugees now residing in east Jerusalem.

much less defensible, from both a moral as well as a practical Israeli point of view, is that during four years of occupation in the Gaza Strip very little has been done toward the "macro" type of solution. The Israeli authorities have been providing more employment, health, and welfare services, as well as training schemes on the spot. They have been helping in modernizing citrus and fish marketing. But none of this solves the problem.

Plans suggesting a gradual removal of refugees from the camps have been suggested by various Israeli experts since the end of the Six-Day War. Although discussed at various government levels and reasonably well received by public opinion, these have so far only been started on a very partial and sporadic basis. The lack of greater progress on this issue partly stems from a weakness already noted—the inability to come to agreement on long-run policies. Partly, no doubt, this is also connected with a reluctance to come to open conflict with the Arab extremist groups who might attempt to foil any Israeli-induced rehabilitation program,[11] or to face the social tensions that an influx of refugees into the West Bank might cause.[12] Still, apparent short-run stability has here been bought at the price of considerable and prolonged instability.

Israel's attempt to apply the noninterference policy to the Gaza Strip has on the whole failed. No recognized political leadership exists locally, and considerable effort has been required by the Israeli army to maintain reasonable security. The cost in human lives, primarily Arabs killed by their own people, but also substantial Israeli casualties, is considerable. After a period of crisis at the end of 1970 and beginning of 1971, the authorities resorted to a more vigorous attempt to improve living conditions (e.g., to supply power and water) in the camps, provide more employment, set up new industrial projects, and safeguard the lives of people going to work. This has

---

[11] A number of new projects in the Gaza Strip have been sabotaged in the past.

[12] One should also keep in mind that during much of this period, people's minds and the country's resources have been preoccupied with two major battles: first the Fatah incursions across the Jordan valley (1968–69) and then Nasser's war of attrition on the Suez (1969–70).

already helped to quiet things down for the time being, but it still remains to be seen whether the more far-reaching "macro" measures will in fact be undertaken.

Let us return, finally, to two major questions that have been implicit all along:

1. In the long run what would be a feasible and humane solution for the two territories that would also serve Israel's self-interest?

2. Has Israel helped to bring about such solutions or in fact preempted any alternative but that of gradual annexation?

Opinions on the first question do, of course, differ in Israel, especially when it comes to the West Bank. Israel is a democracy and all shades of opinion can be heard. The Gahal party on the extreme right and the cross-party-line "greater Israel" advocates—a minority group but a fairly vociferous one—would call for complete annexation plus at least partial Jewish settlement of the West Bank. Opinions within that group would probably differ on the question of equal franchise to all inhabitants of the occupied territories, but what unites them is the principle of territorial continuity of Israel within the old borders of the British mandate and possibly beyond. To this must be added a shade of opinion held most strongly by large parts of the religious parties, which hold the parliamentary balance in the present tenuous government coalition. The religious parties put a great weight on traditional biblical associations with Hebron, to a lesser extent Nablus, and other places of ancient Jewish settlement and worship.

Throughout the years 1967–71 numerous attempts by various private groups were made to settle in the West Bank. In all cases these groups were immediately driven off by the Israeli authorities. In two cases, however, official permission was eventually granted under strong political pressure within the government. One is the resettlement of Kfar Etzion by the surviving descendants of the pre-1948 kibbutz in the Hebron Hills, the site of a heroic last stand by and terrible slaughter of Jewish settlers who warded off the first attack of the Arab invaders at the termination of the British mandate in 1948, thus giving Jerusalem a breathing space of a few weeks to prepare for the long battle. The second, more recent case was the setting up of a small urban and religious center not far away from Kfar Etzion, at the outskirts of Hebron. City of the biblical fathers, Hebron was in recent centuries the center of a thriving Jewish community, which in 1929 was virtually wiped out in a massacre staged by Arab inhabitants.

In both cases sentimental and historical ties, as well as political pressure from within, were so strong that official policy was reversed.[13] But the argument sometimes made by otherwise moderate leaders that "there cannot be a place in which Jews would not be allowed to live" can cut both ways. For if this argument is accepted, why can the same not be said about the right of Palestinian Arabs to return to their former homes? It has been the opinion of many Israelis (myself included) that while the claim to Kfar Etzion or Hebron might be justified in principle, no exception should have been made, if only because of long-run global and political considerations.

It is hard to make estimates on these questions, but I believe it would still be true to say that the great majority in the labor parties, and in fact the majority of Israelis, would still be willing—with the possible exception of the Hebron settlements—to give up the West Bank under some tight security arrangements.[14]

The case of the West Bank exemplifies more than anything else the painful trade-off between two not quite reconcilable goals. The idea that Israel's narrow coastal strip close to Tel Aviv would ever again come under the range of heavy artillery, be it Jordanese, Palestinian, or, God forbid, Russian, is so traumatic that it often dominates any longer-range considerations which in their own way are of at least as great importance to the country's existence. One extreme alternative would be to have secure borders, the way they are now, but at the price of becoming either a binational state or another Rhodesia. The former would not work and the latter would be incompatible with the democratic-socialist-Zionist ideal. In

---

[13] Nor did Arab Hebron stage much of a protest.

[14] The Alon Plan calls for maintenance of bases along part of the Jordan line. The competing Dayan strategy calls for maintenance of such bases along the mountain ridge inland.

the very long run an overall solution might be found in the form of a loose federation of democratic states, Jewish and Arab, but this could only come after, not before, independent neighboring strong nation-states come to an agreement to federate out of their own free will.

It is, of course, virtually impossible to make long-run predictions. A central theme in our discussion has been that the long run consists of a series of short runs and that, in the absence of long-run strategies, these determine the real outcome. There is a danger that while successfully resisting the pressure to take undesirable long shots, i.e., annexation, day-to-day developments may somehow gradually remove any alternative. Our discussion, we believe, shows that so far this is still successfully being avoided.

What Israel has done so far in the territories, primarily in the West Bank, stands largely to its credit—given the inherent dilemmas of "occupied territories." Normalized day-to-day relations build up the kind of mutual trust between people, and realistic life-size images of each other, that will be hard to wipe out.[15] Peace, after all, is not an abstract concept but a condition of mind. There is little that speaks as much in favor of this experience as the growing summer stream of Arab visitors from across the Jordan, and the well-founded knowledge that there are many in Jordan today who would prefer living in the West Bank, even under Israeli occupation, to remaining in the uncertain economic and political atmosphere of Jordan.

Israel's judicial system, welfare-state policies, accumulation of know-how, and socialist traditions have already been put to good use. If and when the territorial and national conflict gets settled in a mutually satisfactory way, there is no end to the scope for cooperation between neighboring sovereign nations.

---

[15] In this respect, at least, the twenty-year experience of relations between Arabs and Jews within Israel bears witness.

Civil Liberties in Israel:
The Problem of Preventive Detention

Alan Dershowitz

ALAN DERSHOWITZ—professor of Law at Harvard University, member of the National Board of the American Civil Liberties Union, author of a forthcoming study of preventive detention, actively engaged in civil liberties litigation.

Times of crisis test the depth of a people's commitment to civil liberties. Nations whose fundamental laws proclaim freedom during times of normalcy often see these protections virtually erased by the exigencies of external or internal danger.

Within the past year numerous countries—some with long traditions of liberty—have suspended, or threatened to suspend, fundamental freedoms in response to perceived threats to their national security. On October 16, 1970, for example, Prime Minister Pierre Trudeau proclaimed a "state of apprehended insurrection" throughout Canada. Pointing to the kidnaping of a Canadian minister and a British consul by members of Le Front de Libération du Quebec (FLQ), he invoked the "War Measures Act," thereby authorizing extraordinary powers of arrest, search, and detention. Before dawn, the police—who had been strategically deployed in anticipation of the announcement—began to round up French Canadians suspected of association with the FLQ. Though most of the 450 arrested were never charged with any crime, many were held incommunicado for considerable periods of time. The Canadian Bill of Rights—which prohibits such detention—was rendered inapplicable by the emergency decree.

And on December 4, 1970, Irish Prime Minister John Lynch announced that a grave emergency existed in his country. Citing information that Saore Eire (a splinter group of the Irish Republican Army) was conspiring to kidnap "prominent" ministers, he declared that "unless this threat is removed," he would, without further notice, empower the police to "intern any citizen without trial." The government issued instructions "that places of detention be prepared immediately" and that the Council of Europe be notified that "these proposals will involve derogations from certain provisions of the European Convention on Human Rights."[1]

Israel has not been immune to this phenomenon. It too has departed from fundamental principles of freedom in the name of national security. And world opinion has not ignored Israel's departures from the norms of liberty. Indeed, the comparative level of criticism directed at Israel might lead one to conclude that no nation had ever taken away more liberties with less justification.[2] My thesis is that precisely the opposite is true—that although Israel has suspended some important liberties during recent crises, it has retained far more than any other country faced with comparable dangers. This is not to say that the suspensions have been justified on absolute terms. I myself have been and continue to be critical of some of Israel's policies in this regard. But comparative analysis is essential to a sense of perspective. I propose, therefore, to compare Israel's response to the dangers it faces with

---

[1] On December 14—in the wake of a kidnapping and demonstrations in support of six Basques on trial for murder—Generalissimo Francisco Franco also granted emergency powers to the Spanish police authorizing them to detain persons for up to six months without a hearing. Franco's proclamation of emergency powers automatically suspended that nation's Bill of Rights. Other countries, lacking traditions of liberty—such as Poland and South Africa—have also suspended "liberties" during recent years in response to perceived crises. Recently, Turkey declared "martial law" after the kidnapping of an Israeli diplomat who was subsequently killed.

[2] See, e.g., *Report* of the Special Working Group of Experts Established Under Resolution 6 (xxv) of the Commission on Human Rights (United Nations).

that of other countries which have faced comparable dangers, particularly the United States.

Among the most fundamental safeguards of liberty is the requirement that imprisonment be predicated on proof that a past criminal act was committed, rather than on speculation that an individual may be dangerous in the future. It is precisely this safeguard that is typically suspended during periods of crisis. This should not be surprising, since the requirement of a conviction for past proven acts entails the possibility that dangerous persons —or even guilty ones—may go free. Accordingly, no civilized nation confronting serious danger has ever relied exclusively on criminal convictions for past offenses. Every country has introduced—by one means or another—a system of preventive or administrative detention for persons who are thought to be dangerous but who might not be convictable under the conventional criminal law.

The Israeli preventive detention[3] law permits the imprisonment—without limit of time—of "any person" whose confinement is deemed "necessary or expedient . . . for securing the public safety, the defense of Palestine, the maintenance of public order, or the suppression of mutiny, rebellion or riot."

The Israeli Knesset has never enacted a preventive detention law. The power to detain derives from a series of emergency defense regulations inherited by Israel from the British mandatory government. Ironically, these regulations, originally promulgated in 1937, were directed at the Jewish underground then operating against the British. Many Jewish freedom fighters—including Golda Meir, Moshe Dayan, and others in the present Israeli government—were detained between 1937 and 1948 (as their entries in *Who's Who* proudly proclaim).

During the mandate period, the Jews bitterly opposed preventive detention. The Federation of Hebrew Lawyers convened a protest convention at which they vowed to do everything they could "to abolish the emergency regulations and restore the elementary rights to the individual."

---

[3] The literal translation of the Hebrew term is "administrative detention"; the words "preventive" and "administrative" are used interchangeably when the subject is discussed in English.

In 1948, however, when Israel was established as a state, the emergency regulations—including preventive detention —remained on the books, to be used sporadically until the Six-Day War of 1967 and more extensively after Israel's victory and the resulting occupation.

Many Jews in Israel still oppose preventive detention, even though it is now their government which employs it. The New Left (known in Israel as Siah) has seized on the case of Fawzi al-Asmar as the symbol of what they claim to be political repression of Arab intellectuals. Wherever preventive detention is discussed in Israel, al-Asmar's name is likely to be invoked by its critics.

Having long opposed preventive detention in America,[4] I was greatly troubled when I learned of its use by the Israeli authorities. While in Israel during the summer of 1970, therefore, I decided to try to interview al-Asmar and to learn all I could about why he and the other Israeli Arabs were being detained. When I set out for Damon Prison, I was doubtful whether the authorities would let me talk to him or whether he would be willing to speak to me. I had read accounts of how uncooperative the Israeli authorities were said to be with "snoopers." Moreover, I had called Felicia Langer—a Jewish Communist who represents many detainees—and asked her to arrange an interview. She laughed: "They won't even let me see my clients about legal matters." I had called the Bureau of Prisons, which granted me permission to tour the facility and see the area where the detainees are held, but nothing had been said about interviews.

When I arrived at Damon, I was taken to the special area where the preventive detainees are separately kept. It was a spacious square courtyard surrounded by three large dormitories and a dining area. The detainees—at that time twenty-three Israeli citizens and seventeen from east Jerusalem—were sitting around in small groups. Most of them were young, in their twenties and thirties. They

---

[4] See, for example, my articles, "Preventing Preventive Detention," *New York Review of Books*, March 31, 1969; and "The Psychiatrist's Power in Civil Commitment," *Psychology Today*, February 1969; and my testimony before the Senate Subcommittee on Constitutional Rights, January 23, 1969, Hearing on Bail Reform at pp. 172–85.

were not dressed in prison garb (a number were wearing Arab burnooses) and they were not behaving like prisoners. There was no genuflecting before the warden; they made demands, rather than requests. And not a few times I heard remarks prefaced with, "Remember, we're not prisoners. . . ."

I walked among the inmates and asked for Fawzi al-Asmar. A tall man emerged, strikingly handsome with a captivating smile. Looking more mature than his thirty-one years, he emitted an aura of confidence, determination, and honesty. I could tell, both by looking at him and by the way he behaved with the other inmates, that Fawzi al-Asmar is a leader of men.

I told al-Asmar that his name had been given to me by critics of preventive detention and that I wanted to hear his story. He put an arm around my shoulder and led me toward the empty dining hall where we began to talk. The governor of the prison made no objection and even provided me with a private room in which I later spoke to other detainees.

I asked Fawzi al-Asmar why he was being detained. He looked me directly in the eye and said, "Because I am an Arab." But there are 300,000 Israeli Arabs, I observed, and only a few handfuls are in prison; why were you singled out? "Because I express the feelings of the three hundred thousand and that makes me dangerous. There are Jews who share my beliefs, maybe even some who express them better. But they are not dangerous because they are Jews, and no Arab will listen to them. That is why I am being detained, and not Meir Vilner [the Jewish head of Rakah, the radical Communist party]."

I asked him what the Israeli authorities had accused him of when they detained him thirteen months earlier. He said that they had concocted a story about his being a terrorist organizer. This time I looked straight into his eyes and asked: "Were you a terrorist organizer?" He smiled: "If they could have proved it, they would have brought me to trial."

Did he support al-Fatah? "I support their ideas, but not all of their means." Would he harbor a terrorist fugitive? "None has ever sought refuge with me, and that is the kind of question one must answer with his heart, not his lips. I cannot know what I would do until I hear the knock on the door."

Al-Asmar had few complaints about conditions in the prison. He writes all he wants to—poems, articles, letters —but he has not tried to publish his prison writings. His greatest complaint is that there is no one to talk to in Damon. I asked him if there is any truth to the charge that Israel is using preventive detention against Arab intellectuals. He laughed and said, "If only that were true, at least I would have someone to talk to. Most of those detained are simple people, half of them can't read or write. There used to be a lawyer here and we talked, but he's been freed."

I asked him why Israel was detaining illiterates; surely not for their political activities? Were they terrorists? "No," came his quick reply, "most of them are here as the result of family quarrels and personal vendettas. If two families are feuding in a village, one will sometimes go to the Israelis and make up a story that someone in the other family is working with Fatah."

I asked how he saw the rest of his life unfolding. Would he remain in detention indefinitely? Did he intend to leave Israel after his release? He told me that he could probably be released whenever he chose to be, that various influential people had offered to intercede on his behalf, but that he did not want "special treatment." No, he would never leave the country. "That's just what Israel wants me to do—go away. But this is my homeland. I would rather write my poetry in Damon than in Paris."

As I was leaving, he told me that he was a man of the pen, not of the lips, and that his views on preventive detention were best expressed in two poems he had just written. I asked to read them. He doubted the authorities would allow that. I asked the governor of the prison, and without having seen the poems, he said that al-Asmar was free to give me any writings he cared to. Translations of his poems follow.

PREVENTIVE DETENTION[5]

I sit in preventive detention.
The reason is that I am an Arab.
An Arab who has refused to sell his soul,
who has always striven, sir, for freedom.
An Arab who has protested the suffering of his people
who has carried with him the hope for a just peace,
who has spoken out against death in every corner
who has called for—and has lived—a fraternal life.
That is why I sit in preventive detention
because I carried on the struggle and because I am an Arab.

THE WAY

I would not despair:
Even though my only way is within a jail,
    Under the sun,
    In the Exile—
I would not despair:
I would not choose but the Right as a retaliation,
For my right is that we behold the sun,
    Destroy the black tent and the banishment,
    Eat the fruit of the olive,
    Irrigate the vineyard,
    Sing melodies, melodies of love,
      In the quarters of Jaffa and Haifa,
    Sow our green soil with seeds;
Since these rights are mine,
I would not choose but the Right as a refuge.

My way is that we would extend hand to hand,
In order to build a castle of dreams,
    Full of flowers,
    Without haste,
    Without unwise manners,
Since this is my way,
And even if the cost,
Of my adherence to my way,
Is to sacrifice the lids of my eyes,
    And my soul,

I would pay,
And would not despair!

---

[5] Al-Asmar has written that he prefers the phrase "administrative detention." I can see no significant difference.

Meir Shamgar, the attorney general of Israel, denies that al-Asmar is being detained because he is an Arab. "He is being detained because he is a terrorist leader who would kill innocent people if he were free. Sure he is a poet, but the cloak of a poet can sometimes conceal deadly bombs."

Shamgar, a career legal official who was formerly judge advocate general of the army, knows all there is to know about preventive detention and about terrorism. He has literally been on both sides of the wall. As a young man, he was a member of Irgun Zvai Leumi (known in the U.S. as the Irgun and in Israel as Etzel). Under the leadership of master terrorist Menahem Begin (now the head of Gahal, the right-wing party which recently left Mrs. Meir's governent), the Irgun's raison d'être was to make life so miserable for the British that they would leave Palestine. (They also made life pretty miserable for many Arabs—which is not to their credit.) Among their most notorious accomplishments was the blowing up of the English high command headquarters in the King David Hotel. Although Begin himself eluded capture, Shamgar was caught and detained without trial by the British under the very same regulation which authorized al-Asmar's confinement. Shamgar remained in British detention camps, both in Palestine and in North Africa, for more than four years.

Nor was preventive detention used against Shamgar's comrades-in-arms only by the British. Within weeks after Israel declared its statehood, a half-dozen Irgunites were detained by the new Jewish government in order to head off an insurrection threatened with the arrival of the *Altalena*, a ship packed with weapons earmarked for the Irgun rather than the Haganah. In the fall of 1948, preventive detention was again used by the Israeli government against another group of Jewish terrorists. Following the brutal murder of Count Folke Bernadotte, about a hundred members of Lohamei Herut Israel (known in the U.S. as the Stern Gang, and in Israel as Lehi) were detained for a number of months. During the next four years, preventive detention was twice again employed against Jewish groups; first against an ultra-Orthodox religious organization that was allegedly plotting to plant a smoke bomb in the Knesset; and then against leaders of an organization suspected of bombing two embassies.

Since 1953, preventive detention has not been used against any Jewish group. Indeed between 1953 and 1967, it was used very sparingly; it served primarily as a short-term "holding operation" against suspected spies until it could be decided whether to deport, to try, or to exchange them for Israeli spies.[6] These were years of relative quiet for Israel, during which numerous attempts were made to repeal, or at least to modify, the emergency defense regulations. When Ya'akov Shimshon Shapiro, the incumbent minister of justice, assumed his position in 1966, he convened a committee to study the regulations with an eye toward repeal. (Shapiro had repeatedly expressed disapproval of these laws while in private practice.) The committee was leaning in that direction when the 1967 war forced the government to turn its attention to more pressing concerns.

Israel's victory, accompanied by its occupation of Gaza and the West Bank, brought about an almost immediate increase in terrorist activities. Israeli Arabs, who had been cut off from direct contact with Jordanian Arabs (except through television which respects no political borders), began to mix freely with Arabs from the West Bank. Indeed, under Israel's "open bridge policy," they were able to establish contact with Arabs from the East Bank as well.

Israel's unwillingness to seal the borders resulted not only in a free exchange of views; it also brought about a traffic in weapons and explosives. Now, for the first time, those Israeli Arabs who had preached terrorism could obtain the matériel with which to practice it. The Israeli authorities, who had always tolerated advocacy of the most extreme ideas, now had the job of keeping potential terrorists from practicing what they had been preaching.

Among those who had been preaching such measures was the family of Fawzi al-Asmar. Al-Asmar's mother was also a writer famous for her anti-Israeli prose. His brother was recently convicted of being a Syrian agent

---

[6] A recent example of this was provided by the detention of the two Algerian security officials who were taken off their airplane at Lod Airport, held for a short time, and then released.

and sentenced to a term of imprisonment. But what about Fawzi himself? Shamgar arranged for me to meet with the chief of the Shin Bet's Arab section in order to learn some details of the government's case against al-Asmar.

The Shin Bet is Israel's small but highly respected counterintelligence organization which is responsible for compiling the dossiers on detainees. The chief, whose name I never learned, was a warm and friendly man in his late forties who, like most Israelis of every rank, wore sandals and an open shirt. He explained the procedure employed in building a case for detention. No piece of information is ever relied upon unless it is corroborated by at least two independent sources. "We know about these family quarrels. We don't want to waste our resources on somebody who is the victim of a grudge." He brought out a pile of thick files and laid them on the table. I picked out a few at random for him to go through. He showed me how each important allegation is corroborated in various ways, how each piece of the puzzle is locked into place.

The file on al-Asmar was voluminous and convincing. In every instance where I could, I myself checked the details with independent sources. Here—on the basis of what I was told by various officials and my own investigation—is what I believe to be the truth about Fawzi al-Asmar.

Early last year, the Israeli army caught an Arab attempting to make an illegal crossing over the Jordan. On his person was discovered a number of papers. One was a coded message to a named person in the city on the West Bank. When decoded, the message proved very revealing; it was a detailed series of instructions to the leader of a terrorist group based in that city. The army went to the courier's destination and discovered an enormous cache of weapons and explosives in the home of the intended recipient and sixteen of his associates. They were all subsequently tried, convicted, and sentenced to prison terms.

While this raid was in progress, the search of the courier's effects continued. Another seemingly innocuous piece of paper was found. It turned out, however, that this paper contained a message written in invisible ink. This paper, when processed and decoded, sealed al-Asmar's fate. It was an instruction to a named person to contact one Fawzi al-Asmar in Lydda about various terrorist activities to be carried out by "the group that he has under his control." Among the activities described in the message was the assassination of certain individuals.

Despite this information, al-Asmar was not yet detained; he was placed under surveillance. Over the next weeks, a number of events occurred which made it plain to the Israelis that more stringent measures would have to be taken: two of those slated for assassination in the instructions turned up dead (apparently duplicate messages had been sent with other couriers); the "middleman" who was supposed to deliver the message to al-Asmar was interrograted and said that although he had never met al-Asmar, he knew from others that he was "very active in the field of sabotage and terrorism"; he also said that but for his arrest he would have contacted al-Asmar pursuant to the instructions. Finally, the Shin Bet received corroboration from an Israeli agent who said that he had heard directly from a Palestinian commander in Jordan that al-Asmar had been active in assassination and terrorism since the end of the Six-Day War. As a result of all this information, al-Asmar was detained in Damon Prison where he remained until his release in the fall of 1970.

The case of Fawzi al-Asmar puts the problem of preventive detention into sharp focus. If the Israeli information is correct, then al-Asmar is an extremely dangerous man whose freedom might result in death and injuries. And the information does seem correct. That the Arab caught crossing the Jordan was a bona fide courier is evidenced by the discovered cache and the conviction of the terrorist group; that the messages found on him were genuine is evidenced by the death of two of those marked for assassination; that Fawzi was not the innocent recipient of a message he knew nothing about is evidenced by the statement of the man who was to contact him and corroborated by the agent's report of his discussion with the commander in Jordan. (It is, of course, possible that the entire file was contrived by the Shin Bet. My own investigation convinces me that this was not done, though I cannot, of course, vouch for the authenticity of every piece of information in the file. I am personally convinced, for whatever that is worth, that Fawzi al-Asmar was the leader of a terrorist group.)

Yet even with this apparently tight web of evidence, it would have been quite impossible—under Israeli law— to charge al-Asmar with a crime and bring him to trial. The courier's document—dramatic as it is—would be inadmissible hearsay; it is merely the statement of an unknown person somewhere in Jordan that al-Asmar was the head of a terrorist group. The statement of the "middleman" would also be inadmissible hearsay, since he knew of al-Asmar's activities from others; in any event, he refused to repeat his statement in open court for fear of his life. (Numerous "collaborators" have, in fact, been killed by Arab terrorists.) The Israeli agent from Jordan could not, quite obviously, be brought into court (even if the power of subpoena extended across the Allenby Bridge).

What then are the options available to a democratic society in a case, like this one, where it seems fairly clear that the suspect is indeed a dangerous terrorist but where a criminal trial under the usual rules of evidence is precluded?

One obvious option is to follow the rules wherever they take you. If al-Asmar cannot be tried and convicted under the established rules of evidence, then he must be released no matter how dangerous he is thought to be. This is what we in the United States do—at least in theory— in ordinary criminal cases: if a suspected murderer cannot be convicted because his confession was coerced or because the weapon was discovered unlawfully, he is supposed to be released. Often, however, ways are found to keep the dangerous defendant in confinement despite the absence of a criminal conviction: if he has "homicidal propensities" he may be committed to a mental hospital; if his crime has sexual overtones, he may be confined as a sexual psychopath; even if he must eventually be released, he may be held in pretrial detention for a year or two before his acquittal. It is true, of course, that some suspected murderers are in fact released even though they are thought to be extremely dangerous.

In times of war, however, the United States does not even purport to follow the usual rules of evidence when these rules would lead to the release of suspected spies or saboteurs. During World War II we used administrative tribunals not only to detain; we actually used them to execute suspected enemy agents.[7] I am not aware of any country in the world that follows the customary rules of evidence during wartime, when those rules would lead to the release of persons who are known to have committed —but who could not be convicted of—serious acts of sabotage, espionage, or terrorism. As one high court correctly observed: "Preventive justice . . . is common to all systems of jurisprudence," especially during times of war or national emergency.[8]

And Israel today is a country at war. Although a ceasefire is currently in effect between Israel and some of the Arab states, Israel is at war with various nations and also with the Palestinian terrorist organizations. The war with the Palestinians is being fought not only on Israel's borders, but also in its marketplaces, it cinemas, its bus terminals, and its civilian airplanes. The fear of a bomb planted in a crowded location is ever-present. The security guard who looks into the purse of every woman entering the concert hall and the Supersol is a constant reminder of the Palestinian terrorists' boast that every Arab living in Israel is carrying a bomb in his heart and perhaps in his pocket.

It is interesting to compare Israel's reactions to the dangers it faces with the reaction of the United States when it faced dangers throughout its history.

The great American President Abraham Lincoln is remembered for having issued the Emancipation Proclamation, but he also issued another, less well-known proclamation which had the effect of virtually suspending the American Bill of Rights. A week after the fall of Fort Sumter, Lincoln authorized the suspension of the writ of habeas corpus in designated areas. (Habeas corpus, though not a part of the Bill of Rights, is the critical safeguard

---

[7] See *Ex parte Quirin*, 317 U.S. 1 (1942).

[8] *Maung Hla Gyaw* v. *Commissioner*, 1948 Burma Law Reps. 764, 766. Compare, for example, the emergency rules recently put into effect by the Canadian government. The infringement of civil liberties authorized under these laws far exceeds that authorized under the Israeli regulations; yet the threat of terrorism is clearly not as serious in Canada—at least not yet—as in Israel.

without which all other constitutional protections would remain largely unenforceable, since its suspension would deny the courts the power to release persons held in violation of other protections.)[9]

A test of the constitutionality of emergency powers arose in the case of Lambdin Milligan, who was arrested in Indiana in 1864. Not content to detain him, the military authorities decided to try Milligan—a civilian—before a military commission, which promptly sentenced him to hang. By the time the case worked its way up to the Supreme Court, the war was over and, in Justice Davis's words, "now that the public safety is assured, this question . . . can be discussed and decided without passion or the admixture of any element not required to form a legal judgment." The Supreme Court held that since the civil courts of Indiana—a loyal state—had been open and "needed no bayonets" to protect them, it had been unconstitutional to try Milligan before a military commission. Recognizing that Milligan was arrested in wartime, when passions run high and "considerations of safety" are deemed all-important, the Court concluded that the framers of our Constitution

> . . . foresaw that troublous times would arise, when rulers and people would become restive under restraint, and seek by sharp and decisive measures to accomplish ends deemed just and proper; and that the principles of constitutional liberty would be in peril, unless established by irrepealable law. . . .
>
> This nation has no right to expect that it will always have wise and humane rulers, sincerely attached to the principles of the Constitution. Wicked men, ambitious of power, with hatred of liberty and contempt of law, may fill the place once occupied by Washington and Lincoln, and if this right [to suspend provisions of the Constitution during the great exigencies of government] is conceded, and the calamities of war again befall us, the dangers to human liberty are frightful to comtemplate.

---

[9] The Constitution specifically authorizes suspension "when in cases of Rebellion or Invasion the public safety may require it," and the Civil War was, of course, a rebellion within the intended meaning of that term.

Having delivered itself of this bold rhetoric about
"irrepealable law," the Supreme Court then proceeded to
suggest that the right to bail could be suspended during
emergencies:

> If it was dangerous, in the distracted condition of af-
> fairs, to leave Milligan unrestrained of his liberty . . .
> the *law* said to arrest him, confine him closely, render
> him powerless to do further mischief; and then . . . try
> him according to the course of the common law.

That is what Congress meant, reasoned the Court, when
it authorized the suspension of the privilege of habeas
corpus.

This view was reaffirmed—and strengthened—by Justice
Oliver Wendell Holmes in a case growing out of a private
war between Colorado coal miners and owners which led
to a declaration of local martial law. In addition to suppressing newspapers, deposing civil magistrates, and closing all saloons, the Governor suspended habeas corpus and
ordered the arrest of certain "objectionable characters."
One of these characters, a leader of the miners, was detained without bail for two-and-a-half months and sued
the governor after his release. Holmes argued that since a
governor can order soldiers to "kill persons who resist"
efforts to put down a rebellion, it certainly follows that
"he may use the milder measure of seizing the bodies of
those whom he considers to stand in the way of restoring
peace."

As the result of Holmes' decision, numerous gover-
nors invoked the magic phrase "martial law" as a kind
of "household remedy" to accomplish such diverse and
illegitimate ends as closing a race track, manipulating a
primary election, keeping a neighborhood segregated, and,
frequently, settling labor strikes to the advantage of management. It was inevitable that the Supreme Court could
not long tolerate such bogus declarations of martial law.
The case that finally made the Court lose patience arose
out of a situation in which martial law was invoked simply to accomplish economic ends. The Supreme Court en-
joined the governor's action, reasoning that unless it did
so "the fiat of a state Governor, and not the Constitution

of the United States, would be the supreme law of the land."

That is where the law stood on December 7, 1941, when the Japanese air force bombed Pearl Harbor, throwing Hawaii into turmoil and generating fear of attack in our West Coast cities. Within hours, the governor of Hawaii, at the insistence of the army, declared martial law, suspended habeas corpus, ordered the civil courts closed, and empowered military tribunals to try all criminal cases. Relative calm returned quickly to the islands as the threat of renewed attack dissipated; places of amusement and saloons were permitted to open in February 1942; and life returned to near normality after our victory at Midway removed any realistic threat of invasion. But the military still insisted that the civil courts remain closed and the writ of habeas corpus remain suspended. Not until after the war (and the restoration of habeas corpus by the President) did the Supreme Court decide that Congress, in authorizing martial law in Hawaii, had not intended to permit the "supplanting of courts by military tribunals." By that time, thousands of man-days of illegal imprisonment had already been served.[10]

Martial law in Hawaii, with all its abuses, did not include the kind of mass detention on racial grounds used on the West Coast from 1942 to 1944. At that time there were about 110,000 Americans of Japanese ancestry living on the West Coast, of whom 70,000 were American citizens (virtually all of them born here, since residents who emigrated from Japan were ineligible for American citizenship under the racial prohibitions then on our statute books). A virulent anti-Japanese hysteria followed Pearl Harbor. Rumors were circulated that Hawaiians of Japa-

---

[10] The main reason why this issue did not reach the Supreme Court earlier was that the Justice Department "mooted" prior cases by releasing the defendants as soon as they filed petitions in the Supreme Court.

An extreme—and absurd—example of the inclination of judges to defer decision until after the emergency had passed was provided by a case growing out of the Hawaiian martial rule. In 1944, a circuit court of appeals had approved the military trial of civilians. Two years later Circuit Judge Stephens filed a belated dissenting opinion, saying he had been reluctant to file it while the war was still going on.

nese ancestry were signaling enemy pilots and submarines;
that Japanese-Americans had intentionally infiltrated the
power and water companies; and that they had formed
sabotage and espionage rings numbering in the thousands.
In fact none of these stories proved true. The records of
"the Federal Bureau of Investigation and army and navy
intelligence indicate that there was not a single instance
of espionage or sabotage by a resident of Japanese ancestry before, during, and after World War II. . . ."[11] The
absence of such activities did not, however, satisfy a hysterical population with deep-rooted racial antagonisms. Indeed Earl Warren, then attorney general of California, expressed the Alice in Wonderland view that it was the very
absence of sabotage that was "the most ominous sign in
our whole situation." It convinced him, he said, "that the
sabotage . . . the fifth-column activities that we are to get,
are timed just like Pearl Harbor," and that the present
inaction by the Japanese-Americans was designed to lull
us "into a false sense of security."[12]

The various intelligence agencies—the FBI and army
and navy intelligence—preferred to approach the problem
of potential terrorism and espionage "on the basis of the
individual, regardless of citizenship, and not on a racial
basis." This was what was done with persons of German
and Italian extraction on the East Coast. Thousands of
aliens "regarded by the Attorney General as dangerous to
the national security if permitted to remain at large" were
preventively detained on an individual basis. But on the
West Coast the prevalent attitude was reflected by General
De Witt, head of the Western Defense Command: "A Jap's
a Jap. There is no way to determine their loyalty. . . ."
Earl Warren agreed: "We believe that when we are dealing with the Caucasian race we have methods that will
test their loyalty. . . . But when we deal with the Japanese
. . . we cannot form any opinion that we believe to be
sound."[13] Accordingly, the decision was made to confine
the entire West Coast population of Japanese-Americans:

---

[11] This is the claim of the Japanese-American Citizens League,
and I know of no allegations to the contrary.

[12] Quoted in Hosokowa, *Nisei: The Quiet Americans* (New
York: Morrow, 1969), p. 288.

[13] Ibid., pp. 287–88.

109,650 men, women, and children were put in detention camps where they remained for nearly the entire war. Virtually no exceptions were made; those detained included veterans of World War I, future soldiers who would die fighting in the famous 442d Regimental Combat Team (the "Nisei Brigade"), and lifelong members of the American Legion (whose monthly publication advocated "putting American Japanese on some Pacific island").

Liberal opinion in the United States was extremely critical of the detention of the Japanese-Americans on racial grounds. Prominent leaders of the American Civil Liberties Union urged President Roosevelt to "constitute a system of hearing boards to test the loyalty" of individual citizens and noncitizens. Those justices of the Supreme Court who dissented from the judicial approval given the exclusion and detention orders criticized the government for not treating "these Japanese-Americans on an individual basis by holding investigations and hearings to separate the loyal from the disloyal as was done in the case of persons of German and Italian ancestry." (Virtually no criticism was ever leveled against the preventive detention of the latter.) Academic criticism centered on our failure to detain Japanese-Americans "on the basis of individual suspicion," and also on our unwillingness to adopt a system of graded restrictions—as the English and French did—whereby only the most dangerous were detained and others "were subjected to certain continuing restrictions especially as to their travel."[11]

What the liberals in the United States urged that we do with our Japanese citizens is essentially what Israel has done with its Arab citizens. It has made an intensive

---

[11] Rostow, "The Japanese American Cases—A Disaster," *Yale Law Review* 54 (1945): 489. After the war ended, Congress enacted an individualized preventive detention law directed against members of "the World Communist movement" and sponsored by such liberal senators as Humphrey, Douglas, Kefauver, and Lehman. That law authorized the "detention of persons who there is reasonable ground to believe probably will commit or conspire with others to commit espionage or sabotage." Since it can come into operation only in the event of a foreign invasion, a declaration of war, or an insurrection to aid a foreign enemy, this detention act has never been employed but has recently been repealed by Congress.

effort to separate out the potential terrorists from the loyal Arabs, or even the "merely disloyal" Arabs. "We are not interested in loyalty," I was told by the minister of justice. "We don't care what they believe in their hearts; we care only about what they conceal under their clothing. Let them pray for Arab victory, as long as they don't work for it."

The Israeli authorities have divided their Arab citizens into four categories. The first covers the loyal and "merely disloyal," which includes more than 99 percent of Israel's 300,000 Arab citizens. They are not subject to any significant restrictions on their liberty. They enjoy the rights of citizenship; they may live and travel almost anywhere (including the occupied territories); they may read the various anti-Israel newspapers published in Jerusalem and elsewhere; they may—as a considerable number of them do—belong to the Rakah party which has three members in the Knesset.[15] The fact that they are Arabs and that Israel is at war with Arabs has not resulted in legal discriminations against them (unless their not being subject to the draft is regarded as discrimination).

The Arab-Israeli is, to be sure, subject to some de facto discrimination. He is stopped more frequently at the roadblocks which the Israeli police routinely set up at the entrance points to every large city. But if his identification is in order—every Israeli, Jew as well as Arab, must carry an identification card—he is politely sent on his way. It is far more difficult for an Arab—even a loyal Arab—to get a job which has any connection with security (a word which has a broad meaning in Israel). And—most unfortunately—it is often difficult for an Arab to find housing in certain parts of the country.

Thus, those Arabs who are not regarded by the security service as potential terrorists, saboteurs, or assassins are not subjected to legal restrictions, even if it is known that their sympathies lie with the enemy. Even those who are regarded as potential terrorists are not all detained. The majority are simply told not to leave their city, town, or village without permission; within that area they are free

---

[15] The day I visited the Knesset it was presided over by the deputy speaker, who is a Christian Arab from Nazareth.

to move about as they please by night or day. Permission to travel to other cities is routinely granted for business reasons and periodically for family and social reasons.

Those who are regarded as especially dangerous—a few hundred—are subject to further restrictions: they may not leave their homes during the hours of darkness without special permission (a kind of personalized curfew), and they must report daily to the local police station.

Only a tiny portion of potential terrorists—twenty-three Israeli citizens during the summer of 1970, and fifteen at the most recent count in the spring of 1971—are actually detained. (The number has never been more than about 100.) The Israeli authorities claim that every one of those detained has, in fact, been involved in serious terrorist activities and that they could not effectively be prevented from carrying on future terrorism by restrictions less total than actual detention.[16]

If there are only two dozen Israeli citizens who are sufficiently dangerous to be preventively detained, would it not be wiser, I asked an Israeli official, to release them

---

[16] It must be pointed out that the fifteen detainees mentioned above do not include the Arabs from occupied territories or from east Jerusalem. A considerably larger number of Gaza Strip and West Bank Arabs—in the neighborhood of 500—are being held in preventive detention. Following the terrorist hijackings in the summer of 1970 an additional 450 West Bank Arabs were detained for a brief period and then released. Residents of the West Bank are Jordanian, not Israeli, citizens. Under the Geneva accords, Jordanian law is supposed to govern their conduct. The Jordanian law applicable to the West Bank derives from the very same emergency defense regulations inherited by Israel and explicitly authorizes preventive detention. When the Jordanian government controlled the West Bank, it made extensive use of preventive detention against Palestinian political opponents. During a visit to the West Bank, I was shown a petition—found by the Israeli army during the war—that had been signed by hundreds of Palestinian women whose husbands, sons, and fathers had been preventively detained by the Jordanian government on "political" grounds. Preventive detention of dangerous members of an occupied population is also authorized by the Geneva accords. It has been practiced by all occupying armies confronting a hostile population. I have, in this article, limited myself to preventive detention as it is practiced on citizens of Israel; I have not dealt with the occupied territories, which present different considerations, both legal and practical.

and take the risks of a few additional acts of terrorism? He responded by telling me the story of Leon Kanner.

Leon was a Hebrew University student who had recently emigrated to Israel from his native Uruguay. His family lived on a kibbutz where they worked in agriculture. Leon shared a small flat in Jerusalem with his friend Edward Joffe, a student who had been twice wounded during the Six-Day War. On the weekend of February 21, 1969, the boys were planning a "trip to the hills to pick flowers," as Edward wrote to his parents. On Friday morning, the roommates went together to the Supersol at Jerusalem's busiest intersection to do some shopping for their trip. The store—which is one of the largest in Israel—was crowded with women doing their pre-Sabbath shopping. As the boys approached the meat counter, an explosion ripped through the store. A bomb containing five kilograms of dynamite had been planted in a biscuit can. Both boys were killed instantly. Many women—including a survivor of Auschwitz—were seriously injured. On another Friday—the eve of the Jewish Sabbath seems to be a favorite time for terrorist activities—al-Fatah planted a massive charge of explosives in an automobile in Machane Yehuda, the always crowded outdoor market in Jerusalem. Twelve shoppers were killed and fifty-two seriously injured.

These are the realities of living in Israel today. They are not rumors, like those which were used to justify our detention of the Japanese. Every Israeli knows a family that has suffered from terrorism, whether it was the blowing up of the Hebrew University cafeteria, the bomb in the Tel Aviv bus station, or the explosions in the Haifa apartment houses.[17] A decision to release a known terrorist who cannot be brought to trial is viewed as a decision to risk the lives of dozens of civilians. Rightly or wrongly, these are the reasons why Israel will not—at least in the most serious handful of cases—follow the usual rules of evidence when these rules lead to release. Indeed, I was surprised that the Israeli population had not de-

---

[17] Indeed, the Dolphin—an excellent fish restaurant in east Jerusalem that is jointly owned by a Jew and an Arab—was blown up shortly after I ate there.

manded detention for more of those under village restriction.[18]

A second obvious option available to a democratic country in a case like al-Asmar's is to change the usual rules of evidence—especially the often anachronistic hearsay rule—so as to allow the introduction of reliable information even if its direct source cannot be produced in court. If hearsay evidence were admissible, a conviction might very well be obtainable against al-Asmar: the invisible-ink document could be introduced if the prosecutor established its authenticity; the statement of the man who was supposed to contact al-Asmar could be admitted without his identity being disclosed; and even the communication from the agent in Jordan might be considered by the judge.

I asked a high-ranking Israeli legal official whether it would not be better to loosen up their hearsay and other evidentiary rules. "We are very proud of our civil liberties," he told me. "It would be absurd to wreck our entire judicial system to accommodate a few wartime security cases." But would you really have to wreck the system, I asked, couldn't you just change some of the rules of evidence? "The rules of evidence lie at the center of our civil liberties and the right to confront your accuser is the heart of any fair system of evidence. If we created a rule allowing into evidence the invisible-ink message and the agent's report, there would be virtually nothing left to the right of confrontation. I would rather see us act completely lawlessly in a few security cases than a little lawlessly in every case." This official felt strongly enough to say that he would "resign in protest" if Israel ever changed its rules to allow hearsay evidence in the general run of cases.

A third option, and the one adopted by Israel, is to create a separate category of cases entirely outside of the judicial system: to handle them administratively; and to apply the flexible rules of evidence traditional in admin-

---

[18] The Israeli authorities publicly belittle the damage done by terrorists, claiming that more Israelis die each year from automobile accidents than from terrorist attacks. But anyone who has driven on Israeli roads can take little comfort from that comparison.

istrative cases. The basic reason why Israel opted for this approach is that the mechanism was there, fully blown; the law establishing this system was on the books of Israel, even though it had been inscribed by a British pen.[19] There is no written constitution in Israel under which the regulations could be invalidated, though one Supreme Court justice, writing in dissent, would have struck down preventive detention as inconsistent with the judicial conscience (a phrase similar to the "shock of conscience test" sometimes applied by our Supreme Court).

The preventive detention regulation inherited from the British is written in the broadest possible terms. There are no restrictions on the military commanders' discretion; no limits on the duration of detention; no rules of evidence; and no judicial review. The regulation does require that there be "one or more advisory committees [whose chairman] shall be a person who holds or has held judicial office or is or has been a senior officer of the government." But the commander is under no legal obligation to follow the advice of the committee.

When the British administered this regulation in Palestine, they did so in the spirit in which it was written. It was a purely arbitrary grant of power to the military unlimited by narrowing rules or practices. The Israeli government, although it has left the broad language of the regulation unamended, has circumscribed it by a series of carefully drawn rules and established practices. Until now these rules were unpublished and regarded as secret (though lawyers had some idea of what they provided). After numerous requests, I was finally given a copy of them. Among other things, they explicitly remove the power to detain for more than three months from any military commander (as provided in the regulation) and give it solely to the chief of the General Staff. In addition to the advisory committee required by the regulations, the

---

[19] It was there as a result of the first law of the state of Israel under which "The Law that existed in the Land of Israel on the Fifth Day of Iyar 5708 [the last day of the British mandate] will be in force" unless repealed or inconsistent with subsequent enactments.

rules establish an internal advisory committee which includes lawyers and professors; no request for a detention order may be made to the chief of staff unless a majority of the committee so votes. Another rule limits any period of detention to six months and requires a complete review at the end of this period. In addition, the advisory committee—which includes a justice of the Supreme Court —is regarded as more than advisory; its advice has never been ignored by the Israeli military authorities in twenty-two years. What is most important, however, is not the language of the regulation or of the narrowing rules; it is the fact—and a fact that is not challenged by Arab or Jewish critics—that the number of Israeli citizens actually detained has been so impressively small.

Despite the fact that so few have been detained, there has been much criticism from students, journalists, leftists, lawyers, and—of course—Arabs. And the criticism has by no means emanated exclusively from the left. Hans Klinghoffer, the intellectual leader of the right-wing Gahal party, told me that he was unalterably opposed to "this unpardonable exception to the rule of law." "Terrorists must be imprisoned," he declared, "but not by means of legal terrorism." He feared that a population gets used to "special rules of war" and has difficulty living without them even when peace returns. He has tried to enact an Israeli security law to replace the "British abomination." Under his proposal, the suspected terrorist would be tried by a court, but the rules of evidence would be specially adapted to security cases. Could a person like Fawzi al-Asmar be convicted under his proposal? "Probably yes."

I asked the minister of justice, Ya'akov Shapiro, why he opposed Klinghoffer's proposal. "I do not want to get the courts involved in the business of the military. The only effect would be to legitimate—to impose a judicial imprimatur of lawfulness—on actions which are taken for military necessity but fall outside the rule of law."[20]

---

[20] He reminded me of the observation made by Justice Jackson in the Japanese-American detention cases: "In the very nature of things, military decisions are not susceptible of intelligent judicial appraisal. They . . . are made on information that would often not be admissible and assumptions that could not be proved. . . .

I asked Shapiro whether it would not be wiser for Israel to enact its own preventive detention law to reflect its narrowly circumscribed practices. He preferred to keep things the way they were. "It is one thing for the military to use somebody else's law. It is quite another thing for the Knesset to enact as its own a new preventive detention law." He told me that he could not vote for a preventive detention law. "I have seen the inside of a prison, and not as a visitor. I know what it means to be preventively detained. How many ministers of justice do you know who have been in jail?" (He described a recent meeting of a committee of distinguished Israeli jurists. "You know that every member of the committee had spent some time in British, German, or Russian jails. People like us could not bring ourselves to vote for an Israeli law of preventive detention.")

I asked the minister how he could speak so sanctimoniously about not wanting to enact a preventive detention law when he readily enforces the present regulation. He was hurt by my question. "I do not enforce that regulation. I have nothing to do with it. That is a matter between the military authorities and the advisory committee. It is not within my jurisdiction. It is not a matter of law. It is a matter of military necessity."

That kind of argument is not very convincing to critics of the New Left, the most prominent of whom is a no-nonsense journalist named Amos Kenan who has long been critical of preventive detention in particular and of Israeli policies toward Arabs in general.

He too had known preventive detention from the other side, having been a member of the Stern Gang as a young man. Kenan had no doubt that most of the Arabs detained were indeed terrorists. He knew, from personal contacts, that numerous Israeli Arabs were working with al-Fatah and with the Popular Front for the Liberation of Palestine. "Before the Six-Day War I know that many Is-

---

Hence courts can never have any real alternative to accepting the mere declaration of the authority that issued the order that it was reasonably necessary from a military viewpoint. . . ."

Jackson went on to conclude that the *judicial approval* of the army order detaining the Japanese was a "far more subtle blow to liberty than the promulgation of the order itself."

raeli Arabs were reporting Israeli troop movements to the Arab government. Our army knew it as well; in fact, they arranged some phony movements with the expectation that they would be reported." I asked him on what he based his information. He told me that he is—and has been for many years—very close to Arab radicals. This began during his days with the Stern Gang, which, he claims, was the "only true anti-colonialist army in Palestine. We had no quarrel with the Arabs. We had a common cause with them against the British. I wept bitterly the first time we were attacked by Arabs and had to fight back. I really did regard them as brothers fighting a single enemy." On the eve of the Six-Day War, a group of Kenan's Arab friends—confident of Egyptian victory—offered his family refuge from the massacre they expected against the Jews. Kenan politely declined the offer and went to join his reserve unit. (Virtually no one in Israel—regardless of his political views—declines to serve in Israel's army.)

I asked Kenan whether in light of his own observations about Arab attitudes and actions, he could really say that Israel was unjustified in detaining the small number of Arabs now in Damon Prison. He told me that his condemnation of preventive detention had to be understood in the context of Israeli-Arab relations over the past twenty years. "Maybe it is needed now. But it might not have been needed if our government had adopted a different policy toward its Arab citizens over the past generation. I could support preventive detention only if I were certain that there had been no other way. But there was another way."

I discussed with him the allegation that people like Fawzi al-Asmar were being detained for their political views. He smiled when I mentioned the poet's name. "I've known Fawzi for a long time. We worked together on many causes. There isn't an honest bone in his body. He's deceitful, he's a parasite, and I think he's a lousy poet. There may be political detainees; Fawzi may even be one of them; but don't believe a word he tells you; don't be taken in by that goddamn smile.

"Fawzi is one of those Arabs," he continued, "who criticizes the hell out of Israel whenever she deserves it; but he doesn't have the balls to criticize any Arab government or group, ever. When I ask him why he doesn't, he says that you have to understand the risks of making such criticism are very great. But that's the goddamn problem with the Palestinian movement. They should take personal risks for their beliefs. The Palestinians will become a real people only after a few of them have been hung for saying what they believe. I'm sorry, but I can't accept a double standard when judging Arabs and Jews."

I asked him whether he himself wasn't employing a double standard by being so vocal in his criticism of Israel's detention practices and so silent about the far more extensive use of preventive detention in Arab countries. His answer was that Israel deserved special criticism because its performance did not match its boasts about human liberty. "In any event, I am an Israeli and therefore I have a special obligation to be critical of my government."

I asked him whether he would advocate releasing the detainees even though he knew that among them were potential terrorists. "Yes," he said sadly, "even if it results in an explosion or two. That's the price we have to pay for our past errors." I asked whether he thought the day would ever come when Jewish critics, like him, would be detained. "I anticipate that happening in your country sooner than mine," he said. "Look at the way you treat your Communists. Ours are elected to the Knesset and practice law."

Felicia Langer is a Communist who practices law in partnership with an Arab Israeli named Ali Rafi. She sees preventive detention as directed primarily against the Communists. "Our people were the first to be detained. That's how I got into this area." I asked Mrs. Langer whether preventive detention was used for political reasons. "Yes, for political reasons against Communists and also as a means of pressure to get Arabs to collaborate." Does it work, I asked? "Not against our people. Not a single Communist has collaborated."

If it is used against political opponents, I asked, why are there no Jews being detained? "It is a racist law, just like in your country the laws are directed against third-world people. Israel is a fascist country, they fight aggressive wars. I am concerned where this is all going to lead."

I asked whether the Communist party was against preventive detention in principle or just when it is directed at Communists. She boasted that there are no such laws in Communist countries. I reminded her that thousands of people are detained in Russian jails without trials, and that we all know what a Russian trial means. "I am not interested in their practices, only their laws," she said with contempt.

My own academic bias leads me to be at least as interested in actual practices as written laws. I set out, therefore, to make an independent appraisal of preventive detention in practice. On the basis of my experience, I find it difficult to understand the criticism leveled against Israel by groups such as Amnesty International and the United Nations Commission on Human Rights who claim that Israel will not open its doors to their investigatory teams. Almost every door in Israel seemed unlocked; all that was needed was some initiative, and, sometimes, a gentle push. The authorities in Israel were aware of my critical attitude toward preventive detention; yet they imposed no restrictions on my activities.

I interviewed numerous Arabs, both in detention and under village restriction. I spoke to their lawyers, to government officials, and to men on the street. I heard both sides of every case. In each instance where I could, I checked these often conflicting versions with third parties or documented records.

My investigation led me to conclude that virtually all of those detained had, in fact, been involved in terrorist activities; that the vast majority could not be tried under Israeli law; and that a considerable number would probably engage in future terrorism if released. Some of the detainees were not bomb throwers themselves; they were recruiters, money raisers, and—like al-Asmar—commanders. Not one of them was a mere politician, or a writer without connection to terrorist activities.[21]

Only one detention case troubled me greatly on its

---

[21] There has been some suggestion by Israeli authorities that preventive detention might be used against convicted terrorists who have served short prison terms, who are due for release, and who pose a danger of renewed terrorist activities. A change in sentencing practices would seem to be a better way to deal with the recidivistic terrorist.

facts, perhaps because it involved a lawyer. It deserves
recitation because it marks, in my view, the boundary beyond which Israel has not gone in preventively detaining
its citizens.

Sabri Jaris is a thirty-one-year-old Arab who began
speaking and writing against the Israeli government when
he was still a teen-age law student at the Hebrew University. Until recently he practiced law in Haifa, sharing office
space with an older Arab lawyer active in Rakah and a
Jewish lawyer affiliated with Maki (the Jewish Communist
party). Jaris divided his time between representing members of the Palestine Liberation Organization charged
with terrorism, and writing books about the plight of the
Israeli Arab.

Early last year, Jaris found himself in need of a lawyer.
He was arrested by the Shin Bet and detained. Preventive
detention was no stranger to Jaris. During the last hours of
the Six-Day War, he—along with a handful of other Arabs
who had publicly called for Egyptian victory—was detained for a short time. (Jaris is fond of remarking: "You
know, the Israeli never would have won the war if they
hadn't detained me.")

For the first month of detention, Jaris was angry but
hopeful of early release. When it did not come, he began
to organize the other detainees. He started a hunger strike
which received international publicity; he brought law-
suits challenging the conditions of detention; he sought
his own freedom by writ of habeas corpus; he notified his
French publisher who came to Israel with a famous con-
tinental advocate; he stimulated protests by other members of the Israeli bar (Jewish as well as Arab). Three
months after his arrest, Jaris was sent home to Haifa.

It was in that city, just a few weeks after his release,
that I spoke to Sabri Jaris. His office, which was on a third-
floor walk-up in the Arab market, was shabby and not
even charming. There was no privacy; three large rooms
—each with a number of desks—simply adjoined one
another without any doors. Loud discussions in Hebrew
and Arabic permeated every corner while a dozen Arab
clients, mostly old, waited to speak with one of the lawyers. Jaris invited me into his room and we began our often
interrupted conversation.

Jaris told me, in his soft fluent English, of his early life in a small Arab village on the Palestinian side of what is now the Israel-Lebanon border. His parents and most of their nine children still live there, and Jaris and his younger brother used to visit them on Christian holidays. During his university years, Jaris became active in various Arab nationalist movements. He was one of the founders of El Ard, an extreme movement which advocated the destruction of Israel. Even before the Six-Day War he had been in trouble with the security service. Once he was briefly detained for investigation after a Lebanese Arab caught trying to cross the border illegally had "mentioned his name." For the past eight years there has been an order outstanding against him which limits his movement outside Haifa without special permission.

I asked him how this restriction affected his life. He told me that it had little or no impact on his professional career, that he could—and does—go anywhere his law practice takes him. His personal life, is, however, severely restricted. He told me that he was recently denied permission to attend a friend's wedding and that his visits to his parents' village near the Lebanon border have been limited to certain religious and family occasions. (Twice he has been caught violating these restrictions and fined.)

We talked about his most recent detention. The Shin Bet had received information that Jaris's younger brother had crossed over into Lebanon and joined al-Fatah. They accused Jaris of harboring him on his way to carrying out a terrorist mission, and Jaris denied all knowledge of his brother's activities. He told me with a smile that was both sad and proud: "I think the authorities are right. My brother is working with Fatah in Lebanon." But he quickly added that he did not harbor or help him. "My brother's activities were the pretext the government has been looking for all along. They detained me because of my political views."

Moving to those views, I asked him what he thought of al-Fatah. "I understand them, I sympathize with the way they are fighting and what they are fighting for." Did he agree with their tactics? "I feel good when I hear that Fatah have attacked an enemy—that is an Israeli—army camp. I don't like the idea of bombs for innocent people.

But how do you expect them to do otherwise when Israel blows up the houses of innocent people in Hebron?"[22] Would he help a member of Fatah who sought refuge in his home? "No, I would not give him a place to stay. But neither would I inform the police that he sought refuge. That would be asking too much." Did he regard himself as a loyal citizen of Israel? "I regard myself first and foremost as a Palestinian Arab. Israel was imposed on me. But I have accepted Israeli citizenship and membership in its bar. I have chosen to remain here. I obey the laws, but no more. I would not fight against my brother Arabs, and that is not required of me by Israeli law. I long for Arab victory, but I do not actively work for it." Why did he suppose they released him after three months? "They had no choice. The pressure was too great. World opinion does not tolerate the detention of a lawyer. In the end they were sorry they had started up with me."

I suspect that Jaris may be right: Israeli officials do seem sorry now that they detained him. The case against Sabri Jaris—as told me by government officials and others—was not nearly as compelling as the case against Fawzi al-Asmar. It was the least convincing of the many cases I had investigated.

It seems that Jaris's native village on the Israeli side of the Lebanon border—Fasuta—was a favorite stopping-off place for terrorists entering Israel from the north. One day early this year, the Israeli police observed a small truck driving suspiciously fast in the area of Fasuta. After a brief chase the truck crashed into a tree, but the occupants escaped into a wooded area. Inside the truck, the police found two large sacks of explosives and detonating devices. They ultimately traced the truck to its owner in Fasuta and were told the driver of the truck was Jarius Jaris, Sabri's younger brother. They also learned from a number of reliable people in the village that Jarius spent both the night before and the night after the truck incident with Sabri (who had traveled from Haifa to Fasuta to meet him).

Within a few days the Shin Bet received a communica-

---

[22] Israel has blown up some houses in which terrorists have hidden. No inhabitants have ever been hurt in these explosions.

tion from an agent in Lebanon corroborating their information about where Jarius had spent the two nights. They also were told by the agent that Sabri and Jarius had planned further sabotage action in the Haifa area. Sabri was then detained—according to the Israeli authority—not for the purpose of punishing him for harboring a member of al-Fatah, but rather to prevent him from carrying out further collaborative work with his terrorist brother who was still at large. The reason Sabri was not brought to trial was because all the evidence against him was obtained from sources that either would not testify (the Fasuta villagers) or could not testify (the agent in Lebanon).

If Jaris was planning future terrorist activities, then why, I asked, was he released after only three months of detention? I was told that something had occurred in May of this year which made it highly unlikely that Jaris could carry out the planned activities. I asked what this occurrence was, and for the first and only time in my numerous interviews, I was told: "This we cannot tell you." My surmise is that the Israeli authorities have learned that Jarius is no longer a threat and have concluded that Sabri himself, without his brother, does not constitute a sufficient danger to justify his continued detention. Accordingly he was sent back to Haifa, restricted in his travel, but otherwise unhampered in the practice of his profession. In September 1970, Sabri Jaris left Israel and moved to Beirut, Lebanon. The reason given for his departure was that he had "probably done all he could effectively do under the prevailing conditions of repression."

Sabri Jaris's case is disturbing to me. I believe that he probably did harbor his brother as the Shin Bet charges. But that does not purport to be the basis on which he was detained. His future dangerousness was evidenced merely by the uncorroborated report of an agent. Moreover, it did not have the kind of specificity contained in the evidence marshaled against al-Asmar. Finally, if the only fear was that Jaris might collaborate with a given person, namely his brother, then it seems to me that careful surveillance might have been adequate to prevent this eventuality.

It must be remembered, however, that the Sabri Jaris

case was not permitted to run its full course. Since his detention ended after three months, it need not have been
approved by the internal advisory committee of the chief
of staff. Nor did the outside advisory committee or the
courts have an opportunity to review its merits. Any one of
these might well have decided to release him, as in fact the
security people decided themselves to do after ninety
days. It must also be remembered that following his release Sabri returned to the active practice of law, despite
his various detentions and violations. Consider whether a
lawyer in this country would, after Jaris's experience, be
permitted to resume his practice unhampered by Bar Association investigation and discipline.

The case of Sabri Jaris leaves me with two impressions:
first, the suspicion that he might have remained in Damon
well beyond the three months if he had not been as prominent and vocal as he was; and second, the confidence that
this is as far as the Israelis will take preventive detention,
and perhaps that they will never again apply it in so ques-
tionable a case.

CONCLUSION

I have attempted to present a fair picture of how a
democratic society faced with real danger from within and
without is coping with the delicate task of balancing the interests of liberty and security. Some critics of Israel,
domestic and external, act as if there were no real threat
of terrorism—as if the explosions at Machane Yehuda and
the Supersol were "Reichstag fires" contrived by the government for the explicit purpose of curtailing liberties. Some
Israeli government officials, on the other hand, speak as if
there were no restrictions on civil liberties. Neither of these
views is correct. Civil liberties have in fact been curtailed
in the face of a genuine threat of terrorism. The curtail-
ment has been considerably less than one might have expected, certainly less than one might be led to believe by
various organizations such as Amnesty International and
the United Nations Commission on Human Rights.

Having attempted to place the problem in context, I am,
of course, entitled to my own personal views. I fully understand the arguments in favor of preventive detention as it

is presently practiced in Israel; I am convinced that it is not being abused and that every good-faith effort is being made to apply it only to persons who have engaged in terroristic activities and are likely to continue to be so engaged. I am impressed with the tiny number of Israeli citizens actually detained. And I, of course, appreciate the danger which Israel faces from terrorism. Nonetheless, I personally favor repeal of the emergency defense regulations and particularly of the preventive detention provisions. Nor is there any paradox in understanding the reasons behind a law, in recognizing that it has been fairly applied, and—at the same time—in favoring its repeal. Although the potential for abuse has not materialized, the possibility of abuse is inherent in the nature of detention laws of the kind now on the books in Israel. Such laws, in the words of Justice Jackson "lie about like a loaded weapon."

If Israel feels that it cannot live with the normal rules of evidence in cases of suspected terrorists, then the Knesset should enact special rules of evidence for a narrowly circumscribed category of cases during carefully defined periods of emergency. All other safeguards should be provided, as in ordinary cases. In the last analysis, such a system might result in the release of some who are now detained. It is in the nature of any judicial system that in order to prevent confinement of the innocent, it must sometimes release the guilty. And those released might engage in acts of terrorism. But risks to safety have always been the price a society must pay for its liberty. Israel knows that well. By detaining only 15 of its 300,000 Arab citizens, Israel today is taking considerable risks. Indeed, what the world must come to realize is that no country throughout recorded history has ever exposed its wartime population to so much risk in the interest of civil liberties.

Modernization and Arab Society: Some Reflections

Shlomo Avineri

SHLOMO AVINERI—chairman of the Department of
Political Science at the Hebrew University of
Jerusalem, author of *The Social and Political
Thought of Karl Marx*.

It has become a truism among political observers and
commentators to discuss Arab society in terms of "under-
development" and to attribute to this its weakness in confronting Israel. If one applies the usual criteria for measuring development, one understandably arrives at indexes
of "underdevelopment" in comparing Arab society to the
Israeli social structure. The picture, however, is much
more complex, and the internal tensions and dilemmas of
Arab society cannot simply be dismissed in such mechanistic terms. The problem is a far deeper one, reaching back
into the history of Arab civilization and the nature of its
initial confrontation with the West.

One of the crucial facts to be remembered in any evaluation of the impact of the West on Arab society is the unusual context of Western colonial rule in the Arab world.
Unlike European imperial rule in most other parts of the
Afro-Asian world, where the Western powers established direct colonial administrations, the Arab countries
(with the exception of Algeria) were never under direct
colonial rule. Though the history of British penetration
into Egypt is different from the history of British rule in
Iraq, there is one common denominator to all European
forms of rule and influence in the Arab Middle East: no
Arab country—except Algeria—has ever been a colony
in the strict sense; nowhere did the Western power put an
end to the social and politico-cultural dominant role of

the traditional local elites, and nowhere did it impose on the country a Western-type colonial administration.

The Arab countries got, in a way, the worst of both worlds. Whatever the sins of imperialism, it did, after all (as has been pointed out very perceptively by Marx) put an end to the old, traditional society. Western economic penetration smashed the autarchy of the old village system; the colonial administration, aiming as it did at its own version of "law and order," managed in the process to introduce rational codes of law, to break up the traditional forms of political rule and societal influence, and to train at least a segment of the population in Western, secular schools so as to enable them to fulfill administrative posts within the colonial system. The colonial power, whatever its own motivation, became the prime mover in the modernization of the non-European world. When in the process of development the ex-colonies became independent states, the only real infrastructure they had which made it possible for them to come to grips with the modern world was the legacy of colonial rule. India, of course, is a prime example: it was only under the British that the historical conglomerate loosely called "India" became a coherent political entity.

None of this happened in the Arab countries. Western influence grew at the expense of the crumbling Ottoman Empire, to which most Arab countries belonged in one way or another. The economic and strategic interest of Britain and France became guaranteed in the process of the dismantling of the Turkish Empire through a complex system of indirect control, without recourse to outright colonial rule. Whether it was called protectorate or mandate, the system ensured the overall paramountcy of the Western power without involving it in direct administration—without, therefore, basically affecting the socio-economic infrastructure of Arab society. The traditional elites were not superseded by new ones; on the contrary, in some cases they even formalized and institutionalized their hold on their society through their reliance on the political paramountcy of the Western colonial power. In other words, Arab society suffered from all the vices of imperialism without benefiting from its achievements. Algeria, on the other hand, whose conquest by the French

was hailed by Engels as "an important and fortunate fact
for the progress of civilization," took a very different turn,
and for this reason Algeria is today the only Arab country in which the traditional elites have no hold whatsoever.

Imperial rule in the Arab countries, instead of pulver-
izing the old society and creating the infrastructure for
modernization (as it did in India or Ghana), only accentuated the dilemmas which Arab society carried over from
its own past. This became especially apparent with regard
to the military.

There hardly exists a political culture whose social
ethos is so much imbued with martial values and the
spirit of the army as is Islam's. Islam, in a way, is the
army of the faithful. If Christianity conquered the Western
world by a combination of proselytism, conversion, deceit,
political considerations, and conquest, Islam conquered
the Mediterranean world by conquest alone. *Din Muhammad bi-seif*—"The Law of the Prophet proceeds by the
Sword"—is both a basic theological tenet of Islam and
an apt description of its historical evolution. The polity
established by the Arabs as they conquered the Mediter-
reanean world was a typical society of *conquistadores*,
and Arab society bears the birthmarks of this as much as
Latin American society is still haunted by Pizarro and
Cortes. These conquerors' states, established as they were
by the sword, ultimately perished by the sword and fell
prey to outside invaders, whose Muslim religion sometimes helped to cover up the fact that they were outsiders
to the Arab world. Since the thirteenth century, the Arab
Middle East has never been ruled by the Arabs, but by a
succession of foreign Muslim military invaders: Seljuks
and Mongols, Osmanli Turks and the slave aristocracy of
the Mamluks in Egypt were the ruling classes of the Middle East prior to Western penetration. Even Saladin was
a Kurd, not an Arab. Much as Arab nationalist ideology
tries to gloss over these somewhat uncomfortable facts,
the brutal truth of Arab history is that when the French
and the British established their hold in the Middle East,
they did not put an end to any Arab form of autochthonous
self-government in the area. The political power that was
pushed away by the British and the French was as foreign

as the Western intruders themselves. Since the thirteenth century, no form of Arab government has existed in the Fertile Crescent.[1]

This military nature of Arab society—and it is immaterial whether the ruling military caste was Arabic or Turkish—also hindered the emergence of an overall differentiated social structure in the Arab world. Social stratification until this day puts the soldier—the fighter (be he the general or the lowliest of the fedayeen)—at the apex of the social pyramid. Arab society, as it confronted the West in the nineteenth and twentieth centuries, had a uniquely vulnerable structure. Due to the high status of military virtues, mercantile activity was looked down upon with deep disdain, and hence no Arab Muslim mercantile middle class emerged. The military elite—mostly Turkish, or (in Egypt) Mamluk—were Muslims; the peasantry were Muslim Arabs; the urban mercantile population was mostly made up of Greeks, Copts, Jews, and members of the eastern Christian denominations. This lopsided social structure was not basically changed under Western rule, except that an Arab Muslim military elite was substituted for the largely non-Arab military caste of the Turks or the Mamluks.

Since what the Western powers needed in the Middle East was a reliable clientele, they obviously pampered the existing social elite of the Arab countries. Since they also needed a reliable military local force, it so happened that the one sector of Arab society that received the greatest care and investment from the British and the French was the army. It is immaterial that today the army is the most anti-Western power in the Arab world: what matters is that the accent the West put on the military only perpetuated the unusually high esteem the army—and military mores—already had in traditional Arab society. The

---

[1] In order to avoid being misunderstood, I want to point out that I put no normative slant to this statement. It is not intended in any way to reflect on the legitimacy of Arab nationalism: this movement draws its legitimacy, as does any other social movement, from the social consciousness of its members. My statement is merely intended to state a fact of history which is of significance in presenting conditions in the Arab world, and which is usually overlooked.

French and the British did little to encourage industrial growth in the Arab world, or to promote literacy, or to lay the foundations for a truly Western type of constitutional state; but they modernized the Arab armies and thus reinforced the most traditional trait in Arab society. The Arab armies that have come to the fore after the demise of Western colonial influence in the Arab world are not, despite their ideology, a modern, revolutionary force. They are, on the contrary, the most traditional element in Arab society and Arab consciousness, the one most connected in the popular imagination with the values of Islam and traditionalism. This also helps to explain how the military regimes in the Arab world are able to survive successive disastrous military defeats. In an achievement-oriented, Western-style military dictatorship, the military rule is, after all, judged by its performance. In the Arab world, military rule *is* political legitimacy; it is the only authentic form of government which has ever emerged in the Arab world. The quasi-parliamentary constitutions imposed on Egypt, Syria, and Iraq by the West were a sorry joke anyway: once the Western powers departed, Arab society very easily, without serious upheavals or civil war, reverted to its traditional form of political legitimacy; hence, also, the relative ease with which the army established itself. No one, after all (and this, of course, includes the intellectuals in the Arab world) ever questions the very basis of the legitimacy of military forms of government in Arab society. One may criticize this general or that colonel. Various factions of the Syrian or Iraqi Ba'ath parties (in each case based on the army) may quarrel among themselves. But the question "What is the army doing in politics?" is never raised. Of course the army is in politics: this has been its business since Muhammad, so to speak.

This is reflected also in the social composition of the army: the social stratification of society is reflected—even reinforced—in the structure of the army. Different laws govern the enlistment procedures of fellahin as against educated (i.e., middle-class) men. While the enlisted men are drawn from the lower classes, the officer corps is drawn from the traditional elite groups—education automatically entitles one to entry into an officers' cadet school. The same traditional social strata that sent their sons to become officers under Farouk do so today, and university graduates are usually exempt from compulsory service and can join the army as officers. The caste nature of the Egyptian army was never better exemplified than in a pathetic incident that occurred in 1967 when the Egyptian officers who became Israeli POWs demanded that their personal servants (enlisted men) be allowed to continue to perform their traditional menial duties for them in captivity also. For how can an officer preserve his honor and dignity if he has to shine his own shoes?

As mentioned earlier, there is only one exception to the obstinate persistence of traditionalism in Arab society—and this is in Algeria. Here, the ruthlessness and cultural messianism of the French almost completely eradicated the traditional structures of Arab society. By confiscating much of the land for their own settlers, the French broke the economic basis of the landowning effendi class and created a modern urban proletariat. By imposing French education, they pushed aside the traditionalist values of Koranic culture. In short, they modernized Algeria brutally, in a way that no other Arab society has ever experienced. As a consequence, the only Arab army that is not weighted down by an oligarchic structure but is truly a fighting army, with strikingly egalitarian values (very reminiscent of the Israeli army) is the Algerian army. Algeria is also the only Arab country that achieved independence not by means of a political deal between the colonial power and the ruling local elite, but through a real war of liberation. The Algerian army is also the only army that has thus, to its credit, victories and not merely defeats.

When Arabs look back on their past history with pride and satisfaction, they reflect on an achievement which was truly remarkable. Medieval Arab culture—a synthesis of Byzantine, Persian, and Arabic Islamic elements—was a magnificent blend, equaled perhaps only by the Italian Renaissance culture. Yet, in terms of the ability to modernize today, this awareness of past glories is dysfunctional. The Arab intellectual who takes pride in thirteenth-century Arab culture tends to overlook the fact that the crucial question is not why thirteenth-century Arabs were so superior in culture to their European contemporaries, but what has gone wrong with Arab culture since the thirteenth century. Past glories are, after all, irrelevant to the present challenges of the modern world, and this sometimes eludes the Arab intellectual who finds in the past a consolation for present difficulties. This escapism finds its way into school textbooks so as to present the Arab child with a totally distorted picture of the world. It is, of course, understandable that Arabs take pride in their medieval achievements in geometry, astronomy, and navigation; but their overall view of Western civilization, as expressed in schoolbooks, sometimes resembles the way the Russians look upon the Tartar invasion.

This ethnocentrism creates obvious blinkers against an adequate understanding of the processes of the modern world. It also creates an illusion that history is bound to repeat itself. The ultimate upshot of this view of world history turns out to be strangely quietistic, fatalistic—and so hopelessly unmodern. It helps the Arabs to come to psychological terms with a hostile world because of the tenacity of their beliefs in their own ethnocentric view of the world.

Arab society thus confronts the challenge of modernization in an intrinsically different intellectual climate than does, for example, an African society. The trouble with Arab society is not that it is underdeveloped, but that it is, in a way, overdeveloped. Its past culture was not simple or primitive; it was and is a culture of unusual depth and sophistication, of finesse and subtlety seldom to be found in the acquisitive and aggressive Western contemporary culture, whether capitalist or Communist. Arab society is a truly baroque society, where manners and style, facade and imagination are all the outgrowth of an overripe culture. Such a society may have greater difficulties in coming to terms with the modern world than a purely tribal, "primitive" society of the African variety.

This overripeness of Arab society was, however, extremely one-sided, and a purely mechanistic analogy with European baroque will again miss the point. It is most astonishing to note that the introduction of the printing press into the Arab world did not occur until the 1830s when American and European missionaries set up presses in Beirut and Jerusalem in order to print the Bible in Arabic. Arab society—and Arab literature and literacy—is today hardly a century away from its first encounter with the printed word and the Gutenberg revolution.

The amazing thing about this is not that the technical know-how was lacking. What was lacking was the cultural and social demand for the printed book. A flowering Hebrew press, specializing in printing Sephardic prayer books and other religious works, flourished in Constantinople centuries before an Arabic or Turkish press was established there. Even in Palestine, where the Jews were a negligible minority, the first Hebrew book was printed in the 1580s—fully two centuries and a half before an Arabic book was printed in Palestine for the first time. The highly verbal nature of Islamic prayer, the different function the Koran plays in Muslim social practice as compared with the Bible in Christian and Jewish religious life, all this must have been part of the reason for this unusual phenomenon in which the dominant culture (Islamic, Turkish, Arabic) does not avail itself of a technological innovation of the magnitude of printing which is available to a marginal minority culture residing within its boundaries. I know of no parallel in history of such striking nature under comparable circumstances.

This lateness in arrival of the printed book in Arab society also accounts for the oral nature of much of Arab consciousness. Again, many unfounded claims have been made about Arab "fantasy," "imagination," and "irrationality." As such, this is loose talk, and these terms do not explain much, especially if they ascribe these attributes to the "underdeveloped" nature of Arab society. Such an identification of Westernism and rationalism is nothing more than wishful thinking. Part of the problem lies in the fact that such views imply that more Western education is a sure guarantee for "rationality." It is not. One striking example may illustrate the complexity of the problem. In a survey done among Egyptian POWs in 1967, the interviewed soldiers were asked, among other questions, whether they had seen U.S. planes participating in combat against their army (it was tacitly assumed that most of them at that stage believed that American planes did participate). It turned out that hardly any of the illiterate fellahin (the enlisted men) had seen such planes with their own eyes. But among the officers (educated, middle-class men), a very high percentage testified that they had seen the American planes with their own eyes. A similar negative correlation between "truthfulness" and education appeared when those interviewed were asked to describe the nature of Egyptian society. Most fellahin gave straight-forward answers attesting to their awareness of Egypt as a highly polarized society of peasants versus townspeople, the poor versus the rich, the have-nots versus the haves. The officers, on the other hand, described Egypt as a classless society, egalitarian and free from any distinction between social strata. Again, in his unsophisticated way, the peasant is more "truthful" than the educated member of the urban intelligentsia—a very unusual phenomenon in other societies.

The tragedy of Arab society is that the conflict with Israel reinforces exactly those traditional traits in the Arab social structure that have already hindered its adap-tation to Western, achievement-oriented standards. If Arab society was to modernize, it would have no difficulty in coming to terms with Israel. But it cannot modernize as long as the conflict goes on, since the conflict gives addi-tional sustenance to the forms that hark back to the his-torical past of "the glorious old days." The real scourge of Arab society is the militarism of Arab and Islamic tradi-tion, which makes honor, pride, glory, form—the vir-tues of chivalry—into the prime motors of the social ethos. When the Syrian or Iraqi army proclaims this or that ver-sion of Arab socialism to be the law of the land, some naïve Western observers think of Castro. But Castro's army was born out of a revolutionary insurrection which became victorious after it had defeated the traditional, oligarchic standing army, whereas all Arab armies (again, with the exception of Algeria) *are* the traditional standing armies with their oligarchic traditions. They now adopt socialist slogans with the same seriousness with which they embraced liberal ideologies under the British and the French—or fascist ideologies during World War II. Their conversion to socialist terminology is largely an outcome of the marriage of convenience with the Soviet Union caused by the Israeli-Arab conflict, much as their fascist inclination in the early forties were born out of viewing England, the enemy of Hitler, as their own national enemy as well.

The same applies, under somewhat different circumstances, to the various Arab Palestinian guerrilla organizations. Trained mostly by regular Arab army officers, financed by Saudi Arabian or Kuwaiti money, they are— for all their left-wing rhetoric—poor substitutes for a real revolutionary force. In order to be able to exist and operate they have to make their peace with the powers that be. Imagine Castro having a tête-à-tête with the Brazilian dictators in the same way in which Yasir Arafat appears together with King Feisal at an Arab summit! The most reactionary Arab rulers pay danegeld to the proponents of social revolution—and it is a shrewd investment on the part of the Saudis—for otherwise dangerous revolutionary fervor is thus channeled into an exclusively anti-Israeli direction. What better way is there than this to divert the revolutionaries from truly revolutionizing Arab society! The parallel would be having the Vietcong financed by the Saigon millionaires or a Che Guevara getting his monthly check from Standard Oil or the Colombian landowners. The coalition (uneasy as it may be, but nonetheless functioning) between guerrillas and oil sheikhs is again a unique phenomenon, expressing the depth and strength of the conservative and traditionalist forces in Arab society.

To this one also has to attribute the centripetal forces that vitiate against any realistic attempt at Arab-political unification. All Arab countries—in their constitutions as well as in their daily rhetoric—declare themselves part of the Arab homeland and base their legitimacy on their being Arab countries. But Arab nationalism is the only national movement that has not succeeded in creating one body politic out of the plurality of political systems that gave rise to it. The Egyptian-Syrian union failed dismally. Yet in Germany and Italy, where nationalism also set out with a plethora of small states, a union was ultimately forged: through diplomacy and war, ideology and Machiavellianism and "blood and iron," unity was finally established. Nothing parallel has happened in the Arab world. The political unification that will create the one Arab state is as far away today as it was on the day the

Arab League was created by the British as an instrument
of their influence in the Middle East. The gap between
the ideology and the rhetoric—between unity and the hard
facts of divergent social reality—has never been
breached. Ideology thus creates and sustains the image,
if not the illusion, of grandeur and unity, which can then
overlook the crying need for real social reconstruction and
political unification.

Perhaps the greatest difference between Jewish and
Arab nationalism lies concealed in their different attitudes
to this issue of social reconstruction. Both the Jews and
the Arabs entered the twentieth century—and the nationalist stage in their own history—with a lopsided social
structure. To put it crudely, the Jews were almost all middle-class, while a middle class hardly existed among the
Arabs. Jewish nationalism—Zionism—very early realized
that a national renaissance would never be accomplished
unless it was accompanied by a radical social transformation of the occupational profile of the Jews. Therefore,
Zionism had to become socialist in order to succeed, and
its aim could not be limited to a mere geographical transfer of the Jews as they were from Europe or the Arab
countries to Palestine. The whole social setup of Jewish
life had to be changed. Zionist romanticism about Jewish
peasants and Jewish workers may sound slightly ridiculous to us today, but it played a crucial role in helping to
evolve a differentiated social structure that became capable of sustaining a national society.

Arab nationalism remained purely political, relying on
traditionalism and the army. Even the most mobile of all
Arab populations—the Palestine refugees—managed to
end up with just another version of the old Arab military
culture, this time called fedayeen. No effort at social reconstruction, no attempt at a real transformation accompanied
even this tragic community. Arab nationalism succeeded
in its initial political aim—independence—because it
could be achieved by purely political means. But it failed
not only to eradicate Israel, but also to achieve political
unification, the most natural desideratum of a national
movement. Social ideas remained a mere ideology, not a
motor for social praxis. The bureaucratic-military nature
of the old Mamluk society in Egypt was preserved under

Nasser, who may one day be recognized for what he really was—a latter-day Mamluk. That a totally unwarlike nation like Israel, which detests bloodshed and sends its officers to the university to study the humanities, is the symbol of military valor in the Middle East, whereas a traditionally militaristic one like Arab society suffers defeat after defeat —would be one of the cruelest ironies of history, if it were not so great a tragedy for the two peoples involved. Unless Arab society comes to terms with itself and with its complex history, unless there emerges something like Arab Zionism that will have the courage to disentangle itself from a millennium and a half of Arab history in the same way as Zionism attempted to emancipate the Jews from two thousand years of Jewish history—unless something of such magnitude happens in the Arab world, the chances for peace in the Middle East are slim indeed.

Trapped in Vicious Circles

Yehoshua Arieli

YEHOSHUA ARIELI—head of the Department of History, Geography and Regional Studies at the Hebrew University of Jerusalem.

The following essay may be said to represent the views of the "responsible doves" in Israeli society—that is, those who are firmly committed to the defense and survival of Israel yet are critical of the policies of the Israeli government in regard to relations with the Arabs, peace negotiations, etc. Though written in 1969 and thereby not touching upon certain developments that have occurred since, Professor Arieli's essay seemed to us very much worth including in this book as a reflection of an important strand of opinion among Israeli intellectuals and as evidence of the vitality and freedom of political debate in Israel.

Precisely these days we have to reiterate and emphasize to ourselves and the world that the state of Israel and Israeli society did not arise by conquest and expropriation, but by the peaceful process of construction. We came to this country to build and to be rebuilt. The Jewish community grew in numbers and strength by creating the conditions for life by its own hands and not by exploiting the other community that had been here for a long time. By labor, stubborn effort, and creative activity it established for itself the beginnings of a homeland, and turned dried-up soil into a fertile land, vibrant with life and creation. We wanted to create things by ourselves and in so doing we shaped the face of the country and the character of the people living in it.

However, the desire for creation and peace was not to

be fulfilled. For more than two decades, we have been engaged in a struggle with the Arab world—a struggle that is growing in bitterness and extent and that has, during the past twenty years, forced us into three wars.

The roots of the struggle lie in the refusal of the Arab world to recognize our rights of return to Zion, to establish there a national home and to maintain our national life in an independent state—the state of Israel. This very refusal to recognize our national existence in Palestine led to the repeated attempts, ever since the British mandate, to eliminate and destroy the Jewish community and the state by force. These attempts, however, failed in every case. The dimensions of the Arabs' defeats grew in the course of the years, until in the Six-Day War they threatened the fall of those Arab countries that had gone to war.

A tragic vicious circle has been created in the Arab world, with every defeat and failure intensifying its desire to destroy Israel, preventing it from looking soberly at reality and impelling it even more to direct all its resources toward the attainment of its goal. In the course of this process the dispute has widened in scope from a limited regional clash into an almost global conflict involving the great powers and the world as a whole. For the sake of this struggle the Arab countries have practically sacrificed their independence and become the clients of foreign powers which desire to dominate the region.

This same period, however, also proved that the dangers and problems facing Israel as a result of the war have increased out of all proportion to the achievements of this war. The areas Israel is holding have become the center of a total crisis. The struggle between the two sides has gone into a new stage, more extreme, more comprehensive, and more fanatic. All the agreements and other balances differentiating between disguised and open war have disappeared. The region has become the focus of a global struggle. While control of the "territories" created a "security zone," it also created a state of actual war and made the state responsible for the fate of a million Palestinian Arabs subject against their will to the Israeli authorities. Though the deterrent force of the Israeli defense army has been increased, the status of the national leadership of the Palestinian terrorist organizations, wearing the garb of a movement for national liberation, has also become stronger. The stability of the Arab countries has been shaken, Israel is paying the price of human sacrifices and is becoming a state living in a state of siege.

The time has, therefore, arrived for both sides to take stock, to learn the lessons of past experience in order to avoid being drawn blindly into the whirlpool and to halt the escalation into another war.

This stocktaking must be done first and foremost by the Arab countries. Israel has never desired to harm or threaten the existence of the Arab peoples, to destroy any one of the Arab states that have attained independence in this century. It is not difficult to comprehend the fears of a small country, the only home of the Jewish people, when it is surrounded by a ring of countries openly and secretly scheming to destroy it. The memories of the Great Holocaust and the other catastrophes that happened to the Jewish people in the course of almost two thousand years are enough to explain them.

In comparison with these fears, the Arab countries' suspicions concerning Israel seem imaginary and almost paranoid. It is time, therefore, that the Arab countries recognize that Israel's strength, her remarkable development, her stubbornness and heroism in clinging to this land, draw on the deepest springs in human life, on the hunger for a homeland and the desire of a homeless, nomadic people to strike roots in the land of its fathers and the land of its dreams.

So long as the Arabs ignore the true nature of the Jewish movement of renaissance and look upon it as a passing phase, an alien growth in the Middle East implanted as an arm of imperialist forces, or a conspiracy of world Jewry to dominate this area, they will be incapable of understanding the reality created before their very eyes and no fertile dialogue between us and the Arab world will be possible.

On the other hand, we, too, are not free of the need to take stock and to learn the lessons of the struggle between the Arabs and ourselves. Like them, we have evaded the need to understand the other side, we have ignored their feelings, the suffering caused the Palestinians as a result of the dispute and wrapped ourselves in our own right-eousness and emotional and rhetorical self-justification.

We have ignored the fact that it wasn't an easy thing for the Arab world and especially the Palestinian Arabs to understand and accept the aims of the Zionist movement. The Zionist movement and the return to Zion came into being simultaneously with the rise of the Arab national movement, and this latter, like all national movements, wanted to attain not only political and cultural autonomy but also exclusive control over the historic lands of the Arab peoples. It was natural and inevitable for the arising Arab national movement not to agree to the Balfour Declaration and the mandate granted by the League of Nations for the establishment of a Jewish national home in Palestine. The immigration and settlement of Jews from all parts of the world, immediately striking roots in the country as people coming home, and the speedy establishment of an autonomous and separate society could only have stimulated the fears and opposition of the Arab inhabitants of the country and implanted the suspicion in their hearts that the Jews had come to deprive them of their homes and rights to this country. This is what led to the disturbances of the twenties and the attacks of the thirties.

This suspicion seemed to be verified in the perspective of the War of Liberation and of the refugee problem that came as its result. From the viewpoint of historic truth it is not hard to demonstrate that this perspective is misleading and that we have a classic case of a self-fulfilling prophecy; that the line of development was not set by us but by the very suspicions and rejection of the other side.

During the years of settlement and the mandate, between 1920 and 1948, not one Arab was expropriated of his land or deprived of his livelihood. No other community in the Middle East thrived and prospered socially, economically, and culturally as did the Palestinian community, thanks to the flow of Jewish capital, Jewish immigration, construction, and settlement that raised the value of land and created a consumers' market and increasing employment. We demanded the establishment of a Jewish state when we became convinced that there was no possibility of bridging between Arab hostility for the Zionist idea and the pressing need to secure the existence of the Jewish people and to save the Jews of Europe from the Holocaust. However, when we demanded the establishment of a Jewish state we also agreed to divide the country, both according to the Peel Report and later the UN partition resolution, in order to do justice to both sides and prevent a war between them.

The War of Liberation was forced on us by the Arab leaders who refused to accept the UN decision, declared war on the Jewish community, and brought on the invasion by five Arab armies into the territory of the British mandate. It was this war, which we didn't want, that led to the flight of most of the Palestinian Arabs from the area under Israeli control and created the problem of the Palestinians. The expropriation of some of the Palestinian Arabs and the great suffering caused the refugees were direct results of Arab antagonism to setting up the state of Israel in *part* of the country. It was that same antagonism that made it impossible to allow the refugees to return except at the cost of giving up Israel's own existence. We have here a typical case of a historic process which cannot be turned back to its starting point. The refugee problem, however, turned into a cause justifying continuing the struggle against the state of Israel and making it possible to unite the Arab world against Israel. In the eyes of the Arab world the Palestinian refugees became a symbol of Israel's implications for the Arabs, a symbol that intensified Arab hatred for the state of Israel.

It seems to me that the serious failure of the Jewish community and of the Israeli leadership to understand the other side and to try to bridge over the contradictions found its first reflection in relation to the refugee question, when the state of Israel made the settlement of the refugee problem dependent on a total peace agreement between the Arab countries and Israel and didn't take any energetic initiative to compensate the refugees for their lost homes and lands. Occupied in absorbing the masses of immigrants, some of them refugees from the Holocaust, and some of them refugees from the Arab countries, Israel wrapped herself in the sureness of the justness of her enterprise and ignored the tragic fate of the refugees and her own moral and human responsibility to solve the problem by political and material efforts in any way possible. The Arabs' hostility was used as an excuse to put off solving the problem and as a rationalization for the lack of action and moral insensitivity.

There have been many situations in history where one justice clashed with another, right with right, without the possibility of being settled by arbitration. That is what happened in the confrontation between the demands of the Jewish and Arab communities in this country. The solution that was found followed Solomon's wisdom in dividing and partially satisfying the demands of both sides. Up until the War of Liberation Israeli leaders had recognized the moral and historic implications of this conflict and accepted the compromise solution of partition as a just one.

They deviated from this path for the first time on the refugee question, and, indeed, it wasn't hard to find the justification for this position. The problem of the existence of masses of refugees isn't a new one in history. All the history of the Jewish people since the destruction of the Second Temple has been the history of a refugee people driven from one land to another and living with the sense of homelessness and insecurity. In the twentieth century the refugee problem became a quite general one involving many tens of millions of human beings. In every case energetic efforts were made by the refugees' own peoples to absorb them and find them homes in their new homelands. In the course of ten years little Israel absorbed more than a million Jews without home or land, the remnants of the Holocaust, most of them Jews from the Arab countries, the Jews from Eastern and Southeastern Europe. West Germany absorbed 7 million refugees from the Eastern-bloc countries, and France a million of Europeans from North Africa. Turkey and Greece did the same, as did Pakistan and India and the countries of the Far East, with their millions of refugees.

Only here in the Middle East the Arab countries refused to accept their refugee brothers and turned their suffering into a weapon and tool of fanatic nationalism and as a justification for waging war against Israel. In no other case was the demand that the refugees return to their former homes made a condition for peace between countries.

However, if Israel's position can be justified by world practice, her lack of action cannot be justified from the viewpoint of her own true interests, which are as far as possible to eliminate the centers of the tension and the reasons for the enmity between her and the Arab world. In any case, instead of the solution for the refugee problem becoming a bridge to peace and cooperation between the two sides, it has become one of the forces perpetuating the enmity toward Israel and spurring on the Arab countries to repeat their attempts, in every way possible, to liquidate her. Israel's reactions to these attempts, the reprisals and deterrent operations on the other side of the border, the Sinai Campaign in 1956 and the Six-Day War, only increased the hatred and over and over again served the Arabs as proof of the aggressive nature of the Jewish state.

However, we too live under the shadow of a vicious circle, of prophecies and estimates that verify themselves, and changing attitudes and positions that will prevent any agreement in the foreseeable future. There is a very serious danger that it won't be too long before our collective personality changes to come closer to the image that the Arab world long since has ascribed to us. The Greater Israel movement is a warning sign. The maze in which we are feeling our way, between security reasons to hold on to the "security zone" and the knowledge that holding on to the territories is preventing an agreement, is another sign.

To the best of my understanding the Arab states are unable to break out of the vicious circle of hatred, frustration, and suspicion, of injured national pride and the feeling of inferiority in the field of modernization. The government of Israel will have to break the circle, to come out with an initiative for peace in order to find a new way to cure the wounds and promote mutual trust between the two peoples. It is not the Arabs but we who have returned to this area and to the Arab world, and our future depends upon our ability to live in peace with the peoples of the region.

If we must persist in the demand that the Arab world recognize the state of Israel's right to exist, and want to open their eyes to the potentialities of peaceful coexistence and of fruitful regional cooperation, we have to convince them first and foremost that we aren't bent on territorial annexations or domination over the Palestinians in Samaria, Judea, and Gaza. We have to break the vicious circle of mutual suspicion impelling both sides to entrench themselves in their positions. That means that we have to declare our readiness to accept in full the Security Council resolution of November 1967. The state of Israel must prepare a constructive program detailing her real security conditions for evacuating the territories and stating the guarantees for the maintenance of a state of peace between the two sides. She must declare that she accepts the right of the self-determination of the Palestinian Arabs in Judea, Samaria, and Gaza, even if she insists on her demand to keep the Gaza area under her security control.

As a national Jewish state Israel must openly waive any territorial demands that will impose an alien rule on the Arabs in the territories, deprive them of their civil or national rights, and at the same time endanger Israel's own Jewish and democratic character. She must immediately and unilaterally propose a plan for the solution of the refugee problem and for their rehabilitation outside the borders of the state, independently of the problem of any inclusive political agreement. The state of Israel must prepare a program for economic and technological cooperation between Jordan and herself, not because she cares for the fate of King Hussein but because of the Palestinian Arab victims of the Israeli-Arab conflict.

I do not underestimate the importance of Israel's security needs which the state must secure to the best of its wisdom and ability. However, when the preoccupation with security becomes a hindrance to any initiative for peace it actually defeats itself.

Those who mistakenly pin their hopes for security only on military power and military and territorial domination are gambling with our future. The dangers facing the Jewish and democratic character of the state of Israel from the perpetuation of the present situation oblige us to look for initiatives for peace even when they involve some risk. The history of Israel from its beginnings has been fraught with risks which we were prepared to face in order to attain our goals.

My faith in Israel's ability to repel any enemy at her gates is too strong for me to fear the risks involved in a peace initiative that would break the impasse.

III

INTERNATIONAL IMPLICATIONS

The Soviet Union and the Middle East

Walter Laqueur

The Soviet position in the Middle East is stronger today than it was ten years ago. This was not the result of invasion, nor of infiltration by stealth: the Soviet Union became a Middle East power by invitation. It has seized no military bases, but was offered the facilities it wanted by the governments of Egypt and Syria, Algeria and the Yemen, of their own free will. Soviet progress has been gradual, unlike its advance into Eastern Europe after 1944. Not one country has been taken over, no attempt has been made to impose from above the Communist political and social system. There have been changes in some countries, but they were the outcome of internal ferment, not outside pressure. Soviet influence has grown not because of the spread of Communist ideology, but as the result of efforts made on different levels to make friends and influence people: loans, arms supplies, political assistance, support of the Arab countries against the West and Israel. It has always been Soviet policy to stress that this assistance, in contrast to imperialist aid, is selfless and free of ulterior motives; neither bases nor oil nor political conformity are expected in return. The Soviet Union has been willing to cooperate with kings and sheikhs as well as ultraradical revolutionaries. The fact that some of these leaders were militantly anti-Communist was no obstacle; it complicated relations in some cases, but on the whole Moscow showed great moderation and patience in the face of Egyptian tantrums (in 1959–61), and turned a blind eye to the suppression of communism in Turkey and Iran. Israel was

the only exception, but in this instance, too, the reasons
for Soviet hostility were not primarily ideological. Having
to choose between the Arab states and Israel, Moscow
opted for the bigger battalions, which it thought were also
the stronger battalions. The anti-Jewish prejudices of the
Soviet leadership should not be underrated, but what in
the last resort prevented a rapprochement between
Moscow and Jerusalem was not anti-Semitism, but the
simple fact that Israel was so small. Size has always been
of great significance in shaping Soviet attitudes to other
countries; more than once this has been the source of
political mistakes.

Soviet objectives in the Middle East are easily defined:
to remove Western influence in the area and to strengthen
the Soviet position there as much as possible. Turkey and
Iran have been to some extent neutralized; with the détente in world politics, the conviction grew in Ankara and
Teheran that the military danger from the north had passed
and that the Soviet Union had given up its old annexationist aims. Soviet policy impressed on both countries the
benefits that would accrue from closer economic relations.
Suspicion of the powerful neighbor did not fade away completely; it emerged again with the appearance of the Soviet
fleet in the Mediterranean and Soviet intervention in East-
Central Europe in 1968. The change in Turkey's and Iran's
foreign policy was not caused by resentment of the West,
though this motive was not altogether absent; it was largely
due to the shift in the global balance of power and the
proximity of these countries to the Soviet Union.

In Syria and Egypt the Soviet Union found more fertile
ground, providing scope for closer political collaboration.
Anti-Western feeling was and is for historical reasons
more intense in these Arab countries, the inclination toward extreme political solutions more pronounced. Ideological affinity played a certain role; Western support for
the "reactionary" Arab states was an aggravating factor,
and Moscow's hostility to Israel was greatly appreciated
in the Arab world. While the emphasis in relations with
Turkey and Iran was mainly on economic collaboration,
Soviet political and military help was the great attraction
for the Arab world. What started in the 1950s as a

"strictly business transaction" later became a fairly close political alliance. Following the deterioration of the Egyptian economic situation and the Arab defeat in 1967, the dependence of the "progressive" Arab countries on the Soviet Union markedly increased. Radical Arab leaders were firmly convinced during the 1950s that while the West and Israel constituted a mortal threat to Arabism, the Soviet Union for a variety of reasons did not. By the middle sixties they were so deeply immersed in the fight against Israel (and in the struggle for their own political survival) that they had little time or energy to ponder the long-range perspectives, an inability compounded by their capacity for self-delusion and their lack of political experience. While not unaware of their weakness, they felt almost unlimited self-confidence: once having coped with the threat of Zionism, they would successfully defend their independence against all comers.

Soviet successes in the Arab world were striking, but not without their problems. Much money and great efforts were invested in Egypt and Syria, yet the loans and the arms have been used in ways that were not always to Moscow's liking. Egypt and Syria became client states, but not satellites; even after the Six-Day War Russia was unable to exert full control in Egypt. It had accepted responsibility, albeit reluctantly, without being always able to impose its will. Soviet help had been provided to make the radical Arab regimes showcases for the superiority of socialism, but their economic achievements were certainly no more striking than those of the "conservative" countries. The weakness of the radical regimes had some indirect advantage, for it strengthened their dependence on the Soviet Union, but it was hardly a good advertisement for the efficiency of communism.

When the Western powers were the dominating force in the Middle East, they had the monopoly of committing mistakes, whereas the Soviet Union, not being involved in Middle East affairs, enjoyed a great deal of prestige precisely because of its apparent position as a dispassionate, seemingly remote onlooker without any specific interests in the area. But as it became involved in Middle East politics, it had to make choices: it could no longer please everyone, and the aura of disinterested altruism began to disappear. It was Soviet policy to extend its influence without provoking a frontal clash with the United States. Frequently this proved only too easy; there was nothing the United States could do about the internal politics of Syria and Egypt, or a coup by radical forces in other Arab countries. Time and circumstances seemed to be working for the Soviet Union in the Middle East, but not always. Whenever the Soviet protégés ran into trouble, direct Soviet intervention became necessary, and this naturally involved risks. Notwithstanding Soviet reservations about its client states, a major setback suffered by any one of them was almost automatically interpreted as a Soviet defeat, and reluctance to come to the help of the "progressives" was regarded as an admission of weakness. The establishment of client states had a logic and a momentum of its own. It is difficult to get out of obligations and cut losses; having gained footholds in the Middle East, the Soviet Union became increasingly involved in crisis situations it could not fully control; having provided considerable economic assistance to Egypt for more than a decade, Moscow could not discontinue its aid, however costly the venture and however unpromising the long-term prospects. In the past, a substantial part of this burden had been borne by the other East European countries, but they were increasingly reluctant to shoulder this load indefinitely. The complications arising from the supply of arms are even more serious. Arms deals were from the Soviet point of view the most effective way of undermining the Western position in the Middle East and winning friends in the Arab world. But the arms were not delivered as a straightforward business transaction; they gave the Soviet Union a vested interest in the fortunes of Egypt and Syria, Yemen and Algeria, and it became identified with them. The Arab defeat in 1967 thus adversely affected Soviet prestige. The reequipment of the Arab armies became necessary, regardless of cost, and has thus involved Soviet prestige even more than in the past. Yet another Arab defeat by Israel must appear well-nigh intolerable in Soviet eyes, but since it has no full control over the armies of the UAR and Syria, and since its capacity to intervene in a war is probably still limited, the Soviet position is not without hazards.

The buildup of a Soviet Mediterranean fleet entails similar problems. The absence of a striking force has served in the past as a plausible reason for refraining from direct if limited military intervention, comparable to the landing of American troops in Lebanon in 1958. With a substantial fleet in the Mediterranean, the Soviet Union can make its presence felt more directly by showing the flag not only in the Mediterranean, but eventually in the Persian Gulf and the Indian Ocean as well. It has raised Soviet prestige and forced all Mediterranean and Middle East countries to recognize the growing Soviet strength in the area. At the same time it enhances the risks: in the event of a conflict, Soviet policy makers face the choice of backing down or of escalating a local conflict into a much wider confrontation.

There are other problems, some of them caused by the uneven advance of Soviet influence in the Middle East. The very fact that Syria had moved so far toward a radical political system frightened Syria's neighbors, and made them more aware of the dangers involved. The Soviet Union would have preferred to encourage Syria without antagonizing its neighbors, but this was not possible. The decision would have been less painful had it been a straightforward choice between "rising" and "declining" forces. But in reality the state of affairs is far more intricate: the basis of the national-socialist regimes in Syria, Egypt, and Algeria, not to mention Yemen, continues to be fragile; their overthrow from within is by no means excluded. National rivalries further complicate the situation: the Soviet Union wants to be on good terms with Greece and Turkey, with Turkey and Syria, with Iran and Iraq, despite the conflicts between these respective pairs. It would like to support Tudeh and the Shah, the Turkish Communists and Demirel, the Iraqi opposition and the Iraqi government. The list of policy dilemmas is long, covering every Middle East country, both on the domestic level and in its relations with other states. In most cases a choice has to be made, and this usually implies antagonizing someone.

There is also the eternal problem of priorities. The Soviet Union has had to pay for its new status as a Middle East power $4–5 billion in military aid alone. In a war the cost in terms of money is hardly ever counted, let alone disputed. In peacetime, on the other hand, the cost of economic and military assistance is open to scrutiny and comparison. Few questions are likely to be asked while the going is good, but when there are setbacks the value of the investment is liable to come up for debate: would the cause of socialism not have been better served by using the billions of rubles given to Egypt for domestic economic purposes? The Soviet Union is a big country, but can it go on providing for a growing number of destitute client states? Financial considerations rarely figure in the discussion of decisive political issues, but there are priorities, and the place of the Middle East in the scale of Soviet political aims is likely to be reexamined from time to time in terms of loss and gain, especially if there should be unforeseen difficulties.

What, then, are the short-term Soviet aims in the area? The rapid transformation of the radical-nationalist regimes into fully fledged satellites is certainly not among them. It would give the Soviet Union few benefits it does not already possess. Further nationalization in the "progressive" countries would not necessarily bring them more securely into the Soviet orbit, whatever the ideologists may claim. It would be desirable from the Soviet point of view if power in the radical Arab countries came to rest in the hands of a disciplined and ideologically trained elite, but this is unlikely to happen in the near future. The present elites are on the whole pro-Soviet; oriental communism is unlikely to be affected by the liberal and democratic deviations of Western communism. The danger of national communism, on the other hand, is equally strong in East and West, and no cure has so far been found for it. There is also the constant temptation for Communists in the third world to play Peking against Moscow and vice versa. These are real problems and the Soviet Union will have to live with them for a long time.

The present state of affairs has many advantages for Moscow, and its perpetuation seems to be the aim of Soviet policy in the Middle East. Important positions have been gained during the last decade and it seems wiser to consolidate them than to press for full satellization of the pro-Soviet regimes. Whether the Soviet Union will have things all its own way is less certain, for Middle East politics have a life of their own; sooner or later outside powers find themselves confronted with situations they did not envisage in their political planning.

The Soviet Union owes its successes in the Middle East in the final analysis to a number of happy coincidences. It did not have to work very hard to realize its aims. The key to success was not a "correct Marxist-Leninist" appraisal, nor the triumph of the local Communist parties; not loans or credits, nor very cunning diplomacy. Moscow did not gate-crash; it was invited to become a major Middle East power by Egypt and Syria. In many respects the Soviet Union was an ideal ally for the radical Arab leaders—powerful, but not so wealthy as to provoke feelings of envy. Ideologically it was far better suited to the radical mood prevailing in the Arab world than Western democracy or liberalism. The Soviet Union became a leading Middle East power because it was militarily strong and geographically close, and it is therefore idle to speculate whether its advance could have been prevented. With the West in retreat, the Middle East became a power vacuum, bound to be filled by the most powerful neighbor. Arab enmity toward Israel was certainly important, but it was an aggravating circumstance, not the decisive factor. The inroads Moscow has made in Yemen and Algeria, in Sudan and Somalia, show that it has improved its position even in countries where Israel was not a major issue. But was not the Arab decision to tie their fortunes to the Soviet Union extremely shortsighted? What if victory over Israel could be achieved only at a formidable price— namely, growing dependence on Russia? In a long-term view, the Arab leaders need the West more than the West needs them, simply because nature has placed them in the vicinity of the superpower with the greater appetite and the fewer scruples. Their chances of remaining independent without the support of an outside power cannot be rated very high. Many Arabs are uneasily aware of the

grave problems they face, but their leaders reassure them:
the Soviet Union is totally different from the Western imperialists, asks for nothing in return, nor does it aspire to
dominate the area. All fears are therefore misplaced.

What direction is Soviet policy likely to take in the
years to come, and how are the Middle East countries
likely to react? There are no certainties, only trends and
possibilities, and about these, too, it is now more difficult
to speculate than before. The Middle East political scene
is forever changing; it cannot be analyzed in isolation from
all other major political and military problems in the contemporary world.

Seen from the present, the future of the Middle East
depends above all on internal developments in the Soviet
Union and, to a lesser extent, on the United States. Essentially, the Soviet Union has become a conservative
society with a superstructure of revolutionary ideological
phraseology; its appeal as the home of communism scarcely
extends beyond its own borders; the idea of world revolution was abandoned long ago. But the Soviet leaders
still feel they have to expand their sphere of influence, their
own cordon sanitaire. Once a sphere of influence is established there is a temptation to look for yet another
beyond it, to make it quite secure: empire building is a self-
generating business. They know that, as a Russian eight-
eenth-century statesman said, "that which stops growing
begins to decay." As the Soviet Union reaches strategic
parity with the United States, there is greater readiness to
follow a high-risk policy in areas thought to be nonvital to
America. It has entered a stage of transformation, but
not, as was widely assumed after Stalin's death, into a
more liberal and democratic system. The Soviet leaders
cannot dissociate themselves altogether from the old beliefs because this would undermine the legitimacy of their
rule. In competition with China for leadership over the
camp, if for no other reason, they are under strong pressure to keep up the revolutionary posture and to pursue a
militant foreign policy.

The paradox of Soviet development is that while militarily the country has become so much stronger during the
last twenty years, politically it is far weaker than under

Stalin, when no opposition was tolerated inside Russia or the Soviet bloc. Power has passed into the hands of bureaucrats, men without any marked interest in ideas or theories. They have no clear concept of the future, but take the existing order of things for granted and want to prevent any major change. The political weakness, the many conflicts inside the Soviet bloc and within the Soviet Union itself, are not necessarily conducive to a policy of détente; there is many a historical precedent for escape into activism.

At the present time Soviet foreign policy seems closer to that of Ivan Kalita and Ivan the Terrible than to that of Lenin. The emergence of one supreme leader is a distinct possibility, but there are a great many others besides. While orthodox Marxism-Leninism was the guiding principle, it was not too difficult to understand and sometimes to predict Soviet attitudes, despite the distortions of the "cult of the individual." It was relatively easy to imagine how a well-disciplined Marxist-Leninist would behave in a given situation, but it is becoming more difficult each year to anticipate the reactions of the latter-day Bolshevik, whose ideology is a mixture of many strange elements, and whose attitude fluctuates unpredictably between extreme caution and surprising recklessness. During the sixties there was an understanding with the United States about spheres of influence, and certain rules of the game are still observed. But with strategic parity the question of the rules of the game and of a redivision of spheres of influence is bound to be reopened. The Soviet Union has pursued a foreign policy that even from a position of relative weakness did not lack drive or self-confidence; how far will it go in a position of strength? The Middle East is in geopolitical terms Russia's back garden; this at any rate is how Soviet leaders see it. They seem to believe that an area so close to their borders should become their sphere of influence.

The stability of the sixties and the rules of the games were based on the credibility of the American deterrent. As strategic parity is reached, some American commitments are bound to be reexamined in the light of a new world situation. It will be asked to what extent American national interest is involved in the defense of the Middle East. Less, no doubt, than Russia's; much less than Europe's. The Middle East has long ceased to be geographically important; there are no crossroads in the air age. Military bases in the area are desirable, but by no means essential; the ICBM has changed all that. The United States is not a major importer of oil; less than 3 percent of the oil consumed in America comes from the Middle East, and this could easily be replaced. True, the production cost of Middle East oil is among the lowest in the world; but this concerns above all the oil companies. As far as American national interest is concerned, Middle East oil does not figure high. There are ties of friendship between the United States and some Middle East nations: Turkey, a NATO member, Israel, and a few others. Neo-isolationists will no doubt argue that their fate is not a matter of life and death for America. Yet the fate of the area as a whole will remain a matter of supreme concern to all American policymakers, for if it were to become an exclusive Soviet sphere of interest the repercussions on the world situation would be immediate and far-reaching. It would decisively shift the balance of power and would have incalculable consequences all over the world.

It was generally believed in Washington during the sixties that, given a strong military presence in the Middle East, the Soviet Union would not deliberately enter on a course of action that would bring about an escalation of the conflict on to the global scale. Despite the traditional Russian interest in the Middle East, the Soviet Union has no vital economic stake in the region, nor does the Middle East constitute a military threat. The Soviet drive to the south is basically a forward political-prestige operation, potentially rewarding, but not essential. Hence there is a good chance in Washington's view that due caution is likely to be exercised in Moscow with regard to the risks involved. But there remain several major question marks. Centrifugal forces have been at work for a long period in both West and East, but the process has not been symmetrical: whereas in the Soviet Union the feeling of political weakness may well lead into an escape into action, it is strengthening neo-isolationism in the

United States. As the Soviet leaders realize that it is becoming more and more difficult to hold the empire built by Stalin, their methods are likely to become more repressive rather than more tolerant. There is not the slightest doubt that they want to keep what they have, and this can be achieved only by extending their spheres of influence. The feeling of weakness adds urgency to this belief.

In America, on the other hand, the Vietnam War has strengthened latent isolationist feelings, to which is added the fear of overcommitment and a growing belief, not only among the pacifists and the New Left, that America should attend to its domestic problems and stop playing the world's policeman. Since the White House, the State Department, and even the Pentagon do not take their decisions in a vacuum, but are influenced by public opinion, it will depend in the last resort on domestic developments whether and how vigorously America will defend its interests in the Middle East.

As Soviet pressure grows, the call for a more active American policy is likely to emanate from Europe, Asia, and the Middle East. In the view of many Europeans and Asians, American interventionism and the cold-war mentality used to be the main threat; in future they may come to regard American isolationism as the main danger. Soviet foreign policy is likely to concentrate on the areas adjacent to the Soviet Union in Europe, on the Middle East and Asia. As a result, Americans now feel less concerned about Soviet policies than those geographically nearer to the Soviet Union who have begun to realize that the roles are about to be reversed and that an immediate threat will affect them far more than the Americans.

The inability of West Europe to overcome its internal divisions, to develop a political will and a policy of its own, and its political and military impotence, is the great tragedy of the postwar period. West Europe still has far more vital interests in the Middle East than America, but it has found itself totally incapable of asserting its influence and pursuing an active European policy in the area. Twenty years after the end of the war, West Europe has abdicated in the Middle East, and this despite the

fact that it is economically stronger than the Soviet Union
and in most other respects potentially its equal. The resistance to European unity, first by the British, later by
de Gaulle, has virtually reduced Europe's influence to
nil; and nowhere is the decline more palpable than in the
Middle East.

A small country, however stable internally, is not nor-
mally able to resist prolonged and determined pressure
by a superior power; Czechoslovakia in 1938 and again
in 1968 is an obvious illustration. The advent of the atomic
bomb changed this, at least for a while, creating a unique
constellation from which the small countries benefited.
The global equilibrium and the overriding threat of nuclear war tied the hands of the big powers and made it
possible even for small countries to retain their independence, sometimes in open defiance of their much stronger
neighbors. But it is by no means certain that this particular
constellation will last forever. It is already argued that
real independence has become impossible in the long run
without a nuclear capacity. The smaller countries are likely
to become vulnerable once more; they will be able to
resist a superpower which is firmly resolved to impose
its political will and has the power to do so only if they
are united and internally stable. On both these counts the
Middle East scores very low. Its internal problems are
immense. Peace and stability seem to be as far away as
ever, and further violent upheavals appear almost inevitable in the Arab world. There will be more revolutions
and quasi-revolutions, but the experience of two decades
has created skepticism about the effects of revolutionary
action: so far it has produced no achievements which
arouse marked enthusiasm. Economic progress and the
rate of modernization in Iran have been impressive, and
substantial advances have been made by Turkey during
the last decade. But the starting point was abysmally low
in both countries, and the time needed to catch up has to
be measured in decades rather than years. Economic
progress by itself will not, moreover, solve the political
problems; on the contrary, it will probably aggravate them
and precipitate social change, nonviolent or violent. It is
doubtful whether the Middle East monarchies will sur-

vive for very long; they are too much out of tune with
the zeitgeist, although they are not necessarily less efficient or more corrupt than the radical elites; the transition from monarchy to military dictatorship will not by
itself resolve many problems. No Middle East junta has
been strikingly successful so far. Only Turkey and Israel
have democratically elected governments. So, within limits,
has Lebanon. Whether the multiparty system will be
able to weather the coming storms in these countries is a
question that cannot be answered with confidence.

No solution is in sight for the crisis of the Arab world.
The conflict with Israel overshadows at present its deeper
problems. There is growing bitterness and frustration, and
as the destruction of Israel does not seem near, the Arab
masses are likely to turn sooner or later against the
Arab governments of the day which have been unable to
fulfill most of their promises. The economic prospects of
some Arab countries are not as unpromising as Egypt's,
but most of their energies are sapped and their resources
squandered on the military buildup. Egypt's long-term economic prospects would no doubt improve if it gained
control over the oil fields of Libya (having so far failed
to do so on the Arabian peninsula). But in view of the
heavy emotional involvement in the Israeli issue, it is not
at all certain how public opinion would react to such a
deflection from a war of revenge. Even an Arab victory
over Israel would immediately create new problems. It
might lessen Arab dependence on the Soviet Union, but
the struggle for domination in the Arab world would become more intense; there are many candidates for ruling Palestine and Jordan. The fight between "radicals"
and "conservatives" (and among the radicals themselves),
submerged at the present time, would immediately enter a new and more bitter phase. Since no one leader
and no one country is strong enough to unite the Arab
world, all indications point to a long period of internal
strife. Future wars between the Arab states and Israel
seem almost inevitable, but a total Arab victory is unlikely. Meanwhile, the drift toward anarchy in the Arab
world seems to be continuing. All immediate political
problems apart, there is a deep-seated malaise through-

out the area, dissatisfaction with established ideologies and institutions, with governments and society, "conservative" and "radical" alike. Among the intelligentsia both Islam and communism are losing ground, democracy is unattainable, planned economy has not worked, military dictatorships have been strong on propaganda, but on little else besides. Nor is Arab nationalism much of a guide to the perplexed. This breakdown of old, established beliefs and values, and the absence of new ones to replace them, is producing a crisis deeper and more intractable than the transient political problems now plaguing these countries, and the growing sense of despair leads them to seek ultraradical solutions, resulting in incessant changes of government, stagnation, and decline. Perhaps one day the vicious circle will be broken by a new idea or a new leader or movement of national and social renaissance. Today no such savior is in sight. This drift toward anarchy may not cause undue concern among the Russians. For Israel it would remove the immediate danger; whether it would be a blessing in the long term is more doubtful. It would mean that Israel would not be able to talk to anyone in authority in the Arab world. But negotiate at some future date they must. The only alternative is a permanent struggle in which they cannot afford to lose a single battle and cannot gain a lasting, decisive victory. Zionism had two basic aims: to restore dignity to the Jewish people and to give it security. It has succeeded in the first part of its program, but security is as far away as ever. Immigration remains the cardinal problem, but a mass influx of American or Soviet Jewry, the two great remaining reservoirs, is highly unlikely in the foreseeable future. That being so, the historical mission of Zionism has come to an end and the state of Israel will have to come to terms with its new function, not on the basis of some ultimate goal, but in its present shape and prospects.

The Arab-Israeli conflict has all but monopolized public interest in Middle East tensions. But there are also Yemen and the struggle for South Arabia, the Persian Gulf, the unsolved problem of Cyprus, and a great many other equally explosive issues. Nowhere are the problems of the area near a solution, and the internal weakness of the Middle East is bound to make it an easy prey. But as the Soviet military presence becomes more palpable, and its political implications more obvious, America (and the West) may find itself in greater demand than at present as a counterforce to Soviet pressure. The Soviet Union was welcomed in the fifties and sixties as a counterforce against "Western imperialism." Since then the political scene has radically changed, and it is gradually coming to be understood that the domination of the Middle East by one great power is not in the best interests of any country in the area. In some capitals it will no doubt take a little time to grasp and digest this, and no radical change in attitude can be expected in a few months or years. But there is a good chance that self-interest and the instinct of survival will eventually make most, though perhaps not all, of these countries recognize these basic facts and act accordingly. If this analysis is correct, the political (in contrast to the military) problems facing the West in the Middle East will ease in the years to come.

Meanwhile, there is the constant danger of local military conflicts escalating into a wider conflagration. Lasting agreement between the two superpowers seems a distant possibility despite the temporary meeting of minds in the talks in New York in 1969 about the Arab-Israeli deadlock. The drive to the south is one of the traditional directions of Russian foreign policy; with the retreat of the West the Middle East has become a power vacuum, and the emergence of China as a great power, hostile to the Soviet Union, has given additional impetus to Soviet activities there and in the Indian subcontinent. Yet it is unlikely that the Soviet Union will be in physical control of the area in the foreseeable future, and there remains a strong element of uncertainty in all these calculations. Moscow may be drawn more deeply than it wants into the problems of the area, whose objective importance is limited. It has been said about Vietnam that it became important mainly because the Americans decided to send an army there. The same applies to the Middle East: the Soviet advance now gives it a significance it would not otherwise have. It is an unfortunate by-product of this advance that it aggravates most of the internal problems of the Middle East. Montesquieu once said: "Happy the nations whose annals of history are boring to read." The boring years in the Middle East were always the happy ones. It would be a great contribution to peace in the area if the world's attention was not permanently focused on it. There may be no cure for its sicknesses, but it would alleviate them if the problems were reduced to their real size: Middle East conflicts flourish in the limelight and begin to wither when ignored. Unfortunately, the Middle East is unlikely to be ignored in the years to come; it will probably get more than its share of attention. There are no certainties: the Soviet Union may be deflected from its preoccupation with the Middle East by increasing unrest in Eastern Europe, by the growing menace of China, or by internal problems that cannot even be foreseen. The struggle for power among the Soviet leaders may sooner or later again enter an acute phase. But all this will rather contribute to instability than to peace. The permanent Middle East crisis will in all probability be further aggravated, and the whole area could be one of the main zones of conflict in the turbulent years that seem to lie ahead.

Vietnam and Israel

Irving Howe

IRVING HOWE—editor of *Dissent*, Distinguished
Professor of English at the City University of New
York, author of numerous books including *Politics
and the Novel, Decline of the New, A World
More Attractive*, and *A Treasury of Yiddish Poetry*.

I

Two days after the outbreak of the third Arab-Israeli
war there appeared an advertisement in *The New York
Times* (June 7, 1967) which, written before the start of
the shooting, called on the United States "to act now with
courage and conviction, with nerve and firmness of intent, to maintain free passage in those waters [of the Gulf
of Aqaba]—and so to safeguard the integrity, security, and
survival of Israel and its people . . ." Among the signers
of this statement were a number of persons who had been
sharply critical of American intervention in Vietnam.
Shortly thereafter, one of the few intellectuals still supporting the Johnson policy in Vietnam was moved to an outbreak of wit, suggesting that the statement—which, it ought
to be stressed, said nothing whatever about any unilateral
United States military intervention in the Middle East—
should have been signed "Doves for War." Predictably,
William Buckley, Jr., joined in the fun.

At the other political extreme, some persons had originally refused to sign the statement in support of Israel
on the ground—they agreed with the logic, if not the
politics, of Buckley—that it would be inconsistent with
their opposition to the Vietnam War. For how, they rea-

soned, could they favor United States involvement in support of Israel if they were opposed to United States intervention in Vietnam? I use these words—"involvement" and
"intervention"—with some hope of precision, intending to
suggest that "involvement" signifies a broad range of possible policies, from diplomatic actions to sending military
supplies to Israel, and "intervention" signifies the direct
engagement of troops.

In regard to this matter, and especially the controversy
that followed the pro-Israel statement, Theodore Draper
has written some cogent paragraphs:

> The issue this raised far transcended the statement which
> occasioned it. The implication was that Vietnam "doves"
> had to be dovish everywhere, or conversely, Israeli
> "hawks" had to be hawkish everywhere. Indeed, one
> merely had to take a position on Vietnam, dovish or
> hawkish, and every problem in every country in every
> region of the world automatically fell into place. On
> principle, one had to be all hawk or all dove in United
> States foreign policy, and there was only one touchstone
> to determine which one it was—Vietnam.
>
> I cannot imagine a more dangerous and pernicious
> doctrine. The difference between Vietnam and Israel
> was not evidence of contradiction on the part of critics
> of the Vietnam war; the disposition to equate them was
> rather evidence of obsession on the part of that war's
> proponents. The cost of the Vietnam war has been high
> enough, but if it is to become the one determining fac-
> tor in United States policy halfway across the globe, in
> totally different circumstances, the result must be war
> everywhere or paralysis everywhere. There is no inherent
> reason why one cannot criticize the abuse of power in
> Vietnam and the abdication of power elsewhere. Indeed,
> this very conjuncture has become the real problem of
> United States foreign policy: our overinvestment and
> overindulgence of power in Vietnam has made it in
> short supply for use elsewhere.

These seem to me eminently sensible remarks, if a trifle
too compressed. Let me try to elaborate a little on the
problem Draper attacks.

In principle, there need be no conflict between favoring rapid withdrawal of U.S. troops from Vietnam and supporting U.S. military and material aid to Israel (something quite different from sending U.S. troops, which the Israelis have repeatedly said they do not want). Leave aside for the moment the criteria one employs for making or proposing such decisions: be it United States national interest, or a universalist commitment to democratic principles, or ethnic loyalty. Whatever the criteria one applies to judging a particular situation regarding a struggle between two other nations or a civil war within one nation, they may be significantly satisfied in one instance and not in another. Or in some situations they may be significantly satisfied, yet other considerations—expediency, possible countereffects, limitations of power—may dictate that they not be acted upon. Thus, by whatever criteria, one may judge that the Israelis merit our support and the war in Vietnam does not.

This seems simple enough in principle, though often exceedingly knotty in practice. There are, however, people who are inclined to take absolutist positions. They say they are against all U.S. involvement with the affairs of other nations (but are they really? Even in World War II, when Hitler threatened to conquer Europe? Even against the racist regimes of South Africa and Rhodesia?) Or they say, in effect, that the United States, by virtue of its overwhelming power or moral obligation, should act as a political-moral arbiter in world affairs. They declare themselves, "in principle," to be in favor of interventionism or against it, in favor of foreign involvement or against it. Neither of these extremes seems to me a very intelligent, or even a tenable, position; nor do I suppose anyone holds to it consistently in practice; yet, in recent years, as a result of justifiable disillusionment with U.S. foreign policy and a consequent trend toward taking moralistic stands, many people of goodwill have moved toward one or the other position. Some say, in effect, that the U.S. is the last bulwark against communism and must therefore intervene steadily and actively in foreign conflicts; others say, in effect, that U.S. foreign policy, since it is inherently and ineluctably imperialist, must be reactionary and therefore persistently opposed. Both of these ultimatistic views can be described, not unfairly, as cold-war positions, though, of course, on opposite sides of the war. For those of us who don't want to be boxed in to such grandiose and apocalyptic position taking, things are admittedly more complicated.

Consider Vietnam. We can say that we oppose the war there on one or more of the following grounds: it is reactionary in consequence, it is an imperialist adventure, it is the result of sadly mistaken policies, it violates the tradition of American commitment to liberalism, it is an act of criminality verging on genocide, it creates domestic costs too great to bear, etc. No one is likely to oppose the war on all these grounds; those of us who are against it choose to emphasize one or more, to the exclusion of others.

Consider Israel. We can say that support for Israel by the United States is urgent in terms of national interest, or because we believe it morally and politically desirable to sustain democratic societies, or because we feel it inconceivable that after Auschwitz the last remaining concentration of Jews outside the United States should be destroyed, etc. These grounds are, again, not mutually exclusive, but for most people some count for more than others. For me, to cite an example, the argument from United States national interest is in this case not a very strong or urgent one; but I am tremendously moved and impressed by the social-political achievement of the Israelis, and I would be lying if I were to claim that the Jewishness of Israel seems a trivial matter.

The internal character of a regime may not always be decisive in determining whether to favor giving it aid. (I, like other socialists, favored helping the Tito regime economically, yet argued against those who tried to veil the fact that it is a dictatorship—in that case, there were factors other than the nature of the Yugoslav regime that seemed crucial.) But for democratic socialists and liberals, as these designations may be used in the most inclusive sense, it certainly matters very much whether we are to provide aid for and take risks in behalf of societies that are politically free and socially progressive or societies that are not. For we believe—and I think, rightly—that the kind of world we want to live in is likely to be realized if there is an increase in the number of nations that are politically free and socially progressive.

I would therefore argue that a crucial—not the only—reason for saying "yes" to support for Israel and "no" to support for the Vietnam war is the enormous difference in character between the two societies. Israel tolerates two Communist parties, as well as numerous groups opposed to its policies; South Vietnam puts political opponents in jail. Israel gains the support of its people through a wide range of social measures and legislation; South Vietnam, under reactionary rule since its formation, fails to provide or enforce such measures and legislation, thereby yielding large segments of the population to the Communists. The result is that not only do we have in Israel a society which, by humane standards, should be helped to survive and flourish; we have also a society which, if provided with material aid, *can* survive and flourish—and indeed, unless subjected to large-scale military assault by a major power like the Soviet Union, can defend itself against its enemies. In Vietnam, political-material involvement has led to a disastrous military intervention, precisely because of the factors I have just indicated. In Israel, political-material involvement obviates the need for military intervention, and again for the reasons I have just indicated.

It therefore seems foolish or demagogic to insist—as have both the more bellicose hawks and the more fanatical doves, the two joined in a tacit alliance of mindlessness—that one must be in favor of intervention in both places or in neither place, ready to send arms and perhaps troops to Vietnam and Israel or to neither country. That, in effect, has been the view advanced by Senator Fulbright who, for all the excellence of his position on Vietnam, has made a good deal of mischief in regard to Israel. For it is a view that settles upon formalities of stance (interventionism per se, isolationism per se), rather than upon the political-moral content of a given problem.

(Sometimes—let us be blunt about it—this inconsistency is attributed to the inclination of some radicals and intellectuals to apply their principles to Vietnam and their ethnic loyalties to Israel. Now, why it is supposed that principle requires that Jews, and Jews alone, refrain from consulting their ethnic loyalties I don't know; but it is surely outrageous to suggest that the possession of such loyalties, which does not in itself distinguish Jews from anyone else, is a ground for dismissing the arguments made by democratic radicals and intellectuals in behalf of supporting Israel.)

II

We know that any policy that dominates the life of a nation for a decade or two is likely to create unexpected and undesirable consequences. The containment of Communist power in Europe after World War II struck most socialists and liberals as a prime necessity; and in my judgment, they were correct. To have "supported" Western policy vis-à-vis Communist expansion in Europe, or to have seen a temporary coincidence of objectives between the Western powers and socialist interests, was not at all to claim that the *motives* of the Western powers were necessarily democratic or humanitarian; it was only to make a careful estimate of likely *consequences* in the given relationships of power, and then to decide that from our point of view it was crucially better for West Berlin to remain a Western city than to fall under Communist domination.

Yet we knew at the time that the application of this policy, while it yielded some major benefits in Europe, also led to styles of political rhetoric, habits of national outlook, and increasingly rigid ideological assumptions about the contemporary world which might, later on, have dangerous consequences. They did. A policy that had significantly positive consequences in Europe, though even there, of course, not without some reactionary effects, proved in Asia to be disastrous. Or more precisely: even if the motives of the U.S. government were not radically different in Asia from what they had been in Europe— that is, to consolidate regimes opposed to Russian and, later, Chinese goals—the consequences in Asia were radically different from what they had been in Europe. And the reasons, of course, were that conditions in Asia were not at all comparable to those in Europe.

Now, certain New Leftists have tried retroactively to argue from the Vietnam War back to the Marshall Plan and the Berlin airlift. They have tried to show that the disaster of the later events was "ineluctably" lodged in the success of the earlier. Whether or not they acknowledge this to themselves, they would have desired a paralysis of American power, for *whatever* purposes (whether to help Berlin or Tito, on the one hand, or to engage in its frequent reactionary policies, on the other). The result, also "ineluctably," would have been to leave Europe helpless before the armies of Stalin and the various agencies of the Communist movement.

Neither in logic nor politics is there any reason, then, to accept this effort to equate Vietnam with Europe. In Vietnam the role of the U.S. has been a reactionary disaster; in Europe it contributed, with, of course, undesirable complications, to saving that continent from totalitarian domination.

Yet it would be disingenuous if we were to say that there was no connection whatever between the policies in Europe and the policies in Asia. It was a connection drawing upon the inevitable excesses, crudities, and simplifications of rhetoric and ideology that accompanied the role of the U.S. in Europe directly after the Second World War. The urgency of holding back Stalin's armies could not always be disentangled from chauvinist or apocalyptic versions of anticommunism. And, as a consequence, one of the deplorable results of the major achievements in postwar Europe was the rise of political rationales that could too easily be exploited in Asia.

Which brings me to my main point:

There may soon be a similar connection between the excesses, crudities, and simplifications of our present Asian policies and future American attitudes toward Israel. The very fact of continued U.S. involvement in Vietnam has already had deplorable consequences in the Middle East. With U.S. energies sequestered in Asia, the Russians have felt themselves emboldened in their pro-Arab policy. And if the U.S. is bogged down in an unpopular war, the Russians can strengthen their positions in the Middle East.

Nor is it only U.S. policy in Vietnam that contributes to a weakening of the Israeli position. So too, it must be said, does a portion of the peace movement. I have in mind that portion which, stirred by the rhetoric of Noam Chomsky, has succumbed to the notion that *anything* the United States does abroad must all but automatically be designated as reactionary and therefore be opposed.

This response within the peace movement takes at least two forms. The first I saw at a recent ADA convention where some fine people were so carried away by their entirely valid opposition to the Vietnam War that they began slipping into a kind of moralistic isolationism. If asked about their feelings on Israel, most of them, I am sure, would have indicated one or another degree of support. But the rhetoric they were employing, the concepts toward which they were moving, propelled them in another direction—toward a refusal of all "entanglements" abroad, toward a politics that would in effect paralyze or negate U.S. power in the world.

And let us be honest about this. We of the democratic left—though we oppose the Vietnam War and the politics that led to it, though we believe that this country needs a radical reordering of priorities, from its gross overemphasis on military expenditure to an increase of expenditure in behalf of social and humane goals—we do not wish for a simple paralysis of United States power *in the world as it now is*. We wish that power to be used with enormous restraint; we wish that power to be used toward democratic social reform rather than to prop up reactionary regimes; we wish that power to be contained by popular and democratic political controls, rather than exercised through executive fiat. But at least as long as totalitarianism, in whatever forms, remains a reality in the world, we cannot simply repeat traditional, old-fashioned pacifist slogans.

The second dubious response that one finds among segments of the peace movement is a coarse version of traditional Marxist-Leninist rhetoric according to which the

U.S. is inherently imperialist and therefore to be opposed at all points. Some of the people who say this are, in fact, mere apologists for the Egyptian and Syrian dictatorships who suffer from a principled distaste for the liberal democracy prevailing in Israel. In a sense, they are right: wherever political freedom exists, they wish to destroy it. But other people who use the argument about imperialism do so with goodwill. They simply fail to understand that the term "imperialism" has by now been employed so promiscuously as to be largely drained of precise content and that even if one does make a serious argument for the view that U.S. conduct is imperialist, that does not necessarily tell people on the left what view to take of a *particular* action or policy. For it is sheer nonsense, and incidentally a parody of Marxism, to suppose that by designating a nation as "imperialist" one thereby solves, with a stroke of denunciation or dismissal, the knotty problem of how to respond to the recurrent crises of foreign policy.

The group employing a coarsened version of Marxism-Leninism seems unlikely to exert much influence on American politics, but the trend toward what I've called a moralistic isolationism—that is another matter. It is a trend flourishing along the entire spectrum of American politics, and flourishing because it can easily be confused with the entirely legitimate and valid opinion that the U.S. has greatly overextended its reach in world affairs, often behaving with brutal indifference to the needs of small nations. This new isolationism flourishes, of course, in the virulently anti-American New Left, which in matters of foreign policy has simply stood the cold war on its head. It flourishes among many liberals who cannot bring themselves to look and think beyond Vietnam. And it flourishes among large segments on the right, which have always been inclined toward "minding our own business" and are not exactly overcome with sympathy for a Jewish state.

Now, try to envisage this situation: a crisis erupts in the Middle East, Russian planes flown by Russian pilots intervene in the fighting, and the survival of Israel is at stake.

What will Americans say? At least some portions of the

left—mistakenly reacting in terms of the Vietnam issue, quite as an older generation mistakenly reacted to Vietnam in terms of the Berlin issue—will scream against U.S. "imperialist" intervention. The liberals will be torn and divided, with at least some persisting in a moralistic isolationism. And this ideology of neo-isolationism will be exploited by the American oil lobby, which does represent a visible component of U.S. imperialism and believes its interests to be aligned with those of the Arab nations.

Meanwhile, the rhetoric now increasingly favored by the peace movement and on the campus will be available to those who are, at best, indifferent to the survival of Israel. Large segments of the right, as well as many ordinary Americans, will feel no intolerable sadness at the thought of refusing help to the Israelis: "Why should we get mixed up with those Jews? Why pay taxes to bail out Tel Aviv? Didn't we have one hell of a time clearing out of Vietnam, and didn't you guys on the left raise the roof so that we should pull out? Why then should we now get mixed up to save Golda Meir? What are those Jews to us?"

The incipient merger of New Left rhetoric with anti-Semitic sentiments, signs of which can already be noticed, could become a powerful and disastrous force at such a moment.

People like Noam Chomsky, whose goodwill is not in question, must now ask themselves whether they are contributing ideologically to this potential catastrophe. *Are they prepared to take responsibility for the consequences of an Arab victory?* If not, they must consider the need for complicating and modulating a politics on the left that would, in effect, deny the employment of U.S. power anywhere in the world. To be sure, we may be told that the Arabs no longer wish to "drive the Israelis into the sea," and an Arab victory would not mean the destruction of Israel. But who is prepared to put that assumption to the test?

Still, let us not make things too easy for ourselves. The people being criticized here might say in reply: "Very well, but how far are you prepared to go in your support of Israel? To the brink of war? Beyond it?" In the immediate moment such questions are not very useful, they can even be deeply malicious; for what is at stake is not a proposal on anyone's part for military intervention in the Middle East—indeed, it is the great strength, the sign of its moral and social viability, that Israel neither asks for nor wants such intervention—but a policy of practical and political support for Israel. Precisely such a policy, I would insist, is the best way of contributing to a negotiated peace in the Middle East and thereby preventing a holocaust there. There are some who insist that to carry through such a policy with success requires that the United States be prepared to show "firmness" toward the Russians in the Middle East, which might even involve international versions of confrontation. Be that as it may; it is, in any case, a problem beyond the scope of this article.

Yet even if we insist that a policy of supporting Israel is likely to be a way of avoiding a world war set off in the Middle East, we must nevertheless be prepared to confront the question, "To the brink of war? Beyond it?" Or rather, to confront the second of these questions. And confronting it means, I think, saying that it is the kind of question that simply cannot be answered, certainly not answered as if it were a matter simply of taking a stand or formulating a position. If indeed the choice facing us were a war between Russia and the United States or the destruction of Israel . . . well, that is not a question which can in advance be answered with a word, *either word*. For there are dilemmas summoned in imagination which are so extreme, so desperate, so intolerable that it becomes pointless to try to resolve them in one's mind. One can only propose courses of action which are seen, in good faith, as ways of avoiding such dilemmas.

Those of us who care both about the survival of Israel and the maintenance of peace must therefore try now, while there is still a little time, to counter the kind of ideology and rhetoric that I have been arguing against. A little caution, a little forethought, a little sense of historical complication, a little skepticism about unqualified slogans —we need these desperately. Nothing, to be sure, in the experience of our time indicates that they are qualities easy to come by.

Imperialism in the Middle East

Michael Harrington

MICHAEL HARRINGTON—National Chairman of the
Socialist Party, U.S.A., author of *The Other
America*, *The Accidental Century*, and *Toward a
Democratic Left*.

There is an American imperialist interest in the Middle East. Its central concern is oil, and it is therefore pro-Arab and anti-Israeli.

I use the term "imperialist" with some trepidation. In recent years it has become the ultimate leftist—and particularly New Leftist—curse and in the process has been drained of almost all content. Vietnam was, of course, a crucial factor in thus turning a serious political term into an empty imprecation. American intervention in that unhappy country began in support of French colonialism's attempt to reestablish its rule after World War II. When a nationalist movement which had been all but driven toward a Communist leadership defeated the French, the United States stepped in and backed the repressive, conservative rule of Diem. Then, following Diem's assassination, Washington sent half a million men to fight for a succession of military regimes led by collaborationists who had previously fought for the French and against the independence of their own homeland.

In rightly opposing this tragic and self-defeating policy, many of the young were emotionally attracted to an oversimplified Leninism as a way of explaining it: the United States, they said, was seeking to maintain the capitalist world system and therefore was necessarily and inevitably opposed to all national liberation movements. This theory was then carelessly applied to the Middle East by means of a preposterous analogy. A democratic Israel with a freely elected government and the overwhelming support of its people in the defense of their right to self-determination was equated with dictatorial regimes in Saigon led by men who had taken up arms against their own country's freedom from colonial rule.

I propose here to examine the thesis that Israel functions as the client state of American imperialism in the Middle East. To do so it will first be necessary to examine the notion of imperialism as it applies, and does not apply, to a post-Leninist world and then to explore its relationship to the specifics of the conflict between Israel and the Arabs. The conclusion that will emerge from this analysis is that, to the extent that the United States has supported the Jewish right to self-determination as it is expressed in the state of Israel, it has followed an anti-imperialist policy. If, however, one wants to find a great power that does act according to Lenin's scenario of imperialism in the Middle East, it is necessary to turn toward the Soviet Union.

In making this argument I am not countering one oversimplification with another and suggesting that America and Israel are unsullied forces of goodness while Russia and the Arabs are incarnations of evil. For while I am in favor of Israel's right to exist and for American policies in support of that right, I do not therefore give uncritical support to the Middle Eastern policies of either the United States or Israel, as I will make quite clear later on. Moreover, I am convinced that there are very substantial Arab rights in this area—the right to self-determination and a just standard of living among them—and I hope that my analysis will contribute to a lasting peace which will permit Israel to share its tremendous social and economic accomplishments with its Arab neighbors. But militant obfuscations about American-Israeli imperialism will not serve that, or any other progressive, end.

I

All left-wing theories of imperialism—Hobson's, Luxemburg's, Kautsky's as well as Lenin's—asserted that metropolitan capitalist powers were driven to colonial expansion because they were structurally incapable of dealing with their domestic problems.[1] After the victory of the Russian Revolution in 1917 it was Lenin's particular version of this theme which became influential on a world scale. And it is his analysis which has preeminent authority today in the third world and among most of the New leftists who hold that Israel is the pawn of American imperialism in the Middle East. So it is necessary, first of all, to restate the Leninist thesis and to see if it applies to the contemporary world in general.

There were, Lenin said, five "basic features" of imperialism as he defined it:

> ... (1) the concentration of production and capital has developed to such a high stage that it has created monopolies which play a decisive role in economic life; (2) the merging of bank capital with industrial capital, and the creation, on the basis of this "finance capital", of a financial oligarchy; (3) the export of capital as distinguished from the export of commodities acquires exceptional importance; (4) the formation of international monopolist capitalist associations which share the world among themselves; (5) the territorial division of the whole world among the biggest capitalist powers is completed.[2]

Parts of this definition were inaccurate at the time even when it was made—Lenin greatly exaggerated the tendency toward the creation of "finance capital"—and parts of it, like the envisioned territorial division of the world, have been rendered obsolete by subsequent events.[3] But the most important change has to do with Lenin's assertion that "the export of capital as distinguished from the export of commodities acquires exceptional importance." This proposition is central to his argument, and it has applied less and less ever since World War II.

---

[1] Tom Kemp, *Theories of Imperialism* (London: Dobson, 1967), passim.

[2] V. I. Lenin, *Imperialism: The Highest Stage of Capitalism*, in *Collected Works* (Moscow: Progress Publishers, 1964), 22:266.

[3] Kemp, *On Finance Capital*, op. cit., pp. 70 ff.

In Lenin's analysis, imperialism is the "highest stage" of capitalism, i.e., it occurs in the period of monopoly and trusts, not in the era of laissez-faire:

> On the threshold of the twentieth century, we see the formation of a new type of monopoly: firstly, monopolist associations of capitalists in all capitalistically developed countries; secondly, the monopolist position of a few very rich countries in which the accumulation of capital has reached gigantic proportions. *An enormous 'surplus of capital' has arisen in the advanced countries.*[4] (Italics added.)

It is the search for investment outlets for that surplus which drives monopoly capitalism to export, not so much commodities, as capital itself. So Lenin maintains.

Whatever the trends before the Second World War (they were often quite in conformity with the Leninist analysis), the advanced capitalist countries have had a steadily declining interest in investing capital in Asia, Africa, and Latin America during the past quarter of a century. I have summarized much of the data for this proposition in my book *Toward a Democratic Left* and there will be more documentation in my forthcoming book, *Socialism.*[5] Moreover, recent research by S. M. Miller, Roy Bennett, and associates has supplied impressive additional statistical proof of the point.[6] So I will only cite a few of the pertinent facts here.

Since 1945, investment in the ex-colonial world by the metropolitan capitalist powers has been of less and less importance to their economic well-being. The percentage of overseas investment in the low-income countries fell from 36.4 percent in 1960 to 31.4 percent in 1964. In 1968 the exports of the high-income nations to the low

---

[4] Lenin, op. cit., p. 241.

[5] *Toward a Democratic Left* (New York: Macmillan, 1968); *Socialism*, to be published by McCalls in 1972.

[6] Miller, Bennett, and Cyril Alafatt, "Working Paper," New York University, Center for International Studies, February 1970, mimeographed; Miller, Bennett, and Ahmed Rhazoui, "Neo-Imperialism Critique: Do the Rich Nations Need the Poor?" Center for International Studies, 1971, mimeographed.

were only a fifth of their total exports, whereas they had
been almost a third in 1948; and the drop in imports from
low-income countries to high was of about the same magnitude. But then these aggregate figures overstate the importance of the third world to Europe and America, for
they lump petroleum with all other economic categories.
When that very special item is taken out of the United
States figures (and it will, of course, be dealt with in some
detail in a moment), then investment in the poor nations
constitutes only one-sixth of American overseas investment and generates only one-seventh of the income from
those transactions. The fact of the matter is that, since
World War II, the affluent economies have been investing in one another and, apart from the major exception of
oil, have been less and less interested in exploiting the
globe's poverty-stricken people.

Why did reality turn out to be so un-Leninist? Lenin
helps provide an answer. In *Imperialism* he wrote,

> It goes without saying that if capitalism could develop
> agriculture, which today is everywhere lagging terribly
> behind industry, if it could raise the living standards
> of the masses, who in spite of the amazing technical
> progress are everywhere half-starved and poverty-stricken,
> there could be no question of a surplus of capital. . . .
> But if capitalism did these things it would not be capital-
> ism.[7]

After the Second World War capitalism did develop agriculture and raise the standard of living of the masses (the
accomplishment was, of course, relative: at best it still
benefited the rich more than anyone else; at worst it
was compatible with a persisting poverty made psychologically more difficult by the existing affluence). And, just
as Lenin said, the problem of the surplus was funda-
mentally changed, for it was now possible to invest capital
most profitably within the advanced welfare states where
huge new markets had been created. Only, as Lenin did
not predict, capitalism remained capitalism while doing

---

[7] Lenin, op. cit., p. 241.

these things—although it is true that the reforms which led to the welfare state were a result of the pressure of the working-class and socialist movements.

Under these conditions one cannot properly argue, as Harry Magdoff does in restating and defending the Leninist theory: "The commonly held notion that the theory of imperialism should be concerned largely with investment in underdeveloped countries just isn't correct."[8] There were, Lenin knew and said, cases of capitalist powers investing in one another's economies and even seeking to annex one another's territory. But since each advanced capitalism was in the process of generating its own surplus, his theory excluded intracapitalist investment as a solution of the common crisis. In Lenin's view, the most developed capitalist nations were systematically faced with a glut of capital and therefore driven to compete for overseas outlets. As it happens, this has not really been true for a generation now.

Yet I do not for a moment want to suggest that the attitude of the advanced capitalisms toward the third world has therefore become benevolent. On the contrary, as I showed in *Toward a Democratic Left,* the trade and aid policies of the big powers are designed to make the starving of the poor nations contribute to the affluence of the fat. The Pearson Committee of the World Bank, to cite a recent documentation, reported that after the Kennedy round of tariff negotiations, the advanced countries were charging higher tariffs on the manufactured goods of the poor nations than on those from the rich.[9]

No, it is not at all my intention to argue that such outrages do not exist. They obviously do. I simply note that they are not *necessary* to the prosperity of the advanced countries, nor, as in the Leninist analysis, are they the only way that such nations can avoid—temporarily—a domestic crisis of overproduction. The capitalist market,

---

[8] *The Age of Imperialism* (New York: Monthly Review Press, 1969), p. 38.

[9] *Partners in Development, Report of the Commission on International Development, Lester B. Pearson, Chairman* (New York: Praeger, 1969), p. 88.

the Soviet economist Varga noted shortly before he died, has grown in spite of the fact that it can no longer reach the more than 700 million people of China.[10] Under such circumstances, he concluded, it was well to abandon the notion that the exploitation of China had been essential to the well-being of world capitalism.

So the general Leninist theory that the United States, or any other advanced capitalist power, must—out of the very necessities of its economic and social structure—export capital to the poor countries is not true. Such exploitation does indeed exist, only it is less and less important to neo-capitalism with every passing year. If American foreign policy in the cold war has often been reactionary—supporting Bao Dai, Diem, Thieu-Ky, Chiang, Batista, Jiménez, Trujillo, Franco, the Greek colonels, and other assorted dictators and despots as members of the "free world"—the causes are not to be sought in Leninist inevitabilities.

But I do not propose to thus hold Lenin to his exact words. For even if one adopts the most minimal definition of the imperialist relationship, it does not exist between the United States and Israel. In such a revised, neo-Leninist model, one would have to assert at least two propositions: that in the given sphere the foreign policy of the advanced power is *significantly* influenced by private economic interests, and that in the dependent state rulers betray the real priorities of their people by subordinating them to the needs of the dominating metropolitan economy. Yet even this minimal thesis about imperialism does not help to explain very much about crucial American policy decisions in recent years, e.g., Vietnam.

II

There is, however, one major exception to the un-Leninist trend: oil. It has become more important to the capitalist West in recent years, not less. In 1968, only 2 per-

---

[10] Y. Varga, *Political Economic Problems of Capitalism* (Moscow: Progress Publishers, 1968), p. 1969.

cent of the world energy came from hydroelectricity, 19 percent from natural gas, 37 percent from coal—and 42 percent from oil.[11] As I noted earlier, oil investments amounted to almost half of American overseas investment in low-income countries and accounted for 71 percent of the profits from them.[12] Of all the commodities in international trade, the greatest gap between average cost and selling price is to be found in crude oil, and partly as a result, among all American corporations the oil companies had the second, third, fifth, sixth, and seventh highest profits.[13]

Indeed, one of the critical flaws in the neo-Leninist theory of imperialism is that writers like Magdoff lump together two very distinct phenomena: nonpetroleum overseas investment, which is of declining importance to the advanced economies, and the empire of oil, which is of great and even increasing significance to them. Then all American policy is seen as if it followed the oil model, which is actually an exceptional, deviant case with a limited application. Magdoff himself notes "that a limited number of U.S. oil companies control two thirds of the 'free world's' oil. At this level of monopoly the involvement of business interests with U.S. foreign policy becomes even more close."[14]

Yet if this is the case, then isn't it obvious that the Leninist theory would lead us to expect that American imperialism in this sphere would be oriented toward the oil-producing nations? The answer is, yes, and the facts bear out the Leninist prediction. The American oil interests have been extremely active politically and have consistently fought for a pro-Arab policy.

In his memoirs Harry S. Truman was marvelously, and somewhat characteristically, candid on this count. A few days after he became President, Mr. Truman tells us,

---

[11] Dick Roberts, "Mideast Oil and U.S. Imperialism," *International Socialist Review*, May 1971.

[12] Miller, Bennett, and Alafatt, op. cit.

[13] Michael Tenzer, *The Political Economy of Oil and Under-Development* (Boston: Beacon, 1969), pp. 6, 42, 48.

[14] Magdoff, op. cit., p. 195.

Secretary of State Stettinius warned him against efforts "by some of the Zionist leaders to obtain from me some commitments in favor of the Zionist program . . ."[15] Two weeks later, Joseph C. Grew, the acting secretary, told Truman that "although President Roosevelt at times gave expression to views sympathetic to certain Zionist aims, he also gave certain assurances to the Arabs which they regard as definite commitments on our part."[16] The State Department, the Joint Chiefs of Staff, the secretary of defense were all, Truman says, hostile to the Israeli cause, in some cases explicitly anti-Semitic and concerned about oil.[17]

Even a very mild proposal for a conference on the issue of Palestine was opposed by the oil lobby within the government. Mr. Truman writes:

> The Joint Chiefs of Staff were also of the opinion that carrying out the findings of the report by force would prejudice British and U.S. interests in much of the Middle East. And if this were to happen, they suggested that the U.S.S.R. might replace the United States and Britain in influence and power through the Middle East. To this they added that control of oil in the Middle East was a very serious consideration, and they concluded, therefore, that no action should be taken that would commit U.S. armed forces or turn the peoples of the Middle East away from the Western powers, since we had a vital security interest there.[18]

And while Truman himself was eventually to favor recognition of the new state of Israel, American maneuvering in the period before its proclamation was widely, and often correctly, interpreted as pro-British and pro-Arab, i.e., pro-oil. In March 1948, when the United States came out for transferring the administration of Palestine from the British to the Trusteeship Council, Andrei Gromyko accused Washington of having "killed partition" by put-

---

[15] *Years of Trial and Hope* (New York: Doubleday, 1956), p. 132.
[16] Ibid., p. 133.
[17] Ibid., pp. 140, 149, 162, 164.
[18] Ibid., p. 164.

ting its "oil and military-strategic interests before the United Nations."[19] It was certainly the intention of the Joint Chiefs and the State Department to do precisely that, but Truman—by obviously going against the American imperialist interest, in part because of his concern with the political power of American Jews—did not follow their advice.

But American recognition of Israel under the Democrats did not in any way end the struggle of the oil interests to win this country to an imperialist policy. When Iranian oil was nationalized by Mossadegh in 1951, the United States first took a relatively conciliatory tone, aimed at ending the crisis through negotiation, not the least because Washington feared that a forceful policy would invite Russian intervention.[20] But in fairly short order President Eisenhower changed his policy and the CIA, under Allen Dulles, played an important part in deposing Mossadegh. Moreover, the United States exacted a price for these subversive activities: in 1951 when Mosadegh took over his nation's oil, British Petroleum owned 51 percent of the Anglo-Iranian company; but after the CIA-sponsored coup, the British share was reduced to 40 percent and five big American corporations were assigned an equal interest.[21]

There are cynics, some of them in the British oil industry, who believe that a similar desire to gain American corporate supremacy was at work in 1956 during the Suez crisis. On that occasion, it will be remembered, Washington made a united front with Moscow in opposing the British-French-Israeli attack upon Egypt. In and of itself, that event should be enough to dispose of the theory that Israel is the pawn of American policy, since it pitted the alleged imperialist tool against its supposed master. What happened was that the United States asserted the primacy of its economic and strategic interest in the Middle East over the attempts of Britain and France to push their

---

[19] André Fontaine, *History of the Cold War* (New York: Pantheon, 1969), 2:140.

[20] Ibid., pp. 149 ff.

[21] Ibid., p. 152; Tehzer, op. cit., p. 326.

special interests and of the Israelis to gain access to the Suez Canal and other basic rights which had long been promised and never delivered. As the *Times* of London commented in late November 1956 about the Suez crisis: "The United States, certainly, could only fear the consequences of an economic crisis in Europe, although such apprehensions seem to have been outweighed until now by a determination to do nothing at the Government level which could jeopardize American oil extraction in the Middle East."[22]

The Eisenhower Doctrine formalized this new American dominance in the Middle East. When Ambassador George Wadsworth testified on it in 1957 he was asked whom we were protecting Saudi Arabia against and replied, "Well, you have got the British and the French and the Israelis who pulled a pretty good intervention in Egypt."[23] The primacy of American oil interest as against Israeli national survival could hardly have been made clearer. And this was particularly true, given the fact that the Saudis, whom the United States thus supported against Israel, were among the most reactionary and feudalist of the Middle Eastern regimes. When Wadsworth was asked about the practice of slavery by this allied power, he answered that such criticisms had been exaggerated.

In 1957, President Eisenhower dramatized the depth of our commitment to oil in the Middle East when he went to the airport to greet King Saud on his visit to the United States, the first chief of state whom he had honored in this fashion. And at the formal White House dinner for Saud, the top officials of the Arabian American Oil Company (Aramco) were prominent among the guests.[24] When the President of Jersey Standard was asked why his colleagues received such special consideration, he responded with commendable candor: "I presume because they are the ones who have the principal interests."[25]

---

[22] Robert Engler, *The Politics of Oil* (New York: Macmillan, 1961), p. 262.
[23] Ibid., p. 254.
[24] Ibid., p. 255.
[25] Ibid.

So oil is the element in the American political structure that lends itself to Leninist analysis. It is responsible for a powerful, and imperialist, lobby in Washington which has consistently struggled against Israel. American support for the Israelis must consequently be seen as the result of a *political victory over the partisans of imperialist politics*. How then, under these circumstances, can those of the left who regard themselves as Marxists, or even Leninists, assert that Israel is really the tool of American imperialism?

The Communist solution to this problem is to ignore it. On the one hand it is argued that "the ruling circles of Israel have come forward almost from the very beginning on the side of imperialism."[26] One can safely assume that "the very beginning" starts precisely at the point where Soviets abandoned both their original support for Israeli nationhood and their attacks on American oil imperialism for being opposed to the Jewish state. On the other hand the Communists do recognize some of the facts of life:

> It is the Arab states, not Israel, which have the oil, which are dominant in the area and which can influence other Moslem countries. Hence the fact that the United States has given more than ten times as much military equipment to Jordan the Saudi Arabis as it has to Israel. And hence the fact that the CIA, as revealed by *The Nation* (May 9, 1966), has funneled money into such a pro-Arab, anti-Israel organization as the American Friends of the Middle East.[27]

The political and logical contradictions of this analysis are mind-boggling. The United States, from an imperialist interest in an alliance with the Arabs against the Israelis, acts, in part at least, against that interest; and the Israelis are designated as pro-imperialist for abetting Washington in this non-, or even anti-imperialist course. In such a view, imperialism is a matter of free choice, not of economic-political necessity, and one should therefore con-

---

[26] Hyman Lumer, *The Middle East Crisis* (New York: New Outlook Publishers, 1968), p. 6.
[27] Ibid., p. 18.

clude that it is precisely Israel which has kept Washington from being imperialist. But then Communist documents, particularly those emanating from the subservient American party, are usually rationalizations of Soviet policies and have little to do with either politics or logic.

The American Trotskyists have been among the most vehement opponents of Israel and advocates of the notion that American policy in this area is imperialistically determined. They are even sophisticated enough to understand that, as Peter Buch wrote,

> . . . the mourning for Nasser in the wood-paneled rooms of the oil companies was almost as great [as the mass outpouring in the streets of Cairo]. As one bewildered oil company executive remarked, "It will be hard for anyone that follows him to be quite as reasonable. They will not have the charisma to suggest an unpopular course, and the masses will not follow."[28]

How, then, relate America's position to the theory of imperialism? Buch reviews all the evidence which shows that America's imperialist policy is pro-Arab and then argues, "The 'conflict' between supporting Israel and protecting oil interests is no conflict at all; U.S. support of Israel is the best guarantee of protection of oil against the Arab revolution."[29]

That is a theory which the men in the "wood-paneled rooms of the oil companies" would most certainly laugh out of court. It is precisely Israel's existence, secured in part by American support, which has been the rallying point for the more radical, oil-nationalizing Arabs. In 1956–57, when the United States opposed Israel, it acted most clearly out of its interest in protecting the flow of oil. In the postwar period there is no question that, had American policy in the Middle East been primarily motivated to support the oil corporations, it would have been pro-Arab.

There is, then, a policy of oil imperialism at work within

---

[28] "The Palestinian Revolution and Zionism," *International Socialist Review*, January 1971, p. 11.
[29] Ibid., p. 12.

the United States, but it is not always successful. It was, and is, oriented toward the Arabs and against Israel. Therefore whatever else one might say about American policy in this area, the one thing which a Leninist analysis clearly proves is that it is not simply imperialist.

III

Finally, let me confront some facts which may seem embarrassing to my argument.

On a number of important issues—self-determination for the Maghreb, the 1956 alliance with France and Britain, silence about or even discreet support for the American intervention in Vietnam—Israel has acted *as if* it were part of an imperialist system. Particularly in some crucial votes in the United Nations on questions of self-determination in the fifties, it behaved as a Western, NATO-oriented nation, not as a Middle Eastern state. And in the attack on Suez it joined with the two traditionally imperialist European countries against its own neighbor.

I was opposed to all of those actions at the time they took place; I am opposed to them in retrospect. But I think it makes a great deal of difference—and not just in terms of abstract considerations of truth—as to how one explains them. They were not the result of an imperialist relationship with the United States; they were a function of a more basic drive: the Israeli determination to survive. Given the most fundamental of aims, Israel made an understandable, if mistaken, calculus: that it had to support the Western powers, first of all the United States and to a lesser degree France, in order to stay alive. In part this orientation was inevitable and, in a harsh world of lesser evils, even legitimate. But I think that the dominant Israeli policy makers (and there were some, including members of the government, who sought other alternatives) did not give sufficient weight to the political cost of their policy. They should not have joined with the British and French in 1956; they should not have opposed Algerian independence.

But, once again, the reason the Israelis acted in this way is related to political considerations of survival, not to involvement in imperialist economics. Still, someone might ask: Isn't that a distinction without a real difference? If you admit that Israel acted on questions which indeed had an imperialist aspect, like Suez or Algerian independence, *as if* it were part of the imperialist system, what practical significance is there in the fact that the precise Leninist, or neo-Leninist, connections are absent?

There is, I believe, a very real difference between these two explanations of American and Israeli policy. For if the United States is structurally compelled to support Israel out of domestic economic considerations and if Israel is therefore a part of an imperialist system, then the possibilities of significant change are slight until there is an anti-imperialist world revolution. But if American and Israeli actions in this area are not thus fated by massive economic imperatives—if the real issue is survival, not imperialism—then one can contemplate, advocate, and work for change both within the United States and within Israel.

Maxime Rodinson, whose study *Israel and the Arabs* is more sympathetic to the Arabs than to the Israelis, understands this point well. I quote him at length precisely because he cannot possibly be dismissed as an Israeli apologist. Rodinson writes:

> Israel is . . . a bridgehead of the industrialized capitalist world in the heart of the underdeveloped world. Yet it does not seem that Israel participates to any major extent in the system of exploitation of the Third World by the industrial world. The opportunities for exploitation conferred by her technical superiority are much reduced by the small extent of her territory, by the difficulties she has with her immediate neighbors, and by her own economic dependence on the European and American capitalist powers. *Israel's membership of the Western world is more a matter of political choice than of economic structure* . . . false and over-schematized conceptions of Israel's membership of and dependence on the Western world must be rejected. Such conceptions are very widely held among the Arabs and elsewhere, and are furthermore frequently linked to Marxism. These notions are of a type which was fashionable in the most vulgar ideological Marxism of the Stalin era.

. . . Israel, with all the limitations which her dependence entails, has a will and purpose of her own. She does not automatically obey all the injunctions of the United States, nor yet those of that indefinable monster which this overschematized Marxism calls "imperialism." She is primarily interested in survival, which some, but only some, of her politicians wish to ensure through some measure of expansion. . . . A different Israel is not an impossibility. If the threat from outside were to disappear for any length of time, the process which began each time during periods of respite could acquire very much greater impetus.[30]

In short, if peace could be achieved in the Middle East —guaranteeing, among other things, secure and defensible borders for Israel—then the Israelis could, and should, act as a Middle Eastern power sharing their technical accomplishments with their Arab neighbors (including perhaps a Palestinian state on the West Bank of the Jordan) and joining with them in the common struggle against oil imperialism. There are no Leninist inevitabilities determining Israel to cooperate in the exploitation of the area: in fact she has fought against the oil imperialists. There is a paramount need for survival and once that is assured, there are exciting and hopeful possibilities for new departures.

---

[30] *Israel and the Arabs* (Baltimore: Penguin, 1971), p. 233–35.

The Middle East Conflict and International Politics

Gil Carl AlRoy

GIL CARL ALROY—associate professor of Political
Science at Hunter College, editor of *Attitudes Toward Jewish Statehood in the Arab World*.

A somewhat reassuring aspect of conventional discourse
on the Middle East is that it bears little resemblance to the
real world. If it did, things would indeed be as ominous
as they are usually made out to be. If the military gap between Arabs and Isaelis were just incremental and amenable to sudden change by the addition of training and
material on the Arab side, as we are told; if the permanently vulnerable Israelis really had to rely for survival
on their foreign friends and international guarantees, as
we again are told; if the United States were indeed prepared to intervene militarily to rescue a foundering Jewish state from the ascendancy of Arab arms, as is generally
presumed; if all that were true, we would indeed be hover-
ing on the brink of catastrophe. Compared to such an envisaged frustration by the U.S. of tens of millions of Arabs
really possessing the capacity to liquidate Jewish statehood
by force of arms, the Vietnam trauma would appear to be
almost a pleasant experience; not to think of the unthinkable, but perhaps inevitable, combat between the two superpowers.

The real Middle East conflict is indeed dangerous—all
armed conflicts are—but not especially so for the conventionally cited reasons. The real conflict is defined by the
absence of a balance in both the Middle East itself and
the international arena. In the region itself the Jews
greatly outweigh the Arabs in military power, while in the

international community the Arabs as greatly outweigh the Jews in diplomatic power. The Middle East conflict represents a tension between contradictory asymmetries in the region and the world, and the dangers derive from that tension, not from imaginary balances. This is why the real military confrontation in the Middle East is not between Arabs and Jews or Americans and Russians, but between Jews and Russians. American official anxiety is rooted not in the alleged fear of having to rush to rescue Israel from Arab invaders, but in the realistic fear that Israel might clash with the Soviets in her continued defiance of unacceptable terms of settlement for the aftermath of the 1967 war, terms already agreed on in essence by all powers, including the United States. There is no question that all the powers endorse one or another variant of the Arab formula for such a settlement—cancellation of the outcome of the last war in return for some Arab semantic exercise—and there could not really have been any other decision in the international community, given Arab diplomatic power. The real question is what the United States would do in a clash between Jews and Russians, since the United States is already committed to an Arab solution, with some window dressing, yet known to resent greatly Soviet assertiveness in an area deemed vital to its national interest. Arabs and Israelis are equally inclined to think that, rather than fight the Soviets for Israel, the United States would join with the Soviets in forcing an Arab "peace" on Israel. The conventional prognostication of doom over superpowers colliding in behalf of their protégés would then serve as a justification for "saving the world."

This is a shorthand description of the tension of asymmetries in the twenty-third year of the Middle East war. But these same dynamics have governed the long war in the past, as now, and will probably continue to do so in the future.

Any analysis of the Middle East conflict must begin with the recognition that Israelis and Arabs do not wage the same kinds of war, nor are they inherently capable of doing so. And when it comes to modern warfare—which in-

volves the coordination of large-scale movement with intense firepower—the gap between Israel and the Arab
states is so large in degree as to become a difference in
kind.

This asymmetry in the capacity to wage war may be
traced through the three instances of full-scale war between Israelis and Arabs in the last twenty years: 1948,
1956, 1967. The first war, involving five times as many
days of actual fighting as the other two combined, is an
especially helpful example, the more so because its initial
phase, from May 15 to June 11, represented the only
period in two decades of war in which asymmetry was not
immediately apparent. During that period Arab armies
seemed to move aggressively forward, while the Israelis
were on the defensive. The Israeli army was just then
being formed; its arms were only beginning to arrive; Israel faced simultaneously the regular armies of Lebanon,
Syria, Iraq, Egypt, the Anglo-Arab Legion of Transjordan,
detachments from Saudi Arabia, and thousands of irregulars in Palestine itself; it had no navy, air force, or armor,
and virtually no artillery: Arab fighters and bombers had
the skies all to themselves.

But even with this unique advantage, Arab military performance by and large concerned itself with the occupation
of undefended land—up to the point of Jewish resistance.
Having "conquered" purely Arab areas of Palestine, each
of the Arab armies concentrated upon the task, not always successful, of taking one or two small Jewish settlements. The Anglo-Arab Legion succeeded at Etzion and
in the Jewish quarter of Old Jerusalem, both long isolated
by Arab irregulars, and took some abandoned settlements;
the Syrians captured the border village of Mishmar Hayarden; the Egyptians captured two isolated outposts in the
Negev; the Lebanese failed entirely.

The essentially static nature of Arab warfare was further
manifested in the lavish bombardments and artillery shell-
ings, unrelated to any real movement of troops, to which
the Arabs often resorted. (The British-officered Legion
pumped no fewer than eight thousand artillery shells into
New Jerusalem within twenty days, killing nearly four hundred civilians and wounding many others.) If Arab cam-

paigns of conquest resembled the storming of open doors, the Arab response to resistance was like the harnessing of a freight train to crack a hazelnut. The lack of "punch" was particularly remarkable. Having traveled several hundred miles to fight in Palestine, the Iraqi contingent, with an entire armored-car regiment at its disposal, could not be moved over the last seven miles to the sea—an operation which would have cut the infant Jewish state in two. Yet these same Iraqis gave an excellent account of themselves in defending Jenin, as did the Arab Legionnaires at Latrun and the Egyptians at Iraq Suidan and Iraq Manshich. Defense, especially static defense, dovetailed with the Arab penchant for sedentary warfare.

The developing pattern of war in the Middle East was demonstrated with greater clarity in the next phase of the 1948 war, when, after a month of truce, the Israelis mounted two major offensives in ten days. These operations involved highly mobile units, greatly concentrated firepower, and the coordination of various branches of the military in the execution of daring and sophisticated plans. The Israelis conquered Nazareth, Ramleh, and Lydda, and occupied a thousand square kilometers of Arab-held land containing scores of villages. By July 1948, although the Arabs and the Israelis were still fighting each other, they were decidedly not fighting the same kind of war. As was to be the case in future hostilities, the Israelis were already fighting against the clock of international intervention more than against Arab military might.

The spectacular difference between the two sides which emerged in the second phase of the 1948 war may be explained not by any discrepancy in respective inputs of manpower and matériel during the preceding truce, but rather by the difference in the social and military structures into which these resources were poured. In fact, additional inputs were nearly equal on both sides, while the respective outputs, in terms of military power, were highly imbalanced. By October and December of 1948, the Israelis required only a little more time than they would in 1956 and 1967 to inflict total routs on Arab armies: three days for the Arab Liberation army in the Galilee; seven days

in October and fifteen days in December-January for the
Egyptian army in the south.

Israeli and Arab military performances in the wars of
1956 and 1967 suggest that the discrepancy between the
sides has, if anything, grown since 1948. When taken separately, to be sure, particular aspects of each war might
appear to contradict this statement. Thus, in 1956 it was
said that the Egyptians were taken by surprise and were
overwhelmed by the combined forces of Britain and
France, not by Israel alone; in 1967, the Israelis wiped out
Arab air power, thereby leaving Arab armies bereft of
protection. But when taken as a whole, the pattern is quite
clear; one may thus explain away each Egyptian rout by
some new ad hoc factor, but one cannot obscure the fact
that the routs get progressively worse while the Egyptians
seem forever taken by surprise. (Actually, the "surprising"
and presumably unprecedented preemption of air power
in 1967 merely repeated a pattern set as far back as October 1948.) The pattern constitutes, moreover, a disturbing reflection on the supposedly revolutionary transformation of Arab society which is said to have taken place in
recent years. In June 1967, unleashed again in sacred jihad
after nineteen years, the Arab legion managed once more
to bombard the civilians of New Jerusalem and elsewhere
and to "conquer" an undefended UN structure. From almost impregnable fortifications high above Upper Galilee,
the Syrian army, nineteen years after Mishmar Hayarden,
once more "charged" the enemy by lobbing shells onto the
settlements below. The conduct of Egyptian forces in Yem-
en has, of course, been equally sedentary in nature.

An adequate understanding of respective military capacities in the Middle East has long been obstructed by a
traditional belief—held not only by the combatants themselves but by most observers—in military effectiveness as a
function of "spirit" (antagonism to the foe, rage against
the enemy, ardor for the cause, etc.). Israelis have attributed their success to "miracles" or to the mystical powers of people who fight with their backs to the wall; they
have sometimes been gratified to see in success a token of

divine support for the Zionist task. Many of them, like some foreign observers have concluded from the evidence of Arab offensive weakness that the Arabs are not really serious in their hostility (the assumption, of course, being that the Arabs could have a strong offensive capability if they so wished). This interpretation has suited those Zionists who have always argued that Arab hostility to Jewish statehood was artificial; it has also suited Western anti-Zionists, who argue that although Arab hostility is indeed implacable, the Arabs would not destroy Israel, presumably out of humanitarian reasons.

As for the Arabs, they have regarded their military shortcomings in ways best suited to defend their own cherished image of themselves. In answering their need to identify an enemy who possesses sufficient strength to undertake the grandiose task of defeating the mighty Arab nation—a task obviously not within the grasp of a small and contemptible people like the Israelis—they have fallen back on numerous explanations, most frequently citing great-power complicity with Israel or, failing that, preposterous population figures for the Jewish state. Other explanations of Arab defeats have taken note of the need for modern skills and technology, and for a radical transformation of the social structure. Proponents of this view, however, most often conceive of modernization as an instrument which will provide the means to satisfy the neuroses of a transitional society in its painful encounter with modernity, without really altering the basic values and orientations of that society.

Hence the insatiable Arab appetite for monstrous quantities of weapons, especially technologically sophisticated ones, which give the Arabs a sense of security and achievement without affecting those aspects of society which must be changed if the Arabs are ever to achieve the kind of military performance they crave. Modern social science has long since disproved the efficacy of such traditional martial virtues as fierceness, hatred, cruelty, and manhood; rather, the roots of modern military effectiveness have been located in factors like social cohesion, affective interpersonal relations, diffusion of trust, integration in the larger society, and cooperative ability. No amount of military

hardware can alter the fact that the Arabs are still exceedingly insecure, living in disintegrating societies suffused
with violence, hostility, and utter distrust of fellow Arabs.
Large amounts of hardware may actually aggravate this
condition: reports from Cairo since 1967 speak of a grim
determination by the Egyptian military to weld its backward manpower to the sophisticated Soviet equipment by
an unprecedented resort to intimidation and physical assault.

Given all this, it is somewhat ironic that Arab society,
with its quaint and ingratiating formalism, should exercise
so much charm upon Westerners, while Israel's unglamor-
ous exterior is found jarring and abrasive. For the truth
is that if the formalism of Arab society is a necessary com-
plement to its essential violence and disintegration, the
brash assertiveness so often complained about by Western visitors to Israel is merely the external skin, not the
essence, of Israeli society. For the latter, one must look to
the intense cooperation, cohesion, and egalitarianism epitomized by the kibbutz, and widely diffused throughout
Israeli society as a whole. Each of the most aggressively
effective units in Israeli military history—the units which
have made up the Palmach—has been in fact a miniature
kibbutz. Members of the Palmach traditionally had no
militaristic outlook in the ordinary sense of the word (they
were actually steeped in left-of-center ideology), and virtually no personal animosity toward Arabs; but their solidarity and egalitarianism were probably matchless. Those
who discuss Israeli military prowess in terms of "militarism" indict their own ignorance.

The pattern of violence which emanates naturally from
Arab society is fedayeen warfare—a variant of the brigandage that is endemic in all premodern societies, and that
stands, as a phenomenon, somewhere between folk he-
roics and banditry, assassination and Robin Hoodism,
highway robbery and political rebellion. The universal gun-
man, who represents the ideal type of the brigand, both
preys on the rural mass and defies its oppressors; he is per-
sonified in the legendary figures of international folklore:

Terente; Schinderhannes; or Antar, the Arab epitome of mustachioed fierceness.

Brigandage requires little or no cooperation. Typically, it is the warfare of loners or of a small group bound together as much by mutual distrust as by anything else. It does not require the qualities of discipline, restraint, or abstraction that characterize industrial man. Its rhythm is as fitful and seasonal as its agrarian matrix; its pattern of authority consists in a tension between abject submission and unbridled anarchy; its aims and achievements are consistent with the blood feuds, honor codes, and erotic aberrations of a culture that is based on the ideals of male vanity.

Fedayeen warfare against Jews was waged with considerable success by the Arabs of Palestine throughout the 1930s and '40s. In conjunction with related forms of communal violence, it helped to effect a steady erosion in the British commitment to the Zionist cause. Since 1948, fedayeen warfare has also been waged intermittently against Israel, not merely in the form of unplanned spontaneous hostilities, but as the kind of planned warfare most likely to be tolerated by the international community. Indeed, after all these decades of fedayeen attacks, there is something terribly spurious about the way in which the Arabs themselves, and even more so the Western press, have now pretended suddenly to "discover" the fedayeen as a military force. The current crop of fedayeen certainly differs in some ways from the older models, but the significance of this difference is not necessarily the obvious one. It is true, for instance, that the current fedayeen include a substantial number of university men, but better-educated fedayeen may paradoxically be even more irrational, or at least more psychologically troubled. The need of such individuals to reassert an Arab identity in the face of the perceived disintegration of traditional Arab society may make their abomination of Israel all the more intimate and compelling, since the very idea of Israel invites demeaning comparisons with their own inability to transform Arab society.

There is something equally spurious about the proposition that the Arabs have deliberately selected the fedayeen mode of hostility against Israel—as if alternative modes of warfare were available to them! And the same may be said with regard to the familiar threat of the Arabs to seek a "military solution" if political means fail to restore the Arab losses of the June war. Of course, these fantasies are not without their uses: they help defend the Arabs' self-respect, and they build international pressure for Israeli concessions. In reality, however, it must be recognized that the Arabs are already waging war on Israel *as best they can.* Unable to generate a real war, a war of movement, they can only intensify the sporadic and static warfare (fedayeen violence, artillery barrages, rocket attacks, etc.) which they are being allowed to wage without serious interference by the international community. As a result, the situation in the Middle East remains now what it has been from the beginning. By virtue of their overwhelming advantage in the international community, as against Israel's relative isolation, the Arabs have been permitted to wage war to the limits of their ability, in a manner consistent with the capacity of the international community to restrain Israel from waging war to the best of *its* ability. Intensified Arab efforts now might take such specific forms as an Egyptian attempt to secure a bridgehead on Sinai, or air and rocket attacks on Israeli ports. Acts like these would not constitute a departure from the habitual forms of Arab warfare; no matter what propaganda or hysterical journalism might term them, they would still be static and sporadic outbursts, not war in the modern sense.

Once it is realized that of the two adversaries in the Middle East conflict, only Israel can wage modern war, the question becomes: under what circumstances is it likely to do so? In the vast literature on the Middle East, there are as many different answers to this question as there have been wars and writers. But the theories tend to fall into two broad categories, depending on the degree of rationality imputed by any one writer to Israel's motives.

The most narrowly rationalistic of all theories, espoused by various leftist sources, regards Israel simply as a tool of the imperialist powers. Israel, according to this theory, makes war in accordance with the requirements of the designs of its masters against the progressive peoples of its area. A classic example of this theory is the official Yugoslav version of the Six-Day War, which is seen as the latest in a series of coordinated strikes by Western reactionaries against anti-imperialist forces (Greece, Ghana, Indonesia, etc.). The specific character of the role played by the Israelis varies in proportion to the proximity of a given writer to Jews. Thus, in the version published by an American Communist of Jewish descent, the Israelis are viewed with a certain degree of sympathy and understanding—their alleged masters emerging all the more sinister for that. In Soviet pronouncements, on the other hand, the Israelis sometimes appear more contemptible than their masters. The constant factor in all these interpretations, however, is the conspiratorial view of history.

It is a measure of the leftist fantasy that the Israeli imperialist-capitalist tool has arrayed against it in firm hostility such progressive forces as Chiang's Formosa, the Vatican, the Greek colonels, Franco's Spain, France, ecclesiastic missionaries, petroleum magnates, and the like. The "anti-imperialist" Arabs, on the other hand, have not ceased urging the imperial powers to intervene in the Middle East, by diplomacy and deployment of troops. While the Jewish state is by definition an "imperialist" base, it actually has no bases on its territory (for the simple reason that no imperial power would wish to antagonize the Arab world by establishing such bases, even if Israel could be persuaded to allow this, which its deep suspicion of foreign powers virtually rules out in the first place). It is the rare Arab country that does not now have imperialist bases on its territory, Soviet, American, or British.

The conspiratorial theory of the left has its natural counterpart on the right. Thus, Lieutenant General Sir John Bagot Glubb, former commander of the Arab Legion, has argued that the Soviets deliberately pushed the Arabs into their last defeat in order to tighten their grip on them more securely. The cast of characters in this particular plot corresponds fully with the author's known sympathies: the Arabs go scot-free; the Israelis are found to be only partly guilty; the wickedness of the Reds is triumphantly confirmed.

Arab versions of the conspiracy theory stress the sinister nature of the Israelis and invariably suggest that it is the Jewish tail that wags the dog of imperialism. Basic to Arab analyses of the situation is the conviction that the Jews really run the world, appearances to the contrary notwithstanding. The strength of this belief can scarcely be overrated. Perhaps the most memorable public enunciation of it occurred in the meeting in May 1948 between the prime minister of Egypt, Nokrashi Pasha, and Count Bernadotte of Sweden, United Nations mediator for Palestine. Nokrashi avowed at that meeting that the Jews actually ran a large number of states, including Egypt, and suggested to Bernadotte that they might be running his own country as well.

The conspiracy theory draws particular strength from the literature dealing with the Sinai War of 1956. The understandable fascination of many writers with the secret French-Israeli collaboration has produced an extraordinary stress on the element of premeditation and little regard for the emotional elements. The sterile conception of Israelis in this literature has effectively obstructed a clear understanding of one really significant factor in Israeli thinking: the hope that an Egyptian leadership in defeat would be more amenable to peace. In order to understand why this expectation was very much alive in 1956, one must look not to what certain statesmen may have said to each other in clandestine conferences, but to the old Zionist illusions about the nature of Arab hostility—illusions which few still share today. Chief among them was the belief that Arab hostility was artificially stimulated by leaders like Nasser, whose demise would facilitate peacemaking.

Corollary to the conspiracy theory is the notion of Israel's expansionism. Some observers regard the history of war in the Middle East as a series of premeditated steps in the fulfillment of a grand Zionist design. Others regard Israeli expansionism as a deeply irrational compulsion driving the Jews instinctively to wars of aggression.

A thorough discussion of Israeli expansionism does not lie within the scope of this analysis. It should be sufficient to point out, however, that the real concern in Israel at present is not with more land, but with the Arabs who live on the land already in Israeli possession. Their very high reproduction rate may threaten the Jewish majority of the state's population in the foreseeable future. Recent public-opinion surveys disclose a substantial consensus in favor of giving up most of the captured territories in return for a contractual peace with the Arab states.

Finally, there is the belief that the Israelis are driven to war simply by their accursed nature. This may well be what most Arabs really believe, at least those not sufficiently sophisticated to follow the esoteric distinctions among Jews, Zionists, and Israelis. Regardless of what finer aspects of the long Jewish-Muslim symbiosis are known to scholars, Jews in the Arab folk tradition are universally regarded as a contemptible people. The extent to which religious contempt for Jews in Christendom generates a similar distrust of Israel in the West is difficult to evaluate, though certainly not negligible.

All these theories have one thing in common: a fundamental ignorance of Jews and Judaism. Although they purport to explain Jewish behavior with regard to a matter of life and death, they are oblivious of the profound anxiety about sheer survival that forms such a large psychological component in the makeup of what is probably the most persecuted people in history. Victimization and slaughter have been an intrinsic part of Jewishness for too long to have been expunged by the recent fact of emancipation in the Western countries. It is unlikely that even sympathetic gentiles really understand the terror, the pain, and the rage of a people so lately ravaged by the most monstrous massacre in human history. Is it surprising that the ignorant and the hostile miss the point as well?

This failure of empathy constitutes an object lesson in the sociology of knowledge, especially in Western societies with large Jewish minorities. While the Nazi Holocaust is almost generally "known" in these societies, the vast majority of people are merely baffled or nonplussed when Jews, as in the period just prior to the Six-Day War, become gripped by fears of catastrophe. Clearly an intellectual understanding of persecution does not stretch far enough to comprehend the impact of persecution on behavior—hence the repeated censures of Israeli reprisal raids even by friendly diplomats, who publicly demand that a people so long victimized be particularly tolerant and kind to others. The resentment occasioned in discussions of Palestine or Germany by Jewish references to past persecution—references which are perceived by others as emotional blackmail—is another example of a cognitive failure to comprehend the roots of Jewish anxiety.

In Israel, the unusually high concentration of Jews with actual experiences of persecution has resulted in a heightened sensitivity to Jewish jeopardy. The early settlers, from whose ranks come most Israeli political leaders, were men whose personalities were formed during the pogroms in Russia and Romania in the early years of this century. Later immigrants included the largest number of Jews anywhere—with the possible exception of Soviet Jewry—who had personally experienced the Nazi nightmare. The Israeli environment is permeated with physical and spiritual commemorations to Jewish martyrdom, and even the younger generation of native-born Israelis, who used to be notorious for their "chip on the shoulder" attitude toward the Holocaust (an attitude that was itself probably a means of compensating for the unbearable thought of Jews being led to slaughter), have in the past few years become profoundly apprehensive about the possibility of genocide, even in the Holy Land.

Arab threats of annihilation, falling upon this collective anxiety, elicit unusually strong reactions, symptomized perhaps by the disproportion between some Israeli actions and what would appear to be the objective conditions of Arab military capacity. Real crises in the Middle East can occur when the mediating trauma of the past overwhelms the Israelis' sense of reality; extreme ones, when they are driven, as in the prelude to the June war, to "relive" the Jews' most terrible ordeal.

Indeed, an analysis of the crises of 1956 and 1967 discloses no simple escalation of the volume of violence into full-scale war, but rather a broader set of interactions, not exclusively between the two belligerents, and involving much more subtle forms of violence.

To begin with, Israel's confinement within virtually indefensible territorial demarcations had not only reduced its capacity to tolerate provocation, but also dictated a "first-strike" strategy. Before the June war, the demarcation lines between Israel and her Arab neighbors were a spectacular example of the maximization of insecurity: they bounded a mere 8,000 square miles of territory with some 600 miles of land border, much of it facing higher ground; they placed the large mass of the country's population within the range of enemy cannon, and a considerable proportion within simple rifle-shot range; they attached the northern and southern halves of the country to a "waist" only nine miles wide; they provided no depth anywhere either for retreat or for normal defensive maneuvers; in short, they virtually invited attack.

Although Israel's narrow territorial confinement was not entirely an involuntary matter (being consistent with the Zionist tenet, "good neighbors rather than good borders"), its effect was to draw heavily on the already meager psychological reserves of the population. The fact of confinement lent credence to the proposition that the state, in the words of General Dayan, was "living under a shadow of imminent destruction"—a proposition upon which Israeli military doctrine was in turn predicated. That the excessive vulnerability of the borders encouraged popular analogies with the exposed position of European Jewry in World War II goes without saying.

Still, to initiate the dynamics of war in this setting, more was required than ordinary manifestations of Arab hostility. For Israelis have long since become inured to random violence, verbal or physical; it has in fact become part of their way of life. This is so much the case that they seem more capable of bearing the actual losses which violence incurs than the *thought* that the act goes unpunished. The government's stern policy of reprisals serves to reassure Israelis that Jewish blood is no longer "cheap," thus paradoxically facilitating their acquiescence in a situation of neither war nor peace. In each of the last two wars, what really got things moving was an extraordinary act of Arab brinkmanship that was intuitively recognized as critical by all concerned. In May 1967, for instance, the *Economist* had little doubt that, in his eviction of the UNEF from Sinai, Nasser was "at it again." The last previous act of this kind, of course, was Nasser's acquisition in 1955 of an unprecedented mass of Soviet arms.

The next phase in the precipitation of war has traditionally taken place not between Israel and the Arabs, but between Israel and the international community. Israel eagerly scans international reactions to the Arab challenge; expecting to find herself abandoned, she is seldom disappointed. The reasons for this are many, but two are basic: most powers, including friendly ones, will not view the Arab challenge from Israel's particularly aggravating perspective, or, if they do, will not act forcefully against the Arabs. In the international community, the Arabs outweigh Israel consistently and overwhelmingly, in numbers, resources, and connections. The resulting bias is even more pronounced and systematic in the United Nations, where affiliations are made more publicly and collectively than elsewhere. As for the great powers, support among them for Israel invariably is more contingent and limited than support for the Arabs. Since close associations with Israel are most often regarded as a passing aberration, especially by the great powers, a premium is placed on clandestine relations, with the result that Israel is made to appear weaker diplomatically than she really is. And even when aid is made available surreptitiously, it does not relieve the Israelis' sense of outrage but rather tends to confirm an already obvious truth: the world does not care about Jewish survival; it has acquiesced in genocide before, and will do so again.

As a reaction to the indifference of the world, Israelis tend to generate an immense solidarity and a grim determination to carry on at all cost. Under conditions of vulnerability and challenge, as in 1956 and 1967, an internal tension builds up that is particularly sensitive to extreme acts of provocation. In both 1956 and 1967 the actual military strike was preceded by ritualistic Arab military agreements, concluded with much fanfare and dire predictions of imminent catastrophe for the Jews. These extreme Arab steps—intended to symbolize the noose tightening around Israel's neck, and so regarded by most Israelis —were prompted in turn by the Arabs' reading of the international situation and the rising mood of nervousness and depression in Israel itself. It is easy to understand why the dominant feeling in Israel on the morrow of each victory was not jubilation but relief.

Developments since the 1967 war have marked no change in Middle Eastern dynamics, but have rather accentuated previous asymmetries even more. The military disparity between Jews and Arabs in the area itself doubtless grows more wide than ever, while an opposite relation of forces in the international community pulls even harder against the Jews. Conventional discourse pretends to the very opposite, showing Israel fatally vulnerable in the immediate area and therefore necessarily reliant on the international community. On this reversal of reality is founded the conventional idea of peacemaking; for if the great powers will ultimately have to secure Israel's survival, they are surely entitled to reimpose on it the grotesquely indefensible borders and other extraordinary disabilities envisaged in the various plans for settlement of the conflict.

If it was difficult enough for common sense to accept the idea of a military ascendancy by a small, demeaned, unmartial people, it has proved virtually impossible to accommodate to the idea that this disparity is not a temporary one. The general assumption since 1948 has been that the gap is closing against Israel, while actually it has continued to widen at a progressively greater pace. Every serious academic student of this disparity agrees that it continues to grow into the foreseeable future, yet no layman, no matter how otherwise serious, is really prepared to accept such a seemingly preposterous proposition. The idea elicits only disbelief and sarcasm from influential men like James Reston and J. William Fulbright; but it is nonetheless true, that, if left alone by foreign powers, the ascendancy of the Jewish state over its rivals would indeed be crushing, and not likely to weaken in the foreseeable future. (Israel's easy access to nuclear weaponry makes an unforeseeable future meaningless.)

Except that the foreign powers have never allowed this to happen. For it is in the international community that the Arabs find the support necessary to continue with any hope of success. The Arabs constitute a really considerable quantum in international politics. They are courted for their numbers, strategic expanses, alliances, wealth, mineral resources, and other values, such as sheer votes (around fifty reliable votes on any issue involving the Jewish state even indirectly in the United Nations). After each disastrous war with Israel, the Arabs can confidently count on the international community to rescue them from having to face their victor in the customary process of peacemaking. The powers rush to interpose themselves between the warmakers and press for the cancellation of the Arab defeat. The ingenuous might actually think that the much vaunted Security Council resolution of November 22, 1967, constitutes some unprecedented and terminal effort at a final conclusion of the long war. Yet, following each Arab-Israeli major war, the same "settlement" as the resolution was imposed by the powers in concert with the United Nations: restoration to the Arabs of their losses in return for some ambiguous semantic exercise. In this fashion the Arab-Israeli conflict had already been "settled" by the powers in both 1949 and 1956. And between the wars, the Arabs were allowed to wage war on Israel to the best of their ability (marauding, harassment, boycotts, fedayeen actions, artillery barrages, etc.). Thus even overt Arab acts of warfare were never censured by the Security Council. Not even the invasion of Palestine in 1948 by several Arab states in open defiance of United Nations resolutions was ever censured by the world organization.

Nor is there in all this necessarily any malicious premeditation. The powers merely pursue what they regard as their national interest, which makes them court Arab favor at Israel's expense. It is for this basic reason that all international guarantees to Israel are inherently worthless. For such guarantees to be effective, some power must in the last resort be prepared to take effective action against the array of Arab states and their allies, and that is a fantastic proposition indeed in international politics. It never happens.

These simple facts of international life are obscured by various popular fallacies.

One which enjoys great popularity, [said Bernard Lewis] is the legal or forensic image, in which the great powers are seen as participants in a law suit, sometimes as judges, sometimes as advocates, with Israel and the Arab states in the role of clients or litigants. Both versions are inappropriate. The great powers are not sitting in judgment to administer the law or to dispense justice, but are there to protect and advance their own interests. All have basically this same purpose but pursue it with varying degrees of wisdom, decency, perseverance and ruthlessness. This fact is well-known to the small powers. The role of the great powers is not that of advocacy either. Great power negotiation is not a courtroom. There is no judge, little law and the adversary runs no risk of disbarment for breaking the rules. And as for the client, if at all, he is so in the Roman, not the modern sense of the word. Forensic imagery, though attractive to lawyers accustomed to the contentious procedures of Anglo-Saxon law and to viewers weaned on television courtroom drama, is profoundly irrelevant. Another such image derives from school and the nursery and depicts relations between powers in terms of big boys and small boys or teachers and pupils. The absurdity of this image of international relations is obvious once it is formulated. Large countries may possibly have wiser leaders than small countries, but this is not a necessary consequence of their size.

The reader can test the pervasiveness of obscurantism in regard to the Middle East conflict by recalling the frequency with which he has been presented with Security Council resolutions, Big Four consultations, or United Nations interventions as undertakings by responsible sources concerned with striking a fair compromise between irresponsible belligerents who threaten to drag the world into holocaust through their intemperate foolishness. By contrast, let him recall whether there have been any presentations of these processes for what they really are: the United Nations and its resolutions and operatives as instrumentalities of belligerency against the Jewish state, so overt by now that the very threat to resort to them is clearly recognized as a pressure tactic requiring concessions; or the great-power consultations as a mechanism invoked by one side in the Middle East conflict and just as clearly dreaded by the other. Yet even the literate public is supposed to hold its breath in anxious expectation of success for this "tireless search for a just peace," and it probably does; for the very language of journalistic reporting is couched in fantastic imagery.

Neither the pattern of international involvement in the Middle East nor the pretense behind it is in any real sense new, unprecedented, or even a mere consequence of the cold war. Both were essentially the same before the cold war or even the emergence of the Jewish state. The British role in mandatory Palestine was also popularly depicted as the hapless travail of evenhanded peacemaking; while in reality the pursuit of imperial interests led Britain into increasingly overt conflict with Palestine's Jews. In the early postwar period, when the Western powers still dominated the region, the pattern was the same. "If one looks at the history of the Israeli State, especially before the Sinai war, one cannot avoid being struck by the extent of the totally inefficient but constant attempts at international interference in and control over the Jewish State: control of frontiers by U.N. Observers; control of Jerusalem by Christian powers; the constant appearances of Israel before the Security Council, usually to be condemned," recalls an Israeli diplomat involved in these events. He describes the British and American response to Israeli anxiety for sheer survival as cynical and contemptuous. Every Anglo-American attempt at settling the Arab-Israeli dispute (the Dulles Plan, the Eden Plan, etc.) involved unilateral territorial and other concessions by the Jewish side—that is, withdrawal not from land occupied in 1967, but from the already grotesquely indefensible lines to which they are now pressing Israel to withdraw. From which it should be obvious that there is no rationale behind any particular demand for Israeli withdrawal, other than the desire of the powers to force Israeli retreat. For if the reasons for the reestablishment of the borders of 1967 are so compelling, why then the relentless pressure for withdrawal from these same borders before 1967?

The United States enjoys an extraordinary position among the powers vis-à-vis the Middle East conflict, as evidenced by the fact that both sides regard American intervention with great anxiety.

Because it is not as dependent on Arab oil as are the countries of Western Europe and because the pro-Jewish element in domestic U.S. opinion maintains some strength, the United States enjoys a relative immunity from Arab pressures. Hence Arab anxiety in regard to U.S. intentions. On the other hand, by turning on Israel the United States could make its isolation total. Hence Israeli anxiety in regard to U.S. intentions. Thus the United States is potentially decisive among all the foreign powers involved in the Middle East conflict, and it is on this fact that two popular, but dubious, interpretations of American policy in the Middle East are based.

The first of these, favored by sympathizers of Israel, may be termed the para-idealist school, which argues the imperative that the U.S., on the grounds of morality and kinship with Israel's democratic ethos, abandon the usual patterns of great-power behavior. This school would make American foreign policy consonant with domestic opinion by declaring a defense of "the bastion of democracy" in the Middle East a basic American interest. One commentary of the naïveté of this theory is the observation made by Secretary Rogers to an American Jewish leader who had argued for greater support for Israel as a bulwark of NATO. But, retorted the American diplomat, the NATO states favor the Arabs. (I term the theory "para-idealist," since the allocation of some weight to moral factors in American foreign policy making is not wholly wrong.)

The other school, popular among the establishmentarian elites of diplomacy, business, ecclesiastics, and related publics, may be termed pseudo-realist. Self-styled "realistic" and unhyphenated "American," this school argues for conformity with the other powers' assiduous courting of the Arabs, where, it contends, our real national interest lies. The realism of this school of foreign policy ends abruptly before the frustrating realization that the United States is at a grave disadvantage in such competition for Arab favor. The disability is, of course, realized; but wished away and denounced. If only, cry the "realists," the United States were different, without millions of Israeli sympathizers, without feedbacks from domestic politics to foreign policy; everything would then be fine, for the U.S.

would be able to compete with the Soviets and others for Arab favor on more or less equal terms in pursuit of the national interest. Thus the two schools blame American foreign policy failures either on the wickedness of oil (the para-idealists disregarding the genuine warmth of our diplomatic Arabists for their foreign protégés) or on the wickedness of Jews who put their Jewishness before American interests (curiously conceived to coincide with specific preferences of minute pressure groups, like Protestant missionaries, with whom the pseudo-realists happen to be intimately associated).

Far from regarding the Jewish democracy as a basic interest in the Middle East, American policy suffers it as a nuisance and impediment to that interest. In the critical year 1948, with millions of Jewish voters in key states in a presidential campaign involving a Democratic incumbent —all this hard on the heels of the Nazi Holocaust in Europe—American policy was directed at preventing the establishment of the Jewish state, up to the very moment of its inception. It then imposed an embargo on arms to that state just as it was being invaded by several regular armies, some led and armed by our British ally. The United States subsequently compensated with lavish economic assistance, the price of which was that Israel, in the realm of diplomacy and strategy, became a virtual outcast; thus no state in the region was excluded from American entreaties for political and military alliances, while absolutely no such entanglement was even to be conceivable with Israel. In fact, Israel was the only state outside the Soviet orbit with which the United States would under no circumstances conclude any alliance. The same applied to arms supply, even in the wake of the massive Soviet-Arab arms deals, when the United States only reluctantly agreed to let others sell some equipment to Israel. Since then, the United States has agreed to sell critical arms to Israel only when alternative sources of supply were disappearing, reluctantly, apologetically, and frankly in the belief that a unilateral and total arms embargo by all the powers would only provoke Israel to strike out in preventive war or push the Arabs into another disaster. How reliable the United States has been as a supplier of critical arms to

Israel is suggested by the latter's desperate effort to secure as much independence in weapons production as possible.

Given the realities of American domestic politics, it is astonishing how far American foreign policy makers have succeeded in moving against their Israeli "friends." A high State Department official, Byroade, in the 1950s even went so far as to endorse in public, with the conventional euphemisms, the elimination of Jewish statehood. But since the Arabs hold the West responsible for the sheer survival of any Jewish state—it being inconceivable to them that a handful of demeaned people should rout them in battle —perhaps even active American collaboration in the elimination of such a state would have little chance at securing continuous influence among the Arabs.

Failure in securing "influence" in the Arab world has resulted from the fact that in regard to Israel we cannot possibly satisfy the Arabs—not with our system of government and surely never so well as the Soviets can. On the other hand, real influence has steadily been wielded by our State Department in many quarters of the Arab world, regardless of our alleged complicity in Israel's successes. But American foreign policy makers keep putting reality on its head: they persuade themselves of a new, illusory Arab moderation toward Israel and then try to connect it with their search for influence. But in regard to Israel there are no real moderates in the Arab world, there are only differences of opinion over the means to its elimination. In the last resort, whether or not the Arabs try to act upon their feelings toward Israel is simply a function of opportunity. Hence, the invariable failure of the American diplomatic approach. Yet, even if Israel were miraculously to disappear, we would still have serious problems in the Arab world, just as we continue to exert real influence in that world even while Israel is aligned with us. The conventional diplomatic pursuit of influence is more compulsive than rational, for it persists in the same direction despite repeated failure. It is manifestly false even on its own premises, since American influence in the Arab world is never stronger than when the Arabs need us most; that is, when it seems that only we can coerce Israel into canceling out an Arab defeat in war. But once we have forced the Israelis to disgorge their gains, it is again others, particularly the Soviets, who outbid us for Arab favor— until the next catastrophic war, when once again the Arabs turn to us.

Soviet sources have publicly stated that their strategy for the recovery of Arab losses is founded on the expectation that the United States, in pursuit of what it considers vital interests in the Arab world, will sooner or later be prepared for all "sorts of deals" at Israel's expense. That several years have passed since the 1967 war, with the United States not yet making Israel disgorge its gains, is a source of puzzlement in the Arab world. With the passage of time, Arab calls for the United States to do its "duty" are becoming more pressing. Why are we derelict?

Not for want of wanting, certainly. American diplomacy has learned little and forgotten almost nothing; it has indicated in every way its readiness to resume the pursuit of "influence" by pushing the clock of history back to June 4, 1967. The story of American "peace" initiatives in the last few years is a series of stillborn attempts at stampeding the Jewish state into what the latter regards as a fatal trap. The well-publicized scandal of the ceasefire-standstill violation was merely one of several such cases. They have failed so far because the clock of history has not really stood still, after all. The tension between the Arabs' capacities in the international community and in the Middle East itself has grown considerably in recent years: their ability to have Arab definitions of the Middle East conflict endorsed by the powers has reached unprecedented heights, but the capacity of the powers to impose their will on the Jewish state has been diminishing. (The conventional code for this phenomenon is "intransigent defiance of world opinion," "arrogant inflexibility," etc.) Not that the full gamut of American and other pressures has yet been applied in that direction. Nor are the Israelis finally immune to pressure. They may well prove more vulnerable on psychological grounds than on material ones—quite a paradox in view of their popular image.

Long habituated to squeezing Israel, the diplomats may now ignore the traumatic impact of the pre-June crisis on the Israelis (the sense of abandonment, the analogy with Jewish victims of the Nazi Holocaust, the collapse of international guarantees). As a result, the pressures to return to the same "vulnerability" become counterproductive—i.e., the Israelis respond in the same traumatized terms, refusing to be led meekly, "like sheep to the slaughter." The Israelis are resisting pressure as never before, and their breaking point may this time be high indeed, perhaps too high for us alone to scale. The Arabs will find it exceedingly difficult, emotionally even more than intellectually, to accept an American failure to "deliver" Israel: emotionally, because their utter rejection of the Jewish state is linked with a conviction of its artificiality, lack of autonomous character and inherent worth. Almost certain to be resisted by Israel are economic sanctions, perhaps even suspension of critical arms deliveries. Whether the Jewish state would be able to withstand the joint pressures of Soviet military action and American intimidation, or some other superpower agreement to save the "peace" or even the world, is another question. The reaction to such jeopardy of a people in whose past one finds Kishinev and Auschwitz, but also Masada and the Warsaw ghetto, may not be a foregone conclusion even then.

The Return of Anti-Semitism as a Political Force

Seymour Martin Lipset

SEYMOUR MARTIN LIPSET—professor of Government and Sociology at Harvard University, author of *The Politics of Unreason: Right-Wing Extremism in America, Passion and Politics: Student Activism in America, Revolution and Counter-Revolution*, as well as numerous articles in scholarly and intellectual journals.

Twenty-five years following the end of World War II, and after the collapse of the most anti-Semitic regime in history and the murder of six million Jews, anti-Semitism raises its head around the world. But unlike the situation before 1945, when anti-Jewish politics was largely identified with rightist elements, the current wave is linked to governments, parties, and groups which are conventionally described as leftist. Beginning with anti-Zionism, some New Left activists in different countries, American black militant groups, Arab "socialist" organizations, and East European Communist governments have moved on to anti-Jewish and fully anti-Semitic statements and acts. And though the extreme right remains relatively weak in Western countries, its newspapers have become much more open about referring to Jewish conspiracies.

It may indeed be suggested that the new more open resort of groups on the right to anti-Semitism (e.g., *American Opinion*, the Birch Society magazine, repeatedly describes a conspiracy dominated by Jewish bankers), as well as the far more significant recent increase in anti-Semitism in the Soviet Union (two virulently anti-Jewish novels have recently been published; Hitler-type cartoons are again evident; and both the Rothschilds and the Vatican are now described as allies in some monstrous Jewish conspiracy), both owe much to the sudden rise of anti-Jewish statements among New Left intellectuals, Arab spokesmen, and black militants. The anti-Jewishness of these groups helps to lift the Soviet Government's inhibitions about appearing anti-Jewish; while even the right can make use of the anti-Jewishness of left and blacks to confirm its own historic anti-Semitic prejudices. Thus Gerald L. K. Smith has written with some satisfaction, even blacks "are disenchanted with Zionism. They look upon the Jews as exploiters . . ." (*The Cross and The Flag*, September 1970).

To say that increasing numbers of New Leftists, black militants, and advocates of the Palestinian cause are not only anti-Israel and anti-Zionist, but more, are moving toward—or have already achieved—full-fledged anti-Semitism is clearly fighting words. Some distinctions are in order. Israel may be opposed, as the policy of any state may be, without being anti-Semitic. Zionism may be resisted, as a movement that created the Jewish state and supports it, without being anti-Semitic. One may point to and criticize worldwide Jewish support of Israel without being anti-Semitic. But when one draws on the age-old hostility to Jews to strengthen a political position, when one gives credence to the charge of a worldwide Jewish plot to rule, when one attacks those with whom one has political and economic differences as Jews, when one implies that Jews are guilty of some primal evil, then one is guilty of anti-Semitism, of appealing to prejudice, and one is engaged in the same racism that all decent men insist on eliminating.

Admittedly it is easy to make these distinctions in theory, but difficult to apply them. Nor are the distinctions so neat in practice. But seeing a rising ferocity in the expression of anti-Zionist and anti-Israeli sentiments, and a rising irrationality in such comments, there is good reason to fear that, even though anti-Semitism may not be at their root, the expression of such sentiments may well stimulate and encourage anti-Semitic feelings. Just as a peculiarly aggressive and unmeasured attack on blacks who commit criminal acts may lead us to suspect the attacker is more antiblack than anticriminal, the same kind of language addressed to Israel and Zionism must arouse the same suspicion, and in view of the murderous possibilities of anti-Semitism, serious concern.

The most important expression of anti-Jewish sentiments in the West takes the form of attacks on "Zionists" and on the state of Israel by every section of the left except the democratic socialists. As the war in Vietnam peters out, the various incarnations of the extreme left, new and old, anarchist, Maoist, Trotskyist, Black Panther, and Communist, have reoriented their international emotional priorities to identify the heroes as the Arab terrorists and freedom fighters, and the villains as Israel and its American ally. Even in Germany, made *Judenrein* by Adolf Hitler, New Left students, in a sickening replay of the behavior of their Nazi predecessors of 1928–33 (the university students were the first stratum in Germany to back the Nazis, giving them majorities in student council elections as early as 1931), chant as they parade, "Mach die Nahe Osten rot; schlag die Zionisten tot" (Make the Near East Red; smash the Zionists dead). More startling perhaps was the effort to bomb the Jewish Community House in Berlin on November 10, 1969, the anniversary of the Kristallnacht, the night in 1938 when the Nazis burned and destroyed synagogues all over Germany ostensibly in revenge for the assassination of a German diplomat in Paris. The German police announced that this vicious action, like many other defamations of memorials to the Jewish dead, was the work of a revived wave of right-wing anti-Sémitic terrorism. New Leftists reacted with resentment, announcing, "These actions can no longer be defamed as some right-wing radical outburst—they are a decisive link in our international socialist solidarity" with the Arab guerrillas. As the German novelist Rudolf Krämer-Badoni reported:

> Police investigating the case seized stacks of incriminating leaflets at the *Republican Club*, a popular meeting-place for members of the [New Left] APO (Extra-Parliamentary Opposition). These proclaimed, under the banner headline "Shalom + Napalm", their authors' intention "to

blow up the *Gemeindehaus* and to deface Jewish memorial stones with the 'Shalom + Napalm' slogan". Such action, the leaflet declared, was called for in view of "the Left's continued paralysis in facing up to the theoretical implications of the Middle-East conflict, a paralysis for which German guilt feelings are responsible. We admittedly gassed Jews and, therefore, feel obliged to protect them from further threats of genocide. This kind of neurotic, backward-looking anti-Fascism, obsessed as it is by past history, totally disregards the non-justifiability of the State of Israel."[1]

More recently, Dieter Kunzelmann, who had played a major role in the SDS demonstrations at the Free University of Berlin during the late 1960s, spent time in the Middle-East with the fedayeen, being instructed, according to his published letters, "in the use of explosives . . . [and] the manufacture of time bombs." He wrote from Amman that the German left must break down the pro-Semitism that emerged out of German guilt at the Holocaust, that Germany must get over "der Judenknax!" (the "thing" about the Jews).[2]

French New Left spokesmen, exhibiting their national passion for logical consistency, have outdistanced their German ideological compatriots by openly defending the need to speak in anti-Semitic terms when supporting the Arab cause. Jean Bauberot, former leader of the French Student Christian Association, and subsequently editor of *Herytem,* a New Left journal, wrote, in the May-June 1969 issue, of the difficulties faced by the left in its effort to "demonstrate the intricacies of the Palestine problem." Leftists find it

. . . necessary to speak about Jewish capitalism, the importance of the key positions held in many countries by Jews. . . . In short, we have to use expressions which, taken by themselves, *appear to resemble* certain lines from *Mein Kampf*. As a result we shall feel the burden of being labelled anti-Semites and will be obliged to live "with" this insult, in the same way that the incurably ill live "with" their "ailment."

---

[1] *Wiener Library Bulletin*, vol. 23, no. 4.
[2] *Encounter*, November 1970.

He declared "that combatting anti-Jewish racism has no eternal and universal value . . . that, like its negative, anti-Semitism, it is an alienated product of Western civilization." The French New Left also has expressed its pro-Arab feeling by violent action. Members of the Mouvement Contre le Racisme Anti-Arabe, formed by people active in the revolutionary movement of May 1968, whose activities are publicized in *Herytem*, were responsible for attacks in October 1968 on the Rothschild Bank in Paris.

The open expression of anti-Zionist and anti-Jewish feelings by important segments of the French left has resulted, for the first time since World War II, in the revival in some quarters of a traditional Catholic religious-based anti-Judaism. An article in *L'Arche* (September 26-October 25, 1970), the monthly journal of the French Jewish community, on "the New Anti-Zionists" reports on the attacks on Judaism and Israel which have diffused from the student New Left to various Catholic groups. The latter express their criticism in theological terms which run counter to the statements adopted at Vatican II. They deny the historic claims of the Jews to Israel on the theological grounds that the Church, rather than contemporary Jewry, is the true heir of ancient Israel. They claim that for a Christian, the only solution of the Jewish problem is "the final conversion of this people to Christ resurrected." It is striking that these ancient concepts have reappeared not among the conservative Catholics, but among the progressives who cooperate closely with the New Left, while the French bishops have criticized these beliefs as counter to Catholic doctrine.

The American New Left largely shares the pro-Arab terrorist views expressed by the movement in Europe. In general, however, the American white left has been more inhibited than the European in expressing anti-Semitic statements, probably because so much of its audience and mass base is Jewish. Nevertheless, some of them also have called for terrorism against American supporters of Israel. Eric Mann, a leader of the Weathermen faction of SDS, writing in the *Guardian* of October 17, 1970, stated: "Israeli embassies, tourist offices, airlines and *Zionist fund raising and social affairs are important targets for what-*

ever action is decided to be appropriate." A student of Weathermen activities, Rutgers Political Science Professor Ross Baker, has seriously raised the question in a recent article whether the bombings in 1969 in Rochester of assorted governmental and establishment targets which included two synagogues "might be the assertion that Weathermen's embrace of the Palestinian Liberation Movement has been translated into depredations against Jewish religious institutions in America." There is, of course, no evidence as to which group was responsible for the bombings in Rochester, but the pattern followed does strongly suggest that it was a leftist or black militant one, and that it is part of the chain already operative in Germany and France.

Overt expressions of anti-Semitism have occasionally appeared in American New Left organs. Thus, in an article, "Jews Riot in the Ghetto," in the underground press weekly the *East Village Other* (October 18, 1968), Philip Anthony fantasized in a crudely anti-Semitic fashion concerning the consequences of the assassination of New York Teachers' Union President Albert Shanker. The article included caricatures of Yiddish expressions and accents. Julius Lester, a regular columnist in the New Left Weekly the *Guardian* until 1970, argued in the issue of October 14, 1967, that "any Jew who does not question Israel's very existence nullifies any meaning his opposition to the war in Vietnam may have." The now defunct paper *New Left Notes*, once the organ of the Students for a Democratic Society (SDS) when it was a viable unified organization, strongly attacked Zionism as an effort of "some leaders in developing world imperialism like the Baron Edmund de Rothschild of France [to foster] his own financial interests, which meant the development of an economic base in the Middle East." The existence of socialist institutions in Israel had no merit in the eyes of these New Leftists since "Israeli 'socialism' was founded on the complete relocation of thousands of people of color" (February 28, 1969). In fact the "Semitic" Arabs are as "white" as the Jews; the description is, of course, designed to eliminate sympathy for "white" Jews as an oppressed people. The same objective has been pursued by linking

Zionism and the Israelis to a complicity with the Nazis in the murder of the European Jews. An article by Tabitha Petran in the November 21, 1969, issue of *FIRE* (the Revolutionary Youth Movement faction of SDS's successor to *New Left Notes*) claimed that after Hitler came to power "Zionist leaders offered the Nazi government their cooperation in finding a solution to the Jewish question." Petran went on to argue that collaboration with "organized Jewry . . . remained 'the very cornerstone' of . . . [the Nazis'] Jewish policy." Supposedly "hundreds of Zionist leaders were permitted to escape to Palestine" during World War II because they collaborated with the Nazis by withholding "from the masses in Eastern Europe the fact that they were marked for shipment to death camps." Such charges, of course, have formed a staple part of Soviet propaganda, which also alleges that Zionists were "seeking to provoke anti-Semitism" in czarist Russia in 1905 and again during the Civil War of 1918 to 1921. The Moscow magazine *International Affairs* (April 1971) quotes General Secretary of the Communist Party of the U.S.A. Gus Hall as its authority for the claim that the international "Zionist center" by "boring underground ideological tunnels" was behind the 1968 "quiet counter-revolution" in Czechoslovakia, prevented only by the intervention of Soviet troops.

Thus, the issue of anti-Semitism, like many others, has turned full circle. The creation of the state of Israel, which many hoped would sharply reduce anti-Semitism by "normalizing" the position of Jews, giving them a national home, has become the focal point for a new international wave of anti-Semitism, and the main intellectual core of this outbreak is not among the traditional enemies of the Jews, the religion-based right, but among the secular left. It is important to recognize, however, that the complicity of the New Left activists is not primarily their occasional overtly anti-Semitic statements; it goes even more to the fact that they explicitly support extremist black and Arab groups who voice naked anti-Semitism. They support those who attack ghetto slumlords, shopkeepers, schoolteachers, the South African economic elite, the owners of diamond and gold mines in black Africa, as "Zionists."

Student and intellectual radicals, whether Jews or not, have historically had a penchant for self-hatred in the form of approval for anti-intellectual populism, and have defined wisdom as coming from the progressive instincts of the masses, of the uneducated, of the poor. If the poor are anti-Semitic, then anti-Semitism has some progressive connotations. Currently, such masochistic populism in the United States takes the form of identifying with the values, statements, and tactics of black militant groups, particularly of the Black Panthers. As Harvard SDS leader Michael Kazin described the process: "S.D.S. has consistently supported the political viewpoints and actions of the most militant segments of the black movement and has consciously shaped its own analysis and program in response to those elements as they have evolved during the sixties from Malcolm X to SNCC to the Black Panther Party."

Many of these have increasingly engaged in anti-Semitic propaganda, often only partially disguised as anti-Zionism. Thus Stokely Carmichael, at one time the leading proponent of black nationalism, who has been a leader both of SNCC, the Student Non-Violent (now National) Coordinating Committee, and of the Black Panthers, before abandoning the struggle in America for residence abroad, accounted for the resentment expressed toward the Jews by black militants as a result of "the exploitation [of blacks] by Jewish landlords and merchants," in an article published in the *New York Review of Books* in 1966. Elsewhere he wrote, "You let just one Negro get a Molotov cocktail and throw it at some Jew's liquor store and they call out the whole damn National Guard." In an interview with David Frost on April 13, 1970, Carmichael declared that in his judgement Adolf Hitler "was the greatest white man." He went on to say that he could not describe men like Johnson, Nixon, Truman, or Churchill as "great people," since they "were doing things against my people."

The *SNCC Newsletter* of June-July 1967, in a two-page spread *"*The Palestine Problem" asked its readers whether they know

. . . THAT the famous European Jews, the Rothschilds,
who have long controlled the wealth of many European
nations, were involved in the original conspiracy with the
British to create the "State of Israel" and are also still
among Israel's chief supporters? THAT THE ROTH-
SCHILDS ALSO CONTROL MUCH OF AFRICA'S
MINERAL WEALTH? (Emphasis in the original.)

And Eldridge Cleaver, the exiled minister of information
of the Black Panther party, was reported in the party newspaper, the *Black Panther*, of January 17, 1970, as explaining that they took so long to understand the Arab cause as
a result of the fact that "the black people in Babylon were
being blocked by forces we did not understand. We found
there were certain people with the U.S. [that is, the Jews]
who wanted to define our struggle for us."

If one wonders why black militants have felt so impelled to attack Jews as such, perhaps one part of the answer lies in the fact, as reported by a participant in SNCC
activities (Mrs. Robert Lautner), that "at the height of
SNCC there were close to 300 staff members . . . around
fifty per cent of these staff members were white and I
would venture to say that seventy-five per cent of the whites
were Jewish." Two of the three SNCC staff members killed
in Mississippi were Jewish (Goodman and Schwerner).

Ironically, it would appear that the very fact of disproportionate participation of Jews in leftist causes is a
major cause of subsequent anti-Semitism (viz., in the East
European Communist countries and Russia where non-
Jewish Communists eventually sought to drive Jews out
of the privileged positions they had gained because of
their early services to the party). In the United States,
the integrationist movement was largely an alliance between Negroes and Jews (who, to a considerable extent,
actually dominated it). Many of the interracial civil rights
organizations, such as the NAACP, have been led and
financed by whites, and the majority of their white members and big financial contributors have been Jews. Insofar
as a black effort emerged to break loose from involvement with whites, from domination of the civil rights struggle by white liberals and radicals, this meant concretely

a break with Jews, for they were the whites who were active in these movements. The black nationalist leadership had to push whites (Jews) "out of the way," and to stop white (Jewish) "interference" in order to get whites (Jews) "off their backs," to eliminate whites from the civil rights movement.

This resentment of the Jewish presence was not limited to their activities within organizations which militant blacks have increasingly felt ought to be totally dominated by themselves. Some black activists have claimed that the disproportionate weight of Jews within the white radical movement generally has hurt the black cause. Harold Cruse, the author of *The Crisis of the Negro Intellectual*, has argued, from his experience within the Communist party in the 1940s, that Jewish Communists were in large part responsible for serious misperceptions concerning the black situation because they erroneously thought that both groups were in a comparable situation as oppressed minorities, and the party generally took this position. And he points out:

> Blacks did not run party affairs inside the black community, but shared this leadership with whites who were predominantly Jewish whites. . . . [A] struggle on the part of any Negro rank-and-file Communist member against "white domination" over black affairs had to be directed simultaneously against elements of Jewish leadership, in order to clarify the exact nature of that white domination, and also against the participation of Jews as a group, acting to negate black political autonomy.

The martyred black leader Malcolm X also resented the presence of Jews in the movement for black rights. He argued in his *Autobiography*, which circulates widely among black militant and white radical youth today, that what he "held against the Jew was that so many Jews actually were hypocrites in their claim to be friends to the American black man." He contended that the misdirection provided by Jews had "a very careful strategic reason: the more prejudice in America could be focused upon the Negro, then the more the white Gentiles' prejudice would keep diverted off the Jew. . . ."

More recently, an article in the *Black Panther* of April 25, 1970, also voiced the complaint that the Panthers are not uncritically supported by the white left because the "White Left in the U.S.A. is comprised of a large percentage of the Jewish population." It charged that many of the Jewish leftists "are Zionists and, therefore, racists."

(Criticism of Jews, the radicals and Communists among them included, for a racist commitment to Israel may even be found among a "white" Communist group, the Maoist Progressive Labor party. Their newspaper, *Challenge*, charged, "Many Jews actually believe Israel has some God-given right to statehood. This argument degenerates into My people right or wrong. Even a few radicals and communists who are Jewish will try . . . to obscure the main question—imperialism.")

The tension between black intellectuals and Jewish radicals and civil rights activists for leadership in movements which affect the black community may account for the anti-Semitic outbursts of men like Stokely Carmichael and H. Rap Brown. The fact that anti-Semitic statements could find a resonance among groups rooted in the ghetto poor, such as Black Panthers, reflects a different source of conflict inherent in the historical fact that most Negro areas in the North were formerly Jewish ghettos. Negroes moved into Jewish areas such as Harlem and Bedford-Stuyvesant in New York, Roxbury in Boston, Boyle Heights in Los Angeles, and other Jewish districts in Washington, Chicago, Philadelphia, and other cities. The reasons for this pattern of ethnic succession attest in part to positive aspects in Jewish racial attitudes—they were less resistant to blacks moving into their neighborhoods, they reacted less violently than other white communities. This process meant, however, that though Jews eventually moved out as residents, some of them have remained as landlords and store owners. Hence many blacks are in a situation in which anti-Semitic propaganda may have an effect.

Reinforcing these consequences of ecological succession has been the effects of the fact that in the 1930s large numbers of able Jews found that the only place they could secure employment was in government service, as teachers, social workers, or other professionals. Thirty years later, many of these same Jews (now in their fifties and sixties) are at the summits of the civil service hierarchy in some cities, as school principals, division heads of welfare departments, etc. And as the blacks follow the Jews into the civil service, they find that the directors of units operating in Negro areas are often Jews. The request that "blacks be given top jobs" in such organizations often has become a demand that Jews be removed from positions which they obtained through merit and seniority. These sources of tension were a major element in the situation which produced the Teachers' Union strike in New York City three years ago.

The role of the Jews as the dominant group within the educational bureaucracy, the classroom teaching situation, and the Teachers' Union was made an overt issue by many blacks at the time. (White leftists, the Socialist party apart, tended to support the so-called black community position and ignored the attacks on Jews.) Thus John Hatchett in an article in the November-December 1967 issue of the *African-American Teachers Association Forum* argued that the Jews "dominate and control [the New York] educational bureaucracy" and regularly practice "misery, degradation, racism and cultural genocide . . . against my people." During the 1968 strike itself, according to an article in the 1969 *American Jewish Yearbook*, handbills, often unsigned, appeared in Jewish districts warning "Middle East murderers of colored people" to help end the strike "or your relatives in the Middle East will find themselves giving benefits to raise money to help you out from under the terrible weight of an enraged black community." In December 1968, the Harlem Tenants Rights party led by Jesse Gray issued a leaflet which said in part:

> Zionists kill black people in their own land in the Middle East. They run the people out of their own communities.
> Now here, SHANKER is trying to use the same tactics and throw us out of our community.
> HARLEM WILL NOT STAND BY WHILE THESE

RACIST, RUTHLESS, ZIONIST BANDITS (SHANK-
ER AND THE UFT) AND HIS PUPPET THE *PO-
LICE* RUN US OUT OF OUR OWN COMMUNI-
TIES.

Gray, who had long been closely allied with Old Left
groups, sought subsequently to capitalize on the fame he
won during the strike. He successfully campaigned in the
1969 primary for the Democratic councilmanic nomina-
tion for Harlem's seat in the New York City Council, a
designation usually tantamount to election. Unfortunately
for him, being a Democratic candidate that year meant
running on Procaccino's ticket, and the Liberal party nom-
inee was swept in on Lindsay's landslide in the black districts.

The perception of the struggle within the schools as one
between the Jews and the blacks continued into the seventies. Thus an article in the June 13, 1970, issue of the
Black Panther by Richard "Dharuba" Moore of the Harlem branch of the party stated: "Albert Shanker who is the
head of the racist reactionary U.F.T. in New York . . .
has been in direct opposition to the desires and needs of
the black community. His actions during the teachers
strike proved that his main interest is that of the Zionists. . . ."

The most overt expression of anti-Semitism has come
generally from the most militant of black organizations,
the one with closest ties to sections of the white New and
Old Lefts, the self-described Marxist-Leninist Black Panther party. The party went out of its way to identify those
in the establishment who opposed it who happened to be
Jews, as Jews. Thus, in the December 21, 1968, issue of
the *Black Panther*, Eldridge Cleaver attacked Judge
Monroe Friedman of Oakland, California, who presided
over a Panther trial, in the following terms: "If the Jews
like Judge Friedman are going to be allowed to function,
and come to their synagogues to pray on Saturdays, or do
whatever they do down there, then we'll make a coalition
with the Arabs, against the Jews . . ."

A Reuters dispatch published in the *Washington Post*
of December 28, 1969, cited Cleaver as saying that "Jew-

ish intellectuals were helping Nixon formulate his domestic policies and . . . that Black Panther leaders Huey Newton and Bobby Seale were sent to prison by Zionist magistrates." The reference to Zionist magistrates was to Judge Friedman, who presided over Huey Newton's trial, and to Judge Julius Hoffman, who sentenced Bobby Seale for contempt during the Chicago conspiracy trial. The Panthers have even argued that Judge Hoffman gave the Jewish defendants in the trial better treatment than Seale. Connie Matthews, international coordinator of the party, wrote in the *Black Panther* of April 25, 1970, that there was an alliance between the Jewish judge and the Jewish defendants:

> It was a Zionist judge, Judge Friedman, who sentenced Huey P. Newton to 2–15 years in jail. It was a Zionist judge, Judge Hoffman, who allowed the other Zionists to go free but has kept Bobby Seale in jail and sentenced him to 4 years for contempt charges. Bobby Seale alone stands trial again in April on conspiracy charges. With whom did he conspire? The Zionists?
>
> The other Zionists in the conspiracy 8 trial [i.e. Abbie Hoffman, Jerry Rubin] were willing and did sacrifice Bobby Seale and his role in the conspiracy trial to gain publicity.

Now clearly Rubin and Hoffman are in no way "Zionists." This is simply a code word for Jew, just as it has become in Eastern Europe, where long-term Communist leaders of Jewish origin are denounced as "Zionists."

Though opposed to all capitalists, the Panthers singled out Jewish business for attack. Thus, a statement in the May 19, 1970, issue of the party newspaper declared that they are against "Zionist exploitation here in Babylon, manifested in the robber barons that exploit in the garment industry and the bandit merchants and greedy slumlords that operate in our communities." In describing a tenants' action in Atlantic City against a landlord, an article in the June 13, 1970, *Black Panther* praised the tenants for "gathering together to form a United Front against Zionist Pig Sobel. . . ." The article, which is headed "People Move on Indecent Housing," concludes with the exhortation: "ALL POWER TO THE PEOPLE—DEATH TO THE ZIONIST PIGS." And as if to prove that the reference to Sobel was not fortuitous, the paper a week later carried a story on "Substandard Housing in America," which referred to buildings "owned by a Zionist by the name of Rosenbaum."

To make Jews (or "Zionists") as a group responsible for the actions of single individuals is anti-Semitism in its purest form. Although it hardly seems necessary to make the case, so many on the left seek to find ways of continued identification with mass-based anti-Semitism that it may be worthwhile repeating Irving Howe's answer to Stokely Carmichael's *New York Review of Books* attack on Jews:

> Exploitative landlords who happen to be Jewish should be condemned, but condemned as landlords, not Jews. They exploit in their social—not religious—capacity, and the same holds true for Christian or Buddhist or Black Muslim landlords. No fair-minded person objects, for example, to demonstrations against such landlords. What is at stake . . . is the *identification* of social oppressors by their religious origin. What is troubling is that the justifiable resentment against slumlords should be diverted, as it sometimes seems to have been, into Jew-Baiting.

The white left, both New and Old, while increasingly anti-Israeli, and occasionally anti-Semitic, does not engage in the kind of virulent anti-Semitism which may be found among the black militant left and the white extreme right. But it is important to reiterate that the white left *does not challenge* black anti-Semitism. This is not because it fears to criticize the black militants. Most of the left-wing publications, *Challenge* (Maoist), the *Militant* (Trotskyist), the *Daily World* (Communist), the *Guardian* (ecumenical left), have carried articles, sometimes lengthy ones, which are highly critical of various aspects of black nationalism, and of the Black Panthers in particular. Such articles usually criticize the militants for their lack of emphasis on class as distinct from race, and often involve highly esoteric discussions of Marxist-Leninist analysis concerning concepts of nationalism, colonialism, and the like. The Panthers for one, do not take kindly to such criticism, and have replied with violent rhetoric concerning the revolutionary bona fides of those who dare challenge their revolutionary purity. Yet in all of this criticism, anti-Semitism is never mentioned. The white left acts as if it is of no consequence, or as if no one on the left is capable of it.

The same double standard with respect to anti-Semitism voiced by groups identified as part of the revolutionary left or third-world anti-imperialist struggle is seen in much of the American leftist press response to the propaganda themes of the Arabs. On one hand, they accept the self-description of a number of Arab states and movements of themselves as socialist, even though Communists are outlawed in all Arab countries except for Lebanon, and occasionally Syria, though little is nationalized or socialized in these countries, and though the inequality of income and land ownership is greater in all the Arab nations than in Israel. More significant, however, is the fact that the American left-wing press also ignores the fact that the Arab militants as well as a number of governments have been ready to use whatever sources of anti-Semitic, anti-American, anticapitalist, or anti-Israeli feelings exist to foster their cause. Before and during World War II, the equivalent to the Arab guerrillas of today worked closely with Nazi and Fascist groups, repeated Nazi propaganda about Jews, and identified with the cause of Axis victory against Allied imperialism, much as their descendants currently purport to a leftist anti-imperialist position. But even today, many of the Arab groups continue to reiterate anti-Semitic themes taken from Nazi handbooks, and cooperate with various European and American right-wing extremist groups.

The Arabs, of course, like other critics of the Jews on the far left and right, insist that they are only anti-Zionist, not anti-Semitic. This distinction is a valid one, which applies to the views of many critics of Israel, Arabs and others. Yet there is clear evidence that anti-Semitism—not simply anti-Zionism—has deeply penetrated Arab groups and governments. Such sentiments have been spurred on by their Soviet allies who have translated and widely distributed blatantly anti-Semitic works in Arabic. Thus, Old Leftist Jewish historian Morris Schappes reported that "in Moscow Yuri Ivanov's primitive anti-Zionist work that often sinks to anti-Semitism has been translated into Arabic and 35,000 copies are to be exported to Arab states" (*Jewish Currents,* November 1971, p. 46). Now there are many official Egyptian books and pamphlets dealing with the Palestine problem which have reprinted or cited as factual the hoary mythological *Protocols of the Learned Elders of Zion*, a document put out in the nineteenth century initially by the tsarist police, which purports to contain the details of the Jewish worldwide conspiracy to control the world. It was circulated extensively in this country by Henry Ford during his vitriolic anti-Semitic campaign in the 1920s, by the Ku Klux Klan, and by Gerald Winrod and Father Charles Coughlin, two pro-Nazi demogogues of the 1930s. Nasser himself, in an interview in 1958 with the editor of *Blitz*, a left-wing Indian paper, advised him to read the *Protocols*, which "will tell him all about the Jews" (*al-Aharam*, September 1958). Hasan Sabri al-Huli, the head of the Palestine department of the Egyptian Presidential Office and an Arab Socialist, Nasser style, wrote detailing the expulsions of Jews from various countries since 1290. He explains such anti-Semitic outbursts: "The history of the Jews demonstrated that they were always welcomed into each country . . . but in the end they became *hated* and were expelled because of their arrogance and intriguing nature" (*The Palestine Problem*, 1965). In an official Egyptian publication, *World Zionism*, which includes the *Protocols* as an appendix, the author, al-Aqad, ascribes a number of evils to the Jews: sociology is a well-known plot founded by a rabbi's son, Émile Durkheim; psychoanalysis was initiated by the Jew Sigmund Freud, "whose aides and disciples were *only* Jews"; and nuclear physics was begun by the Jew Albert Einstein, who acquired dominance over the scientific world. *Free Palestine,* an al-Fatah paper published in London, referred in its January 1970 issue to the old anti-Semitic jibe that after the Cherbourg gunboat affair RF no longer stood for République française, but for Rothschild Frères. This paper, while nominally taking a left line, has also published contributions by Hans Katzner, who consistently denounces Israel in his capacity as a regular writer for the German neo-Nazi NPD weekly *Deutschen Wochen-Zeitung*. Arab groups emphasize the economic role of the 100,000 Jews in South Africa, and argue the existence of a Jewish-backed conspiracy, linked to the Rothschilds, to protect the two "white settler" states, South Africa and Israel, against black and Arab native populations. The South African millionaire Harry Oppenheimer is frequently mentioned as the Jewish head of this plot. (In fact, Oppenheimer's father converted, his mother is Christian, and he is an Anglican.)

Although most left-wing defenders of the Palestinian Arab cause usually insist that the militant Arabs are not anti-Semitic, and that in fact they are desirous of co-operating with Jews, at least one prominent New Left spokesman, Jean Bauberot, editor of the French magazine *Herytem*, has acknowledged and sought to justify the repeated anti-Semitic statements in Arab propaganda.

> To be against all forms of racism is as stupid as being against all forms of violence. We must begin by saying that the Palestinians have the right at present to appear antisemitic to us. . . . The [Middle East] situation is a racist one, and if we refuse the Palestinians the right to name their oppressors, this accounts to a right to disband them culturally.[3]

Not surprisingly, Arab spokesmen have been willing to work with extremist groups on the right as well as the left. Speakers and propaganda material from the Palestine Liberation Organization have shown up in different parts of the political spectrum. The Austrian neo-Nazi *Klartext* offers to supply "the facts about Israel" as received from the Research Center of the Palestine Liberation Organization in Beirut. And important segments of the extreme right have resembled the extreme left in giving support to al-Fatah and other Arab militants. The neo-Nazi German youth group *Bund Heimattreuer Jugend* (League of Patriotic Youth) competes with New Left student groups in

---

[3] *Herytem*, May-July 1969.

recruiting young Germans for service with the Arabs. It "calls upon young men (from 18 up to 40) to join the Auxiliary Corps Arabia. You too must do your share in restoring, through hard personal action, the good German name." (See *Der neue Aufbruch*, no. 1, 1968.) The most widely circulating neo-Nazi paper in Germany, *Deutsche National und Soldaten Zeitung*, has always been extremely pro-Arab, and has published a number of long interviews with Nasser and with representatives of the Arab League in Germany. When the Belgian Jean Robert Debbaudt, a veteran of the German SS Walloon Legion, announced the re-formation of the fascist Rexist movement founded by the Belgian Quisling Léon Degrelle, he concluded his announcement with the words: *"Vive Léon Degrelle! Vive El Fatah! Rex Vaincra!"* The West European neo-fascist magazine *La Nation Européenne*, which stands for a unified anti-Communist fascist Europe, has only two foreign representatives, one in Algiers, and the other in Cairo. It has carried many advertisements from Arab sources, e.g., publicizing fairs in Algeria and Iraq, or French language anti-Zionist books published in Egypt. The Italian neo-fascists strongly back al-Fatah and (like the New Left) reprint much of its propaganda.

The ultra-rightist racist American National States Rights party has also repeatedly expressed pro-Arab, pro-guerrilla sentiments in its newspaper, the *Thunderbolt*. Its issue of December 1969 called attention to the presumed fact that "Israel is the only country in the Middle East with a legalized local Communist Party," while "every single one of the Arab nations has outlawed the Communist Party and placed its leaders in prison." The paper displayed an al-Fatah propaganda poster, and said: "The time has come for us White Christian Americans to come to the aid of our good anti-Communist Arab friends and demand that the government stop aiding the Jews." Party headquarters, e.g., in Baltimore, carry al-Fatah posters on their walls. The long-enduring violently anti-Semitic magazine *Common Sense* also publishes the writings of Arab spokesmen. In May 15, 1970, an article by a London-based Arab lawyer, Issa Nakhlen, refers to the "Jew gangsters of Tel Aviv" who are "completely eradicating Christianity and Islam from the Holy Land." An article in the ultra-rightist anti-Semitic magazine the *American Mercury* (Fall 1970) also defends the Arabs by pointing out that "Kibbutz living is communal living. Yet pro-Communist tendencies are attributed [by Zionists] to Arab states, where the Communist Party is barred. . . ." Being on the same side as the Communists, of course, disturbs many right-wing extremists, but some, like the American Liberty Lobby, have been able to explain it. "Soviet global strategy is working out perfectly. In the Mid-east the Communists take an anti-Zionist position while in America they always support Jewish interests. This isolates America from the Arabs, forcing the Arabs to seek 'protection' from the Soviets" (*Liberty Lobby Newsletter*, July 1969). Thus Arab materials increasingly appear in left-wing, right-wing, and black nationalist papers which share an antipathy to Israel and to Jewry. Both SNCC and the National States Rights party published such propaganda under their own auspices, as the following material demonstrates.

(Paragraph numbers correspond to those used in the original documents identified below)

Student Non-Violent Coordinating Committee	Palestine Liberation Organization
(SNCC *Newsletter*, June-July 1967)	(*Do You Know? Twenty Basic Facts About The Palestine People*, September 1966)

DO YOU KNOW:

6. THAT the British Mandate Government of Palestine, along with the Zionists, immediately began to encourage European Jews to immigrate to Palestine . . . in spite of the fact that, in 1917, more than 90 per cent of the population of Palestine were Arabs . . . and there were no more than 56,000 Jews in Palestine?

DO YOU KNOW:

1. THAT, when the Palestine Problem was created by Britain in 1917, more than 90 per cent of the population of Palestine were Arab? . . . And that there were at that time no more than 56,000 Jews in Palestine?

7. THAT more than half of the 56,000 Jews living in Palestine at that time were *recent immigrants*, who had come to Palestine only a few years before to escape persecution in Europe and had been welcomed by the native Palestinian Arab people with open arms, living in peace side-by-side with the Arabs? That, in 1917, less than 5 per cent of the population of Palestine were native Palestine Jews?

2. THAT more than half of the Jews living in Palestine at that time were *recent immigrants*, who had come to Palestine in the preceding decades in order to escape persecution in Europe? . . . And that less than 5 per cent of the population of Palestine were *native Palestinian Jews?*

8. THAT Arabs of Palestine at that time owned 97½ per cent of the land, while Jews (native Palestinians and recent immigrants together) owned only 2½ per cent of the land?

3. THAT the Arabs of Palestine at that time owned 97½ per cent of the land, while Jews (native Palestinians and recent immigrants together) owned only 2½ per cent of the land?

9. THAT during 30 years of British occupation and rule, the Zionists were able to purchase only 3½ per cent of the land of Palestine, in spite of encouragement by the British government? And that much of this land was transferred to Zionist bodies by the British government directly, and was not sold by Arab owners?

4. THAT, during thirty years of British occupation and rule, the Zionists were able to purchase only 3½ per cent of the land of Palestine, in spite of the encouragement of the British Government? . . . And that much of this land was transferred to Zionist bodies by the British Government directly, and was not sold by Arab owners?

10. THAT therefore when Britain passed the Palestine Problem to the United Nations in 1947, Zionists owned no more than 6 per cent of the total land area of Palestine? At that time there were 1.3 mil-

5. THAT, therefore, when Britain passed the Palestine Problem to the United Nations in 1947, Zionists owned no more than 6 per cent of the total land area of Palestine?

lion Arabs and 650,000 recent Jewish immigrants living in Palestine.

11. THAT in spite of these facts, the General Assembly of the United Nations, in 1947, recommended that a "Jewish State" be established in Palestine? . . . And that, furthermore, the U.N. granted the proposed "State" about 54 per cent of the total area of Palestine, which included the coastal fertile and irrigable lands leaving the Arabs dry mountainous areas with little or no irrigation possibilities.

12. THAT the Zionists (Israeli) armies immediately occupied (and still occupy) more than 80 per cent of the total land area of Palestine?

13. THAT this conquest of Arab land took place, for the most part, *before* May 15, 1948 *before* the formal end of British rule, *before* the Arab armies entered to protect Palestinian Arabs, and *before* the Arab Israeli War?

18. THAT under the Charter of the United Nations, the U.N. General Assembly had no legal right to recommend the 1947 Partition Plan which created the "Jewish State?"

6. THAT, notwithstanding these facts, the General Assembly of the United Nations recommended that a "Jewish State" be established in Palestine? . . . And that the Assembly granted that proposed "State" about 54 per cent of the total area of the country?

7. THAT Israel immediately occupied (and still occupies) 80.48 per cent of the total land area of Palestine?

8. THAT this territorial expansion took place, for the most part, *before* 15 May 1948: i.e., *before* the formal end of the British mandate and the withdrawal of British forces from Palestine, *before* the entry of Arab armies to protect Palestinian Arabs, and *before* the Arab-Israeli war?

9. THAT the 1947 recommendation of the General Assembly in favour of the creation of a "Jewish State" was outside the competence of the Assembly under the Charter of the United Nations?

19. THAT all attempts by the Arab States and other Asian countries to have the U.N. Assembly test the legality of this plan before the International Court of Justice were rejected or ignored by the Assembly?

10. THAT all attempts by the Arab States and other Asian countries to have the Assembly submit the question of "constitutionality" of its recommendation to the International Court of Justice for an "advisory opinion" by the Court were rejected or ignored by the Assembly?

20. THAT the original 1947 Partition Plan was approved, at the first vote, only by white European, American and Australasian states, that every African and Asian state voted against it? And that, in the second vote, urgent United States pressures (which a member of the Truman cabinet called "bordering onto scandal") had succeeded in forcing only one Asian country (the Phillipines) (*sic*) and one African country (Liberia) both controlled by "Uncle Sam," to abandon their opposition. IN OTHER WORDS, ISRAEL WAS PLANTED AT THE CROSSROADS OF ASIA AND AFRICA WITHOUT THE FREE APPROVAL OF ANY MIDDLE-EASTERN ASIAN OR AFRICAN COUNTRY!

12. THAT that original 1947 recommendation to create a "Jewish State" in Palestine was approved, at the first vote, only by European, American and Australasian States . . . for every Asian State, and every African State (with the exception of the Union of South Africa) voted against it? . . . And that, when the vote was cast in plenary session on 29 November 1947, urgent American pressures (which a member of the Truman cabinet described as "bordering onto scandal") had succeeded in prevailing only upon one Asian country (the Philippines) and one African country (Liberia), both of which had special vulnerability to American pressures, to abandon their declared opposition? . . . And that, in other words, *the "Jewish State" was planted at the point-of-intersection of Asia and Africa without the free*

approval of any Middle
Eastern, Asian or African
country except the Union
of South Africa, itself
ruled by an alien minor-
ity?

21. THAT Israel has re-
mained a total stranger in
the Afro-Asian world,
that Israel has never been
allowed to attend any conference of the African,
Asian, or Afro-Asian
states?

13. THAT Israel remained,
ever since its inception, a
total stranger in the
emerging world of Afro-
Asia; and that Israel has
been refused admission to
any inter-state conference
of Asian, African, Afro-
Asian, or Non-Aligned
States ever held?

22. THAT, ever since the Armistice Agreements were
signed in 1949, Israel has
continued to cross the
Demarcation Lines, in-
vade the neighboring Arab
states, and make com-
mando raids against the
Arab People? And that
the U.N. has condemned
Israel for these attacks on
at least eleven occasions.

14. THAT, since the Gen-
eral Armistice Agreements
were signed in 1949, Is-
rael has maintained an aggressive policy of waging
military attacks across the
Armistice Demarcation
Lines, repeatedly invading
the territories of the
neighbouring Arab States
. . . And that Israel has
been duly *rebuked, cen-
sored*, or *condemned* for
these military attacks by
the Security Council or
the General Assembly of
the United Nations on
eleven occasions—five
times by the Security
Council and six times by
the General Assembly?

23. THAT no Arab State has
ever been condemned by
the U.N. for military at-
tacks against Israel.

16. THAT no Arab State has
ever been condemned by
any organ of the United
Nations for military at-
tacks upon Israel (or any
other state)?

25. THAT Israel segregates those few Arabs who remained in their homeland, that more than 90 per cent of these Arabs live in "Security Zones" under Martial Law, are not allowed to travel freely within Israel, and are the victims of discrimination in education, jobs, etc.

18. THAT Israel has additionally imposed a system of *apartheid* upon the Arabs who stayed in their homeland? . . . More than 90 per cent of these Arabs live in "security zones"; they alone live under martial law, restricting their freedom to travel from village to village or from town to town; their children are denied equal opportunities for education; and they are denied decent opportunities for work, and the right to receive "equal pay for equal work"?

National States Rights Party

(*The Thunderbolt*, August 1967)

Palestine Arab Delegation

(*Jewish War Crimes and Genocide*, July 14, 1967)

The Jewish hate for the Christians and Muslims of Palestine was demonstrated in 1948 in six large scale massacres of disarmed men, women and children by Jewish terrorists, the products of the ghettos of Central and Eastern Europe. The same hatred was displayed again in 1967 by acts of genocide committed by Jewish forces in the Gaza Strip, the Sinai, the Western Bank of Jordan and in Syria. Jewish forces rounded up thousands of Arab young men in the Gaza Strip and shot in cold blood more than 3000 of them. In most brutal meth-

The Jewish hate for the Christians and Muslims of Palestine was demonstrated in 1948 in six large scale massacres of disarmed men, women and children by Jewish terrorists, the products of the ghettos of Central and Eastern Europe. The same hatred was displayed again in 1967 by acts of genocide committed by Jewish forces in the Gaza Strip, the Sinai, the Western Bank of Jordan and in Syria. Jewish forces rounded up thousands of Arab young men in the Gaza Strip and shot in cold blood more than 3000 of them. In a Nazi-like

ods, Jewish forces compelled their victims to dig mass graves, then shot them and buried them in those graves.

The Jewish murderers repeated their acts of genocide in the occupied Syrian territory. Many Syrian civilians who were found carrying a booklet—"Service to the Flag"—were shot immediately after their capture. Jewish forces rounded up many Syrian young men and shot them and buried them in mass graves as they did in the Gaza Strip.

Acts of genocide were committed in Jenin, Tulkram and Qalzilya where many Arab young men were shot because of their fierce resistance to the Jewish invaders.

Jewish forces committed the most heinous forms of crimes against the civilian population in all sectors of the war. In the Syrian territory, Jewish aggressors forced all civilian population out of their homes compelling them to sit in the sun for hours without food or water, torturing and screening men, and raping women and young girls particularly in Jolan.

Jewish inhuman practices of hate and insults were poured out against the civilian population in Jenin and Tulkarm districts and the old city of Jerusalem. The in-

method, Jewish forces compelled their victims to dig mass graves, then shot them and buried them in those graves.

The Jewish murderers repeated their acts of genocide in the occupied Syrian territory. Many Syrian civilians who were found carrying a booklet—"Service to the Flag"—were shot immediately after their capture. Jewish forces rounded up many Syrian young men and shot them and buried them in mass graves as they did in the Gaza Strip.

Acts of genocide were committed in Jenin, Tulkram and Qalqilya where many Arab young men were shot because of their fierce resistance to the Jewish invaders.

Jewish forces committed the most heinous forms of crimes against the civilian population in all sectors of the war. In the Syrian territory, Jewish aggressors forced all civilian population out of their homes compelling them to sit in the sun for hours without food or water, torturing and screening men, and raping women and young girls particularly in Jolan.

Jewish inhuman practices of hate and insults were poured out against the civilian population in Jenin and Tulkarm districts and the old city of Jerusalem. The inhabhabitants of many towns and villages were forced out of their homes and made to sit in the open fields without food or water while Jewish forces looted their possessions and destroyed their homes.

The same inhuman acts were committed in the Gaza Strip where thousands of civilians were assaulted, insulted and forced to sit in the burning sun without food or water for many hours while Jews were screening men and looting homes and possessions.

itants of many towns and villages were forced out of their homes and made to sit in the open fields without food or water while Jewish forces looted their possessions and destroyed their homes.

The same inhuman acts were committed in the Gaza Strip where thousands of civilians were assaulted, insulted and forced to sit in the burning sun without food or water for many hours while Jews were screening men and looting homes and possessions.

Given the clear-cut anti-Semitic character of much pro-Arab propaganda, given the extent to which criticisms of Zionism by various left and black militant groups have become anti-Semitic, the question arises as to why so many on the left, including many of Jewish origin, have accepted such policies as their own, or more commonly have abstained from criticizing groups such as the Black Panthers, no matter how explicit their bigotry. The answer is obviously not simple.

The most immediate sources of the reaction seem to result from the diverse results of the Vietnam War and the Six-Day War. The conflict in Indochina clearly alienated most people on the left, whether moderate or extreme, from the United States as an international force. For many on the left, particularly the young who never knew and do not understand the horrors of Nazism, Stalinism, totalitarianism generally, the United States has become the epitome of international reaction, the stronghold of all that is evil. Hence, any government, any society, any movement which has the strong backing of the United States must be almost as wicked. And conversely, people opposed by the United States must be good or at least better, particularly if they are also backed by China, North Vietnam, Cuba, Russia, and the various leftist third-world countries. The support given to the Arab cause by the black nationalists is an additional argument in the same direction, since many young white leftists take their domestic cues from the black radicals.

More specific, however, in changing the outlook of many on Israel and the Jews was the impact of the Six-Day War. Israel by its rapid and decisive victory ceased being an underdog nation. Liberal and leftist egalitarian values, as well as Christian religious sentiments, tend to make common cause with the weak against the more powerful. Many seem to believe that anybody who looks underprivileged and poor must be right, and should be supported morally. Before the Israeli military triumph, Jews and Israel still possessed their traditional image as victims, as the oppressed, which had been strengthened by Nazi persecution and the fact that Israel was surrounded by a hundred million hostile Arabs. Since then Israel is seen as the strong and wealthy nation, backed by the power, influence, and financial resources of world Jewry, while the Arabs are weak, underdeveloped, and poor.

It may be, however, that these explanations are too rational, or that they only serve to explain the specific content of the current revival of anti-Jewish feelings. What may be more abnormal, more peculiar, than the presence of anti-Semitism, is its absence for a quarter of a century within Western civilization. Reactions to the Holocaust repressed overt expressions of the normal vein of anti-Semitism which has existed in Christendom for close to two thousand years. To attack Jews became an unspeakable act following the revelations of the mass murders committed by the Nazis. But it is not very likely that one of the most stubborn cultural conventions of Western civilization could disappear that quickly. The French Revolution did not succeed in obliterating the cultural continuum of anti-Semitism, but only invested it with new secular forms. The Russian Revolution failed even more dramatically. Not even the creation of culturally and ethnically pluralistic societies in the New World could eliminate it. The generationally transmitted reservoir of cultural anti-Semitism is best conceived of as a kind of collective consciousness, a *common* reservoir, built almost ineradicably into our literature, into our language, into our most general cultural myths. The memory and significance of the Holocaust inhibited the willingness to use anti-Semitism, even to express it, but it still persisted. And over a quarter of a century, the events of 1939–45 have retreated into history, have become increasingly irrelevant, particularly to those who came of age since 1945. For new generations what happened just before they reached political consciousness has almost as little direct impact as events which occurred a century ago, or even longer. Hence as time goes on, the chances that the persistence of cultural anti-Semitism, of folk anti-Semitism, will be picked up and used for political purposes increases.

The fact that this time the predominant weight of the anti-Semitic thrust is on the left rather than the right will only surprise those who are unaware of the considerable literature on anti-Semitism in the socialist and other leftist movements. The identification of the Jews with international finance, with capitalism, with the status of businessman, with Shylock, has long replaced the image of the Jew as anti-Christ for many on the left and right. Karl Marx, himself, accepted the stereotype which linked Jews with capitalism. Thus in his early essay on "The Jewish Question," he wrote: "What is the worldly cult of the Jew? *Bargaining*. What is his worldly God? *Money*. . . ." A decade later in 1856, in an article in the New York *Tribune,* reprinted in 1897 in a work edited by his daughter, he commented "we find every tyrant backed by a Jew, as is every Pope by a Jesuit," and referred to the corrupt business activities of "the small Jew fry," "the Jew jobbers," the "Jew financial circles," that "the loan-mongering Jews derive much of their strength from these (extended international) family relations . . . (which) in addition to their lucre affinities, give a compactness and unity to their operations which insure their success." Marx concluded this essay by linking economic criticism of Jews with the traditional antagonism of Christianity.

> Let us not be thought too severe upon these loan-mongering gentry. The fact that 1855 years ago Christ drove the Jewish money-changers out of the temple, and

that the money-changers of our age enlisted on the side of tyranny happen again chiefly to be Jews, it perhaps no more than a historical coincidence. The loan-mongering Jews of Europe do only on a larger and more obnoxious scale what many others do on one smaller and less significant. But it is only because the Jews are so strong that it is timely and expedient to expose and stigmatize their organization.[4]

Much of Marx's anti-Semitic comments were censored by various editors of his published works, although as Dagobert Runes notes, they are now being published in full "by the decidedly anti-Jewish-oriented State Publishing House in Moscow." Marx clearly was unable to inhibit his strong feelings about Jews, sentiments which may have reflected his desire to free himself from the stigma of Jewish origins, a reaction that has characterized many who have sought to flee Judaism by conversion either to Christianity or to a form of radical universalistic secularism. Thus in *The German Ideology*, Marx arued that "it is the circumvention of law that makes the religious Jew a religious Jew." In 1849, he referred to the Polish Jews as "the smeariest of all races"; in 1862 he described his socialist rival, Ferdinand Lassalle, as "Judel Itzig—Jewish Nigger."[5] Marx was repaid in kind by his anarchist rival, Mihail Bakunin, who often described him by the pejorative adjective *jevrejcik*, little Yid.

Some leftists have been willing to accept or tolerate anti-Semitism since the mid-nineteenth century as some sort of groping toward a progressive anticapitalist position by masses in contact with Jewish businessmen. Since leftist movements invariably received considerable support from Jews who properly resented the anti-Semitic politics of the assorted conservative and monarchical regimes of

[4] In Karl Marx, *The Eastern Question*, Eleanor Marx Aveling and Edward Aveling (London: 1897) eds., p. 606. For a more comprehensive analysis of the phenomenon of left-wing anti-Semitism historically with bibliographic references, see S. M. Lipset, *Revolution and Counterrevolution* (Garden City: 1970, rev. ed.), pp. 375–400.

[5] For detailed citations see Karl Marx, *A World Without Jews*, Dagobert D. Runes, ed. (New York: 1959), pp. vii, xii.

Europe, this often meant that anti-Semitic movements included Jews among their activists. The Russian nihilist-populist *Narodnaya Volna*, for example, had many Jewish youth in its leadership and membership, while openly welcoming peasant pogroms against Jews as evidence of the emergence of mass revolutionary antibourgeois consciousness. Similar favorable reactions to popular anti-Semitism among German and Austrian socialists led August Bebel, the famous German socialist leader, to describe anti-Semitism as "the socialism of fools."

The task of analyzing the sources of these sentiments among the left is further complicated by the fact that, as we have seen, Jews play a very great role in various radical groups, both new and old, both student and adult. Some who have tried to analyze the special appeal of leftist universalistic ideologies to Jews have argued that identifying with a universalistic movement, one which rejects all forms of religious or ethnic particularism, and all group loyalties, as the extreme leftist movements do, appeals to members of minority groups who seek to escape the stigma of belonging to an unpopular minority. To some degree the literature on "Jewish self-hatred" and on "Jewish anti-Semitism" suggests adherence to radical causes has been a way of escaping one's Jewishness. Hence, one finds youth of Jewish origin who react with fervor to every nationalist cause but that of the Jews, who are sensitive to every slight against every minority, but not to overt attacks against Jews, not even when directed against Abbie Hoffman and Jerry Rubin.

In expressing directly or indirectly a disdain for Jewishness, the young New Leftists are following in a classic tradition set by a number of prominent Marxists of Jewish origins who could find it in their hearts to be concerned about many national groups, but *not* the Jews. The famous Polish Jewish revolutionary Rosa Luxemburg specifically repudiated any concern with the plight of the Jews in a letter written in 1917, in which she indicated that the exploited of Asia and Africa were "so much closer" to her than the Jews; that "I cannot find a special corner in my heart for the ghetto; I feel at home in the whole world." In *Are the Jews a Race?* the only book on the Jewish question written by a major Marxist theoretician, Karl Kautsky, who was not of Jewish origins, criticized Judaism as the major source of medieval thinking left in the modern world, one which must "dissolve . . . and disappear." And like Marx, Kautsky wrote about Judaism: "The sooner it disappears, the better it will be, not only for society, but also for the Jews themselves."

The American Communist party, though always having a significant membership of Jewish origins, has rarely shown concern for the plight of Jews, except during periods in which Russia was strongly anti-Nazi. In his book *The Social Basis of American Communism* (1961), Nathan Glazer concluded that

> . . . in general there was no group in the population for which the party showed more contempt and disdain, in its formulations of specific party positions, than the Jews. Melech Epstein has told the incredible story of the party's treatment of the Arab massacres of Jews in Palestine in 1929. This was initially referred to in the Yiddish *Freiheit* as a "pogrom." The party then severely castigated the *Freiheit* for not seeing the Arab uprising as a "class war . . . against British imperialism and their Zionist agents." The *Freiheit* immediately corrected its error by resorting to a treatment of the Palestine events not very different from that of an anti-Semitic newspaper—indeed, the cartoons it ran of hook-nosed and bloated Jews sadistically attacking Arabs could have appeared in any German anti-Semitic newspaper.

The Jews have suffered severely in the past from the insensitivity to the consequences of anti-Semitism exhibited by many "internationalist" leftists, both Jewish and non-Jewish. Isaac Deutscher, a leading Marxist analyst, and himself of Polish-Jewish background, wrote in his book *The Non-Jewish Jew:* "If, instead of arguing against Zionism in the 1920s and 1930s I had urged European Jews to go to Palestine, I might have helped to save some of the lives that were later extinguished in Hitler's gas chambers." Today, the revival of anti-Semitism or of a tolerance for it when expressed by "progressive," proletarian, third-world, or racially oppressed people, not only increases the insecurity of Israel (which for the moment seems capable of taking care of itself), but severely endangers Soviet Jewry. There is some evidence that the post-Stalin rulers of the Soviet Union have been inhibited in supporting or expressing anti-Semitism by the fact that until recently opinion in the non-Communist world, including Western Communist parties themselves, reacted strenuously against evidence of anti-Semitism. The relaxation of concern about the Jews exhibited by a growing sector of intellectual and left-wing opinion gives the Soviet leadership freedom to treat the Jews as they will.

In fairness, it should be noted that some factions and major intellectual figures on the left continue to find a basis for strongly supporting Israel and for stressing the significance of the Holocaust as an overriding experience which dictates a special concern for any expression of anti-Jewish or anti-Zionist sentiments. Thus many older black militant leaders, such as A. Philip Randolph, Bayard Rustin, Roy Wilkins, and the late Whitney Young, have strongly condemned black nationalist anti-Semitic and anti-Israel statements. Opinion polls clearly indicate that the large majority of blacks are not anti-Semitic, that groups like the NAACP which include Jews prominently among their leaders have always had much more support than the Panthers and other nationalist organizations, even before the latter weakened themselves through internecine warfare. The democratic socialist movement, represented in this country by the Socialist party, the Young Peoples Socialist League, and the magazine *Dissent*, defends Israel as the one democratic state in a sea of Middle East authoritarianism, and has been critical of anti-Semitic tendencies among the more authoritarian sections of the left in the United States. A large group of former Communist Jews continue to maintain a variety of secular Jewish institutions, including the magazine *Jewish Currents* and the daily Yiddish paper *Freiheit*, which sharply criticize the anti-Jewish policies of the Soviet government and are positive toward Israel. Isaac Deutscher, though sympathetic to the New Left and closer to the severely anti-Israel Trotskyists than to any other group, wrote that the Jews of Israel "have the feeling—how well justified—that the 'civilized world,' which in one way or another has the fate of European Jewry on its conscience, has no moral ground to stand on when it tries to sermonize or threaten Israel for any real or imaginary breaches of international commitments." The editors of the "independent socialist magazine" *Monthly Review*, Paul Sweezy and Harvey Magdoff, who have the admiration of many young revolutionaries for their maintenance of a radical Marxist organ during the lean years of American radicalism, also felt it necessary in a recent issue (July-August 1970) to remind others on the left that whatever the history of Zionist relations with the Arabs, Israeli

> . . . nationalism is nevertheless a reality, one that was deeply affected by the Nazi holocaust and is constantly refreshed and sustained by anti-Semitic thought and practices in various capitalist and socialist countries. Thus, the nature of the Jewish experience has generated a national consciousness in which the nightmare of forced emigration to a hostile, closed world and the dread of extinction by violence are ever present.

And though he has been ignored on this issue by many who identify with his writings on other matters, it should be recorded to the credit of the intellectual theorist of the New Left, Herbert Marcuse, that he, too, recognizes that anti-Semitism is not just another prejudice. Speaking in Germany to a New Left audience, Marcuse said:

> I cannot forget that during centuries, Jews were persecuted and oppressed and that not so long ago six million of them were annihilated. This is an objective fact.
> The Jews finally found a land where they must no longer fear persecution and opposition and I identify myself with the aim reached by them. I am happy to be in agreement, in this case also, with Jean-Paul Sartre who said: "The only thing that we must prevent at any cost is a new war of extermination against Israel."

And Marcuse concluded by saying that "the preventive war (for this was in fact the character of the war waged against Egypt, Jordan and Syria) can and must be understood and justified."[6]

---

[6] Cited in *Jewish Currents*, June 1970.

What characterizes these radical leftists so concerned with anti-Semitism and Israel is that all of them, Deutscher, Sweezy, Magdoff, Marcuse, and Sartre, were adults, politically conscious and involved, during the era of Nazism and experienced the impact of the Holocaust. But they have signally failed to convey their experiences, their shock, the lessons they learned, to a new generation of revolutionary radicals. Hopefully, the latter will have less impact on the future of the Jews than earlier generations who required Auschwitz and Dachau to prove to them that anti-Semitism was more than a foolish prejudice.

EPILOGUE

Since this article was written in the early fall of 1970, the situation with respect to the activities of New Left and black nationalist groups, and the image of the Palestinians has changed considerably. Since that time, much of the New Left has declined in the United States and other countries. The academic year 1970–71 was the most peaceful experienced by American universities since the Berkeley Revolt of 1964–65, and 1971–72 bodes to be even quieter. Opinion polls of students revealed that not only were there many fewer demonstrations and protest meetings last year, but that considerably fewer students identified with "radical" positions than in previous years.[7] The splits in SDS were not followed by the formation of any new viable campus groups. The decline in American troop strength and military activity in Vietnam seemingly undercut the anti-war movement. The growing activities of committed Jewish students who took the offensive with respect to support for Israel and Soviet Jewry appeared to have helped reduce the anti-Jewish campaigns on the Left.

The other major source for anti-Israeli and anti-Jewish propaganda, the Black Panthers and assorted black nationalist organizations, also suffered a drastic falling-off

---

[7] For an account in the changes of opinion and action among American students from the beginning of the Republic to the present see S. M. Lipset, "The Dimensions of Student Involvement," Part 1 of S. M. Lipset and G. Schaflander, *Passion and Politics: Student Activism in America* (Boston: 1971).

in strength and public activities. Similar to SDS, the Panthers divided into two bitterly hostile factions. By the end of 1971, the remnants of each proclaimed to the few who would listen that the other faction did not exist. Both appeared to be right. The attacks on these groups for fostering anti-Semitic doctrines appeared to have sharply reduced financial contributions from white liberals, many of whom are Jewish. Open resort to violence, the arrest of a number of leading activists for clearly criminal activities, hold-ups and robberies, also contributed to a decline in sympathy for them among both the black and white communities.

In Europe, also, with the exception of West Germany, the militant New Left groups suffered sharp reversals. Internecine warfare among the *groupuscules*, as to which was the most revolutionary, the most militant, interested few within or outside of the university. The waning of the Vietnam War, the opening of Sino-American negotiations, had effects comparable to those in America, in weakening the student-based protest movements. Only in Germany did the New Leftists, now closely linked to the official Communists, remain an important force.

The weakening of the extreme Left and militant groups in America and Western Europe was paralleled by the disasters that affected the Arab guerrilla movement. The civil wars in Jordan, which witnessed the almost total collapse of the fedayeen—topped by the efforts of a number of them to flee for refuge in Israel—destroyed the image of the Arab revolutionaries as the Middle East version of the FLN. Many on the Far Left had clearly begun to see in the fedayeen a new international cause which would supplant that of the Vietnamese. But nothing is less attractive than failure. And as the weakness and lack of support for the fedayeen became clear, the leftist groups of America and Europe began to lose interest in the Arab cause. Stories about Israel, the inequities of Zionism, the mistreatment of Arabs, and the glories of the Mid-East revolution disappeared from the New Left press. The remnants of the Black Panthers rarely mentioned the Middle East during 1971. The Maoist Progressive Labor party discovered that the al-Fatah is not a revolutionary organization, that it is linked to the ruling classes in the Arab world and the Soviet

Union. The Trotskyist Socialist Workers party also changed its line. It continued to attack Israel as a reactionary clerical state which discriminated against oriental Jews and Arabs. But its paper, the *Militant*, increased dramatically its attacks on the Arab states as reactionary and under the leadership of "racist demagogues." The December 27–31, 1970, convention of the Trotskyist youth group, the largest section of the movement, did not even bother to pass a resolution on Palestine or Zionism. In Europe also, one finds little interest in the Middle East among Far Left groupings. Occasionally, however, they continue to publish articles exposing the mistreatment of some oppressed group in Israel.

The decline in interest in the Middle East and the Arab cause, the reduction of negative commentary about wealthy Zionist and their power does not mean, however, any revival in positive attitudes toward Israel among Left-inclined youth generally, or among militant blacks. If anything, some evidence would suggest that underlying attitudes continue to change for the worse. The young socialist organizations, the youth affiliates of the various socialist, social democratic and labor parties of Europe, parties generally pro-Israel, show a growing disdain for Israel's position. In so far as they comment on the Middle East, they are generally and increasingly more likely to support the Arab position. Although clearly not anti-Semitic, these young socialists born after the war, and coming of age long after the holocaust, exhibit little awareness of the historic plight of the Jews. In America, opinion polls conducted among students in 1971 indicate that black students are less inclined to favor American aid for Israel than white undergraduates. And among students generally, the more liberal or Left-inclined they are on issues, the less they are disposed to endorse a policy of support for Israel.

Thus as the memory of the holocaust continues to recede, as new generations of youth become aware of an international scene in which the Arabs continue to be underdogs, seemingly part of the less developed Third World, in which the Jews of America and other Western countries continue to contribute their wealth and influence to Israel, the stage remains ripe for a revival of popularly supported leftist attacks on Israel and its Western Jewish supporters. This danger will continue until a genuine peace is made between Israel and its Arab neighbors. No one concerned, therefore, with the elimination of anti-Semitism as a potential political force can rest easy, for the tensions between Jewry and the Communist world, and between Israelis and Arabs, can yet kindle a new racist fire.

The Campus Left and Israel

Irving Howe

That some academics, students, and intellectuals have dropped their support for Israel is hardly news. In part it seems a quite normal development. A power struggle rages in the Middle East; both sides make passionate claims; the arguments grow complicated. Serious people, it follows, may find the Israeli case not entirely persuasive. Agree or disagree, such a judgment is entirely proper in a democratic society.

But there's another side to the growth of anti-Israel sentiment on the campus. Anyone who keeps an eye on our intellectual life must know that the turn against Israel reflects a complex of values and moods verging on the pathology of authoritarianism.

Of course there are aspects of Israeli public life (e.g., the marriage laws) that require criticism. Of course Israeli officials sometimes violate the democratic norms proclaimed by their government—something that can occur only in countries where democracy exists. Such failings are repeatedly criticized by Israelis themselves.

But I don't really believe that it is Israel's shortcomings which explain the turn in sentiment among portions of our "left" academics. Part of that turn may be the result of a century-old sentiment always at work in our civilization: as someone has remarked, in the warmest of hearts there's a cold spot for the Jews. A more immediate reason for this shift in feeling toward Israel has to do, however, with the growing distaste, the downright contempt, a portion of the New Left intellectuals shows toward the very idea of democracy.

428

That the Israeli press can attack its government with a freedom utterly beyond the reach of the Arab press; that the Communists in Israel function openly through two parties while Egyptian Communists languish in jail; that the Israelis have a vigorous multiparty system while their Arab opponents are ruled by rigid dictatorships—such arguments register only with those who care about democracy in the first place.

But suppose you dismiss democratic values as "bourgeois." Suppose your heart quickens only to visions of bloody apocalypse in which "the party" takes power and throws dissidents into "the dustbin of history." Suppose you yearn for a charismatic-authoritarian Maximum Leader who will replace laws with decrees. Then you will despise Israel not because of her flaws but because of her virtues. And you will heap contempt upon a country which, under extreme difficulties, remains about as good a model as we have for the democratic socialist hope of combining radical social change with political freedom.

So one wonders, can Israel do anything to gain the favor of the campus Guevarists, Trotskyists, Maoists, and Panthers who lead the assault against her? Yes, she can, and here is a scenario:

In the name of a Provisional Revolutionary Junta, General Moshe Dayan removes the Israel government and disperses the Knesset. Golda Meir is forcibly retired to an old-age home. ("Enough of government by grandmothers," snarls a young aide of the junta.) Yigael Allon appears to have suffered a regrettable accident and Abba Eban has been exiled to the London School of Economics. Ben-Gurion mutters in the desert, but who can say whether it's a blessing or a curse?

Dayan abolishes all existing parties (including the Communist parties). The Histadrut—dissolved. The kibbutzim—dispersed. The Hebrew University—cleansed. Strikes outlawed. The press—muzzled. But, announces the Revolutionary Junta, "elections will be held as soon as tranquillity is restored." Meanwhile, a little blood flows, for without a little blood how can you have a revolution?

Everywhere the New Left rejoices. Brigades of youth from Scarsdale, Evanston, and Palo Alto race to Israel to help with "the planting." The *New York Review* plans a special issue. And Jean-Paul Sartre and Mme. de Beauvoir take the next plane to Israel, prepared to write a thousand pages in four weeks on *the Achievements of the Israeli Revolution* (while getting the street names of Tel Aviv wrong).

I told this bitter fantasy some time ago to an elderly lady from the Israeli government. She laughed and said, "Not such a foolish scenario, though you're unfair to Moshe. . . . But you know, for the blessings it promises us, the price is too high."

Index

Acheson, Dean, 172
Adler, Friedrich, 25
Administered territories, 236–37,
    249–65
    annexation of, 252
    conditions in, 255–58, 260–61
    holy places in, 252–53
    military-civilian control of, 254–
    60
    resettlement in, 263–64
    strategies for, 251–52, 263–65
Al-Alami, Zuheir, 226
Al-Asmar, Fawzi, 269–73, 274–77,
    287, 289, 291–92, 293, 297
Al Fatah, see Fatah
Al-Huli, Hasan Sabri, 406
Al-Hut, Shafiq, 246
Al-Qamhawi, Walid, 215n
Al-. See also El-
Alafatt, Cyril, 353n, 357n
Alexandrowicz, Charles, 211–12
Algeria, 50, 189, 195, 235, 300,
    409
    Arab guerillas and, 232–33
    army in, 305
    French conquest of, 301–02
    independence of, 243, 363–64
    Soviet Union and, 323, 329
Ali, Tariq, 120
Allon, Yigael, 429
AlRoy, Gil Carl, 155, 366–89
Americans for Democratic Action
    (ADA), 346
An-Nashashibi, Nasir ad-Din, 217
Anarchists, 47, 392
Anglo-Arab Legion, 368
Anthony, Philip, 395
Anti-Semitism, 29, 44, 120, 141n
    of black militants, 390, 391, 395,
    396–404, 422
    in Germany, 25, 33
    of Jews, 420
    neo-fascism and, 407–08
    reaction to Zionism, 16–17
    return of, 390–427
    socialist movement and, 22–24,
    27–32, 418–22
    in the Soviet Union, 35, 390
    in the United States, 358, 390
Anti-Zionist Committee, 40

Antonius, George, 139n, 144n,
    147n
Arab guerilla movement, 120, 158–
    59, 175, 180, 189
    anti-Semitism and, 406
    contradictions of, 309
    development of, 231–40
    failure of, 224–58
    goals of, 240–41
    internal conflicts of, 225–29,
    240–42
    military methods of, 372–74
    myth of, 224
    propaganda claims of, 227
    relationship of to Arab states,
    241–42
    Six-Day War and, 224–25, 234,
    235
    terrorism of, 231, 274–77
    as "vanguard," 231
    See also Arabs; Fatah; Palestine
    Liberation Organization
Arab-Israeli conflict, 119–24, 200,
    202, 311–20, 334–36, 339
    administered territories and,
    249–65
    Arab intransigence and, 152–57
    Arab-Jew cooperation and, 147–
    49, 156, 177
    Arab social structure and, 307–
    09, 371
    binational state as solution for,
    188–90
    conspiracy theories of, 374–77
    "early conquest" criterion and,
    210–11
    historical basis of, 137–56, 203–
    09
    international opinion and, 380–
    81
    international politics and, 366–
    89
    Israel as scapegoat in, 218–20
    Israeli "expansionism" and, 150–
    52, 376–77
    Israeli fears of, 314, 377–78
    military performance in, 368–72
    oil interests and, 357–63, 365,
    385, 386

431

Arab-Israeli conflict (*continued*)
  problem of nationalism and, 185–99
  refugee problem and, 157–85
  Soviet Union and, 323–39, 343, 346, 347
  vicious circle of, 311–20
  See also Arabs; Israel; Six-Day War
Arab League, 210, 216, 226, 310, 408
Arab Liberation Front, 238, 245
Arabs, 20, 52
  anti-Semitism among, 405–09
  detention of in Israel, 269–72, 274–78, 283–99
  effect of Western imperialism on, 300–05
  exodus of from Israel, 159–66, 179, 208
  expropriation of, 315–16
  history of in Palestine, 140–56
  internal conflict of, 219, 220
  intransigent enmity of, 152–56
  Islam conquest and, 302
  in Israel, 65, 183–84
  land abandoned by, 63
  medieval culture of, 305–06
  military nature of society, 303–05, 310–11
  modernization and, 300–11, 334
  nationalism of, 41, 171–76, 188, 195–99, 200–23
  non-acceptance of Zionism by, 313, 315–20
  prosperity of during Jewish settlement, 177–78
  rights of in Palestine, 210–14
  Soviet alliance with, 36–37, 167
  technology in society of, 306–07
  warfare methods of, 371–74
  See also Arab guerilla movement; Arab-Israeli conflict; Refugees
Arafat, Yassir, 120, 226, 238–40
  in development of guerilla movement, 231–33
  ideology of, 242
Arieli, Yehoshua, 312–20
Auriol, Vincent, 27
Austria, 23, 209
Avineri, Shlomo, 300–11
Axelrod, 28

Ba'ath parties, 173, 238, 304
Baker, Ross, 395
Bakunin, Mikhail, 419
Balfour Declaration, 139–44, 147, 172, 174–79, 315

Bao Dai, 356
Barkai, Haim, 69–99
Batista, F., 356
Bauberot, Jean, 393–94, 407
Bauer, Otto, 24–25, 29, 41, 49
Beauvoir, Simone de, 430
Bebel, August, 420
Begin, Menahem, 273
Bellow, Saul, 117
Bengal, 193
Ben-Bella, Ahmed, 232
Ben-Gurion, David, 45, 47, 60, 127, 140, 207*n*, 429
Bennett, Roy, 353, 357*n*
Ben-Zvi, Yitzhak, 47
Berkeley revolt (1964–65), 424
Bernadotte, Folke, 273, 376
Bernstein, Edward, 18, 28, 49
Biafra, 157, 193, 194
Bialik, Chaim Nachman, 109
Bible, Holy, 307
Binational state, proposal of, 188–90, 196–99
Birobidzhan, Jewish settlement in, 30–31
Black Panther Party, 392, 397, 398, 400, 402–04, 416
  splits in, 424–25
"Black Panthers" of Israel, emergence of, 126, 128, 130–31
Blacks
  militant groups of, 390, 391, 395, 396–404
  opposition to anti-Semitism among, 422
  relationship of with Jews, 398–401
  Teachers' Union strike and, 400–01
Bloch, Josef, 27
Blum, Léon, 18
Bolsheviks, 23, 32, 36, 40, 105, 331
Borochov, Ber, 47, 50
Borokhov, 38
Boumedienne, Houari, 232
Brandeis, Louis D., 60
Breitscheid, Rudolf, 27
Bridmead, A. J., 162–63
Britain, 36, 150, 151, 172, 218, 309, 333, 363
  imperialism of, 36, 144, 149, 155, 301–05, 375
  legal administration by, 287–88
  nationalities in, 202–03
  oil policy and, 359
  policy of in Palestine, 178
  role of in Arab-Israeli conflicts, 162
  in war against Israel, 370

Brouckere, Louis de, 27
Brown, H. Rap, 400
Bruno, Michael, 249–65
Buber, Martin, 5–15, 97n, 102, 197
Buch, Peter, 362
Buckley, William F., Jr., 339
Bulgaria, 210
Bunche, Ralph, 169
Byroade, Henry, 387

Canada, 266, 278n
Capitalism, 107
  centralization under, 5
  imperialism and, 353–56
  Zionism and, 38
  See also Imperialism
Carmichael, Stokely, 397, 404
Castro, Fidel, 308, 309
Catholic Church, 16
Catholics, anti-Semitism among,
  394
Central Intelligence Agency (CIA),
  359
Chiang Kai-shek, 356, 375
China, 50, 167, 195, 242, 344, 356,
  416
  conflict with Soviet Union, 330,
  337, 338
Chomsky, Noam, 176, 346, 348
Churchill, Winston, 141n, 397
Class consciousness, 59–60
Cleaver, Eldridge, 398, 402–03
Cohen, Aharon, 144n, 148n, 149n
Cohn-Bendit, Daniel, 120
Communist Party (U.S.), 399, 421
Containment policy, 344
Cooperative movement
  history of, 6–7
  in Palestine, 8–15, 52–53
  nature of, 5–6
  See also Kibbutzim
Coughlin, Charles, 406
Cruse, Harold, 399
Cuba, 50, 308, 416
Cyprus, 164, 336
Czechloslovakia, 191, 209, 334, 396

Dayan, Moshe, 120, 156, 227, 268,
  379, 429
Debbaudt, Jean Robert, 408
De Gaulle, Charles, 334
Dier Yassin massacre, 160, 161,
  166
Degrelle, Leon, 408
Democratic Popular Front for the
  Liberation of Palestine
  (DPFLP), 238, 240, 241, 246
  See also Arab guerilla move-
  ment

"Democratic secular state" pro-
  posal, 189–90
Dershowitz, Alan, 266–99
Deutscher, Isaac, 40–42, 421, 422–
  23, 424
Diem, Ngo Dinh, 350, 356
Dimanshtein, 30
Disraeli, Benjamin, 41
Dohrn, Bernardine, 40
Douglas, Paul, 283n
Doukhobors of Canada, 7
Draper, Theodore, 340
Dulles, Allen, 359
Dulles Plan, 384
Durkheim, Emile, 406

Eban, Abba, 184, 215n, 429
Eden Plan, 384
Education
  integration and, 133
  kibbutzim and, 85–86
Egypt, 51, 121, 166, 169, 209, 229,
  242, 347, 375
  aggression by, 200, 205, 218,
  368–70, 374
  Arab guerillas and, 229–31, 233
  attack on, 359–60
  class distinctions in, 307–08
  economy of, 335
  Mamluks in, 302, 303, 310–11
  military dominance in, 304–05,
  347
  nationalism in, 309
  Six-Day War and, 249–50, 253–
  54
  Soviet Union and, 323–27, 329
Einstein, Albert, 406
Eisenhower, Dwight D., 359, 360
El-Hassan, Hani, 237
El-Hawatmeh, Na'if, 238
El-Kadumi, Faruk, 228
El-Sa'ika, 238, 245
El-. See also Al-
Engler, Robert, 360n
Engels, Friedrich, 17–18, 104, 302
Epstein, Melech, 421
Eshkol, Levi, 227
Eytan, Walter, 140n

Faisal, Emir, 147, 155, 174
Fanon, Franz, 158, 243
Farouk, King of Egypt, 166
Fascism and Nazism, 105, 308–09,
  416, 417, 424
  Arabs and, 405
  ideology of, 17
  Jewish reactions to, 33–35
  victory of, 23, 25, 33

Fatah, 120, 181, 189, 219n, 228, 229–36, 245, 270, 290, 295
conflict of with PFLP, 225
founding of, 232
ideology of, 238, 242–44
Israeli measures against, 236
raids by, 233, 258
sense of mission in, 154
strategy of, 235–36
terrorism of, 286
See also Arab guerilla movement
Fedayeen, See Arab guerilla movement; Fatah
Feisal, King of Saudi Arabia, 309
Feminists, 47
Fontaine, André, 359n
Ford, Henry, 406
France, 144, 151, 333, 363, 375
anti-Semitism in, 393–94, 407
imperialism of, 155, 301–05, 350
New Left in, 393–94, 407
refugees in, 209, 317
in War against Israel, 370
Franco, Francisco, 267n, 356, 375
Frankenstein, Ernst, 142n
Frankfurter, Felix, 175
Franklin, Benjamin, 167–68
French Revolution, 5, 417
Freud, Sigmund, 41, 406
Friedman, Monroe, 402, 403
Front de Libération du Quebec, Le (FLQ), 266
Frost, David, 397
Fulbright, William, 343, 381
Fyvel, T. R., 115–24

Gahal party, 263, 273, 289
Gandhi, Mohandas, 16, 197
Germany, 43, 196, 209, 233, 309, 317
extermination of Jews in, 40, 377–78
Jews in Communist movement of, 23
neo-Nazi groups in, 407–08
New Left in, 392–93
planned emigration of Jews from, 33–34
rise of anti-Semitism in, 392–93, 407–08
Gershman, Carl, 224–48
Ghana, 302, 375
Glazer, Nathan, 421
Glubb, Sir John Bagot, 375
Gordon, A. D., 47
Gordonia, 56
Gray, Jesse, 401–02

Greece, 191, 192, 196, 317, 375
Grew, Joseph C., 358
Gromyko, Andrei, 146, 358
Guevara, Ernesto "Che," 309

Habash, George, 238
Hadrian, Emperor, 212n
Haganah (Zionist defense force), 57, 162, 165, 273
Haj Amin, 149–50
Halaf, Salah, 226
Hall, Gus, 396
Halpern, Ben, 45–68
Halutzim (pioneers), as leaders in communes, 9–11
Harkabi, Yohosafat, 138n, 201n, 202n, 215n, 217n, 235, 244
Harrington, Michael, 350–65
Hashomer, 54, 56
Hatchett, John, 401
Hebrew language, 30, 307
Hedjaz, Kingdom of, 175
Heine, Heinrich, 22, 41
Heller, Otto, 31–32, 33, 40
Henderson, Arthur, 27
Herzl, Theodore, 21, 26, 37, 39, 60, 177
Hess, Moses, 18, 104–05
Heykal, Mohammed Hassanein, 231
Hisadrut (Israeli labor organization), 54–67, 85n, 107, 252
functions of, 56–57
labor unions and, 59–60, 64–65
organization of, 58–59
socialism of, 59–60
See also Labor unions
Hitler, Adolf, 25, 33, 105, 141, 181, 187, 309, 341, 396, 397
Hobson, J. A., 350
Hoffman, Abbie, 403, 420
Hoffman, Julius, 403
Holmes, Oliver Wendell, 280
Hourani, Cecil, 152
Howe, Irving, 339–49, 404, 428–30
Humphrey, Hubert, 283n
Hungary, 50, 51, 209
Hurst, Sir Cecil, 148n
Hurwitz, J. C., 142n
Hussein, Abu Haled, 227n
Hussein (King of Jordan), 170, 219, 224, 225, 226, 231, 319
administered territories and, 259–60
guerilla movement and, 239, 259
Six-Day War and, 250
Hussein, Sherif, 144, 147
Husseini, Jamal, 137n
Huysmans, Camille, 27

Imperialism, 155, 175, 218, 337
British, 36, 144, 149, 155, 301–05, 375
effect of on Arab society, 300–02
French, 155, 301–05, 350
Israel and, 41, 350–51, 361–65, 375–76
Lenin's definition of, 352
modernization and, 301
in Middle East, 350–65
oil interests and, 356–63, 365
Soviet Union and, 323, 329–30
theories of, 351–56
of United States, 341–42, 347–48, 350–51, 354, 356–63
India, 62, 192, 195, 301, 302, 317
Soviet Union and, 337
Indochina, 50, 157, 209
See also Vietnam
Indonesia, 210, 375
Industrial Workers of the World (IWW), 58
Iran
oil nationalized in, 359
Soviet Union and, 323–27
Iraq, 51, 62, 139, 145, 193, 208, 217, 408
aggression by, 368–69
guerilla movement and, 238
Jews in, 206, 210
military dominance in, 304
Soviet Union and, 323–27
Ireland, 267
Irgun Zvai Leumi, 273
Irish Republican Army, 267
Islam, conquests of, 302
Isolationism, Vietnam War and, 346–48
Israel
administered territories of, 236–37, 249–65
"Afro-Asian" Jews in, 125–34
as "agent of American imperialism," 351, 356–65, 374
Arab exodus from, 159–66, 169
assimilation process in, 128–31
civil liberties in, 266–79, 298–99
critics of, 40–41
"expansionism" of, 150–52, 376–77
fears of, 314
founding of as state, 102, 178, 200
"image" of, 100–14
imperialism of, 41, 350–51, 363–65, 375–76
Law of Return to, 196–98
leadership of, 56
no longer "underdog," 417
peaceful nature of, 312, 314, 318
policy of toward occupied territory, 236–37, 249–65
preventive detention in, 269–79, 283–99
problems of socialism in, 45–68
resettlement by, 207, 221–22
settlement of with Arab states, 229
social democracy in, 102–06
social organization in, 57–68, 103
Soviet Union and, 46, 323–38
United States and, 46, 339–49, 386–87
Vietnam involvement of U.S. and, 339–49
writers of, 115–17
youths of, 125–26
See also Arab-Israeli conflict; Jews; Palestine
Italy, 309, 408
Ivan the Terrible, 331
Ivanov, Yuri, 406

Japanese-Americans, 281–83, 289n
Jaris, Sabri, 294–98
Jewish National Fund, 61, 178
as bourgeoisie, 51
ethnic division of, 125–34
extermination of, 23, 40
internationalist spirit and, 42–43, 187
liberation of, 47–48, 120, 199
nationalism and, 186–88, 195–99, 203–04
oriental, 2, 125–34, 158, 168, 181
problems in assimilation of, 24, 43
role in socialist movements, 18, 23
self-defense of, 50
self-hatred among, 42, 119, 420
Sephardic, 131
in Soviet Union, 34–37, 119
stereotypes of, 418
See also Israel: Zionism
Jiménez, Marcos P., 356
Joffe, Edward, 286
John Birch Society, 390
Johnson, Lyndon, 339, 397
Jordan, 121, 139, 169, 175, 276
administered territories and, 252, 256, 259–60, 264
aggression by, 200, 368
conflict within, 335

Jordan (*continued*)
  establishment of, 180, 205, 218–19, 222
  guerilla movement and, 234, 241
  occupation policy of, 236–37
  refugees in, 209

Kalinin, M. I., 31
Kalita, Ivan, 331
Kamenev, L. B., 23
Kanner, Leon, 286
Karmi, Y., 201n
Katzenelson (*or* Kaznelson), Berl, 14, 47, 60
Katzner, Hans, 407
Kautsky, Karl, 41
  anti-Zionism of, 19–22, 24, 27, 29, 32, 37, 40, 420–21
  imperialism theory of, 350
Kazin, Michael, 397
Kaznelson, Berl, *see* Katzenelson
Kefauver, Estes, 283n
Kemp, Tom, 352n
Kenan, Amos, 290–92
Kenya, 195
Khidr, Mohammed, 232
Kibbutzim, 58, 61, 69–99, 103–04, 107, 372
  child care in, 85–87
  communal dining in, 84–85
  control of, 59
  "crisis" of, 62–63
  early role of, 55–57
  economics of, 74–79
  equality among, 94–96
  housing in, 87–88
  income distribution in, 83–88
  industrialization in, 90–94
  personal budget controversy in, 88–90
  population of, 62, 69–70
  production in, 74–80
  "self-labor" in, 78, 79, 80–83
  socialism and, 13–15, 73–74, 108
  structure of, 71–73
Kimche, Jon, 225
King-Crane Commission, 176
Kisch, F. H., 149
Klinghoffer, Hans, 289
Knesset, 61, 268, 273, 284, 290, 292
Koran, 307
Krämer-Badoni, Rudolf, 392–93
Kristallnacht, 392
Kropotkin, Peter, 7
Ku Klux Klan, 406
Kunzelmann, Dieter, 393
Kurds, 191, 193
Kuwait, 241, 309

Kvutzah (village commune), 8–15, 58

Labor unions
  in capitalism, 5
  dominance of in Israel, 45–46
  Hisadrut and, 59–60, 64–65
  Jewish, 48–49
  See also Hisadrut
Labor Zionism, 38, 49–63, 102–03
Langer, Felicia, 269, 292–93
Lansbury, George, 27
Laqueur, Walter, 16–44, 147n, 323–38
Laski, Harold, 28
Lassalle, Ferdinand, 22, 41, 104, 419
Lautner, Mrs. Robert, 398
Lavon, Pinhas, 47
Law of Return, 196–98
Lawrence, T. E., 143n, 146–47, 228n
Lazare, Bernard, 19
League of Nations, 145, 148n, 218, 315
Lebanon, 139, 155, 159, 175, 180
  aggression by, 368
  Arab nationalism and, 173, 174
  democratic government in, 335
  guerilla movement and, 233
  refugees in, 209
  United States and, 327
Lehman, Herbert, 283n
Leftwich, J., 31n
Lenin, V. I., 24, 36, 50, 102, 331
  anti-Zionism of, 29
  imperialism theory of, 350–56, 361, 363, 364, 365
Leon, A., 38
Lestchinsky, 31
Lester, Julius, 395
Liberty Lobby, 409
Libya, 51, 335
Lincoln, Abraham, 278
Lindsay, John, 302
Lipset, Seymour Martin, 390–427
Lohomei, Herut Israel, 273
Longuet, Jean, 27–28
Lumer, Hyman, 361n
Luxemburg, Rosa, 18, 41, 49–50, 420
  imperialism theory of, 350
Lynch, John, 267

Macdonald, Malcom, 178
MacMahon, Sir Henry, 144, 176
Magdoff, Harry, 355, 357, 423, 424
Magnes, Judah, 197
Maki party, 294

Malcom X, 397, 399
Mamluks, 302, 303, 310–11
Mandelstam, Nadezhda, 186
Mann, Eric, 394–95
Mao Tse-tung, 234
Maoists, 392, 404, 429
Mapai, 61, 64
Marcuse, Herbert, 423–24
Marshall Plan, 345
Marx, Karl, 22, 40, 104–05, 107,
  301
  on industrialization, 47–48
  on Jews and Zionism, 17–18,
    101–02, 418–19
  on national self-determination,
    20–21, 24, 191, 192–93
  See also Marxism
Marxism
  in Israel, 52–53
  Israeli imperialism and, 364–65
  national self-determination and,
    20–21, 24–26, 29, 48, 187
  reaction to Zionism of, 17–44,
    48–50, 418–21
  theory of imperialism of, 49
  Zionist response to, 22–23
  See also Marx; Marxism-
    Leninism; Socialism
Marxism-Leninism, 329, 331, 346–
    47, 402, 404–05
  solution to Jewish question by,
    24
  See also Lenin; Marx
Matthews, Connie, 403
Meinertzhagen, Richard, 149n
Meir, Golda, 182, 184, 248, 268,
    273, 348, 429
Mensheviks, 105
Miller, David Hunter, 148n
Miller, S. M., 353, 357n
Milligan, Lambden, 276–77
Mongols, 302
Montesquieu, 338
Moore, Richard "Dharuba," 402
Morocco, 62, 109
Moshavim, establishment of, 63–
    64
Mossadegh, Mohammed, 359
Muslim Brotherhood, 232, 234
Mutual aid, 8

Nakhlen, Issa, 408
Nasser, Gamal Abdel, 180, 226,
    262n, 376, 406, 408
  guerilla movement and, 229–31,
    238–39, 241
  "irregulars" organized by, 231
  pan-Arab ideas of, 232

Six-Day War and, 249, 251,
    378–79
National Association for the Ad-
    vancement of Colored People
    (NAACP), 398, 422
National States Rights Party, 408,
    409
  propaganda of, 414–16
Nationalism, 191–99
  Arab, 41, 171–76, 188, 200–23,
    310–11, 336
  binational state proposal and,
    188–90, 196–99
  immigration policies and, 196
  Jewish, 186–88, 203–04, 310–11
  marginal groups and, 195
  Marxism and, 20–21, 24–26, 29,
    48, 187, 191–93
  See also Zionism
Nazism, see Fascism and Nazism
Nehru, Jawaharlal, 192
Netherlands, 209–10
New Left, 205, 224, 333, 345, 420
  anti-Semitism of, 391, 392–96,
    404–05, 407, 423–27
  anti-Zionism of, 22, 38–40, 121,
    187–88, 390
  in France, 393–94, 407
  in Germany, 392–93, 425
  imperialism and, 352
  isolationism of, 347
  Israel and, 105–07, 269, 428–30
  Jews in, 51–52, 119
  nationalism and, 188
  nondoctrinaire attitude of, 46
  in United States, 394–96, 424–
    25
Newton, Huey, 403
Neyer, Joseph, 137–56
Nigeria, 193
Nixon, Richard M., 397
Nokrashi Pasha, 376
Nordau, Max, 21, 39
North Atlantic Treaty Organiza-
    tion (NATO), 385
Nuclear powers, 334

Oil interests, 356–63, 365, 385, 386
Oppenheimer, Franz, 60
Oppenheimer, Harry, 407
Oriental Jews, 2, 125–34, 158, 168,
    181
Osmanli Turks, 302
Oz, Amos, 115–24

Pacifism, 16, 47, 333, 346
Pakistan, 157, 193, 199, 317

Palestinian National Covenant, 189, 213, 214n, 221, 222, 242, 244–45
Palestine
Arab concept of, 172–75, 200–03, 220–23
early Jewish settlement in, 20–21, 52–54, 138–44
establishment of communes in, 54
establishment of Jewish state in, 144–46
self-determination question and, 200–23
See also Arabs; Israel; Refugees
Palestine Liberation Organization, 138, 154, 174, 226–34, 238, 242, 294
agreement with Nasser, 229–31
anti-Semitism and, 407
ideology of, 244
power struggle within, 238–39
propaganda of, 409–14
See also Arab guerilla movement
Palestine National Fund, 226
Parkes, James, 139–40, 141n, 142n, 143n, 203
Pearson Committee, 355
Peel Commission, 122, 316
Peretz, D., 201n
Pernerstorfer, 25–26
Petran, Tabitha, 396
Plekhanov, G. V., 19, 102
Pogroms, 47, 53, 141n, 378, 420
Poland, 23, 24, 48, 51, 191, 196, 209, 267n
Popular Front for the Liberation of Palestine (PFLP), 225, 228n, 229, 239, 290
conflict of with Fatah, 225, 234
ideology of, 238
See also Arab guerilla movement
Populists, 47, 397, 420
Preventive detention, 266–99
of Arabs, 269–72, 274–78, 283–99
in Canada, 266
in Ireland, 267
in Israel, 267–79, 283–99
of Jewish groups, 273–74
theory of, 268
in United States, 278–83
Printing press in Arab society, 306–07
Procaccino, Mario, 402
Progressive Labor Party, 400, 425

Rabikowich, Dalia, 116
Radek, Karl, 23
Rafi, Ali, 292
Rakah party, 270, 284, 294
Randolph, A. Philip, 422
Rees, Elfan, 170, 209
Refugees, Palestinian, 157–85, 187, 213–14, 316
in administered territories, 254, 260–62
Arab evacuation and, 159–66, 208
comparison of with other refugee problems, 209–10, 317
condition of, 169–70, 260
number of, 168–69, 171, 207n
resettlement of, 184–85, 207
"restoration" of, 183–84
Rejwan, Nissim, 125–34
Renner, Karl, 24, 25–26, 49
Reston, James, 381
Revolutionary Youth Movement, see Weatherman
Rhazour, Ahmed, 353n
Rhodesia, 341
Ricardo, David, 41
Rodinson, Maxime, 137n, 364–65
Rogers, William, 231, 385
Roman rule of Palestine, 139, 174
Romania, 51, 109, 110, 378
Roosevelt, Franklin D., 283
Rosenberg, Alfred, 17
Rostow, W. W., 283n
Rothschild, Edmund de, 395
Rothstein, Theodore, 26
Rouleau, Eric, 225n, 240n
Rubin, Jerry, 403, 420
Rudd, Mark, 40
Runes, Dagobert, 419
Russia, 29, 48, 105, 378
See also Soviet Union
Russian Revolution, 352, 417
Rustin, Bayard, 422

Sadat, Anwar, 230–31
Saidam, Mamduh, 228
Salah Halaf, 228
Samuel, Maurice, 126–27
Sanders, Ronald, 100–14
Sartre, Jean-Paul, 424, 430
Saud, Ibn Abdul Aziz, 360
Saudi Arabia, 139, 170, 241, 368
aid for guerillas, 242, 309
oil interests and, 360
Sayegh, Fayez A., 137n, 154n
Schappos, Morris, 406
Schechtman, Joseph B., 150n
Seale, Bobby, 403
Second International, 27, 29

"Self-labor" principle, 78, 79, 80–83
Seljuk Turks, 302
Shamgar, Meir, 272–73, 275
Shamir, S. 201*n*, 219*n*
Shanker, Albert, 395, 401–02
Shapiro, Ya'akov Shimshon, 274, 289–90
Shin Bet (counterintelligence organization), 275–76, 294–96
Shukairy (*or* Shukeiri), Ahmed, 173–74, 232, 234, 239, 244
Six-Day War, 40, 115, 151, 200, 276, 313, 317, 416, 417
administered territories of, 249–65
Arab guerillas and, 224–25, 231, 234, 235, 290, 294
Israeli strategy in, 378–79
Jewish fears and, 377–78
losses during, 250
Soviet Union and, 325
Zionism and, 117
See also Arab-Israeli conflict; Refugees
Smith, Gerald, L. K., 391
Sneh, Moshe, 151–52
Socialism
anti-Semitism in, 418–22
approval of Zionism by, 27–29
communes and, 9, 13–15
criticism of Zionism by, 16–27, 36–44
of Histadrut, 59–60
internationalism and, 187, 199
Jewish question and, 48–50
in kibbutzim, 13–15, 73–74, 97–99, 102–04
problems of in Israel, 45–68
religious, 47
See also Marxism
Socialist Committee for Working Palestine, 27
Socialist Party (U.S.), 422
Socialist Workers Party, 426
Somalia, 329
South Africa, 267*n*, 396, 407
Soviet Union, 46, 94*n*, 103, 107, 120, 264, 293, 344–46
anti-Semitism in, 390–91
Arabs and, 36–37, 167, 180–81, 253, 254, 308, 372, 375
Egypt aided by, 251
emigration from, 37
Jewish colony established in, 30–31
Jewish policy of, 29–31, 35–37, 336, 422

Middle East policy of, 323–39, 343, 346, 347, 349, 375, 388–89
military aid costs, 328
See also Russia
Spain, 24, 267
Spinoza, Benedict, 22, 41, 104
Stalin, Josef, 23, 331, 345, 364
anti-Zionism of, 29–30, 36, 105
Stein, Leonard, 143*n*, 144*n*
Stern Gang, 273, 290–91
Stettinius, Edward, 358
Stone, I. F., 166–67
Stone, Julius, 200–23
Student Non-Violent Co-ordinating Committee (SNCC), 397–98
propaganda of, 409–14
Students for a Democratic Society (SDS), 394, 395, 396, 397
splits in, 424–25
Sudan, 329
Sweezy, Paul, 423, 424
Switzerland, 172
Sykes, Christopher, 137*n*, 143*n*, 146, 176
Syndicalists, 46
Syria, 139, 155, 159, 178, 219, 153
aggression by, 368, 370
Arab nationalism and, 173
guerilla movement and, 180, 233, 238
military dominance in, 304, 347
nationalism in, 309
Palestine and, 148
radical political system of, 327
Soviet Union and, 323–27, 329
Syrkin, Marie, 157–85
Syrkin, Nahman, 47
Szanto, Alexander, 27

Tabenkin, Yitzhak, 47
Tanzania, 195, 199
Teveth, S., 255
Tito, Josip Broz, 342, 345
Tolstoy, Leo, 16
Tories, evacuation of, 167–68
Toynbee, Arnold, 172
Tripartite Declaration (1950), 151
Trotsky, Leon, 231*n*
anti-Zionism of, 18, 37
See also Trotskyism
Trotskyism, 362, 404, 426, 429
anti-Zionism of, 22, 37–40, 392, 422
See also Marxism; Trotsky
Trudeau, Pierre, 266
Trujillo, R. L., 356

Truman, Harry S, 357–58, 397
Trumpeldor, Joseph, 52
Tunisia, 51
Turkey, 26, 51, 62, 139, 144–145, 148, 174, 317
  democracy in, 335
  distribution of former territories of, 203–04
  military caste of, 303
  nationalism and, 191–92, 196
  refugees in, 210

"Underdevelopment" of Arab society, 300–01, 306–11
United Arab Republic, 232, 309, 326–27
United Federation of Teachers (UFT), 401–02
United Nations, 146, 170, 173, 184, 200–01, 209, 230, 359, 380, 383
  Arab votes in, 382
United Nations Partition Resolution of 1947, 137, 142, 158, 160, 167, 200, 316
United States, 107, 120, 144, 151, 176, 218
  civil liberties in, 268, 269, 277–83
  as epitome of reaction, 416–17
  Hussein supported by, 259
  imperialism of, 341–42, 347–48, 350–51, 354, 356
  Jews in, 51–52, 359, 385, 386
  Middle East policy of, 326, 330–33, 357–65, 367–68, 384–88
  New Left in, 394–96, 424–25
  oil interests and, 357–63, 385, 386
  populism in, 397
  preventive detention in, 281–83
  spheres of influence and, 331
  support for Israel by, 46, 339–49, 386–87
  Vietnam intervention of, 339–49, 356, 363
Utopianism, 48, 50, 52, 102
  cooperative movement and, 6–9

Vandervelde, 27
Varga, Y., 356
Vegetarians, 47
Vietnam, 333, 337, 339–49, 350, 363, 366, 392, 416, 424
  imperialism and, 356
  isolationism and, 346–48
  U.S. support for Israel and, 339–49
  See also Indochina
Vilner, Meir, 270

Wadsworth, George, 360
Walzer, Michael, 186–99
Warren, Earl, 282n
Weatherman (revolutionary SDS faction), 394–95
Weinstock, N., 38n
Weizmann, Chaim, 61, 147, 155, 174, 177
Wilkins, Roy, 422
Wilson, Woodrow, 176
Winrod, Gerald, 406
World Zionist Organization, 54–57, 63

Yaari, Ehud, 232n
Yaari, Meir, 47
Yehia, Abdul-Razzak, 228–29
Yemen, 206, 210, 242, 327, 329
  conflict in, 336, 370
Yiddish language, 30, 101
Young, J. Douglas, 207
Young, Whitney, 422
Young Peoples Socialist League, 422
Yugoslavia, 209, 342, 375

Zhitlovsky, Haim, 31
Zinoviev, G. Y., 23
Zion, Poale, 28
Zionism, 172
  administered territories and, 251, 256, 264–65
  aims of, 336
  anti-Semitism and, 390–92
  Arab non-acceptance of, 313, 315–20
  birth of modern, 140–41
  "class interests" and, 39
  communal organization and, 52–57
  contemporary Israelis and, 117–24
  illusions of about Arab hostility, 376
  Jewish statehood and, 186
  kibbutzim and, 97–99
  Labor, 38, 49–63, 102–03
  myth of expansionism of, 137–56
  proponents of, 27–29, 176
  response to Marxism by, 22–23
  social reconstruction and, 310–11
  socialist criticism of, 16–27, 29–44, 188
  view of Palestine, 177
  See also Jews; Nationalism
Zukerman, William, 33–35, 40